The German Question

SECOND EDITION

The German Question

A Cultural, Historical, and Geopolitical Exploration

Dirk Verheyen

Loyola Marymount University, Los Angeles

Westview Press
A Member of the Perseus Books Group

Copyright © 1999 by Westview Press, A Member of the Perseus Books Group

Published in 1999 in the United States of America by Westview Press, 5500 Central Avenue, Boulder,
Colorado 80301-2877, and in the United Kingdom by Westview Press, 12 Hid's Copse Road, Cumnor
Hill, Oxford OX2 9JJ

Find us on the World Wide Web at www.westviewpress.com

Library of Congress Cataloging-in-Publication Data
Verheyen, Dirk.
  The German question : a cultural, historical, and geopolitical
exploration / Dirk Verheyen. — 2nd ed.
     p. cm.
  Includes bibliographical references and index.
  ISBN 0-8133-6878-2
  1. German reunification question (1949–1990).   2. Political
culture—Germany.   3. Germany—History—Unification, 1990.
4. Germany—Foreign relations—1945–   . I. Title.
DD257.25.V47   1999
943.087—dc21   99-22456
                                                                         CIP

The paper used in this publication meets the requirements of the American National Standard for
Permanence of Paper for Printed Library Materials Z39.48-1984.

10   9   8   7   6   5   4   3   2   1

Contents

Preface

The end of the sixteen-year chancellorship of Helmut Kohl after the Bundestag elections of September 27, 1998, leading to the advent of an unprecedented coalition of Social Democrats and Greens, has raised new questions about Germany's future direction in domestic politics as well as foreign policy. Even prior to this historic election, however, the turbulent aftermath of the country's reunification in 1990 had already raised many similar issues among German and non-German analysts and commentators alike.

In an attempt at providing a broader framework for an examination of Germany's contemporary condition and the country's possible future prospects, I have presented in this book an analysis of what has tended to be called the "German Question" from four different angles: German identity, German national unity, German power, and Germany's role in European and world affairs. Special emphasis is placed on a variety of cultural, ideological, psychological, as well as geopolitical factors.

While preparing the first edition of this book, I benefited tremendously from the advice, support, and hospitality of many. Kenneth N. Waltz, the late Paul Seabury, and Wolfgang Sauer at the University of California–Berkeley, and Alfred Grosser at the Sorbonne in Paris, provided valuable criticism and suggestions. Kenneth Jowitt introduced me to the concept of political culture and was a constant source of moral and intellectual support. Christian Søe not only provided excellent feedback on the manuscript but also has become a much-appreciated friend and scholarly collaborator.

During research visits to (West) Germany and (West) Berlin in the course of the 1980s and 1990s, I enjoyed the hospitality of Werner Geisberg in Köln, Albrecht and Lore Tyrell in Bonn-Bad Godesberg, Rainer Zäck and Juergen Gebhard at the Akademie für Internationale Bildung in Bonn, and Abraham and Cathy Ashkenasi in (West) Berlin. The Deutsche Gesellschaft für Auswärtige Politik in Bonn graciously agreed to host me as a visiting researcher in 1984 and enabled me to utilize its superb staff and library resources. Colette Myles and the late Serge Millan of U.C. Berkeley's Institute of International Studies Library were always a source of excellent assistance and cordial friendship.

At Loyola Marymount University, I have received generous research support, especially in the form of several summer grants from the University Research

Committee. My faculty colleagues inside and outside the Department of Political Science at LMU have been a constant source of encouragement and support. Dina Ng, Claire Twomey, Cathy Trent, Bridget Carberry, Christoph Hupach, and Olga Badilla, along with the staff of the LMU library, provided valuable assistance in tracking down a variety of materials. Leo Wiegman and Kristin Milavec at Westview Press have been most helpful throughout the manuscript preparation and production process.

All those mentioned here, as well as many others, have contributed greatly to whatever merits this study might have. Any flaws or shortcomings remain properly mine.

—*Dirk Verheyen*
Los Angeles

Introduction

Defining the German Question

In 1983, the late Italian journalist and commentator Luigi Barzini wrote: "The future of Europe appears largely to depend today once again, for good or evil, whether we like it or not, as it did for many centuries, on the future of Germany."[1] In view of the truly momentous changes and transformations that have swept Europe, both East and West, and Germany in particular, since the fall of 1989, such words were both accurate and prophetic.

In Western Europe, the process of integration (especially in the economic sphere) picked up speed again after the mid-1980s, apparently reversing many years of slow-down and impasse. The vision of EC'92, of a truly Common Market without internal boundaries and restrictions, firmly seized the popular imagination, followed by the historic Maastricht Treaty on European Union concluded in 1991.

In Eastern Europe in the late 1980s, Gorbachev's Soviet reform program triggered a significant spillover into the politics of countries like Poland, Hungary, East Germany, Czechoslovakia, and Romania, where Communist rule collapsed, while Gorbachev himself continued to intrigue European public opinion with his vision of a "Common European Home." The pressures for reform, if not revolution, in East Germany ate away the roots of the very existence and *raison d'être* of the state created on the eastern shore of the Elbe river in the early years of the Cold War. In Austria and Hungary, old ideas of *Mitteleuropa* (Central Europe) were resurfacing, indicating that at least on a psychological and political level the "blocs" of the Cold War were steadily losing their erstwhile rigidity. Contacts between East and West in Europe continued to proliferate. Perhaps most important, the question of a divided versus reunited (or at least confederated) Germany was also coming back to life in this changed European climate. In short, there were many indications of a Europe moving beyond the postwar era with its Cold War characteristics, and into an exciting but also uncertain and perhaps even unsettling phase of its history. The process of transformation reached its climax in the spectacular yet by and large astonishingly nonviolent demise of both the Soviet Union and the Warsaw Pact.

Old policies and assumptions eroded, but new ones were slow to crystallize. Germany clearly occupied a central position in this rapidly changing geopolitical, military, and economic landscape. Any transformation of the old Cold War status quo on the European continent implied a recasting of what tends to be called the German Question.[2]

But that raised a very fundamental issue: What really is the German Question? Is it German reunification and its consequences, or the oft-mentioned historic weakness of liberalism in Germany, or the genesis and legacy of the Nazi disaster, or Germany's historically aggressive diplomatic and military behavior, or something else? I will suggest in the chapters that follow that the essence of the German Question lies in four interrelated dimensions. First, there is the question of *German identity*. What is "German" and what is "Germany"? It will be shown that most discussions of aspects of this question tend to include such issues as Germany's historic alienation from some important Western cultural and ideological traditions, the many illiberal aspects of the country's political legacy, the profound political and cultural changes in postwar Germany, and the psychological burdens of a troubled past. These elements of the German Question are addressed primarily in Chapters 1 and 2, but also in Chapter 8. But we shall also explore the controversial quality of much of this analysis by examining the critique of the so-called *Sonderweg* thesis, that is, the idea that Germany's troubles during the past century can be understood as the result of a "special" or "separate" German developmental "path." In addition, this issue of identity requires that we consider evolving patterns of German attitudes in politics and foreign policy; we shall do this at various points in all the chapters.

Second, there is the question of *German unity*. In this context, Germany's delayed unification, its illiberal and uncertain sense of nationhood after 1871, the discontinuities in its national political experience, the troubled legacy of its nationalism, and its post-1945 predicament as a divided nation become issues of great importance. They are examined in varying contexts throughout this book. This aspect of the German Question corresponds most closely with the way in which that Question has been most commonly defined after 1945, namely as the issue of German reunification.[3]

Third, there is the question of *Germany's place and role* in international affairs in general and European affairs in particular. The different diplomatic options that the Germans have pursued, or have been allowed to pursue, in this regard since 1871 are of central importance, as will be shown especially in Chapters 4 and 9.

Fourth, there is the question of *German power*. Here we are interested in the impact of that power (political, military, and economic) on European and international politics, and in the ways that both the Germans and others (friend and foe) have sought to manage it. This theme is taken up at various places in Chapters 4 and 5. It also resurfaces prominently in Chapters 6, 7, and 9.

As the discussion of the German Question unfolds, it will become clear that the essence of this Question manifests itself in a somewhat different way for Germans and non-Germans.[4] The basic argument is that the German Question as perceived and experienced by the Germans themselves revolves significantly around the issue of *identity*, whereby issues like national unity and Germany's role and power in world affairs are important as related concerns. For non-Germans, however, and especially for Germany's neighbors, it is the question of German *power* and the need to "manage" it that is most decisive. I would suggest that these somewhat divergent conceptions of the German Question by Germans and non-Germans have been, and frequently continue to be, instrumental in causing difficulties in Germany's diplomatic relations with other nations.

In addition, *identity* and *role* on the one hand, and *unity* and *power* on the other hand, can also be viewed as connected analytical pairs. The Germans' search for a national cultural and political identity, including questions of ideological orientation and choice of political system, matches the concern of the country's neighbors regarding the consequences of that search for identity for the role that Germany might play in international affairs. For example, throughout the Cold War years, the question was raised whether the Germans would continue to play a pro-Western role based on a firmly grounded pro-Western political-cultural national identity, or whether a sense of cultural "intermediacy" would induce a tendency to "float" between East and West in the affairs of Europe. This issue resurfaced in a changed international setting after 1990, as Chapter 9 shows. Similarly, the Germans' historical quest for national unity, and its recent recovery after four decades of division, matches the concern of their neighbors regarding the implications of the presence of a powerful Germany in their midst. Put most simply, a united Germany is inevitably a powerful Germany.[5]

In addition, it may be suggested that the issues of *identity* and *unity* are perhaps first and foremost cultural and ideological in nature, while the issues of German *power* and Germany's *role* in international affairs combine considerations of both ideology and policy. In both cases, *geographic* factors must be considered: "geocultural" in the case of Germany's search for identity and unity, and "geopolitical" or "geostrategic" with respect to the country's power and role in world affairs. In sum, the German Question becomes a matter of culture as well as policy, placed in a geographic and historical context.

To understand the complexities of the German Question, one must venture beyond a straightforward, traditional foreign policy analysis, because the German Question as defined above is not just a matter of foreign policy and international politics. A variety of questions pose themselves. What made prewar Germany "tick," what made West Germany and East Germany "tick," and what makes post-1990 Germany "tick"? What are the traditions and historical experiences we should be aware of when trying to understand Germany before 1945, West Germany after the war, and the united Germany since 1990? Are there, as many observers have claimed, dominant facets of a German "worldview"? What makes Germany "Germany"? What kinds of general cultural orientations do we encounter? What is the nature of political culture and tradition in Germany? What are the decisive experiences, traditions, and perspectives in the area of foreign policy (what one might call "foreign policy culture")? And how did East Germany fit into this picture? By examining these issues, especially in their historical context, we shall gain a better insight into the complex interaction of identity, unity, role, and power that constitutes the German Question.

Although this study does not pretend to offer a refined or comprehensive *theoretical* framework for an understanding of the German Question, some basic theoretical orientations should nevertheless be spelled out. The book is based on the assumption that the German Question is best understood through the complex interplay of what might be formulaically expressed as "mind, time, and space (or context)." We are interested in beliefs, values, and other relevant orientations ("mind"), but with adequate sensitivity to the factors of historical context and generational differentiation ("time") as well as domestic and international context or "space" (including geography). One consequence of this particular approach is a less primary emphasis on material (especially economic) factors, except in the general context of German power (for example, in Chapters 7 and 9).

Thus we will seek to trace the development of beliefs, values, and attitudes over time, looking for continuities and discontinuities, at times especially across generations. We will see how such mental orientations have interacted with factors of a more contextual or environmental kind. Thus we are interested in the ways in which geostrategic location and placement within international-structural configurations have affected mental orientations and created opportunities as well as constraints, with a constant need, especially since 1945, to adapt to the latter. Contextual sensitivity also implies a consideration of the ways in which patterns in German orientations are or have been matched by similar patterns among other Europeans, whether in postindustrial cultural values or in diplomatic tradition or in postwar foreign policy.

The reader will notice that *historical experience* is in many ways the "glue" that binds "mind," "time," and "space" (or "context") in this analysis of the German Question. This does not amount to any tyranny of historical inevitability when we consider the prospects for the future. It does, however, suggest the basic prudence of a contextualized awareness of the past for a proper understanding of both present and possible future. Furthermore, the historical focus of much of the discussion is also intended to provide what is essentially a "retrospective" survey of aspects of the German Question ("how did we get here?") that may assist us in grasping more clearly possibly enduring facets of that Question as we move into a new period of history with a reunited and transformed Germany in the center of a changing Europe.

The structure of the book is as follows: The first three chapters focus centrally on the issues of *identity* and *unity*. Chapter 1 looks at the pre-1945 German past, emphasizing Germany's historical search for identity, its legacy of conservative nationalism, the illiberal aspects in its political tradition, and the ongoing debate concerning the true extent of Germany's alleged developmental *Sonderweg* (special path). Chapter 2 focuses on postwar West Germany, and discusses manifestations of profound change and occasional continuity in both general culture and political culture, in addition to the persistent burdens of a troubled past and the crucial question of national identity in a context of Cold War national division. Chapter 3 addresses the issue of identity and national unity from the East German viewpoint between 1949 and 1989. The next two chapters turn more directly to the issues of Germany's *power* and *role* in world affairs, by shifting our focus from the realm of domestic culture and political tradition to the area of foreign policy, although the issues of identity and unity remain present as a persistent undercurrent. Chapter 4 deals with Germany's prewar diplomatic traditions, the different visions of power management and diplomatic role in the history of prewar Germany and postwar West Germany, and the impact of a troubled past on the foreign policy of the Federal Republic. Chapter 5 examines postwar West German diplomacy from an explicitly ideological point of view by delineating Conservative, Liberal, and Social Democratic conceptions in foreign policy, particularly with respect to the question of national unity in the Cold War context.

In Chapter 6, we look at the decade of the 1980s, especially the nature of foreign policy attitudes in West Germany and the perceived resurgence of a "new" German Question during the Reagan era. Questions about identity, unity, power, and Germany's role in Europe and the world at large converged quite dramatically in a context of renewed East-West Cold War. Chapter 7, which reviews the major domestic and international aspects of Germany's reunification process in 1989–1990, sets the stage for Chapters 8 and 9, which analyze contemporary developments in the united Germany's domestic political culture and foreign policy, respectively. Insofar as it presents a partially chronological survey of the development of the German Question, this study aims at providing the reader the overall historical background against which current developments in Germany can be better understood. Finally, a brief word about sources and notes: Each chapter contains a considerable range of endnotes, in which, in turn, I provide additional comments, observations, and suggestions for further reading and study.

The German National Journey: A Sketch

Since this study presupposes a basic familiarity with German history, the following pages attempt to provide a brief sketch of the evolution of modern Germany for those readers who would find such an overview useful as an introduction to the material that follows.[6]

In 1803, Ernst Moritz Arndt, in his *Germanien und Europa,* wrote: "Let's take Germany then as a united entity, which it could have become just like France and Great Britain, but which it did not have to become: which are the natural boundaries of [this united Germany]?" In 1867, the Prussian Prime Minister Otto von Bismarck, striving to bring about a united German Reich, suggested that "without a doubt there is something in our [German] national character that resists the unification of Germany." In a memorial speech in 1919, Hermann Oncken argued that "it is we Germans, among the peoples on earth, who have been destined time and again to experience in moving and symbolic fashion the fate of the individual human being: ecstasy and agony, victory and death." Amid the 1972 debate on West Germany's new *Ostpolitik,* the prominent Social Democrat Carlo Schmid mused: "The fact that one can even pose the question: What is the German's fatherland?, that one can ask: What then is actually the condition of the [German] nation, of the possibility of [a] German nation? This [fact] shows how different our [German] situation is from that of other [nations]."[7]

These random historical snapshots are indicative of the turbulent and traumatic national experience that characterizes modern Germany, this "'tragic land' of the twentieth century," to use the expression employed in an influential book on German history.[8] The search for stable nationhood and identity stands at the center of postmedieval German history. The (potential) impact of a united Germany on the rest of Europe has been a crucial theme in the international politics of the Old World for at least the last two centuries.[9]

The area that became known as "Germany" did not develop into a modern nation-state when other entities such as France, Spain, Great Britain, or Sweden came into being. The center of Europe emerged from the Middle Ages in the form of what was known as the Holy Roman Empire of the German Nation, which was in reality a crazy quilt of small states (duchies, princedoms, and so on). The Empire lacked a strong central authority, and its continued weakness and division played an important role in the dynastic balance-of-power politics of the early-modern European great powers. The highly disruptive impact of the Reformation during the sixteenth and seventeenth centuries, culminating in the disastrous Thirty Years' War (1618–1648) pitting Catholic against Protestant states, further enhanced an already strong tendency toward regional fragmentation. Greater economic unity among the various states was forestalled by uneven levels of development and by jealously maintained tariffs, duties, and other protectionist policies.

It was not until well into the eighteenth century that the early stirrings of a more fully developed sense of German nationalism began to emerge alongside more regionally focused identities (Saxon, Prussian, Bavarian, Westphalian, Hessian, and so on). As part of the Enlightenment, writers and intellectuals like Herder and Fichte assisted in the genesis of a stronger "German" cultural identity, giving rise to the idea of a German *Kulturnation.* Crucial political impulses were added by the French and American Revolutions and the Napoleonic era, as we shall see in Chapter 1.

The wars unleashed by Napoleon caused the collapse of the old Holy Roman Empire in 1806, and the development of modern German nationalism became significantly affected by a sense of resistance against revolutionary France. Several German states formed a Confederation of the Rhine, which was essentially a Napoleonic protectorate, while Prussia suffered defeat at the hands of the French emperor. In many German states, liberalism and nationalism became intertwined in emancipatory reform programs pushed especially by middle-class groups, aiming at the creation of a modern German nation based on liberal democracy, featuring constitutionalism, representation, and popular sovereignty, rather than absolutist rule.

Although the German experience of revolutionary nation-building in the eighteenth and nineteenth centuries was not completely different from similar processes in neighboring Western European states, there were nevertheless distinctive aspects in the German developmental process. These included the more delayed formation of national consciousness in Germany, the relative weakness of the German bourgeoisie as a carrier of modern liberal nationalism, the uncertainty regarding the boundaries of the emerging German nation, the profound rivalry between Prussia and Austria, and the considerable foreign influences (not just Napoleonic) in various German regions.

At the conclusion of the Napoleonic wars, the European powers met at the Congress of Vienna (1814–1815). The old German Reich was not reconstituted, nor was the liberal dream of a modern nation-state realized. Instead, several dozen German states and free cities (including Prussia and Habsburg Austria) were linked into the German Confederation, a construction devoid of any meaningful federal institutions aside from a *Bundestag* (chamber of representatives) led by Austria. Prussia became Austria's main rival for leadership among the German states. The Confederation turned into a reactionary political instrument, undermining any liberal reform efforts, even those unleashed in various states in response to the French Revolution of July 1830. Increased economic interdependence among the German states culminated in the formation of a customs union (*Zollverein*) in 1834, a development promoted especially by Prussia. As a result, the side-by-side existence of a Prussian-dominated *Zollverein* (excluding Austria) and an Austrian-dominated Confederation further deepened the antagonism and rivalry between these two most powerful German states.

The revolutionary year 1848 and its aftermath turned into a watershed epoch in modern German history. Liberal political reforms were initially achieved in a number of states, and the bourgeois nationalist movement succeeded in convening an all-German parliament in Frankfurt in May 1848. But in the search for a new German national constitutional foundation, the parliament became entangled in the Prussian-Austrian hegemonic rivalry. The deputies opted for a "small-German" solution (that is, a German Reich without Austria) and offered the imperial crown to the king of Prussia. The latter's refusal to accept the offer effectively unraveled the 1848 liberal-constitutional nation-building effort. A

decade of conservative reaction ensued. The creation of a modern German nation-state seemed farther away than ever.

From the late 1850s onward, the Prussian-Austrian rivalry intensified, with a
number of other German states caught literally in the middle. Meanwhile, Bismarck had become prime minister in Prussia, and proceeded to block all Austrian attempts to join the *Zollverein*. The Prussian-Austrian contest became one
between "small-German" (excluding Austria) and "great-German" (including
Austria) solutions to the national question. Each solution had its supporters, who
in turn fueled an intense public debate.

In the end, Prussia won the contest over German hegemony. The three successful "wars of unification" against Denmark (1864), Austria (1866), and France
(1870) enabled Prussia to consolidate its leadership among the German states. In
1871, the new German Reich was formed, by means of warfare instead of revolution, and excluding Austria. Northern and southern German states merged in a
new empire that was permeated more by Prussian authoritarianism than by
bourgeois liberalism, and this time the Prussian king did accept the imperial
crown.

The new German Reich inevitably shook existing international power configurations in Europe. The precarious balance of power that Bismarck's diplomacy
was able to maintain after 1871 disintegrated after 1890. The growing rapprochement among Britain, France, and Russia resulted in Germany's equally growing
isolation. The reckless and aggressive diplomacy of a Germany whose economic
clout was rapidly increasing steadily heightened international tensions, both in
Europe and in various colonial areas. A clearly irredentist attitude regarding German-speaking minorities in neighboring countries generated mounting foreign
concerns over the Reich's possible revisionist intentions.

The powder keg exploded in 1914. Although the causes of World War I, and the
issue of "war guilt," remain a matter of keen dispute, there can be little doubt that
the war saw Germany's first explicit bid for continental hegemony, as it aimed to
break the fetters imposed on any European power (including Germany) by a balance-of-power arrangement. The 1919 Treaty of Versailles that followed the carnage
of World War I punished Germany severely by imposing reparations payments, loss
of territory, and extensive demilitarization. To its neighbors, a weaker Germany was
quite simply a safer Germany. The old Kaiserreich had collapsed, and the somewhat
shaky liberal-bourgeois Weimar Republic was formed in 1919. Its acceptance of the
Versailles treaty, which was seen as a *Diktat* by many Germans, undermined the new
republic's political legitimacy right from the start, however. Meanwhile, the demise
of the old Habsburg Empire had resulted in the creation of a series of newly independent states in Central and Eastern Europe, several of which contained significant German-speaking minorities. A serious irredentist attitude now began to make
itself felt in certain intellectual and political German circles.

Multiple economic and political crises ultimately doomed the Weimar Republic. Anti-Versailles nationalist revisionism was widespread. German and Austrian

Social Democrats dreamed of a new great-German merger, and liberals like Naumann envisioned a future *Mitteleuropa* growing out of a German-Austrian customs union. The most aggressively revisionist plans were drawn up by the steadily growing Nazi party, whose leader was offered the chancellorship of the moribund republic in 1933.

Hitler proceeded to overturn the *Diktat* of Versailles, setting Germany on a course that could only lead to war. With remilitarization in progress, the *Anschluß* with Austria was brought about, as well as the incorporation of the Sudeten area of western Czechoslovakia. A series of assaults on neighboring countries ensued, inspired by an ideology containing geopolitical, social-darwinist, and racialist dimensions, but Germany's second twentieth-century bid for absolute hegemony had failed by 1945.

Allied conferences at Tehran, Moscow, Yalta, and Potsdam during and right after World War II determined Germany's postwar fate. Large sections of German territory east of the so-called Oder-Neisse line were placed under Polish and Soviet control, while the remainder of Germany was divided into four occupation zones, to be administered by the United States, Britain, France, and the Soviet Union, respectively. Although a joint allied administration of Germany by means of an Allied Control Council was envisaged, in reality the growing atmosphere of East-West Cold War soon led to the de facto 1949 division of Germany into a Western-oriented Federal Republic (FRG) and a Soviet-dominated German Democratic Republic (GDR), with the unsuccessful 1948–1949 Soviet blockade of Berlin (which had also been divided into four occupation sectors) as a crucial turning point. The division prevented the conclusion of a formal allied peace treaty with Germany. Such a treaty has never been signed, although the 1990 agreement between the FRG, the GDR, and the four wartime Allies, on the eve of reunification, turned out to be a fairly close substitute. The Oder-Neisse line, and Germany's territorial losses, became essentially permanent.

Before 1949, the West German territory had already benefited from the U.S.-financed Marshall Plan for the economic recovery of war-torn Europe. The Soviet Union prevented the GDR and the rest of Eastern Europe from receiving similar economic assistance. In the years after 1949, the FRG was able steadily to regain its sovereignty and status by means of participation in a variety of Western integration schemes, both in the area of security (NATO, WEU) and economic cooperation (European Coal and Steel Community, Euratom, EEC, and OECD). As we shall see in more detail in Chapters 4 and 5, this emancipation-through-integration strategy formed the core of the *Westpolitik* of West Germany's first post-1949 chancellor, Konrad Adenauer. We shall also notice that it was a controversial diplomatic course in terms of domestic politics, however. The Christian Democrats and the Social Democrats became the main protagonists in a lengthy ideological and electoral contest, elements of which persist in today's Germany.

Meanwhile, the GDR was steadily incorporated into the Soviet camp by joining the Warsaw Pact in 1955, following the FRG's entry into NATO. Inside the

GDR, a forced merger of the Communist (KPD) and Social Democratic (SPD) parties laid the foundation for a new German Socialist Unity Party (SED). Inasmuch as Germany was the ultimate prize in the East-West Cold War contest, a growing sense of stalemate on the reunification issue was inevitable: In spite of occasional designs and frequent statements of support for German reunification, the two-state "solution" of the German Question took on an increasingly permanent character. East and West simply had incompatible conceptions of the domestic political nature and international strategic status of a reunited Germany. The construction of the Berlin Wall in 1961 by a GDR regime desperate to stem the continued outflow of its disillusioned citizens merely heightened the sense of definitive division.

In retrospect, however, the Berlin Wall really was the beginning of East Germany's end. Not only did it demonstrate the GDR's ideological bankruptcy and political artificiality, but it also brought about an important shift in West German diplomacy. Throughout the 1950s, the West German government had made its support for East-West detente efforts dependent on progress in the area of German reunification, based on a policy known as *Politik des Junktim,* or "linkage." The so-called Hallstein Doctrine threatened a break of diplomatic relations with any country that would recognize the GDR as a sovereign state. By the end of the 1960s, however, the West German position was essentially reversed. The new *Ostpolitik* and *Deutschlandpolitik,* pursued especially by Willy Brandt and his fellow Social Democrats after 1969, envisaged a gradual change in the direction of reunification by means of a steady FRG-GDR rapprochement and normalization in the larger context of East-West detente and the creation of a European "peace order" transcending the Cold War alliance blocs. The new West German diplomacy culminated in the conclusion of a series of historic treaties in the early 1970s between the FRG and the GDR, Poland, and the USSR, while the Conference on Security and Cooperation in Europe, leading to the 1975 Helsinki Accords, appeared to finalize the international recognition of Europe's postwar political and military order, including the reality of two essentially sovereign German states.

Yet, an East German willingness to engage the FRG in a mutual detente effort could only run counter to the GDR's post-1961 preoccupation with *Abgrenzung* ("separation") and socialist nation-building. Inter-German detente helped create a growing sense of shared intra-German interest, particularly vis-à-vis the two superpower patrons, and could easily call into question the GDR's already shaky legitimacy. The renewed sense of Cold War after the late 1970s made this abundantly clear: Any East-West conflict in Europe would have Germans as its first and maybe even only victims. In retrospect, the detente era made a resurgence of an effective, shared German national identity all but inevitable. And under such circumstances, a prosperous and democratic West Germany could only be an irresistible magnet for the population of an increasingly oppressive and stagnant GDR. Consequently, the disintegration of East Germany had its roots well before the Gorbachev era, although there can be little doubt that the Soviet leader's refusal to bail out East Berlin's faltering and aging Stalinists was highly instrumental in providing the needed final push that toppled the SED regime in late 1989 and unexpectedly brought the issue of German reunification back to the top of the international agenda.

Notes

1. Luigi Barzini, *The Europeans* (New York: Penguin Books, 1984), p. 69.

2. See, for example, F. Stephen Larrabee, ed., *The Two German States and European Security* (New York: St. Martin's Press, 1989).

3. See the excellent collection of materials, with commentary, on the evolving issue of German reunification provided by Hans Edgar Jahn, *Die deutsche Frage von 1945 bis heute* (Mainz: v. Hase & Köhler Verlag, 1985).

4. William D. Zuckerman, in "The Germans: what's the question?" (*International Affairs*, vol. 61, nr. 3, Summer 1985, pp. 465–470), also distinguished between a "German" and a "non-German" German Question. Whereas he identified the non-German German Question as involving international concern over "the potential for instability in Europe created by the continued enforced division," the German version of the German Question was seen as an FRG desire "to overcome the division of Germany imposed in the aftermath of the Second World War." A somewhat similar approach, with particular emphasis on the ways in which the German Question is embedded in general European frameworks, was offered by Eberhard Schulz, "Unfinished business: the German national question and the future of Europe," *International Affairs*, vol. 60, nr. 3, Summer 1984, pp. 391–402. My approach to the German Question is not completely dissimilar, but is much broader in conception and historical framework.

5. The interplay of unity, identity, and power is also very much emphasized by Anne-Marie LeGloannec, *Die deutsch-deutsche Nation. Anmerkungen zu einer revolutionären Entwicklung* (Munich: printul Verlagsgesellschaft, 1991; updated edition of *La Nation orpheline. Les Allemagnes en Europe*, Paris: Fondation Saint-Simon/Calmann-Levy, 1989). The same mixture of factors is also central in Wolf D. Gruner's *Die deutsche Frage in Europa, 1800 bis 1990* (Munich/Zürich: Piper Verlag, 1993).

6. The following discussion is especially indebted to the Introduction and sources provided by Peter Longerich in *"Was Ist des Deutschen Vaterland?" Dokumente zur Frage der deutschen Einheit 1800–1990* (München/Zürich: Piper, 1990).

7. These four quotations are taken from Longerich, ed., *"Was Ist des Deutschen Vaterland?"* pp. 41, 93, 121, and 247, respectively.

8. David Blackbourn and Geoff Eley, *The Peculiarities of German History: Bourgeois Society and Politics in Nineteenth-Century Germany* (Oxford/New York: Oxford University Press, 1984), p. 292.

9. See Rudolf Vierhaus, "Die 'Deutsche Einheit' als Problem der deutschen und europäischen Geschichte seit der Französischen Revolution," in Karl-Ernst Jeismann, ed., *Einheit—Freiheit—Selbstbestimmung: Die Deutsche Frage im historisch-politischen Bewußtsein* (Frankfurt/New York: Campus Verlag, 1988).

1

A Troubled Identity and a Difficult Fatherland

Before World War II, Charles de Gaulle once depicted Germany as "a sublime but glaucous sea where the fisherman's net hauls up monsters and treasures."[1] The purpose of this chapter is to begin our examination of the German Question by addressing a basic question. What has made Germany "Germany"? In the final analysis, many have argued that this is a question about German culture, and perhaps more specifically about the German *Weltanschauung*, or worldview (if such a thing exists), and German identity.

Any attempt to describe purportedly dominant facets of German identity immediately runs into a number of difficult problems, however. First, there is the question of what is German and what is Germany. It is the kind of question that historically evokes strong feelings of one kind or another. Thus the nineteenth-century German philosopher Friedrich Nietzsche once argued that "[i]t is characteristic of the Germans that one is seldom wholly wrong about them. The German soul has corridors and interconnecting corridors in it, there are caves, hiding-places, dungeons in it; its disorder possesses much of the fascinating and mysterious; the German is acquainted with the hidden paths to chaos. . . ." The poet Heinrich Heine would even suffer insomnia on account of his native land: "When I think of Germany in the night, I am robbed of my sleep!"[2] Closer consideration will show that the answers to this inevitably controversial question are by no means obvious. Charles E. McClelland and Steven P. Scher argue, for example, that "[a]nswers to the question 'What is German?' are at least as complex as those to the question 'What is culture?'" They conclude that "[a]ny closer knowledge of the modern political and social history of the German-speaking peoples must lead to serious doubts whether one can make any binding and continuous statements about 'the Germans' or their 'character.'"[3] Perhaps it all merely confirms Goethe's lament: "The Germans make everything difficult, both for themselves and for everyone else."[4] The question is not only relevant to the divided Germany of the postwar era. It is a question of identity that has a long historical legacy, as we shall see presently.

Second, there is the issue of profound historical discontinuity in the German experience, and its consequences for German identity. Richard Löwenthal has noted "a very special lack of chronological continuity, geographic unity and intellectual form and coherence." He notes the crucial discontinuity of both state and nation in the German historical experience and concludes that "[t]his lack of unity across time, in space, and in the mind is in fact the central problem—or if one wishes, the central secret—of German history."[5]

Third, one may raise some questions about the quality and usefulness of some discussions of German cultural and political identity. Any cultural analysis runs the risk of careless overgeneralization and exaggeration. But in the German case there is the additional problem that much of the cultural material was written in an attempt to find answers to the "German Problem" or "German Question." Why has Germany been so involved in warfare, and why was a liberal-democratic political order unable to emerge indigenously? These two questions have often been connected, and the answers have frequently been sought in sociocultural factors. There has been a particular predilection for "national character" explanations, with the Germans as patients in need of a cure.[6] Many of such national character analyses have focused on Nazism and World War II, and the pressures and emotions of war often had a clearly negative impact on their quality. The result frequently was a constantly reinforced German stereotype.[7]

Perhaps the importance of such stereotyping lies more in its frequency and persistence than in its definitive accuracy.[8] Its utility for an understanding of the German Question must be considered strictly limited, however. It tends to stress "negative" character traits like arrogance, aggressiveness, authoritarianism, mindless discipline and obedience, and ideological extremism, at the expense of "positive" ones like artistic creativity, diligence (Fleiß), orderliness, thoroughness, or loyalty.[9] It often involves generalization across politically, culturally, socially, and economically very dynamic periods of history, thereby losing a much-needed sense of nuance. Yet equally significantly from a social-psychological point of view, the world's perception and conception of the Germans and Germany have undergone considerable historical evolution, from an image of Germans as poets, dreamers, and peasants in the days of Madame de Staël's De l'Allemagne (1810), to a succession of negative images, ranging from the "Huns" of World War I and the unredeemable Nazi barbarians of World War II, to a post-1945 foreign image of the Germans that often mixes elements of (potential) neo-Nazism, pacifist neutralism, and/or domineering but efficient capitalism, depending on the observer's particular inclinations.

It is certainly appropriate to keep in mind Hermann Eich's insistence that "[o]ne will come nearer to a just assessment of a nation by recognising its contradictory nature rather than by branding it wholly black or wholly white."[10] Or, as Willy Hellpach once suggested in *Der deutsche Charakter*, "[e]very nation is in a perpetual state of transformation."[11] In addition, "national character" generalizations run the risk of neglecting very real sources of cultural and attitudinal variation, based on region, generation, or social class.[12]

Describing the "pitfalls of domestic explanations," David Calleo has argued that

> [f]inding the key to the German Problem in the country's domestic character has been a major preoccupation of postwar studies. . . . Often a series of stereotypes is patched up into a collective German "character." The result seems a composite projection of those qualities that people dislike most about their own societies. In many instances, the characteristics seem misinterpreted in their German context and, moreover, are easily found in other societies. At their worst, such attempts at definition seem reminiscent of the very racist techniques made notorious by anti-Semites.[13]

One does not have to agree completely with Calleo's critique; one might even consider his condemnation of sociocultural explanations too radical and absolute, and his own international-structural answer to the German Question too narrowly focused. His essential point is nonetheless an appropriate one. It is the aim of this and subsequent chapters to demonstrate that although sociocultural factors cannot be neglected in any serious exploration of the German Question, broader ideological but also historical, international-structural, and geographic elements must be duly incorporated into an analysis.

A Troubled National Identity

The history of nineteenth- and twentieth-century Germany, prior to the complete defeat of 1945, shows evidence of a basically uncertain self-identity and a simultaneous assertion of an alleged German historical mission and uniqueness, all of this connected with a constant attempt to define the essence of *Deutschtum* ("Germanness").[14] A proper understanding of the significance of this theme of troubled German identity requires a somewhat extended historical perspective, particularly focused on the rather incomplete impact of Liberalism and the Enlightenment in Germany, the influence of Romanticism, and the country's historical lack of unity and sense of failure. In the total context of the German Question, this is a truly fundamental theme.

It has often been argued that German culture was characterized historically by a basic ambivalence, if not enmity, vis-à-vis many of the revolutionary ideas of the seventeenth and eighteenth centuries. According to Löwenthal, we should remember "that Germany in the age of the French Revolution was the great 'developing country' of the West." The new ideas and discoveries of the new age that came to Germany from outside at that time induced a fundamental German ambivalence regarding the process of modernization in culture and politics: "on the one hand the excitement about the new ideas and the wish to be equal to [foreign] examples in the development of liberal constitutionalism and modern forms of life, indeed, if possible to surpass them—on the other hand the fear regarding the impact of foreign influences, the loss of one's own soul, and of one's national identity in the process of a diligent imitation of envied examples."[15]

The weak or incomplete impact of the Enlightenment on Germany should be understood in its historical context. According to George Bailey,

> [h]istorians generally hold that German national resistance [to] the Napoleonic invasion unfortunately evolved into German nationalist rejection of the Enlightenment. It was as if the whole ethical corpus of the Enlightenment had stumbled into the line of fire and suffered mortal wounds. The Prussians—and indeed the majority of Germans awakened into some sort of national consciousness by the French invasion—threw out the Enlightenment with the invader and persisted in rejecting most of what the Enlightenment involved because it was French and therefore anti-German.[16]

The Enlightenment did not affect a unified Germany but instead a crazy quilt of little states and principalities in which, so the argument goes, the sociopolitical preconditions for a sympathetic reception of Liberal ideas were largely absent, with the possible exception of certain western and southwestern areas such as the Rhineland and Baden.

The German reaction to the Enlightenment became most clearly embodied in Romanticism.[17] The differences between the two cultural and philosophical movements were profound. The Enlightenment gave expression to an optimistic sense of progress, worshiped human individuality, stressed a rationalist and empiricist approach to life and its problems, and focused on human rights and freedoms as well as questions of basic human equality. The Romantics, however, were animated by a greater sense of pessimism and tragedy. At times such attitudes could be joined to a strong sense of terror, excitement, and foreboding. Instead of rationalism and empiricism, many of them tended to stress the irrational, the metaphysical, the mysterious or mythical, and the poetic.

The importance of the Romantic epoch for the historical German worldview cannot be understood when divorced from the quest for German unity and identity. Disunity and a lack of clear identity have been mutually reinforcing aspects of the German experience. Thus Bailey suggests that

> [i]dentity has always been the main aspect of the German Problem. The Germans have shown a remarkable lack of the sense of identity: they have fought each other in full enmity down the ages. They have banded together with foreigners against other German tribes as often as they have allied themselves against foreigners: Germans have always been more than willing to fight Germans. They have never been united in the sense that the classic nation-states of Europe were and remain united.[18]

Initially, Romanticism was a largely cultural and intellectual phenomenon and fairly apolitical in orientation. The historian Thomas Nipperdey, for example, points out that "Romantic nationalism is based on culture, not on the state."[19] The Napoleonic wars and the resulting efforts at national liberation caused a clear politicization of Romantic thinking, however. National unity and identity were increasingly sought along Romantic lines. In the words of Nipperdey, "the cultural conception of the nation was politicized. . . . Romantic nationalism became the legitimating idea and one of the driving forces behind the claim to national self-determination. [This nationalism] was connected with the idea of popular sovereignty and liberal rights, [acquiring] a revolutionary character."[20]

Emphasis was placed on the importance of the *Volk*, a concept that implied a mixture of "nation," "race," and "people."[21] Insofar as a sense of German identity was sought that was felt to be distinct from the modernizing neighbors to the West, however, elements of an often ill-defined, antimodern, and "anti-Western" notion of *Deutschtum* ("Germanness") developed, alongside persisting liberal conceptions.[22]

The idea gradually took hold that Germany, as "land of the middle," bearer of a higher form of *Kultur*, had the exceptional historical destiny of being either the bulwark against or the bridge between the (decadent) West and the (uncivilized) East. In this Central European geographic area, where the liberal bourgeoisie was particularly conspicuous in its weakness, the mere achievement of national unity became more important than the political nature of the regime that would govern the new realm. This was especially true in the years following the failed liberal revolution of 1848, when, according to Nipperdey, "Romantic nationalism [was increasingly] connected with a new conception of the State which emerged [in the work of] Rousseau and Hegel—independently of Romanticism and nationalism," whereby the State was frequently seen "more as [the expression of] collective power than as instrument of individual liberties."[23]

But the sense of German identity, as it developed in the nineteenth century, notably after 1848, was fundamentally flawed, which itself had crucial consequences for the German worldview. There were rather clear elements of artificiality, self-deception, and unreality in the search for identity. National unity was to be imposed on regions that had had often markedly different historical experiences, and that were by no means culturally homogeneous, aside from a common language. Fundamental inspiration was derived from the old ideal of the *Reich*, particularly the Holy Roman Empire.[24] Unfortunately, that ideal was as much based on fiction as on fact. Moreover, the Reich could never be a mere nation. It stood for a larger vision. And even if it meant something more than a nation, its geographic boundaries were fundamentally ambiguous. And when it finally came, in 1871, national unity was achieved along "small-German" (*kleindeutsch*) lines (that is, excluding the German-speaking parts of the Austrian empire) and had little in common with the old Holy Roman Empire.

Thus unity was not achieved on the basis of an integrative national experience such as revolution, but rather in large measure by force, conquest, and imposition. As Alain Clement has put it, "Germany reached the goal [of national unity] faster than the Germans. Political unity was not achieved in the heart of Germany, but in the palace of Versailles, on foreign soil, sealed by virtue of [warfare]. The 'miracle' of 1871 became a matter of national self-evidence, accompanied by the suppression of a real national [identity]."[25] Thus, the problem of identity was never fully resolved, and continues to play a central role in German politics and culture to the present day. Bailey, therefore, concludes:

> This is the German Problem: what, where, and when is, was, or will be Germany? "Germany" was never more or less what it should have been; it was always less or more than it should have been. The "Germans" have always been more than a nation and therefore always less than one. They were, in fact, many nations and tribes, but the whole was always less than the sum of its parts.[26]

Germany was late in achieving national unity, compared with most other Western countries, although *not* when compared with its neighbors to the East and Southeast. Having come late as a nation-state and sensing a continued degree of artificiality in their national identity, many Germans developed a worldview with some notable traits. There was a pervasive sense of failure. Bailey calls this the "almost factor" in German history. "Except for Bismarck's half-century, German history is an unbroken chain of failures-by-a-hair, of maddeningly near misses and no cigars."[27] Many Germans acquired an image of their own history marked by a high degree of discontent and dissatisfaction. According to Clement, "from the very beginning the Germans were dissatisfied with Germany and, therefore, with themselves. From century to century drags this oppressive feeling, that Germany falls short of its developmental potential, short of its duty of self-determination."[28] One finds considerable evidence of pervasive self-pity and a deep sense of inferiority, although this runs clearly counter to a more common international perception of the Germans as arrogant and self-confident. In Germany, political and cultural pessimism became very much intertwined.[29]

Hans Kohn has sought to point to the linkage between this historical German sense of tragedy and failure and a simultaneous desire to assert a German exceptionalism.

> From the Hohenstaufen to the Hohenzollern, Germany has written some truly tragic pages in the history of Europe. Perhaps for this reason Germans have claimed to feel the tragic character of history more strongly and to meditate more intensely about it than do others. This pessimistic attitude toward history divides the Germans from the English-speaking peoples and has made mutual understanding in the realm of political thought difficult indeed. The Germans easily succumb to the strange fascination which words such as *Schicksal* (fate) or *Verhängnis* (doom) exercise upon

them. These are both words which are used as a matter of course in their scholarly writings and among the general public. They convey an untranslatable overtone of inevitability. They endow many Germans with the certainty of understanding the course of history in a deeper way than the more superficial peoples of the West. In this higher spirituality these Germans found a compensation for Germany's allegedly undeserved national misfortunes.[30]

Writing of this tendency toward a compensating response, Clement has suggested that "[t]he foundation of the Prussian-German view of history consisted . . . of a permanent urge to prove oneself, an urge that often expressed itself in demands made on the outside world." Löwenthal observes that "due to this situation of historical discontinuity, the philosophy of history has acquired for the Germans, to a greater extent than for other peoples, a special, quasi-religious meaning, . . . a salvific connotation."[31] The result was a "political messianism."

It is important to stress this *importance of the past*, whether real or mythical, as a source of inspiration, roots, and identity for today and tomorrow, in the German experience. Many of the historically dominant German attitudes regarding the past, the present, and the future have been amply shared by other European countries. In this worldview, the world of one's ancestors can still speak to the present. History may be full of discontinuity for almost all European countries, but memories linger, monuments and some institutions remain, traditions are passed on, and reminders of the past constantly appear.

The German perspective on the past is strongly connected with the uncertainties of German identity, however. Germany has experienced more historical discontinuity than most major nations in recent times. Hence, the meaning of history and its lessons are perhaps less self-evidently conceived in German culture. This fact may help to explain the traditional popularity of philosophy of history in Germany.[32] When history's designs do not seem to spring naturally from the national experience, the purposes of history must be constructed and imposed by means of human intervention. When the national experience seems to be one of frequent or constant political retardation and failure, explanation and amelioration may be found by discovering the nation's true mission in history. Historiography can drift into ideology.

German orientations toward the past have by no means been devoid of illusionary idealizations. This is what I would call the "imaginary golden age" phenomenon. The leading German historical ideal, certainly until World War I, if not World War II, was probably the Holy Roman Empire, with the perspective very much fixed on assumed medieval conditions, and tied to a conception of a positively "special German path" (*deutscher Sonderweg*).

The idealization of the past, including a purported German *Sonderweg*, focused on the Wilhelmine era, was quite pronounced during the Weimar years, for example. The historian Wolfgang J. Mommsen has argued that a consistent German misconception of the past helped doom the Weimar Republic.

The democratic new beginning of Weimar had, right from the start, but little chance of survival. This new beginning was overshadowed not so much by the past itself, but by the image that the great majority of Germans had of that past and to which they clung with remarkable stubbornness. Consequently, it was impossible to put an end to the authoritarian and imperial traditions of the Kaiserreich, which would have permitted the construction [of a democratic system] on new foundations. Rather, all shortcomings of the present were blamed on the Versailles 'Diktat' and the [political] Left. . . . The unwillingness and inability of the Germans to risk a true confrontation with their own past, and their satisfaction with a superficial idealization of the Kaiserreich, thus ended in a catastrophe of worldwide proportions.[33]

Mommsen points out that "the collapse of National Socialist rule in the wake of military defeat in 1945 deprived the Germans of the possibility to entertain any further illusions about their own history."[34] But that is when new problems of historical interpretation and evaluation began.

A Difficult Fatherland

The issue of identity and fragile, delayed unity in the German historical experience may be still more clearly understood from an explicitly *political* perspective. Many analyses of what is commonly referred to as the German Question or Problem have been deeply concerned with its political-cultural aspects. We first turn to an overview of the commonly identified aspects of Germany's troubled political tradition. After that, we examine separately the important debate about Germany's sociopolitical history that has emerged in recent years. This dispute has centered on the twin questions of whether the path of German political development was truly "unique" or even "deviant" in a negative sense and whether the pre-1945 German political tradition was really as illiberal as is usually suggested. Both conservative and more left-wing historians have staked out their positions in this debate, with the argument emphasizing either a stronger bourgeois-liberal tradition in Germany than is commonly assumed or a more illiberal political legacy in those nations, such as Britain and France, compared with which Germany is so often seen as negatively deviant.

It has become a commonplace in postwar discussions of German history that the experience of German Liberalism has been a troubled one. Although no one can deny that both Liberalism and Socialism (or Social Democracy) constitute significant ideological elements in the political history of modern Germany, nevertheless one scholar after another has stressed the consequences of Germany's growing alienation from the philosophical and political legacy of the eighteenth-century Enlightenment in the course of the nineteenth and early twentieth centuries: a strongly statist, authoritarian, conservative political tradition.[35] Whereas Liberalism spread through most of Western Europe during the nineteenth century, so the argument goes, the movement failed repeatedly to take full root in German political life.[36]

In German history, the achievement of nationhood and the cause of democracy became fatefully separated. Germany's fledgling Liberal movement surrendered its hopes for freedom and democracy in return for the realization of its second dream: national unity.[37] In the century that followed, German Liberals would remain seriously split into two major factions: the National Liberals, who largely made their peace with the German Reich and its troubled political system, and the Progressive Liberals, who continued the quest for further political liberalization and democratization. It was a split that was still visible in the post-1945 West German Free Democratic Party. This defeat of Liberalism after 1848, together with the victory of its illiberal opponents, helped to shape a political tradition that was shaken but not shattered by World War I. Its persistence, in spite of the presence of other political traditions in Germany (Liberalism and Social Democracy in particular), doomed the Weimar experiment and created a political climate that at least indirectly made the Nazi assumption of power possible.

Several facets of this illiberal political tradition deserve closer examination.[38] Perhaps the most commonly noted characteristic is the political supremacy of the state. In the Liberal understanding, the state is seen as essentially artificial, set up by means of social contract and subject to the control of society's elected representatives. The Liberal conception of citizenship makes political obedience contingent upon the state's recognition of and respect for each citizen's inalienable natural rights.

Such ideas have historically been much less common in central Europe. Karl Dietrich Bracher's classical contrast between the Anglo-American and the continental European (especially German) political experience is worth quoting at length. He points to

the historical difference between the forms of democratization adopted on the continent and by the Anglo-Saxons. In Britain and America democratization amounted to 'adoption of the state by the people'; on the continent it was 'integration of a self-governing people into a state', although, as opposed to France, the state in Germany still only existed as an idea [before 1870]. After the failure of 1848 the liberal movement, strong though it was, gave increasing preference to foreign policy based on the ideal of national freedom and unity over internal policy based on the ideal of individual liberty and the constitution; as a result it became subject to the reactionary authority of the princely courts, the military and the bureaucracy. Bismarck and Prussia, both pillars and symbols of this reaction on the part of the old-established order, contrived to impose on the people their long-sought German nation-state by means of revolution from above. The result was a Prussian authoritarian substitute for the liberal democratic nation-state which had been the object prior to 1848. It satisfied the longings of the unity movement, however, and so was able at the same time to absorb the bourgeois-liberal emancipation movement into the structure of an ostensibly constitutional, semi-absolutist state based on feudalism, the military and officialdom.[39]

Before the Enlightenment, the German states had shared in the prevalent European tendency of royal absolutism and its notions of *Staatsräson* (reason of state) and divine right. This tradition persisted in Germany into the nineteenth century, however, while it was in noticeable decline elsewhere. The spread in Germany of cultural Romanticism and philosophical Idealism undermined the Liberal potential of the German *Aufklärung*.[40] The state was not seen as the artificial creation of an emancipated society, but rather as an abstract, at times even anthropomorphized, entity with a life and purpose of its own.[41] Hegel's Idealist theory, neo-Platonic in inspiration, was very influential in this regard. According to Bracher,

> even among the majority of liberals, the German idea of freedom was constricted from the outset and increasingly by the concept of the state as the law-and-order authority standing above party. Initially under this concept of the state a place was to be found for freedom of the individual within society but ultimately concessions were made to defensive conservative forces and so there came about that concept of the state which has increasingly governed the juridical and political thinking of the citizenry since the age of romanticism and which places an exaggerated emphasis on the theories of Hegel.[42]

The conception of *Staat* was continuously contrasted with the realm of *Gesellschaft* (society), that is, the arena of selfish interests and private pursuits that should not be permitted to interfere with the higher realm of *Staatsräson*. In the words of Bracher, "the state was presented as something either contrasting with or superior to the realities of party politics, parliamentary government and pluralist democracy."[43] Political life was to be guided by what was known as *das Primat der Außenpolitik* ("the primacy of foreign policy"), and in this realm of foreign policy the state reigned supreme. As a result, the German military establishment acquired increasingly preponderant influence over German political affairs, which has led some to characterize the Second Reich as a *Militärstaat*. The extent to which this development was influenced by Germany's particular geopolitical location and late unification, rather than some more purely domestic set of factors, is difficult to determine.[44]

From the point of view of political culture, the most common way to describe the German political tradition has been the notion of the *obrigkeitsstaatliche Tradition* ("the tradition of the authoritarian state"). The state was seen as neutral and politically independent, staffed by a conservative, authoritarian *Beamtentum* (civil service).[45] The attitudes of the general population, faced with the state's traditional *Obrigkeit* (authority), constituted what is called an *Untertanenkultur*, roughly equivalent to what Gabriel Almond and Sidney Verba identified as a "subject" political culture.[46] Its characteristics were an emphasis on duty, loyalty, obedience, and a worship of power (*Macht*), tied to an apolitical frame of mind, and a deep-seated yearning for consensus and harmony.[47] The power of the state and the weakness and incompleteness of any modern sense of competent citizenship were perhaps the most central facet of the German illiberal political tradition.

Another, and related, aspect of this tradition is the idea of the *Rechtsstaat*. The *Rechtsstaat* aims at the creation of a legal system of governance, especially in a constitutional sense, that provides for executive "neutrality" on the part of the state and political predictability for the citizen. Although the emphasis is on legal order, this order need not necessarily be undemocratic. The sources and extent of citizen rights become the decisive issue. These rights were rather limited in traditional Germany, and characterized by a fairly formalistic definition. They were part of a democratic façade that was firmly embedded in a predominantly traditional sociopolitical setting. In the *Rechtsstaat*, the citizens were essentially dependent on the state for their rights, and that same state could change, restrict, or suspend those rights by claiming the prerogative of *Staatsräson*.[48] Allegedly neutral and above vulgar politics, the state, and the conservative elites who were its mainstay, could silence those who sought to alter the German political order as *Reichsfeinde*, enemies of the Reich.

The argument can be made that the *Rechtsstaat* tradition has left a conservative legacy in German political culture, a predilection for legalistic formalism,[49] a tendency to absolutize and rigidify existing political (and even socioeconomic) foundations, and a predisposition to employ inflexible juridical fictions in political life. It is also a tradition that is revealing of what is often judged to be the rather paternalistic German conception of politics: Rights and reforms are expected to come from above, resulting in a thoroughly unrevolutionary political frame of mind. This feature of recent German political experience is further highlighted by the fact that actual attempts at revolution have tended to fail and major domestic changes have come as a result of defeat in war and, most recently, by means of foreign occupation, although the 1989–1990 events in East Germany would seem to represent a significant exception to this general legacy. The notion of legitimate political resistance could not develop in such a political-cultural climate.

A further aspect of the illiberal German political tradition is the German tendency toward *Konfliktscheu*[50] or limited *Konfliktfähigkeit*, that is, an unwillingness and inability to tolerate or cope with manifestations of conflict in political life, even if in the form of debate or nonviolent competition.[51] This resulted in intolerance vis-à-vis dissidents, a utopian search for sociopolitical harmony and consensus, exaggerated defamation of political opponents, a constant hunt for political scapegoats, and a tendency toward ideological absolutism resulting in an inability to compromise. Fearful of controversy and yearning for security, harmony, and predictability, the citizen "escapes" into the sheltering embrace of the "neutral" but omnipotent state and turns into an apolitical subject.[52] The idea then takes hold that politics is best left to those who "know best." Hence arose the strongly Platonic and elitist conception of politics that seemed to characterize traditional German political culture.

An interesting manifestation of the paradoxically apolitical quality of traditional German mass political culture involved a separation between *Kultur* and

Geist ("spirit") on one side and *Politik* and *Macht* (power) on the other side. At first, *Kultur* and *Geist* involved an escape from political responsibility into the lofty realm of true self-fulfillment by means of *Bildung* ("education" with a connotation of "formation") and a developed sense of *Humanität* ("humanity," linked to a cultivation of the liberal arts). This was the realm where ethics and innocence dwelled beyond the reach of the tough and compromising world of politics. This conception of *Kultur* and *Geist* was essentially aristocratic and elitist. But it was accompanied by a conception of *Volk* (people) and *Gemeinschaft* (community) that was at first equally apolitical, while referring to the cultural traits and qualities of the German people (the idea of the *Kulturnation*).[53]

Both conceptions, involving a separation of politics and culture, were increasingly politicized in the course of the nineteenth century, especially after the *Reichsgründung* (foundation of the empire) of 1871. The idea of *Kultur* shed its earlier, purer association with philosophical Idealism and developed into what Fritz Stern has called a *Vulgäridealismus*.[54] German *Kultur* became strongly associated with German *Realpolitik*. Attitudes of cultural darwinism and messianism spread, with profound consequences for the course of German foreign policy. An anti-Western, romanticized sense of *Deutschtum* emerged in German political life. The conceptions of *Volk* and *Gemeinschaft* were driven to their racial extremes in the Third Reich. The politicization of both conceptions (*Geist/Kultur* and *Volk/Gemeinschaft*) occurred on a thoroughly illiberal basis and under conservative, authoritarian auspices.[55]

Finally, this troubled, illiberal legacy in German political life must be placed in the context of the development of German nationalism and the prevailing conception of German nationhood. Nationalism is probably the most decisive ideology in modern history. The impact of nationalist fervor on domestic political life and foreign policy has not by any means been unique to the German experience. The quest for nationhood is a central theme in all modern Western (even world) history. Yet there are historical aspects of German nationalism that clearly differentiate it from developments in neighboring Western European nation-states.[56]

In post-1871 Germany, nationalism was not the ideological by-product of a successful revolution or war of independence, as had been the case in, say, France, England, or America. Until the *Reichsgründung* of 1871, German nationalist sentiment had contained both liberal and conservative strands. The former tendency was more favorable toward the emancipatory political quality of modern nationalism, whereas the latter tendency was more hostile regarding any association of radical Enlightenment beliefs with the idea of German nationhood. The German bourgeoisie proved to be too weak and divided to make the liberal form of nationalism prevail. Their greatest chance came in 1848, but the attempt at a national, liberal revolution failed. As a consequence, conservative, authoritarian nationalism prevailed, and German national unity was established by means of warfare, under the auspices of illiberal, reluctant Prussia. Germany's *delayed* national unification separated the idea of nationhood and nationalism from the Enlightenment.[57]

The idea of the nation-state was gradually emptied of any modern political connotations and infused with culturally antimodern and anti-Western sentiments. It should also be remembered that many German or Germanic peoples (especially the Austrians) remained outside the Second Reich. The latter fact implied that a potential nationalist irredentism was built into the Reich's psychological foundations, the power of which was demonstrated by subsequent German history.

It was precisely the delay in national unification, together with the identity problems brought on by the Reich's apparent artificiality and its weak *Staatsidee* ("conception of state"), that imparted to post-1871 German nationalism its ideological virulence. It was a reactionary nationalism, based on a conservative anxiety regarding the socioeconomic changes that were being experienced by all nation-states in industrializing, nineteenth-century Western Europe. Consequently, it was a nationalism with a decidedly illiberal political content, implacably opposed to competing political ideologies, such as Liberalism or Socialism. It was a cultural nationalism that stressed the purported virtues and mission of the German *Kulturnation*, leading to political intolerance toward those who were considered (potentially) *un-deutsch*, such as Catholics or Socialists.

It was perhaps above all a compensatory nationalism, dedicated to seeking Germany's rightful "place in the sun." Together with the political irredentism of the incomplete Reich (especially after the disintegration of the Habsburg empire in 1919) and the assertive messianism of the *Kulturnation* ideology, this compensatory nationalism was a driving force behind Germany's increasingly aggressive diplomatic behavior in the first half of the twentieth century.[58] In summary, in the words of Bracher, the genesis of German unity in the course of the last decades of the 1800s

> brought into the open the great cleavage which ultimately destroyed any foundation, based on the communal freedoms, which the democratic national emancipation movement might have possessed; this was the cleavage between the principle of an internal political structure based on democracy and that of nationhood considered in terms of foreign policy, between the internal and external political connotations of the concept of freedom, between the rights of the citizen and the power-policy demands of the nation-state. . . . The newly awakened national consciousness was directed primarily to the attainment of national power-policy ends and so internal liberty and organization were subordinated to the concept of external freedom. Nationalism was consequently used to further a spurious defensive ideology in the service of existing power relationships; instead of giving concrete political expression to the interest of the people it degenerated into a non-political metaphysical concept of the absolute importance of the nation. A German ideology serving the ends of reaction and the patriarchal state was able to restrain or divert the democratic tendencies inherent in the concept of the nation and even to make use of the concept in the fight against democracy.[59]

In an interesting study, Harold James ventures in a somewhat different direction and seeks to trace some of the links between Germany's *economic* development in

the course of the nineteenth century and the evolution of its national *political* identity. His analysis focuses on "the emergence in the mid-nineteenth century of a doctrine of nationality that justified the existence of the nation primarily by reference
to the inexorable logic of economic development. . . . [T]he nation became the
framework for an economic process that would in turn create political and cultural
consciousness." In addition, he stresses that these developments must be placed in
the context of the evolving "state of international politics."[60]

According to James, "[i]n the nineteenth century and for most of the twentieth, Germany was a political territory in which institutions failed to provide any
true stability and continuity. Germans looked to foreign models for inspiration,
and attempted to assimilate these in a theory of Germanness. Each process of
adoption proved to be problematic, and gave rise to a generational reaction and
rejection." He concludes that

> German nationalism had appeared first without any political content, as an expres-
> sion of a sense of cultural community. As a reaction to the French Revolution, to in-
> vasion and occupation by the revolutionary and Napoleonic armies, and to consti-
> tutional upheavals in the 1800s, it acquired a political edge. Nationality defined itself
> in opposition to the contemporary order of international politics, rather than as a
> more positive doctrine. . . . In the middle of the nineteenth century, economics be-
> came the central consideration for nationalists. Prosperity alone could sustain the
> social community essential to national integration.[61]

Economic calculations, blended into a conservative nationalism, came to play a
major role in the creation of the Second Reich, but by the early twentieth century
a culturally oriented reaction against this preoccupation with economic success
by elements of younger generations became noticeable, akin to what would later
happen in the West Germany of the 1960s and 1970s. According to James, German "national identity" over the past 200 years has tended to move "from cultural, to political, to economic, and then back to a series of cultural claims." And
for him it is this "peculiar cycle that justifies a German claim to uniqueness."[62]

The importance attached to the troublesome aspects of this political tradition
for an explanation of the course of modern German history can, needless to say,
be exaggerated. Richard J. Evans has argued that

> [t]here is no reason either in theory or in practice to deny the existence of continu-
> ities of social attitudes and institutions or political values and ideologies from the
> age of Prussian absolutism in the eighteenth century up to the parliamentary
> democracy of the Weimar Republic. What is at issue, surely, is the interpretive weight
> that should be placed on these continuities. The real problem with recent work on
> German history is that much of it has enlarged the weight of these "feudal" continu-
> ities beyond the bounds of usefulness or plausibility, until they have come to domi-
> nate the whole explanatory procedure.[63]

It is certainly appropriate to emphasize that a potential for Liberalism persisted in some German areas, especially the southwest. Nor can it be denied that the Weimar Republic was a genuine attempt on the part of some segments of German society to establish a more truly liberal-democratic political system. Nor is it proper to suggest that Nazism and its crimes were the inevitable outcome of German political development. Although the main aspects of the German political tradition as sketched above are noted by a great number of observers, there is not an absolute consensus. In fact, some have argued that the Germany of the Second Reich and the Weimar Republic was not nearly as illiberal as it has often been portrayed.[64] In the context of this study, the facets of the illiberal tradition are subject to special emphasis, however, since they point to the Germans' historical difficulties with regard to their political culture and identity.

This general survey of the pre-1945 German political tradition contains at least two important implications in the context of this study. First, one can argue that various aspects of this tradition were crucially related to the nature and development of German foreign policy. Whether domestic political conditions shaped foreign policy or were themselves shaped by the exigencies of Germany's international setting is still open to debate. Perhaps influences flowed in both directions simultaneously. At any rate, the relation between both realms seems to have been very significant. The worship of *Staat, Macht,* and *Realpolitik,* the sociopolitical preeminence of the military establishment, the friend-foe style of political life, and the relative passivity of the citizenry— these features of German political life, together with an increasingly militant nationalism, had an important impact on the conduct of German diplomacy, especially during the Wilhelmine and Nazi epochs. Thus, suggesting a direct link between this troubled political tradition and German diplomacy, Fritz Stern has written that

[t]he domestic tensions of an illiberal regime had profound repercussions on German foreign policy as well. It is my contention that the conditions of illiberalism at home prescribed an aggressive stance in German policy abroad and that the illiberal style at home bred a similar style in the conduct of foreign policy so that, quite aside from the substantive antagonism that Germany would inevitably have encountered, her mode of operation enhanced her dangers and contributed to the coming of the Great War.[65]

Second, this political tradition has had an important influence on political life in the Federal Republic—on the one hand, in terms of partial continuity and persistence; on the other hand, as a source of "lessons" and consciously negative contrast. As far as the latter point is concerned, Wolfgang J. Mommsen has suggested that "a free [political] order in the west of Germany has only been possible by means of a break with essential elements of the German tradition and a free adoption of Western European and American examples."[66]

Beyond the Illiberal Tradition:
Voices of Doubt and Dissent

Much of the writing on Germany's illiberal political legacy that appeared in the decades after 1945 was the result of a desire to explain Germany's fatal susceptibility to Fascism in general and the occurrence of the Nazi disaster in particular. Early postwar attempts to account for Nazism as an "accident" in German history, a deviant episode largely unconnected with earlier epochs and traditions, gave way to the widely accepted idea of the negative German *Sonderweg* ("separate/special path") in modern Western history. It was suggested that the Third Reich and Germany's pre-1933 sociopolitical heritage were intimately connected, whereby the fateful consequences of the country's illiberal political tradition received a great deal of emphasis. In the final analysis, the idea of the German *Sonderweg* implied a disastrous degree of illiberal continuity.

In recent years, the "orthodoxy" of the German *Sonderweg* has been subjected to important challenges in both historiography and social science, in Germany as well as abroad. Richard J. Evans sees this as the "*normalization* of German historiography" after a long period of scholarly distortions.[67] Questions have been raised about the notion that an experience of "flawed modernization," whereby Germany supposedly underwent a modern capitalist transformation without completing the "normal" liberal-bourgeois political revolution, preconditioned German society for the Nazi outcome, unlike countries such as England, France, and the United States, which were treated as "normative" Liberal success stories. It is clear, therefore, that a full consideration of Germany's political legacy must consider some of the important critiques and attempted revisions put forth in recent years.

Arguably one of the most influential books to appear in this debate over Germany's purported sociopolitical *Sonderweg* has been *The Peculiarities of German History* by David Blackbourn and Geoff Eley.[68] According to Evans, this book "mounts a new and explicitly Marxist challenge to recently developed liberal interpretations" of German history.[69] Blackbourn and Eley see as the "major theme" of their work the attempt "to address some critical questions to the notion of the peculiarity of German history—the idea of a German *Sonderweg* which diverged from the history of other (western) countries."[70]

As far as the central notion of the *Sonderweg* is concerned, the two British historians point out that "[b]y and large, those who talked before 1945 about a German *Sonderweg* were more often inclined to endow this with a positive value,"[71] as we saw in the discussion of the idea of superior *Deutschtum.* "Notions of a positive German *Sonderweg* were given a fillip by the First World War (the 'ideas of 1914'), and they retained a powerful purchase through the years of the Weimar Republic."[72] Popular as well as scholarly conceptions of the German *Sonderweg* underwent a fundamental change as a result of the Nazi disaster, however. Blackbourn and Eley note that many post-war German historians have taken over the old view of a special German development and turned it on its head. The positive view of the German *Sonderweg* was largely discredited, at least in its overt form, by the Third Reich and the total defeat of 1945. When the idea reappeared in the 1950s, and still more in the 1960s, it had negative connotations. How, it was asked, had the German catastrophe been possible? The answer was found in the fatefully aberrant pattern of German history, by western standards. Thus the German *Sonderweg* was reinstated with all the moral signs reversed. With 1933–1945 understandably regarded as the awful culmination of modern German history, the roots of Nazi success were now located in the peculiar pattern of German ideological, institutional, and political development, stretching back into the previous century.[73]

Most scholarship based on this idea of the Germans' fateful *Sonderweg* stresses important facets of sociopolitical continuity between the Imperial, Weimar, and (early) Nazi eras, focused on the persistent predominance in German political and social life of the "traditional preindustrial elite." In this interpretation of modern German history, the Nazi period and World War II mark a decisive watershed. "Only the Third Reich and the total defeat of 1945 finally dislodged this stubborn elite from its anachronistic, but commanding, heights. In this sense, 1945 really was *Stunde Null*, or year zero. Only after 1945 did German society— at least in the west—finally come into its own, its non-western peculiarities sloughed off and its political life and social values now cast in the image of those earlier, more successful western bourgeoisies."[74]

In their study of nineteenth-century German society, economics, politics, and culture, Blackbourn and Eley present some criticisms and propose some revisions of this dominant view of German history, because they feel that "the critical edge which arguments about the *Sonderweg* have lent to the study of modern German history" has "become blunted."[75]

First, they challenge the very idea of a *Sonderweg* for any country.[76] They argue that "[i]n order to have an aberration it is clearly necessary to have a norm." Noting that "it was 'western' and most particularly Anglo-American and French developments that were taken as a yardstick against which German history was measured and found wanting," they suggest that "this kind of approach . . . can easily come to rest on a misleading and idealized picture of historical developments in those countries that are taken as models."[77] Instead, they prefer to look "in new ways at what actually did happen in German history."[78] Or, as Evans puts it, "both authors argue that the Kaiserreich must be looked at on the basis of its own conditions, not as the arena of an interplay of pre-industrial continuities, nor as a simple curtain-raiser to the later Weimar period and the Third Reich."[79]

Second, Blackbourn and Eley seek to revise one of the most central elements of the alleged German *Sonderweg*: "the failure of a proper bourgeois revolution."[80] Eley deplores the extent to which "the assumption that Germany did not have a bourgeois revolution in the nineteenth century has structured our general understanding of the German past."[81] The basic point they wish to make is that "the gaping hole where the bourgeoisie should have been was something of an illusion: the German bourgeoisie had not been quite so absent from the historical stage." Consequently, they seek to identify and describe "a less abject bourgeois role in modern German history."[82]

Blackbourn and Eley suggest that "we can make a reasonable case for arguing that Germany did, after all, experience a successful bourgeois revolution in the nineteenth century."[83] Their research focuses on "the unfolding of an authentically bourgeois society in nineteenth-century Germany, looking especially at property rights and ideas of competition, the rule of law, the emergence of voluntary associations and public opinion, and new patterns of taste, patronage, and philanthropy." They feel that one can speak of a distinct "embourgeoisement of German society," and add that the "social rapprochement between bourgeoisie and landowning class in Germany from around the 1870s" was by no means fully unique to Germany but was instead perhaps part of a more general European pattern of social development at the time.[84]

Turning to the German bourgeoisie's alleged failure to consolidate itself as a truly dominant political force commensurate with its socioeconomic significance, Blackbourn and Eley note that "the idea of a failed bourgeois revolution requires some notion of bourgeois revolutions elsewhere that succeeded," but then they proceed to "question whether one can in fact talk plausibly of a bourgeoisie anywhere which seized power and recast the state and politics after its own image."[85] Eley concludes that "national forms of bourgeois revolution may vary considerably, and certainly can't be identified straightforwardly with either the British or French examples."[86] They essentially suggest that an explicit and definitive bourgeois *political* revolution resulting in a fully developed liberal parliamentary democracy did not occur anywhere in the West. Instead, they define the notion of a "bourgeois revolution" primarily in socioeconomic, cultural, and legal terms, and they question the extent to which *any* nineteenth-century bourgeoisie was truly committed to "democracy" in the full sense.

The political failure of Germany's nineteenth- and early twentieth-century bourgeoisie is judged to be not its absence from the political stage but rather its "division and weakness" as a political actor in spite of clear socioeconomic power.[87] Bourgeois socioeconomic and cultural unity and power paralleled bourgeois political division and weakness. In addition, the extent to which the German bourgeoisie drifted into the embrace of conservative, illiberal political forces in order to escape the (perceived) radical threat and popular discontent emanating especially from the Left (Social Democrats during the Empire, Communists during the Weimar Republic) is reemphasized by the two British historians. It is in the weakness and internal political division of the German bourgeoisie, and the resulting "unstable and febrile nature of German political culture" during the Empire, that Blackbourn and Eley see a crucial degree of "continuity" shaping pre-1933 German history. They conclude that "the popular social and political roots of National Socialism must be sought in the period before war [1914–1918] and revolution [1918]." At the same time, however, they insist that "German history from 1848 to 1945 was not a one-way street which came to an end with the Third Reich and allowed the new post-war departure."[88]

Revisionist interpretations of modern German history like the one provided by Blackbourn and Eley have been eagerly received by more conservative historians in (West) Germany who have long sought to counter the scholarly as well as political dominance of the liberal *Sonderweg* approach.[89] It should be remembered that historiography is an integral part of present-day political dispute and controversy in a country that is so obviously burdened by the legacy of its own troubled and violent past. The irony that the Blackbourn and Eley revision had neo-Marxist roots and was produced in England, the purported model of liberal "normalcy" that had inspired so many of the liberal West German adherents of the *Sonderweg* explanation, did not diminish its impact among more conservative historians like the late Thomas Nipperdey.

In a collection of essays, Nipperdey takes on an issue that is clearly central to the whole *Sonderweg* debate: the alleged continuity in modern German history generated by an exclusively illiberal modernization experience.[90] Although many of Nipperdey's arguments actually do not radically diverge from much of the *Sonderweg* perspective, his conclusions are nonetheless different in a number of important ways. He rejects the notion that the "discrepancy" between socio-economic and political modernization, plus the accumulation of modernization crises, in nineteenth- and early twentieth-century Germany provide the "key . . . to the history of National Socialism," and considers the idea that the "missing democratization" explains "the instability of the Weimar Republic . . . and the victory of Hitler" to be "misleading." He suggests that "the political-social system in Germany before 1914 was in no way as immobile as it is often depicted," and maintains that "the authoritarian tradition made the Nazi seizure of power easier, but cannot explain the genesis of the revolutionary Fascist mass movement."[91] Nipperdey sees the roots of National Socialism in a specifically German version of a historically more widespread "crisis of modernization," but not as the outgrowth of a deformed capitalism: "National Socialism was an answer to the fundamental [German] ambivalence vis-à-vis modernity," although adequate attention to the multiple crises affecting the Weimar Republic, plus some of the more accidental aspects of history, should be added for a full explanation.[92]

The conservative historian is particularly interested in correcting what he considers to be a "stereotypical" conception of Imperial German society as a mere *Untertanengesellschaft* ("society of subjects"). In the final analysis, he argues, Wilhelmine Germany must be analyzed with a sense of balance and fairness, whereby negative features and evidence of genuine change and reform are considered side by side. In view of standard interpretations of traditional Germany, particularly in the context of the *Sonderweg* idea, his conclusion aims clearly at a serious revision:

[Pre-1914] German society was [undoubtedly] a society of subjects, oriented towards authority and obedience; the phenomenon of militarism should by no means
be downplayed. . . . And yet: German society before 1914 was also a society of right
and law, of relative liberalism and labor. [Pre-1914 society] was segmented in old-
fashioned ways but at the same time on the road to modern pluralism. It was a society of reforms, of departure from the nineteenth century, and above all of social reforms, and it was a critical society. [It was a society] that [steadily] became more
bourgeois and liberal, and that developed within itself the growing potential of a future democracy.[93]

He concludes that "[i]f all this was the case, then it seems much more important
to me today not to be fixated, [as has been done] over the past 80 years, on the
phenomenon of the subject [German], but instead to analyze the [pre-1914] crisis of the authoritarian political system [*Obrigkeits-Untertanensystem*] and its potential for change. Only then will we capture the true historical character of Wilhelmine society."[94]

Finally, Nipperdey takes issue most explicitly with supporters of the negative
German *Sonderweg* thesis when he calls into question their alleged inclination to
postulate a fundamental continuity in modern German history, whereby the Nazi
era helps explain the pre-1933 period while, arguing in an opposite direction, the
Third Reich is also seen as in many ways the (inevitable?) outcome of the recent
German past. Nipperdey concludes that "1933 is not the result of 'the' continuity
of German history, but rather that 1933 is connected with the majority of dominant (although varied) continuities of German history; without recourse to these
continuities no historical explanation [of Nazism] is possible."[95] In his view,
"[r]eality is not so unequivocal, it is not, as the [analytical] perspective predicated
on essential continuity would wish, particularly homogeneous; rather, [reality] is
contradictory and ambivalent. . . . History based on [the idea of] continuity in
practice tends . . . towards an overestimation of the inevitability of [historical]
developments and an underestimation of the possibilities for a different development [or outcome]. . . . The meaning of the German *Sonderweg* must be weighed
more precisely than has been done so far against European commonalities. . . .
The past is more than [mere] pre-history."[96]

In conclusion, an examination of recent critiques of the liberal *Sonderweg* argument reveals four primary analytical directions. First, some analysts have questioned the very validity of an allegedly unique German *Sonderweg*, for example
by arguing that "in important respects Germany had been no less bourgeois than
Britain." They ask: "Was there really one Western norm from which Germany diverged?" and conclude that "[u]pon scrutiny every nation had its own exceptionalism." If each country is in some way unique and if an appropriate norm or standard of comparison does not really exist, then the whole notion of any country's
Sonderweg becomes "meaningless." One is left with inevitable "differences" instead of fateful "deviance."[97]

Second, as Charles S. Maier points out, "abandoning the *Sonderweg* as a starting point let historians do justice to the strengths of German civic life. The facile notion that Germans had no self-governing tradition crumbled as historians reemphasized a tissue of occupational associations, municipal self-government, and economic organization. Germany was hardly a feudal society bereft of urban institutions."[98] In other words, elements of a German liberal tradition were "rescued" from what has tended to be presented as a predominantly illiberal political history.[99]

Third, the thesis of National Socialism as an unfortunate "accident" (*Betriebsunfall*) in modern German history, without direct causal connection with the general German past or the intrinsic nature of German culture and/or society, could enjoy a partial revival.[100] This notion of a Weimar Republic succumbing to the demonic Nazis amid economic and political crisis, but not as the result of a particular German historical *Sonderweg*, had been a popular approach among conservative historians immediately after 1945, until it was overtaken by the liberals who placed more stress on the inevitable consequences of Germany's overall historical deviance. The *Betriebsunfall* argument has often had a distinctly apologetic quality, attractive to those who wish to present the Third Reich as a fundamentally deviant period in German history, thereby assisting in the lifting of some heavy national burdens. Its popularity in some quarters of the German political Right clearly persists.

More generally, Mommsen has suggested that much of the conservative critique of the liberals' *Sonderweg* thesis has been aimed at enabling the German people to acquire a less traumatic and more "positive" image of Germany's national history. "[These conservative interpretations] aim at pushing back the front-line of the [liberal] critique of the recent German past to such an extent that the general public may be enabled once again [to develop] an unembarrassed or at least less embarrassing identification with its own national past."[101] The neoconservative historian Michael Stürmer has played a particularly prominent role in this regard.[102]

Fourth, as Maier indicates, "[s]ome conservatives have refurbished a rival historical paradigm, one first proposed in the late nineteenth century. This is the quasi-determinism, not of social structures, but of geographic situation." This argument implies that "German historical identity has emerged from the nation's central position in Europe with exposed frontiers to east and west."[103] Historians like Michael Stürmer and Hagen Schulze have basically argued that "[t]he exposed geography . . . is the alleged source of German political difficulties."[104] Not only is the attempt made to explain Germany's domestic political fate by means of geographic factors, but the course of German diplomacy is also frequently interpreted with explicit reference to the nation's geopolitical situation in the center of Europe.[105]

The unification of West and East Germany has generated a resurgent debate about the nature, meaning, and implications of the German national past, as rejoined East and West Germans seek to define a clear overall national identity, beyond Cold War rhetoric, for the first time since 1945. In this debate, if we are to follow the thinking of Mommsen,

> [t]he basic question is whether the symbiosis of German and Western European thinking achieved during the 1960s and 1970s in the area of historical research and historical consciousness will survive into the future, or whether the Germans in the Federal Republic are also in the area of historical consciousness more or less beginning to go their own way again.[106]

It may well be that in this context the idea of a uniquely deviant German *Sonderweg* has lost much, if not most, of its former strength. Yet, the consistency with which the notion of a "German Question" returns to both the scholarly and the diplomatic agenda should serve as sufficient evidence that Germany is not (yet) considered a "normal" country, and that some critiques of the *Sonderweg* thesis have almost certainly overshot their target. What is meant here is not an affirmation of Germany's "deviance" but of the "uniqueness" of its historical experience. When all is said and done, this uniqueness is the essence and the secret of the German Question, and it is in search of that uniqueness that this book has been written.

Conclusion

We conclude this exploration of the issue of identity and national unity in pre-1945 Germany by reviewing briefly some of the major forces that helped shape the country's history. First, there is the fundamental significance of the German reaction to the Enlightenment, particularly in the form of Romanticism. It is important to remember that a more sympathetic reception of the Enlightenment had been more than a mere possibility before the Napoleonic wars, in the age of Goethe, Kant, and Lessing. Enlightenment philosophy had enjoyed a certain popularity in Prussia. However, Germany's historical fate separated it in crucial respects from trends in other Western European countries.

A second factor is the impact of the historical lag in Germany's national development, again compared with most other Western European nations. This basic fact has had tremendous consequences for Germany's identity and self-image, thereby affecting historically prevailing views of the world at large. Self-pity, perceived inferiority, the need for compensation, fear of further failure, an anxious search for identity, and a fear of weakness tied to a preoccupation with security have been some of the important effects of Germany's late and broken historical development. These first two sources, then, are key components in Germany's national experience.

A third and historically very significant factor has been Germany's geographic location in the center of the European continent. The country is often referred to as "land of the middle" (*Land in der Mitte*). As far as German culture in general is concerned, the country's location has imparted a considerable degree of cultural complexity and insecurity, further enhancing the uncertainty of identity. In many ways, Germany lies astride a fault line between some fundamentally different political, social, and cultural traditions. The country itself has often been the expression of conflicting cultural pulls and pressures. Its mixed cultural exposure, especially toward East and West, has given it a rather Janus-faced outlook.

A fourth important source of the traditional German worldview is the Lutheran heritage.[107] For the sake of accuracy, it is relevant to note that not all Germans are or ever have been Lutheran. The Lutheran *Evangelische Kirche* has been most prominent in northern and eastern Germany, while western and southern Germany have been predominantly Catholic. Since decisive power was historically exercised by Protestant Prussia, however, Lutheranism was able to acquire significant influence.

In Germany, the Lutheran tradition helped shape a rather pessimistic, socioculturally authoritarian outlook on life. According to Gordon Craig,

> Luther . . . believed that the existing political and social order, with all its inequalities and injustices, was an expression of the will of God, Who had also created government by secular authorities for the enforcement of law and order. The secular world was not a Christian order; most men were unregenerate sinners and had to be controlled by worldly wisdom or by force. But it was a necessary one, since, without an imposed order, chaos would result, and the existence and spread of Christianity would become impossible. Therefore, the individual Christian, who lived in a community of mercy and love, also had to fulfill his duty in the world of violence and sin. Bound by his conscience to an ethics of love, he also owed allegiance [to] the secular order, whose preservation was ordained by God; and, if he were called upon to serve it, as a soldier or office-holder, he must do his duty and regard his service as a form of worshiping his Maker.[108]

The Romantic era in Germany did not affect German Lutheranism in the way the Enlightenment modified or even undermined traditional religious forces elsewhere in the West. Thus, from a religious point of view, traditional German culture was quite unreceptive to modern Liberal ideas.

Finally, one should note a fifth source of culture: Prussia. This most powerful German state, largely responsible for the country's unification in the years after 1864, has become a prime historical villain, although Hermann Eich has urged us to remember that "[t]he Prussian character is more complex than many foreign critics suppose."[109] Prussia came to be seen as the root of German authoritarianism and militarism. The degree and extent to which Prussia was either a mere reflection or a basic source of German culture constitute an important but very complicated question, and one that this study will not attempt to answer.[110] It may be suggested, however, that, in view of its preeminent position among the

German states, Prussia was probably bound to become a cultural and sociopolitical model in many important areas. The Lutheran, authoritarian ethos was quite prevalent in Prussia and adjacent areas. The same can be said of many of the other cultural traits discussed earlier. It is possible to argue that the Romantic legacy has been less evident in Prussian culture. The martial spirit commonly associated with Prussia should be seen in the context of the historical roots and geographic location of that state. Insofar as Prussia was a somewhat artificial entity, created by an army rather than the reverse, largely landlocked and subject to a combination of cultural, military, and political pressures, its historical preoccupation with questions of identity and security is perhaps but a reflection of the more general German experience.[111]

Notes

1. Quoted in *The Economist*, 27 January 1990, p. 32.

2. Nietzsche's statement comes from his *Beyond Good and Evil* (paragraph 244), while Heine's famous lament appeared in his *Deutschland, ein Wintermärchen*. It was also Nietzsche who once suggested that "the profound and icy mistrust which the German arouses whenever he gets any power into his hands is the aftermath of that vast horrible fear with which, for long centuries, Europe dreaded the wrath of the Teutonic blond beast" (quoted in *Time*, 9 July 1990, p. 66).

3. Charles E. McClelland and Steven P. Scher, eds., *Postwar German Culture* (New York: E. P. Dutton, 1974), pp. 6, 8.

4. Quoted in Gordon A. Craig, *The Germans* (New York: G. P. Putnam's Sons, 1982), p. 15.

5. Richard Löwenthal, "Geschichtszerrissenheit und Geschichtsbewußtsein in Deutschland," in his *Gesellschaftswandel und Kulturkrise* (Frankfurt: Fischer Taschenbuch Verlag, 1979), pp. 240–242.

6. For a (controversial) illustration of enduring speculation about German "character" tendencies, see Leopold Bellak, "Why I Fear the Germans," *The New York Times*, 25 April 1990. But as a counterargument, see also Jeane Kirkpatrick, "Evil Lies in System, Not in the Race," *Los Angeles Times*, 18 February 1990.

7. See, for example, the rather stereotypical description of German prisoners-of-war by H. V. Dicks, "Some Psychological Studies of the German Character," in Tom H. Pear, ed., *Psychological Factors of Peace and War* (New York: Philosophical Library, 1950), p. 199. Sweeping stereotypes are by no means concocted only by non-Germans. In his *X-mal Deutschland* (München: Piper, 1961, pp. 15–18), Rudolf W. Leonhardt reports some negative German character traits that are often encountered in German analyses (including arrogance, extremism, authoritarianism, aggressiveness). See also Hermann Eich, *The Germans* (New York: Stein and Day, 1980; published originally in 1965 in the U.K. as *The Unloved Germans*), pp. 39–89.

8. Probably the best illustration of the persistence of this kind of "national character" thinking occurred in July 1990, when a British government minister was forced to resign after making highly provocative statements about the Germans (and the French and the EC). A subsequently leaked British government memo, which listed purported German

character traits ("bullying," "egotism," "angst," "aggressiveness," "inferiority complex," and "sentimentality"), only added fuel to the fire.

9. Some of these more positive features are mentioned by Hellpach, quoted in Eich, *The Germans*, p. 38.

10. Eich, *The Germans*, p. 10.

11. Willy Hellpach, *Der deutsche Charakter* (Bonn: Athenäum-Verlag, 1954), quoted in Eich, *The Germans*, pp. 10–11.

12. On the connection between national character and social class, see Hans Detlef Werner, *Klassenstruktur und Nationalcharakter* (Tübingen: Huth Verlag, 1967). As far as regional variation is concerned, Hermann Eich has argued that "[the] broad spectrum of regional characteristics which a German may possess . . . has seldom caused anyone, at least since 1945, to falter when pronouncing on the Germans or to take care in distinguishing between their numerous types and characteristics." Eich, *The Germans*, p. 24.

13. David Calleo, *The German Problem Reconsidered* (Cambridge: Cambridge University Press, 1978), pp. 123–124.

14. For a fundamental exploration of this theme, see Otto Dann, *Nation und Nationalismus in Deutschland, 1770–1990* (München: Verlag C. H. Beck, 1996).

15. Löwenthal, "Geschichtszerrissenheit und Geschichtsbewußtsein in Deutschland," p. 247. Craig also stresses the "relative failure in Germany of that great intellectual movement of the eighteenth century known as the Enlightenment." Craig, *The Germans*, p. 26ff.

16. George Bailey, *Germans* (New York: Avon Books, 1972), p. 188.

17. On the Romantic heritage in German culture, see especially Craig, *The Germans*, Chapter 9; Hans Kohn, *The Mind of Germany* (New York: Harper & Row, 1965), Chapter 3.

18. Bailey, *Germans*, p. 341.

19. Thomas Nipperdey, *Nachdenken über die deutsche Geschichte* (München: Verlag C. H. Beck, 1986), p. 121.

20. Nipperdey, *Nachdenken über die deutsche Geschichte*, p. 121. He concludes that "Romantic nationalism was closely related to the classical Liberalism of the 19th century. . . . The Romantic nationalists were politically all liberals, and they were, especially in Germany, the left-of-center [political] opposition" (p. 123). He suggests that the "separation of nationalism from the liberal tradition [in Germany]" occurred only toward the end of the nineteenth century (p. 124). Nipperdey's characterization of the liberal dimensions of Romantic nationalism certainly is not uncontested, however.

21. For further discussion, see George L. Mosse, *The Crisis of German Ideology* (New York: Grosset & Dunlap, 1964), especially Part I.

22. As Nipperdey reminds us, however, it is important to keep in mind that "Romantic nationalism . . . originally had a universalistic, cosmopolitan, humanitarian root; all national cultures, and all peoples have a similar right to [their own] cultural identity and self-determination. . . . Although [the Romantic nationalist would] stress the 'mission' of one's own people, in the context of a conception of [general] humanity all peoples [were seen as having] a mission." Nipperdey, *Nachdenken über die deutsche Geschichte*, p. 121.

23. Nipperdey, *Nachdenken über die deutsche Geschichte*, pp. 122, 123.

24. A longing for the true German Reich was strongly fueled by the medievalist predilections of the Romantic era. On the Reich ideal (and its historical reality), see Johannes Gross, *De Duitsers* (Baarn: Uitgeverij In den Toren, 1968), Chapter 4; and Bailey, *Germans*, p. 332ff. See also Franz-Josef Jakobi, "Mittelalterliches Reich und Nationalstaats-

gedanke," in Karl-Ernst Jeismann, ed., *Einheit—Freiheit—Selbstbestimmung: Die Deutsche Frage im historisch-politischen Bewußtsein* (Frankfurt/New York: Campus Verlag, 1988).

25. Alain Clement, *Gibt es ein deutsches Geschichtsbild?* (Studien & Berichte der Katholischen Akademie in Bayern, Heft 14, 1961), pp. 19–20.

26. Bailey, *Germans*, p. 340.

27. Bailey, *Germans*, p. 32.

28. Clement, *Gibt es ein deutsches Geschichtsbild?* p. 17. Preoccupation with their country's misfortune and vulnerability has a long tradition among Germans. In the early 1980s, for example, Günter Gaus, the FRG representative in East Berlin during the era of the SPD's *Ostpolitik*, lamented Germany's Cold War vulnerability and significantly entitled the first chapter of his book *Wo Deutschland liegt: eine Ortsbestimmung* (Hamburg: Hoffmann und Campe, 1983) "Altes Unglück" ("Old Misfortune").

29. In this context, see especially Fritz Stern, *The Politics of Cultural Despair* (Berkeley: University of California Press, 1963), particularly pp. xi–xxx and 267–298.

30. Kohn, *The Mind of Germany*, pp. 7–8.

31. Clement, *Gibt es ein deutsches Geschichtsbild?* p. 23; Löwenthal, "Geschichtszerrissenheit und Geschichtsbewußtsein in Deutschland," p. 249.

32. McClelland and Scher point to the fundamental German interest in historical study throughout the post–World War II period (*Postwar German Culture*, pp. 48–49). A general discussion of traditional German historicism may be found in Georg G. Iggers, *The German Conception of History: The National Tradition of Historical Thought from Herder to the Present* (Middletown, CT: Wesleyan University Press, 1983).

33. Wolfgang J. Mommsen, "Die Vergangenheit, die nicht vergehen will," in his *Nation und Geschichte: Über die Deutschen und die deutsche Frage* (München/Zürich: Piper, 1990), pp. 111, 112.

34. Mommsen, "Die Vergangenheit, die nicht vergehen will," p. 112.

35. On the roots of German conservatism, see Klaus Epstein, *The Genesis of German Conservatism* (Princeton, NJ: Princeton University Press, 1966). See also Helga Grebing et al., *Konservatismus—eine deutsche Bilanz* (München: Piper, 1971); and Martin Greiffenhagen, *Das Dilemma des Konservatismus in Deutschland* (München: Piper, 1971). On German authoritarianism, see the interesting collection of essays in Carl G. Schmidt-Freytag, ed., *Die Autorität und die Deutschen* (München: Delp Verlag, 1966). On the illiberal tradition in German politics, see especially Fritz Stern, *The Failure of Illiberalism* (New York: Alfred A. Knopf, 1972).

36. On the failure of nineteenth-century German Liberalism, see Kohn, *The Mind of Germany*, Chapter 6. See also Friedrich Sell, *Die Tragödie des deutschen Liberalismus* (Stuttgart: Deutsche Verlags-Anstalt, 1953).

37. On the issue of Liberalism and national unity in nineteenth-century Germany, see Alexander Schwan, "Deutscher Liberalismus und nationale Frage im 19. Jahrhundert," in Manfred Funke et al., eds., *Demokratie und Diktatur* (Bonn: Schriftenreihe der Bundeszentrale für Politische Bildung, 1987). The failed revolution of 1848 is usually seen as a crucial turning point. For a critical evaluation, see Michael Stürmer, "1848 in der deutschen Geschichte," in his *Dissonanzen des Fortschritts: Essays über Geschichte und Politik in Deutschland* (München: Piper, 1986). See also "'Es lebe die Republik,'" *Der Spiegel*, nr. 7, 9 February 1998, p. 44ff.

38. The following discussion of the German political tradition is especially indebted to several sources: Kurt Sontheimer, *Grundzüge des politischen Systems der Bundesrepublik*

Deutschland (München: Piper, 1971), pp. 76–80; Martin Greiffenhagen, "Vom Obrigkeitsstaat zur Demokratie: Die politische Kultur in der Bundesrepublik Deutschland," in Peter Reichel, ed., *Politische Kultur in Westeuropa* (Bonn: Schriftenreihe der Bundeszentrale für politische Bildung, 1984), pp. 53–56; Martin Greiffenhagen, *Die Aktualität Preußens* (Frankfurt: Fischer Taschenbuch Verlag, 1981), especially pp. 18–112; Hans Kohn, *The Mind of Germany*; Stern, *The Failure of Illiberalism*; Karl Dietrich Bracher, *The German Dilemma* (London: Weidenfeld and Nicolson, 1974), especially Chapter 1; Martin and Sylvia Greiffenhagen, *Ein schwieriges Vaterland* (Frankfurt: Fischer Taschenbuch Verlag, 1981), pp. 65–101. See also Hermann Lübbe, *Politische Philosophie in Deutschland* (Basel: B. Schwabe, 1963); and Jean Edouard Spenle, *La Pensée allemande de Luther à Nietzsche* (Paris: A. Colin, 1967).

39. Bracher, *The German Dilemma*, p. 7.

40. For a discussion of German Idealism, see Hajo Holborn, "German Idealism in the Light of Social History," in his *Germany and Europe* (Garden City, NY: Doubleday, 1970).

41. On the German Romantics and the state, see Kohn, *The Mind of Germany*, p. 63ff.

42. Bracher, *The German Dilemma*, p. 6.

43. Bracher, *The German Dilemma*, p. 15.

44. In this context, see especially the interesting essay by Peter Gourevitch, "The Second Image Reversed: the international sources of domestic politics," *International Organization*, vol. 32, nr. 4, Autumn 1978.

45. See the dicussion of the dual German tradition of *Beamtenstaat* and *Rechtsstaat* in Gregg O. Kvistad, "Radicals and the State: The Political Demands on West German Civil Servants," *Comparative Political Studies*, vol. 21, nr. 1, April 1988, p. 99ff.

46. Gabriel Almond and Sidney Verba, *The Civic Culture* (Boston: Little, Brown & Co., 1965).

47. On the traditional German separation of private and public values and virtues, see Ralf Dahrendorf, *Society and Democracy in Germany* (New York: W. W. Norton & Co., 1979), Chapters 19–21.

48. In this context, see the excellent discussion of the German tradition of *Libertät* in Leonard Krieger, *The German Idea of Freedom* (Chicago/London: University of Chicago Press, 1957).

49. See Sontheimer, *Grundzüge des politischen Systems der Bundesrepublik Deutschland*, pp. 79–80; Heinz Rausch, *Politische Kultur in der Bundesrepublik Deutschland* (Berlin: Colloquium Verlag Otto H. Hess, 1980), pp. 23–26.

50. See, for example, Sontheimer, *Grundzüge des politischen Systems der Bundesrepublik Deutschland*, pp. 78–79.

51. In this context, see especially Dahrendorf, *Society and Democracy in Germany*, Chapters 9–13.

52. On the character of the "apolitical German," see Stern, *The Failure of Illiberalism*, pp. 3–25.

53. It is important to note that the ideology of *Volk* and *Gemeinschaft* in traditional Germany was in many ways un-Prussian. The Nazi use of *völkisch* ideological referents is but one example of the many un- or even anti-Prussian features of National Socialism. In this context, see the interesting essay by Wolfgang Wippermann, "Nationalsozialismus und Preußentum," *Aus Politik und Zeitgeschichte*, 26 December 1981.

54. Stern, *The Failure of Illiberalism*, p. 17ff.

55. For a general discussion of some of these ideological developments in nineteenth- and early twentieth-century Germany, see Mosse, *The Crisis of German Ideology*.

56. In addition to the sources cited in subsequent notes, the reader may wish to consult Paul Joachimsen, *Vom deutschen Volk zum deutschen Staat. Eine Geschichte des deutschen Nationalbewußtseins* (Göttingen: Vandenhoeck & Ruprecht, 1967); and Christian Graf von Krockow, *Nationalismus als deutsches Problem* (München: Piper, 1970).

57. On Germany's delayed unification, its meaning and implications, see especially Helmuth Plessner, *Die verspätete Nation* (Stuttgart: W. Kohlhammer Verlag, 1959). On the nature of late nineteenth- and twentieth-century German nationalist chauvinism, see *Die verspätete Nation*, p. 22. On the Romantic dimension of traditional German nationalism, see Kohn, *The Mind of Germany*, Chapter 4.

58. Characterizing the nationalism of this period, Abraham Ashkenasi suggests that "[t]hree mystiques, Empire, romantic irrationalism, and ethnocentrism, merged to give the nationalist principle an extreme vitality; this irrationalism influenced the development of a pseudorealistic posture. This is a fourth element of German nationalism, its adherence to statism and to a mystique of power, specious realism and militarism." Ashkenasi, *Modern German Nationalism* (New York: John Wiley and Sons, 1976), p. 37. Cultural and political elements mixed in German nationalism to produce virulent anti-Western (especially anti-French) and anti-Slavic sentiments. It is important to note the link between this aspect of German nationalism and the country's geopolitical and "geocultural" position between East and West. See Louis L. Snyder, *Roots of German Nationalism* (Bloomington: Indiana University Press, 1978), pp. 246–247. See also the discussion of Germanophilism in Kohn, *The Mind of Germany*, Chapter 11.

59. Bracher, *The German Dilemma*, pp. 10–11.

60. Harold James, *A German Identity, 1770–1990* (London: Weidenfeld and Nicolson, 1990), pp. 3, 5.

61. James, *A German Identity*, pp. 216–217.

62. James, *A German Identity*, p. 217.

63. Richard J. Evans, *Rethinking German History* (London: Allen and Unwin, 1987), pp. 108–109.

64. See, for example, Gottfried Dietze, *Deutschland—Wo bist Du?* (München/Wien: Günter Olzog Verlag, 1980), Chapter 1. In this context, see also Alfred Rapp, "The Untrue Myth," in Walter Stahl, ed., *The Politics of Postwar Germany* (New York: Praeger, 1963).

65. Stern, *The Failure of Illiberalism*, p. xxiv.

66. Mommsen, "Die Vergangenheit, die nicht vergehen will," p. 117.

67. Evans, *Rethinking German History*, p. 15 (emphasis in original).

68. David Blackbourn and Geoff Eley, *The Peculiarities of German History* (Oxford/New York: Oxford University Press, 1984).The book originally appeared in German in 1980 under the title *Mythen deutscher Geschichtsschreibung. Die gescheiterte bürgerliche Revolution von 1848* (Frankfurt/Berlin: Ullstein, 1980). There is also a collection of essays by Geoff Eley that appeared in 1986 under the title *From Unification to Nazism: Reinterpreting the German Past* (Boston: Allen and Unwin, 1986) that also addresses the *Sonderweg* issue. See also the review of this work by Jürgen Kocka in *The Journal of Modern History*, vol. 62, nr. 1, March 1990, pp. 200–202.

69. Evans, *Rethinking German History*, p. 119.

70. Blackbourn and Eley, *The Peculiarities of German History*, p. 2

71. Blackbourn and Eley, *The Peculiarities of German History*, p. 3. See also Kurt Sontheimer, "Der 'Deutsche Geist' als Ideologie," in Funke et al., eds., *Demokratie und Diktatur*.

72. Blackbourn and Eley, *The Peculiarities of German History*, p. 3. See especially Bernd Faulenbach, *Ideologie des deutschen Weges. Die deutsche Geschichte in der Historiographie zwischen Kaiserreich und Nationalsozialismus* (München: Beck Verlag, 1980); and also Faulenbach's essay "Die Frage nach den Spezifika der deutschen Entwicklung. Zu neueren Interpretationen des 19. Jahrhunderts," in Wolfgang Michalka, ed., *Die Deutsche Frage in der Weltpolitik* (Stuttgart: Franz Steiner Verlag Wiesbaden, 1986).

73. Blackbourn and Eley, *The Peculiarities of German History*, p. 4.

74. Blackbourn and Eley, *The Peculiarities of German History*, pp. 7–8.

75. Blackbourn and Eley, *The Peculiarities of German History*, p. 12. Support for the arguments by Blackbourn and Eley can also be found in James, *A German Identity*, p. 210ff.

76. In this context, see also Klaus Hildebrand, "Der deutsche Eigenweg," in Funke et al., eds., *Demokratie und Diktatur*. Hildebrand suggests that national developmental *Eigenwege* ("individual paths") are part of history's "normality."

77. Blackbourn and Eley, *The Peculiarities of German History*, p. 10. Eley concludes that "we should speak not of German peculiarity, but of British, French, and German *particularities*" (p. 154).

78. Blackbourn and Eley, *The Peculiarities of German History*, p. 11. Later in the book, Blackbourn suggests that a questioning of a German *Sonderweg* "does not mean that we should write the history of Germany as if it were like the history of everywhere else; only that we should not write it as if it were quite unlike the history of anywhere else. The distinctiveness of German history is probably best recognized if we do not see it (before 1945) as a permanent falling-away from the 'normal.' In many respects . . . the German experience constituted a heightened version of what occurred elsewhere. . . . [The] unevenness of economic, social, and political developments was not in itself peculiarly German: Germany was much more the intensified version of the norm than the exception" (pp. 291–292).

79. Evans, *Rethinking German History*, p. 101.

80. See Blackbourn's discussion of alleged "German peculiarities" in Blackbourn and Eley, *The Peculiarities of German History*, pp. 159–175, with particular focus on the purported "sins of omission" of "the German bourgeoisie" (p. 159).

81. Blackbourn and Eley, *The Peculiarities of German History*, p. 51, and pp. 51–61 generally.

82. Blackbourn and Eley, *The Peculiarities of German History*, p. 13, and also p. 42ff. See also the discussion of the Blackbourn and Eley argument by Evans in his *Rethinking German History*, p. 100ff.

83. Eley, in Blackbourn and Eley, *The Peculiarities of German History*, p. 144. Wolfgang J. Mommsen, although not in complete agreement with the Blackbourn/Eley argument, does agree that "indeed one must admit that the political and societal development of Germany, when seen in European perspective, did lie more or less in the middle of progressive tendencies, and can hardly be considered exclusively as a developmental trajectory, deformed by authoritarianism, which [inevitably] had to lead to the political catastrophes of the two world wars." Mommsen, "Die Deutschen und ihre Geschichte," in his *Nation und Geschichte*, p. 178.

84. Blackbourn and Eley, *The Peculiarities of German History*, pp. 13–14.

85. Blackbourn and Eley, *The Peculiarities of German History*, pp. 52, 15.

86. Blackbourn and Eley, *The Peculiarities of German History*, p. 144.

87. Blackbourn and Eley, *The Peculiarities of German History*, p. 15ff.

88. Blackbourn and Eley, *The Peculiarities of German History*, pp. 20, 22ff., 147, 23, 34.

89. See, for example, Michael Stürmer, "Jede Nationalgeschichte verläuft anders: Welche ist Sonderweg?" in his *Dissonanzen des Fortschritts*, pp. 259–264.

90. Nipperdey, *Nachdenken über die deutsche Geschichte*. The following discussion is based primarily on three essays in this book: "Probleme der Modernisierung in Deutschland," "War die Wilhelminische Gesellschaft eine Untertanen-Gesellschaft?" and "1933 und die Kontinuität der deutschen Geschichte."

91. Nipperdey, *Nachdenken über die deutsche Geschichte*, pp. 54–55.

92. Nipperdey, *Nachdenken über die deutsche Geschichte*, p. 58.

93. Nipperdey, *Nachdenken über die deutsche Geschichte*, pp. 184–185.

94. Nipperdey, *Nachdenken über die deutsche Geschichte*, p. 185.

95. Nipperdey, *Nachdenken über die deutsche Geschichte*, p. 197.

96. Nipperdey, *Nachdenken über die deutsche Geschichte*, pp. 200, 202, 204.

97. Charles S. Maier, *The Unmasterable Past: History, Holocaust, and German National Identity* (Cambridge, MA: Harvard University Press, 1988), pp. 105, 108, 109.

98. Maier, *The Unmasterable Past*, p. 108.

99. See, for example, Dietze, *Deutschland—Wo bist Du?* especially pp. 21–36.

100. There is more than a flavor of this in Dietze, *Deutschland—Wo bist Du?* especially pp. 36–47.

101. Mommsen, "Die Deutschen und ihre Nation," in his *Nation und Geschichte*, p. 134.

102. See especially Stürmer's essay "Deutsche Identität: Auf der Suche nach der verlorenen Nationalgeschichte," in his *Dissonanzen des Fortschritts*.

103. Maier, *The Unmasterable Past*, p. 115.

104. Maier, *The Unmasterable Past*, p. 116. See Michael Stürmer, "Mitten in Europa: Versuchung und Verdammung der Deutschen," in his *Dissonanzen des Fortschritts*; Hagen Schulze, *Wir sind was wir geworden sind. Vom Nutzen der Geschichte für die deutsche Gegenwart* (München/Zürich: Piper, 1987). See also Hellmuth Rössler, *Deutsche Geschichte. Schicksal des Volkes in Europas Mitte* (Gütersloh: C. Bertelsmann, 1961); and Ernst Jäckh, *Deutschland. Das Herz Europas* (published during the Weimar Republic; Stuttgart/Berlin/Leipzig: Deutsche Verlags-Anstalt, 1928).

105. See, for example, Calleo, *The German Problem Reconsidered*. Calleo mixes considerations of geopolitics with developmental timing to explain modern Germany's diplomatic difficulties and tragedies. A similar emphasis on the geopolitical factor for an understanding of modern German history can be found in Sebastian Haffner, *The Ailing Empire: Germany from Bismarck to Hitler* (New York: Fromm International Publishing Corp., 1989); and in Renata Fritsch-Bournazel, *L'Allemagne: un enjeu pour l'Europe* (Brussels: Editions Complexe, 1987).

106. Mommsen, "Die Deutschen und ihre Geschichte," p. 183.

107. On Luther and the Lutheran legacy in German society, culture, and politics, see Craig, *The Germans*, pp. 83–90; and Bailey, *Germans*, p. 182ff.

108. Craig, *The Germans*, p. 84.

109. Eich, *The Germans*, p. 22.

110. For a German speculation on this point, see Greiffenhagen, *Die Aktualität Preußens;* and Rudolf von Thadden, *Fragen an Preußen* (München: Deutscher Taschenbuch Verlag, 1987).

111. In this context, see Michael Stürmer, "Preußens Erbe an die Bundesrepublik: Entscheidung in Deutschland" and "Mitten in Europa: Versuchung und Verdammnis der Deutschen," in his *Dissonanzen des Fortschritts*.

2

Cultural Change and National Identity in West Germany, 1945–1990

Discussions of the German Question that focus on cultural and political facets of modern Germany generally treat 1945 as a definitive watershed in the country's development. Does this mean that the traumas and upheavals of Nazism and World War II did indeed bring about such a fundamental and decisive break in German history that German culture was completely and forever changed? In this chapter, we explore this question. We shall look at the significant cultural changes that West Germany experienced after 1945 and prior to unification with the former German Democratic Republic (GDR, or East Germany) in 1990. A similarly fundamental transformation in the area of political culture will be discussed. At the same time, we shall see how the burdens of a troubled past continued to affect the lives of West Germans after 1945. In addition, special attention will, of course, be given to evolving West German attitudes regarding German unity (prior to 1989–1990), in view of the country's postwar division.

Postwar West Germany and the Question of Cultural Change

Politically and socially, postwar West Germany underwent tremendous change.[1] Writing almost three decades ago, Paul Schallück suggested that "if there has been an abundance of discontinuities in German history, there is definitely continuity between 1945 and today. Everything that makes Germany an enigma to its neighbours in 1970 has its origin in 1945, when Hitler's Reich, founded to last a thousand years, came to an enforced and ignominious end after only twelve years. . . .

For Germany, far more than its neighbours, 1945 was an historical caesura—sentimentally and morally, economically and politically, in technology, sociology and art. There had never been a comparable break in the history of this country." The consequences of this condition were decisive. "In the year zero [1945] the German nation . . . was empty, unresistant, impressionable, receptive. It learnt eagerly, sometimes voluntarily, sometimes under compulsion, it imitated, and very gradually began again to think for itself. This was, at least in Germany, an unprecedented historical process."[2]

As a result, there were important value changes, especially among the younger generations, away from older traditions of authoritarianism and toward a greater valuation of individualism. As far as the Federal Republic is concerned, there is much to be said for Ralf Dahrendorf's conclusion that Nazism turned out to be the means by which Germany radically dismantled the barriers that a traditional society had placed on the road to modernity.[3] The thorough modernization and "bourgeoisification" of German society was perhaps the most important unintended consequence of Hitlerite totalitarianism. The Nazi experience paradoxically cleared the ground for the possible creation of a more liberal-democratic sociopolitical order.

Dahrendorf also stressed, however, that many traditional German sociocultural characteristics and institutions were only partially affected or dominated by Nazi power. As a result, he and others emphasized important manifestations of historical cultural continuity.[4] It is important, then, not to exaggerate the break represented by the "year zero." Germany cannot fully escape or ignore its cultural legacy, historical experiences, or the enduring psychological effects of its geographic location.

Yet subsequent scholarship suggested that even Dahrendorf's influential analysis, with an emphasis on certain cultural (illiberal) continuities, was in need of some basic adjustment. Thus Russell J. Dalton wrote in 1989 that

> Germany is one nation where the stereotype of the culture is well known; in fact, too well known in some ways. German culture has been analyzed in extensive detail, with attention focused on the negative culture norms inherited from earlier periods. Dahrendorf's description of the social consciousness in postwar Germany provided the most comprehensive view of the German psyche, and the problematic traits that others had noted. . . . While these negative characterizations of popular values and cultural norms were widely applicable during the immediate postwar years, many aspects of this social consciousness changed in the new environment of the Federal Republic.[5]

Dalton suggested, for example, that the "authoritarian legacy was inconsistent with the postwar social system, and social norms gradually changed to reflect the new reality," with the result that "West German culture now encourages its citizens to be more independent and less deferential toward all forms of authority." Yet Dalton also pointed out that although "[a] mass of public opinion data documents the growth of civic tolerance among the West German public," such tolerance "still remains a questionable aspect of German *social* norms."[6] He also suggested that the legendary German work ethic (*Fleiß*) may be somewhat diminished today. Altogether, Dalton concluded that

> [t]he evidence . . . suggests that many of the negative aspects of West German social norms noted by Dahrendorf have improved in the past forty years. The nation has shed much of its premodern social consciousness. . . . Despite this progress, however, the transformation of social norms has been incomplete. . . . The partial change in social norms also contrasts with the rich literature documenting a fundamental transformation in the political culture over the past forty years. This imbalance between social and political change reflects the unequal pattern of socio-political development in the Federal Republic. . . . Changes in social norms thus have lagged behind the changes in political norms.[7]

One additional manifestation of important value change that may be mentioned here concerns the emergence, not just in preunification West Germany but in the West generally, of what are often called "postmaterial" values.[8] According to Dalton, "[t]he modifications in the social norms identified with the 'German question' are the most important changes in the German social consciousness during the past four decades, but in recent years a new aspect of social change has become apparent. Once substantial progress was made in addressing traditional socioeconomic needs, the public broadened their interests to include a new set of personal and political goals."[9] These developments aided in the emergence of countercultures in the 1960s, the feminist and ecological movements of the 1970s, and the phenomenon of the Greens in political life during the 1980s.

Beyond the question of German cultural change, there is also the related problem of international perceptions of German change. What is Germany's image in the world today? Are the Germans today seen as having changed? How many non-Germans would agree with the following statement by Luigi Barzini (made in the mid-1980s), particularly in light of the dramatic transformations of 1989–1990?

> It is therefore once again essential for everybody, the French, the British, the Italians, the other Europeans, as well as the Americans and the Soviets, to keep an eye across the Rhine and the Alps and the Elbe in order to figure out, as our fathers, grandfathers, great-grandfathers, the ancient Romans, and remote ancestors had to do, who the Germans are, who they think they are, what they are doing, and where they will go next, wittingly or unwittingly. This, of course, was always impossible to fathom.[10]

Most observers appear to agree that some pre–World War II culture and experience live on in the Germany of today, both in terms of continuity and contrast. Gordon A. Craig suggests that "the attitudes and thinking of today's Germans continue to be affected, to a greater or lesser degree, by history and tradition.

There is no way, natural or contrived, of divorcing a people completely from its past." However, he adds that the precise "influence of historical memory and cultural tradition in contemporary German life is difficult to measure with any hope of accuracy, and so is the degree to which the German people can be said to have assimilated their recent past and come to terms with the atrocities committed in their name by the Nazis." In many ways, "contemporary German attitudes show the effect of old but stubborn assumptions and prejudices," particularly expressed in "an inconsistent attitude toward modernity." Based on extensive research, Craig concludes that "no people is harder to generalize about than the Germans, perhaps because they have not always been as obedient to the laws of logic as other peoples."[11] The historically weak impact of the Enlightenment and Liberalism still makes itself felt in a variety of ways and degrees.[12] The Romantic legacy has not by any means been purged completely.

It is particularly important to note that the traditional preoccupation with German identity and the country's place in Europe and the world at large remains and was, if anything, enhanced by the traumatic Third Reich experience and the Cold War division of the nation. Different generations and people of divergent political persuasion have dealt differently with this issue of German identity.

An awareness of "traditional" cultural orientations in Germany is also vital if one is to explain the causes of some postwar cultural changes in the Federal Republic: The latter often occurred in direct (perceived) *reaction* to the former. The persistent preoccupation with individual rights and Liberalism, alternatives to nationalism, democratic practices, personal achievement and success, and so forth, can be more fully understood if seen as a continuous reaction against what were considered to have been the failures of the past.

Although shifts in general cultural orientation varied markedly from generation to generation in postwar West Germany, it is quite appropriate to conclude that, perhaps more than ever before, the western part of Germany became more fully integrated into the Western cultural mainstream. Amid this cultural convergence between Germany and the West, some differences remain(ed), however. These lie (or lay) in the persistence of some older traits and traditions, in the continued burden of the Nazi crimes of the past, and (until recently) in the country's Cold War division. Awareness of these continuing differences will be needed in any proper evaluation of the cultural and psychological bases of the Federal Republic's foreign policy, both before and after unification. The sociocultural character of the former GDR and its inhabitants is, of course, yet another issue with important implications for the German future, as we shall see in Chapters 3, 7, and 8.

Political Culture in West Germany

The mixture of profound cultural transformation and partial cultural continuity in West Germany after World War II was quite clearly reflected in developments

in the Federal Republic's political culture. There are some key questions to consider. Was the illiberal component in Germany's historical identity as a nation
transformed by thorough democratization and liberalization in the Federal Republic? Were there ways in which the illiberal legacy still lingered? And what does
all this mean for the political and ideological aspects of the German Question as
we reach the end of the twentieth century?

One important fact must be immediately emphasized. After 1945, Germany
was an occupied country. Although that occupation gradually disappeared, with
the 1949 Petersberg agreement, the 1952 Bonn accords, and the 1955 Paris treaty
as milestones, West Germany's dependence on the West (especially the United
States) continued, while taking on new forms. This facet of dependence in the
Federal Republic's development, in socioeconomic, political, and military affairs,
must be clearly borne in mind. It suggests that the political leadership of the West
German state had to maneuver within the confines of available room, although it
is also true that this room expanded with the passing of time.

With respect to West German political culture, the importance of this dependent development was threefold. First, the Federal Republic as a state was in large
part the product of international developments, specifically the Cold War. Although there was considerable popular support for the creation of a West German state in 1949, the ideological and security considerations accompanying the
state's creation, aimed at making the FRG a strong anti-Communist bulwark, left
a deep imprint on West German political culture.

Second, dependence heightens the influence of foreign "models." The development of West German political culture cannot be fully understood unless we recognize especially the profound impact of the U.S. model on West German beliefs
and values. Hence has arisen the facet of pro-U.S. admiration in West German
political culture. As political mentor and guarantor, the United States became the
model of what the new Germany aspired to be: a modern, trustworthy democratic republic. But this fact also helps call attention to the importance of German anti-Americanism. According to Andrei S. Markovits,

> the special nature of America's position in the Federal Republic has largely been a
> corollary to and consequence of the interrupted and complicated development of a
> German identity in a post–World War II Europe. It is in the context of this "German
> exceptionalism" that relations with the United States and all things American have
> experienced a qualitatively different existence in the Federal Republic as compared to
> elsewhere in Europe. Thus, Americanism and anti-Americanism are rather *sui
> generis* in their texture and meaning to the political culture of the Federal Republic.[13]

Consequently, as a third facet we should note that dependence breeds resentment. This is more than a matter of bitterness upon defeat or of lingering *Kultur*
arrogance, although these were certainly important. Dependence entails a feeling
and reality of limited control over one's destiny and development and of uncertainty and anxiety regarding one's identity. It helps explain why anti-Americanism

became a notable ingredient in West German political culture (and in the political cultures of other Western European countries). In the midst of the Cold War (1958), the European predicament led Leo Moulin to observe:

> For the first time in centuries, Europe is starkly aware of the fact that she is no longer the leading power. And not only is she no longer the leading power, but her deep-seated confusion also dooms her to impotence. She broods morosely over her past splendors. Disunited Europe is nothing and Europe knows it. . . . The United States . . . is in a good position to threaten Europe's ancient mastery precisely because she is close to Europe. In fact, she has already acquired hegemony in a number of economic, military, technical, financial and even political spheres. Now such a development appears to Europe, or at least to a part of European public opinion, as a brash attempt at "usurping the inheritance." Whence a feeling of inferiority (excessive in some respects), and of decadence and disgrace.[14]

The subsequent development of German- and European-U.S. relations eliminated or mitigated many of the sentiments described by Moulin, but there was an unmistakably persisting legacy here as well.

We saw earlier that 1945 had many characteristics of a "year zero." The sense of a break with the German past was felt as profound. It is indeed true that the shock and upheaval of the Third Reich and World War II brought about vast and probably lasting changes in German political life. Many facets of West German political culture were quite novel, and often a conscious reaction against prewar political orientations.

Numerous observers pointed to the persistence of certain traditional German elements in West German political culture, however.[15] They noted evidence of a continued mutual estrangement between state and society, and state and democracy, in West German political life. The Germans presumably had not yet fully surmounted their traditional *Staatskultur* (state-oriented political culture). The frequent tendency of the state to overwhelm the individual, the continuing predisposition to see the state as source of citizen rights, the dedication to legalistic, bureaucratic politics and *Staatseffizienz* (efficiency of the state), and the trend toward ideological absolutism with regard to the Federal Republic's purported *Grundwerte* (basic values)[16]—these were some oft-noted facets of West German political culture with roots in pre–World War II Germany.

To these one might still add the persistence of the *Rechtsstaat* ideal, continued elements of a subject political culture (or *Untertanenkultur*), a preoccupation with order and security, a tendency toward *Verfassungsvergottung* ("deification of the constitution"), a fear of change and debate, a yearning for consensus and harmony but also continued friend-foe thinking in politics, and enduring elitism and *Beamtenherrschaft* (bureaucratic rule).[17] According to Martin Greiffenhagen, it was especially the legacy of Prussia that is still very much in evidence in the Federal Republic today.[18] Karl Dietrich Bracher concluded that the "[a]pplication of concepts of state and democracy is still an uncertain process today, showing that the old German dilemma still exerts a powerful influence."[19]

It would be grossly inaccurate, however, to describe preunification West German political culture as no more than a collection of traditional German ingredients covered with a formal democratic veneer. There is widespread agreement that a clearly democratic political culture developed in the Federal Republic after the late 1940s.[20] David P. Conradt, for example, pointed out in the early 1980s that

> [t]he much-discussed postwar political stability of the Federal Republic is now rooted in a solid attitudinal consensus on the values, processes, and institutions of liberal democracy. Bonn, in contrast to Weimar, is not a Republic without republicans. Moreover, since the mid-1960s there has been an increasingly closer fit between citizen attitudes and values and actual behavior. Germans at elite and general public levels are becoming more interested in politics and more inclined to use politics as a means of social change and personal development. . . . In short, the institutions and processes of liberal democracy are being used extensively without any perceptible stress on the basic structure of the political system. The stability of the West German political system has been supplemented by a vitality in political life not apparent during the Republic's early years.[21]

Before we look at this political culture, we should note that, in direct opposition to the alleged persistence of traditional German political orientations, much in West German political culture was understandable only when seen as a (generally conscious) *reaction* against undemocratic elements in the past (and present). Thus, according to Rudolf Wassermann, "[t]he state of the Federal Republic became something new not just in contrast to the perished National Socialist regime, but also in contrast to the Weimar Republic. For the first time a political order was created on German soil along middle-class lines in the Western sense."[22] Paradoxically, however, this very reaction could itself assume certain undemocratic qualities.

Thus, an awareness of the (partially) illiberal nature of the old *Rechtsstaat* tradition led to a purposive attempt to infuse this concept with elaborate, constitutionally guaranteed basic rights, in order to strengthen the foundations of democratic citizenship. Haunted by the specter of the politically fragmented and crisis-ridden Weimar Republic, the Federal Republic's founders drew up a *Grundgesetz* (Basic Law) that contained elaborate provisions intended to forestall excessive partisan pluralism and destabilizing political crises. But this very fear of political instability and crisis in turn led to a preoccupation with governability, order, and stability that permitted older, illiberal German attitudes to resurface and harm democratic rights.[23] According to Johannes Gross, "the Basic Law (Constitution) attempts to eliminate actually existing or merely perceived sources of danger and seeks to block disruptive influences on the business of politics as much as possible, in order to [enhance] the protection against crises. To protect against as yet unknown threats, the Basic Law provides a rich arsenal of stabilizing mechanisms and obstructionist measures."[24] The fear of subversion and crisis on the one hand, and the fear of political illiberalism on the other hand, became equally important elements in West German political culture.[25]

Given the virulence of political extremism of Left and Right in the Weimar Republic, the trauma of National Socialism, and the neighboring presence of East German Communism in the decades after 1949, ideological antitotalitarianism became a vital aspect of West German political culture.[26] This fear of totalitarianism was pervasive, although the West German Left generally placed relatively greater emphasis on anti-Fascism than the Right, which tended to be more preoccupied with Communism. The Nazi past led to extreme sensitivity concerning possible neo-Nazi revivals, such as the *Sozialistische Reichspartei* (SRP) in the 1950s, the *Nationaldemokratische Partei Deutschlands* (NPD) in the 1960s, and the *Republikaner* led by former SS officer Franz Schönhuber in the 1980s and beyond, a sensitivity that was amply shared, if not surpassed, outside the Federal Republic. There was distinct concern that Nazism might yet leave a largely submerged legacy in German political life, despite all postwar efforts at de-Nazification, "re-education," and democratic *politische Bildung* (political education).[27]

The ideological predicament of anti-Communism was more complicated. During the Cold War, it could imply hostility against a considerable number of fellow Germans in the GDR. What is more, its potential link with the anti-Bolshevism of the Third Reich could serve to provide (unintended) post-facto legitimacy to some key ideological elements of Nazism. In addition, among German conservatives anti-Communism historically tended to spill over into anti-Socialism, focused largely on the Social Democratic Party (SPD) as *Reichsfeind*. This legacy burdened postwar relations between the Christian Democratic Union (CDU) and the SPD.

When analysts looked at the development of West German political culture from decade to decade,[28] they tended to reach a number of important conclusions. First, the legitimacy of the Federal Republic in the eyes of its citizens was strong and had steadily increased. Second, West German political culture had acquired increasingly democratic traits. Third, the sense of a West German "national consciousness" (prior to the events of 1989) had been expanding. Fourth, the burdens of the Nazi past remained noticeable in German political life. Fifth, some elements of the illiberal German political tradition persisted. Sixth, ideological polarization between West Germany's two leading parties, the SPD and the CDU/CSU, strongly diminished, although clear differences remained. And seventh, the profound discontinuities in recent German history led to major differences between the various generations.

Under the impact of total defeat and destruction, foreign occupation, and the basic needs of economic reconstruction, a political culture developed in West Germany during the pre-1949 period and the Adenauer era that had some characteristic traits.[29] There were profound changes in political and philosophical orientations, a renewed focus on freedom, a questioning of state power and ideological politics, an antitotalitarian fear of Communism, and a widespread tendency to withdraw from active involvement in political life. These developments were understandable especially as a reaction to the excesses of the Nazi era.[30] It was the age of the *skeptische Generation* (skeptical generation).[31] Hermann Eich concluded in 1963:

> Politically today's German is passive rather than active. Looking back over the last few decades of his history he feels that he has had more than his share of the consequences of great-power politics. Three changes of regime, two currency devaluations, the division of the country, the loss of a quarter of the national territory, the destruction of the expansionist dream in the Russian winter—this was enough. Equally shattering for the Germans was the realisation that the harder they had striven the deeper they had fallen into the abyss.

To many foreigners, "[t]he Teuton had finally cast off his bearskin and was behaving himself."[32]

The initial pessimism and anxiety that had revealed themselves in a pervasive uncertainty about the possibility of progress soon gave way to new optimism as the *Wirtschaftswunder* (economic miracle) unfolded. A preoccupation with the ethical dimensions of political life went hand in hand with increasingly antiideological, pragmatic attitudes. Conscious of past failures and Weimar instability, a mood of sociopolitical conservatism set in, heavily focused on the maintenance of political stability at home and an image of reliability abroad. Nationalism appeared to be a largely discredited ideology. The legitimacy of the new state seemed to be based primarily on economic performance and Cold War anti-Communism, however. The democratic aspects of the evolving political culture were as yet rather weak and formal. Nostalgia for earlier regimes lingered, and many observers claimed to detect a process of gradual "restoration."

The characteristics of West German political culture prevailing in the 1950s were still very much in evidence in the early 1960s, when Gabriel Almond and Sidney Verba published their observations on the Federal Republic's weak civic culture.[33] They suggested that

> [t]he high level of development in the communications and educational fields is reflected in the fact that most Germans are aware of and well informed about politics and government. In a number of ways they take part in the political system. The frequency of voting is high, as is the belief that voting is an important responsibility of the ordinary man. And their level of exposure to political material in the mass media of communications is high. Furthermore, German political culture is characterized by a high level of confidence in the administrative branches of government and a strong sense of competence in dealing with them.[34]

Yet they added that "the contemporary political culture also reflects Germany's traumatic political history. Awareness of politics and political activity, though substantial, tend to be passive and formal. Voting is frequent, but more informal means of political involvement, particularly political discussion and the forming of political groups, are more limited. . . . Germans tend to be satisfied with the performance of their government, but to lack a more general attachment to the system on the symbolic level."[35] They concluded that "the balance of the political system is weighted in the direction of the subject role and of passive forms of participation. The government is viewed largely as an agency of administration. And the attachment to the political system is closely related to the ability of the government to satisfy pragmatic needs."[36]

The decade of the 1960s turned out to be an age of transition and paradox, however.[37] It was a period of important generational change, with a younger generation both less directly burdened by Germany's traumatic past and more willing to raise uncomfortable questions and shatter taboos. There was a distinct re-ideologization of political life. Precisely at a time when the Federal Republic appeared to have achieved considerable political stability and economic prosperity, protest movements, radical ideas, increased anticonservatism, and a counter-culture emerged.[38] It turned into an age of identity crisis, neonationalism, uncertainties in thought and belief, fading pre–World War II memories among an increasingly post-Nazi population, and constant calls for reforms. The antibourgeois and anticapitalist protest, anger, and frustration had facets in common with developments in other Western nations, but in the German case some of the elements of idealism, utopianism, and irrationalism were particularly tied to a powerful Romantic legacy. In addition, the earlier image of Communism appeared to be "softening," thereby reducing the effectiveness of anti-Communism as a domestic ideological "glue" to maintain political consensus and stability.[39]

The great hopes and ideals of the 1960s were largely disappointed, however. The coalition between the SPD and the FDP (Free Democratic Party) under Willy Brandt after 1969 was for many a disillusionment. As a result, there was a good deal of political withdrawal in the 1970s, continuing into the 1980s (with some exceptions).[40] Ideological skepticism, a "silent revolution" in political values, a widespread loss of faith in progress, a search for more authentic forms of political participation (especially so-called Bürgerinitiativen, or "citizens' initiatives"), individual alienation in modern mass society, a neoromantic search for German identity, a neoconservative quest for effective moral standards, ecological and cultural pessimism, and "nuclear fear"—these were some of the trends that were noted in West German political culture during the fifteen years prior to unification.[41] At the same time, West Germany's overall political culture continued to be marked by rather exceptional liberal-democratic stability and regime legitimacy, with a well-entrenched and broad-based political center. Many of these trends were amply shared by other Western democracies.[42]

In order to acquire a more complete picture of post-1945 West German political culture, however, it is essential to move beyond the broader picture of overall developments, and draw special attention to two important sources of attitudinal diversity in the Federal Republic: political parties and political generations. As we shall see in several subsequent chapters, it is impossible to acquire an accurate picture of the foreign policy aspects of the German Question without noting the differences in historical experience, ideology, and constituency of the Federal Republic's major political parties.[43] (West) German political life has been dominated by the SPD and CDU. Their philosophical differences are genuine, rooted in partly diverging historical experiences and worldviews, and not merely a result of political posturing.

The SPD's historical experience has been quite traumatic. Persecuted as *Reichsfeind* (enemy of the state) in Bismarck's Second Reich, alienated from the prevailing conception of nationhood in traditional Germany,[44] burdened by the stigma of having accepted the Versailles *Diktat* and cosponsored the Weimar fiasco, and driven into concentration camps or exile during the Third Reich, the SPD developed a considerably more nationalist outlook after 1945, especially due to a desire to be no longer accused of being *vaterlandslose Gesellen* ("fellows without a fatherland"). It is impossible to understand the attitudes of the postwar SPD without noting this historical experience and, in addition, the party's strong ideological anti-Communism, the loss of its prewar bulwark in eastern Germany (until 1989, at least), the strong Protestant element in its membership, and its extensive international socialist and social-democratic contacts.

The SPD's historical experience is not merely traumatic, however. There is also a long and proud ideological tradition dating to the 1870s. In fact, the SPD is Germany's oldest party. In addition, the SPD can look back on a heroic record in the anti-Hitler resistance. But the party went through a fundamental identity crisis after World War II. In the course of the 1950s, the more dogmatic Marxist heritage eroded, as the SPD developed from a traditional *Arbeiterpartei* (workers' party) into a modern, catch-all *Volkspartei* (mass party). The great turning point came with the party conference at Bad Godesberg in 1959: Older Marxist elements dissipated as a more pragmatic orientation broke through and helped redefine the party's positions on many of the issues that had led to bitter CDU-SPD controversy in prior years. And in the course of the 1960s, as the party acquired greater self-confidence and public trust and support, it finally gained political power and became what Kurt Klotzbach called a *Staatspartei* ("governing party").[45]

Its gradual ideological moderation, resulting from a postwar search for national credibility, brought about the alienation of many groups on the political Left from the "new" SPD. Although the SPD disproportionately attracted those in the younger generation who are the main supporters of the New ("postindustrial") Politics, it was not able to retain them completely. This partly explains the emergence of the Greens in the early 1980s. As a *Volkspartei*, the SPD expanded its membership and electoral constituency beyond its traditional (but still significant) working-class base, into white-collar, middle-class segments of society.

Generationally, the SPD displays some interesting divisions. Rapidly dwindling numbers of older members were socialized in the Weimar Republic and the era of the old *Arbeiterbewegung* (labor movement). They are followed by a slowly retiring generation of reform-oriented, "antiideological pragmatists." Some of them are still among today's SPD leaders, socialized by the Third Reich, World War II, and post-war reconstruction experiences. Finally, there is the younger, more critical *Wohl-standsgeneration* ("prosperity generation"), basically socialized in a postwar environment of economic abundance and a mixture of Cold War and detente. They have been especially prominent in the left wing of the SPD, but they can now increasingly be found in the party's leadership circles, with the new federal chancellor, Gerhard Schröder, as a striking example.[46] Some of these younger SPD members left the party during the 1980s to join the ranks of the Greens, a new party/movement focused particularly on pacifism, neutralism, and ecological issues.[47]

The Federal Republic's second major party, the Christian Democratic Union (CDU), was founded after World War II, partly as successor party to the old Catholic Center party of the pre-1933 period.[48] As a confessional *Volkspartei* it succeeded in bridging the gap that had traditionally separated Catholics and Protestants in German life. The loss of the largely Protestant eastern zone unintentionally resulted in a more stable Catholic-Protestant balance in West Germany, but there is awareness within the CDU that Germany's reunification has increased the influence of eastern (Protestant) elements on German political life (including internal CDU affairs).[49] The CDU has also been able to provide a political home for some conservative, nationalist elements of the past, and for the millions of refugees who came into the Federal Republic from the once-German eastern territories.

After initial tendencies in the direction of socioeconomic socialism (for example, in the 1947 Ahlen Program), the more conservative wing in the party, led by Konrad Adenauer and Ludwig Erhard, gained the upper hand by 1949. The Christian Democrats fully dominated the first fifteen years of the Federal Republic's existence. It is especially in the CDU that some traditional, at times illiberal, German attitudes can still be found. Officially, the CDU espouses what one might call a "Christian realism" along conservative lines. Excessive state power and socioeconomic egalitarianism are disliked, the individual is the focus of attention, and political *Grundwerte* (basic values) are to be asserted. There is also considerable preoccupation with problems of security, individual duty and loyalty, German national identity, and the potential of a philosophical and spiritual vacuum that might be invaded by Communism and Socialism.[50] In the 1950s, this led to the emergence of the notion of a *streitbare Demokratie* (militant democracy) in the face of totalitarian Communism.

The CDU has lived in a sometimes uneasy alliance with its Bavarian sister-party, the Christian Social Union (CSU). Almost entirely Catholic, this party tends to be clearly more conservative and nationalist than the CDU. A deep ideological gap separates it from the SPD.[51] Its anti-Communism was and remains especially strong. Under the leadership of the late Franz-Josef Strauss, the CSU left its mark on the course of West German foreign policy.[52]

The Free Democratic Party (FDP) is a postwar phenomenon, although the frequent ambivalence of its conservative and liberal, and nationalist and internationalist, orientations is reminiscent of the ideological drift that characterized the old German Liberal movement and led to the split between Progressive and National Liberals. Generally, however, the party moved in a more leftward direction during the 1960s and 1970s, especially away from old-German nationalism, but back to economic conservatism in the 1980s.[53] On the German political scene, the FDP played a pivotal role as a strategically placed coalition party (prior to the elections of 1998).

In the course of this survey of West German political culture, we have repeatedly observed the importance of *generational* differences. The course of modern German history has been marked by such discontinuity and upheaval that the normal manifestations of generational heterogeneity in political culture have been increased even more. Differences among generations are natural, because different age groups have been socialized by different sets of experiences. But in Germany, not only common experiences diverge. Different German generations have lived under radically different political regimes and been exposed to some vastly different ideologies. In German political life, the "chronological fragmentation" of the population plays an important role.[54]

According to Helmut Fogt, by the early 1980s there had been eleven periods in twentieth-century German history that had produced identifiable generational units: the pre–World War I period, World War I, revolution and economic crisis (1917–1924), the stable Weimar period (1924–1929), economic and regime crisis (1930–1933), established National Socialism (1933–1941), World War II, the immediate postwar reconstruction era (1945–1953), the established Adenauer era and its decline (1953–1966), the age of student protest movements (1966–1971), and the age of "alternative" cultural tendencies (after 1971). Martin Greiffenhagen made largely similar observations. He identified four general generations instead of Fogt's eleven smaller units. He also stressed that the lessons drawn by one generation from its experience can be passed on to subsequent generations by intricate processes of socialization. In this way, a society may develop elements of a "collective memory." Historical experiences will thus produce a mixture of cultural homo- and heterogeneity.[55]

The Federal Republic was created under the auspices of those whose formative experiences reached back to at least the Weimar era and World War I, if not the Wilhelmine era. The post–World War II reconstruction was accomplished by those who were primarily socialized by the Nazi experience and World War II. Some had been old enough to serve in the military. They made up the "skeptical generation" of the 1950s. Distrustful of ideological politics and concerned with political stability and economic security, they were still the most dominant political stratum in western Germany when the GDR collapsed. They are now increasingly succeeded by those whose awareness and memory of the Third Reich and World War II, if present at all, are far more limited. These newer generations were essentially socialized by the postwar occupation period and/or the economic miracle of the 1950s and 1960s. Some are frequently critical, rebelling against parents and grandparents whose past they question and reject, and are often also forgetful. The strong intergenerational divergence of experience in part produced appeals to different lessons and political evaluative criteria. Political objectives tended to be formulated based on an intention to help avoid repetition of past evils and failures, and the perceptions of these varied from generation to generation.

The unification of West and East Germany in 1990, signaling the rise of a "new" Germany in the heart of Europe, immediately raised questions in the area of political culture. For example, would unification destabilize West Germany's democratic political culture? If so, why and how? What political and ideological impact would the East Germans have on the united Germany? What lingering effect might East Germany's Communist legacy have on the all-German political process? Might the world yet witness a resurgence of an illiberally flavored German nationalism and national identity?

In an early speculation, David P. Conradt offered some reflections on these and other questions. He argued that "two general explanations of what will happen to German political culture after reunification can be extracted . . . [f]rom the existing scholarly and journalistic treatment of these questions."[56] One perspective stresses "the differences between [the FRG and the GDR] largely as a result of the forty-year division. It sees in the [GDR] today many of the same traits which characterized prewar Germany, i.e., the [GDR] as a 'cultural museum'." After unification, such traditional German political cultural features as "idealism," "statism," "unpolitical 'innerlichkeit'," "avoidance of conflict," "legalism-formalism," and "security" [Geborgenheit] would be expected to "have a greater weight in the total culture."[57] East Germans would have to "catch up" with changes in political culture that occurred in West Germany earlier after World War II. Another perspective, labeled "democrats without a democracy" by Conradt, "suggests that [GDR] citizens were pre-socialized to liberal democracy through their knowledge and vicarious experience of the Federal Republic's development, most of which was based on media exposure and in recent years visits to the West."[58] As a result, many if not most East Germans would be relatively well-prepared to join West Germany's liberal democracy.

Conradt summed up his investigation by suggesting that "[t]he limited data base precludes any definitive conclusions about the impact of unification on German political culture. The rapid pace of the unification could also mean that any [GDR]-specific orientations could remain latent for a number of years. Intra-German migration, however, could well reduce the weight of any regional differences." More specifically, he believed that the legacy of East Germany's socialism may well lead to "the emergence of a substantial left subculture in a unified Germany."[59] We will attempt in Chapter 8 to measure and evaluate these and other speculations against a near-decade of postunification developments.

Burdens of the Past

The cultural and political problems and uncertainties created by the profound discontinuities in recent German history are central to the riddle called the German Question. The historian Wolfgang J. Mommsen has argued that "the Germans [have] had difficulties all along in coming to terms with their history."[60] A search for identity, intergenerational communication problems, and an illiberal legacy are some of the issues that arise in this context. We are dealing here largely with difficult *problems*, however.

In addition, German history has also saddled postwar Germany with profound and seemingly insoluble *moral burdens*. These burdens are an integral part of the identity of Germany in the world at large, and they are thus vitally connected to the overall German Question. The issues in this case are not merely difficult, they are painful. How was Nazism possible? How was the Holocaust possible? Why did only few Germans actively resist National Socialist tyranny? How responsible for the Nazi past should the different German generations be? How to come to grips with such a traumatic historical past?[61]

In 1990, with the rush toward unification of East and West Germany gathering ever more speed, despite predictable and unpredictable obstacles that would inevitably tend to slow the astonishingly rapid pace, the German past became again the focus of much international attention and even concern. Neofascist activity in a GDR liberated from Communist control, Chancellor Helmut Kohl's equivocations on the issue of the Polish-German border, the "discovery" of mass graves in East Germany (dating from the early postwar years), accusations hurled at GDR politicians concerning their alleged past collaboration with the hated Stasi secret police, the reassertion of Allied legal prerogative in the context of the "2-plus-4" talks between the two Germanys and the old wartime allies (the United States, the USSR, Britain, and France)—these were but the most visible signs of an important dimension of the evolving German Question as Europe entered the 1990s. When the subject is Germany, the past always somehow seems to haunt and complicate the present.

While attention is focused on the Germany of today and tomorrow, the inclination (if not temptation) is widespread to apply implicit or explicit interpretations of Germany and the Germans based on their recent and not-so-recent past. In this regard, as in so many others, the Cold War years permitted the development of a distinct atmosphere of almost disingenuous unreality. As long as Germany was divided, and as long as reunification seemed but a distant or perhaps even unlikely prospect, concerns about the legacy of the German past could be conveniently downplayed or ignored. This was true internationally, as each German state was eagerly transformed into a valued alliance partner in its respective "camp." It was also true domestically in both German states, since alliance loyalty and ideological dogmatism in the Cold War context permitted many to forget that the great ideological confrontation of the twentieth century has not been a bipolar contest between Liberalism and Communism but rather a triangular struggle between Liberalism, Communism, and Fascism/Nazism, in which the latter was merely the first clear loser.

The controversial Bitburg episode of 1985, involving President Reagan's visit to a West German military cemetery containing some SS graves, was a telling reminder of this fundamental predicament. Years of East-West Cold War and loyal NATO membership on the part of the FRG could not obfuscate the underlying persistence of international unease about the German past. The subsequent letter to Congress written by the prominent West German CDU politician Alfred Dregger, suggesting that in a Cold War context it should be remembered that the Germans had also fought against Communism during World War II, equally betrayed a fundamental misunderstanding of the enduring significance of Germany's past in the perspective of our present age.[62]

Another dramatic example of the West Germans' confrontation with the burdens of their Nazi past came in the form of the so-called *Historikerstreit* (historians' dispute) in the mid-1980s, focused particularly on some writings by (neo)conservative historians like Andreas Hillgruber, Ernst Nolte, and Michael Stürmer. The essence of the debate revolved around the question of whether German Nazism and its systematic persecution and murder of Jews and others during the Holocaust were truly unique or perhaps comparable to, connected with, and/or preceded by other totalitarian phenomena in the twentieth century (for example, Stalinism or Pol Pot's Khmer Rouge). The conclusion could be that Germans were or are less uniquely guilty if their totalitarian experience was comparable to other cases. Critics of this analytical tendency, led especially by Jürgen Habermas, denounced the dangerous implications of such thinking and continued to stress the "uniqueness of Auschwitz." Incidentally, there are some clear connections between this dispute and the more general debate about a purportedly deviant German *Sonderweg*, or "special path," in modern history, which we examined in the previous chapter.[63]

The steady erosion of the Cold War's institutional rigidities and ideological certainties after 1985, culminating in the turbulence of 1989–1990, posed anew the question of Germany's past in the context of a seemingly unstoppable unification drive. Questions about the fate of democracy in a united Germany or about the future role of Germany on the European continent were ultimately flavored by assumptions and expectations rooted in perceptions of the German past. As world events moved us toward a new Germany, many minds continued to be haunted by the old Germany.

Let us step back for a moment from these still recent events and look briefly at how the past in general, and the Nazi era in particular, affected the general political, cultural, and psychological climate in West Germany over the years. For most of the postwar period, German consciousness, if at all preoccupied with the past, tended to focus on the Third Reich and the questions posed at the beginning of this section.[64] The interest in regaining international trust and respect sprang almost entirely from a desire to overcome the moral stigma left by Nazism and its crimes. The efforts to develop a more fully liberal-democratic German political culture resulted largely from a sense that political orientations must be definitively transformed in order to eliminate the sociocultural sources of Nazism. The postwar development of the Federal Republic was accompanied, both at home and abroad, by a persistent fear of a possible totalitarian relapse.

It is possible to argue, therefore, that in the context of German history in general, the National Socialist era constituted the decisive historical legacy for the Federal Republic after 1949. Consider the following observations by Martin and Sylvia Greiffenhagen:

> Although almost any European country has periods in its recent history that look pretty bad in the history books, none among them has an identity that is so fundamentally damaged as does the German people. In no country on earth has there ever been such a heavy discussion about collective guilt or responsibility. National-Socialism was of "constitutive" importance for the history of the German nation since 1945 until the present, and this will probably continue to be so for some time to come.[65]

The creation of the Federal Republic was in many ways the direct outcome of the Third Reich disaster. The Nazi Reich haunted West Germany like a nightmare, and served as a source of contrast and lessons in the development of a new, democratic German political culture. Nazism was a key cause of Germany's division and the destruction of Prussia. It helped shape the nature of political debate in the Federal Republic by generating taboos and anxieties. It caused profound intergenerational differences that burdened postwar German political life. It severely damaged German identity and self-image and Germany's international image, and for many it delegitimized national pride and power.

Despite a widespread willingness (and initial need?) to avoid the uncomfortable, controversial, and complicated aspects of German guilt and personal responsibility, the idea of *Vergangenheitsbewältigung* ("mastering the past") came to play a crucial role in West German public life.[66] Its international moral and material dimension was the focus of a broadly supported government policy of *Wiedergutmachung*, or reconciliation, often tied to financial compensation. But the domestic dimension was far more controversial, hampered by residual resentment concerning the victors' de-Nazification and reeducation policies and by generational and partisan disagreements.

A well-known critic of the whole idea of *Vergangenheitsbewältigung* has been Armin Mohler. He has argued that the very notion of "mastering the past" has been increasingly subjected to often partisan political manipulation. It is no longer focused on those generations that were actually in some way responsible for what happened, but instead on the Germans in general, young and old. It allegedly has become a tool in the hands of foreign, anti-German elements to harm the Federal Republic by means of propaganda, manipulation, and blackmail. According to Mohler, the concept increasingly has lost its original meaning and purpose. In addition, he claims that the constant attempt to somehow "master" the past tends to stifle the will to face up to existing political needs and realities. He believes that the obsession with the potential return of Nazism is psychologically paralyzing and destructive of the supposedly still fragile legitimacy of the young (West) German democracy. Mohler's critique has found a considerable resonance among fellow (West) German conservatives.[67]

The general West German attitude toward the idea of *Vergangenheitsbewältigung* in the postwar period can be characterized as fundamentally ambivalent. It is a concept that acquired many connotations, some positive and some negative. Is it possible to "master" one's past? Is it desirable? What part of the German past needs to be mastered? Only the Third Reich? Should all generations share in the effort, or does it apply only to the "responsible" generations? How should it be done, and for how long? What are the lessons to be learned from the past? Should one speak in terms of "collective German guilt" or, as some have suggested, along the lines of "collective responsibility" or "collective liability"?

Attitudes regarding the Nazi past and the question of *Vergangenheitsbewältigung* changed over time, especially as a result of differences among generations.[68] According to Greiffenhagen, by the late 1970s

> [i]n a biographical sense National-Socialism [had] been of "constitutive" importance for at least three generations: [first], those who grew up during the Weimar Republic, who served the Nazi regime as adult or young men, who undertook the reconstruction after the war, and who founded the Federal Republic and made it into one of the most powerful states on earth; [second], the generation of those who experienced their youth during the Third Reich and in its organizations and military, and who today lead the West German state; and [third], the generation of those for whom, despite a postwar birth, the theme of National-Socialism has remained alive until today. Only now is a generation growing up which is far removed from this theme.[69]

During most of the Adenauer era, there was an ambivalent mixture of genuine guilt feelings, psychological avoidance, and limited rejection of Nazism. Beginning in the mid-1960s, however, some new attitudes emerged. These were in large part a reflection of the rise of younger generations, whose mental world was oriented more exclusively to the postwar world and less burdened by problems of personal responsibility. According to Mommsen, "[t]he [sense of] trauma, which led the older generation of Germans to keep silent about their own recent past and thereby often about history as a whole, has today been broken. Similarly, the taboos, which induced many simply not to talk about particular aspects of the German political tradition, like anti-semitic tendencies, have become weaker."[70] The new attitudes were also in part the result of West Germany's resurgence as an international power with renewed self-confidence and of a marked decline of effective all-German consciousness.

The political consequences of this changed psychological climate were at times paradoxical. The new generations were (and are) less encumbered by considerations of taboo, more willing to pose certain fundamental and uncomfortable questions, but also potentially more forgetful of certain lessons of the past. Whether fairly or not, the burdens of history continue to weigh on the different German generations, and in the coming chapters, the issue of Germany's past will resurface with almost predictable regularity.

Some final, yet preliminary observations may be illustrative of the enduring difficulties experienced by the Germans when it comes to dealing with their nation's past. The 1989–1990 collapse of the GDR and that state's absorption into the FRG triggered questions of *Vergangenheitsbewältigung* of a particular kind. In the east, it implied a day of reckoning: Who was guilty of misdeeds under the old regime, who had collaborated, and what were the moral implications of the evidently very widespread acquiescence throughout the postwar era? For Germans in the east, *Vergangenheitsbewältigung* thus concerns the need to come to grips with a dual dictatorial past: the Nazi era and the four decades of Communist rule.

In the west, the need for *Vergangenheitsbewältigung* with respect to the former GDR was (and is) no less important, though rarely officially admitted. Had not West Germany, especially since the 1960s, engaged in considerable interaction (even cooperation) with the now-maligned SED regime in the GDR? Attempts by some Christian Democrats to pin the guilt and blame as exclusively as possible on the Social Democrats were (and are) rather disingenuous, because they obscure the fact that by the 1980s, if not already much earlier, the CDU, SPD, and FDP had all reconciled themselves more or less with what was seen as an inevitable two-state situation in Germany for the foreseeable future, including the need to deal with the existing GDR regime.

In addition, any postunification policy of "de-Communization" in the east was bound to have an inescapable air of awkwardness (to say the least), in view of widespread German complaints and resentment in the early postwar years with regard to what were seen as hypocritical and/or misguided Allied attempts at "de-Nazification." FRG-style "Nuremberg Trials" of former GDR officials would raise serious legal as well as ethical questions. Would not the spectacle of West Germans trying East Germans for complicity, collaboration, or other misdeeds under a Communist dictatorship with which many in the West had had dealings pose again those haunting questions of complicity and collaboration with dictatorship that overshadowed the past of *all* Germans? Who is to judge whom and what is to be judged, and by what ethical norms or legal principles? We return to this crucial theme in Chapter 8.

Nationalism and National Identity in Postwar West Germany

In Chapter 1, we encountered some of the problems associated with the idea of nationhood in the German historical experience. The uncertainty of what is and is not Germany, the persistent mystique of the Reich, the delayed national unification, and the illiberal nature of traditional German nationalism were some of the issues introduced at that time. We now look more closely at the fate of nationalism in postwar Germany, and the thorny question of national identity in West German political culture between 1949 and 1989. In doing so, we shall gain a better understanding of the postwar importance of the issue of *unity* as one of the four key dimensions of the German Question, in addition to the elements of postwar West German cultural and political *identity* that we have examined thus far.

The traumas of Nazism and World War II in numerous ways produced a break with the illiberal, nationalist past. There was a widespread desire after 1945 to escape from history and its painful burdens. The old nationalism was one of the prime casualties of the war. It became a thoroughly discredited ideology and a liability for a new Germany that sought reconciliation with victims and enemies and acceptance in the Western community of nations.[71] This does not mean, of course, that nationalism completely disappeared from German political life. Thus Bracher suggests that

> [a] glance back into the history of [the] German problem shows that in relation to democracy and the concept of the state, nationalism has always been in an ambivalent position *and still is so today*. The development of a national consciousness has contributed to the rise of democratic movements; it has also, however, become unpolitical and so supported and deified authoritarian regimes; on occasions it has depoliticized and diverted the demands of the masses for freedom and democracy and used them for ideological, imperialist and power-policy ends.[72]

The question of nationalism ought to be seen in the broader context of the problem of *German national identity* after World War II, however.[73] Although identity crises have been experienced by most, if not all, nations in the twentieth century, Germany has faced, and still faces, some unique problems. There are three general and important aspects to the German identity question since World War II.

First, German identity has been burdened by the traumas of German national historical experience. The desire to leave behind the past has produced a harmful, and some would say dangerous, *Geschichtslosigkeit*, roughly translatable as a "loss of historical consciousness."[74] It may well be that much, if not most, of German history has lost its functional utility for the creation of a modern German identity. This may especially be the case because the traditional German approach to nationhood was so suffused with illiberal, anti-Western elements. A national identity for a liberal-democratic, Western-oriented Federal Republic could only with great difficulty be rooted in such a heritage.[75] Yet no complete German identity can or will emerge if national historical experiences are ignored or avoided. An attempt to focus on purely cultural aspects of German nationhood will lead only to an incomplete sense of identity, because it would tend to be devoid of any firm political foundation.[76] What is more, a preoccupation with a German *Kul-*

turnation could resuscitate foreign concerns regarding culturally based political irredentism and a new German unity-before-freedom mentality.

Second, the question of German identity was made even more complicated by the nation's division into two ideologically competitive republics. The ideological hostility between the FRG and GDR during the Cold War meant that any attempt to have both states share in a purportedly common German *Kulturnation* would end up begging many political questions. But the Federal Republic was always hesitant to claim to be a full-fledged German *Staatsnation*. The West German self-understanding after 1949 became explicitly "provisional." The Federal Republic claimed to be the legitimate successor of the old German Reich, but destined to be dissolved once all Germans regained their national unity. The preamble to the West German state's Basic Law enjoined all federal governments to strive for the restoration of German unity. Attempts to eliminate this preamble in the face of the bitter reality of two independent German states were met by a mixture of vigorous protest and deafening silence. This provisional West German self-understanding produced an elaborate array of legal principles and fictions that played a central role in the Federal Republic's foreign policy. Unfortunately, as the French have reminded us, "il n'y a que le provisoire qui dure" ("it is only the provisional which endures"). As a result, a fairly explicit West German *Staatsbewußtsein* ("state consciousness"), sometimes referred to as *Verfassungspatriotismus* ("constitutionally focused patriotism"), did emerge with the passing of time.[77] Amid the turbulent events of 1989–1990, some observers wondered whether a specific West German consciousness would persist in a reunited Germany, and what its consequences would be.

The very idea of a specifically West German national identity constituted a far-reaching development, of course. In a rather influential study, published in the 1970s, Gebhard Schweigler noted that national sentiment, though still quite pronounced in the 1950s, had shifted significantly during the 1960s. He suggested that popular expectations of national reunification had declined, coupled with an increased willingness to recognize the Oder-Neisse line and the GDR as a separate German state. He noted an apparently reduced sense of an all-German *Staatsnation* and a growing national consciousness focused more exclusively on the Federal Republic. Identification with West German democratic institutions seemed clearly strengthened, along with an increased pride in the West German political system, although, as Almond and Verba showed in the 1960s and Richard Rose in the 1980s, the traumas of the past continued to inhibit a more fully developed German national pride and confidence.[78] Schweigler concluded that this increased West German *Staatsbewußtsein* did not (yet) translate into any explicit form of nationalism, and that the new West German sense of identity could play a major role in the solution of the German Question.[79] A similar development was allegedly occurring in the GDR, according to Schweigler.

Research by Silke Jansen on West German public opinion carried out during the 1970s and 1980s (prior to the events of 1989) appeared to support some of

Schweigler's suggestions. Jansen noted a growing sense of distance between the FRG and the GDR and concluded:

> Parallel to this feeling of distancing one sees the development of a growing identification of West German citizens with the Federal Republic as their state. This specific [West] German identity is today being strengthened by the many opportunities for travel and communication in the German-German relationship. The political, social, and economic differences between the West and East German systems become clear in the course of encounters with GDR citizens. For the Germans in the Federal Republic a "West German" national consciousness (in everyday usage reduced to a "German" national consciousness) is no longer a taboo. This does not prevent the West Germans from preserving a sense of membership (however diffuse) of a single [all-German] people, which leads back again and again to the same formula: "two German states of a single German people."[80]

The decade that followed upon Schweigler's study witnessed the growing popularity of political culture research in the Federal Republic. Most writers were much less sanguine, however, about the decline of national consciousness and the rise of a more distinct West German identity. Many of them noted that the search for identity constitutes an old and continuing theme in German political life. Although acknowledging that evidence for a growing West German *Staatsbewußtsein* could be found, they also tended to stress that an all-German national consciousness persisted and that the identity question was still in many ways wide open. The noticeable interest in Prussia, Luther, Bismarck, and other facets of German history that was observed in the Federal Republic (and in East Germany, as we shall see in Chapter 3) during the 1980s[81] was seen as evidence of a continuing search for German identity.

Jansen's research cited previously permits us to acquire a sense of some basic trends in West German opinion on some of the important issues over the past several decades, prior to the collapse of the GDR and the rush toward unity that followed in its wake. Several tendencies appeared to be noticeable. Jansen wrote: "The Germans desire a reunification but do not expect one. This means that the Germans operate with a realistic perspective on a contemporary political situation that does not offer a short- or medium-term possibility for any type of reunification."[82]

Jansen found that most West Germans tended to prefer a united Germany along Western lines (around 60 percent), but a sizable minority (from 34 percent in 1979 to 41 percent in 1986) would opt for a neutral united Germany. As of early 1989, Jansen was able to conclude:

> The citizens of the Federal Republic differentiate between two German states of one German people, and a majority is unwilling to give up the shared [German] historical roots. In this context, the GDR is not perceived as a foreign land by the popula-

tion, although the citizens in the Federal Republic exclude the GDR and its citizens from the notion of "Germany" in their day-to-day language. In this respect one can notice a greater sense of distance among the younger generation, since it is they who to a considerable extent perceive the GDR as a foreign country and the populations of both German states as two separate peoples. [The younger generation] perceives the GDR as an unfamiliar state with a different social order, and thus not as part of Germany.[83]

A third aspect of postwar German identity concerns the fact that this identity has to an important extent been dependent on the ebb and flow of world affairs in general and European integration in particular.[84] A product of the Cold War in many ways, and animated by a strong sense of anti-Communism because of the proximity of its East German opponent, the Federal Republic's sense of identity was always far more sensitive to changes in the international environment than any other Western country. West Germany's identity came to depend a great deal on the country's membership in and acceptance by the Western alliance and the general community of Western nations. The fear of being the ultimate victim of an East-West political and military bargain (a "Potsdam complex") produced a persistent strain of anxiety and insecurity, thereby heightening the uncertainties of identity.

For much of the postwar period, it seemed that the Federal Republic's participation in the process of European integration would provide it with an ersatz European identity. Many Germans eagerly supported this hopeful opportunity. As the expectation of a soon-to-be-united Europe faded in the course of the 1960s and 1970s, however, and nationalist sentiments in Europe appeared to remain more influential than expected, the Federal Republic's identity problems returned. It is possible to argue, then, that West Germany's identity over the years involved an attempt to focus on both the democratic values shared with the West and the sense of Germanness shared with East Germany.

The Third Reich helped discredit nationalism as an ideology, particularly in its more virulent and extremist form. The Federal Republic sought to develop a sense of identity that would overcome the illiberal legacies of the past. Yet all this did not mean that all nationalist sentiment had disappeared in West Germany.[85] As was the case after World War I, the resurgence of nationalism as a reaction to defeat could not be ruled out in the early post–World War II period. The trauma of national division could only add to this potential ideological powder keg. The shock of Nazism and the totality of defeat seemed to have been sufficiently great to forestall any full-scale nationalist revival, however. More problematic was the fact that Cold War anti-Communism had an apparent and awkward affinity with the anti-Bolshevism that had played such a prominent role in the extremist nationalism of the interwar period. The slow process of social change in the Federal Republic, and continued evidence of traditional regionalist sentiment, permitted the older spirit of nationalism to survive in some quarters.

The persistence of some pre–World War II nationalism was well reflected in the slow rate of change in public opinion concerning the Second Reich and the Nazi regime, especially in the late 1940s and early 1950s. Emotional identification with the Federal Republic tended to be fairly low and increased only very gradually, although it became quite considerable, as we saw earlier. Also noticeable in this context were (and are) differences between older and younger generations. The latter are much less likely than the former to be animated by the illiberal nationalism of the past. Nationalist sentiment has tended to be strongest on the right end of the political spectrum. There have been some small neo-Nazi parties, but none have been fully successful. Most nationalist elements appear to have been absorbed by the CDU and its Bavarian sister-party, the CSU.[86] But sparks of nationalism have not been absent in the SPD, either. And a romanticized, left-wing nationalism can be encountered within the ranks of the Greens.

In this context, we might also note the observation made during the mid-1980s by Rose that the level of "national pride" has varied considerably between Right and Left in most Western countries, especially in West Germany. Of those who identified themselves as "right-wing" in the Federal Republic, 83 percent acknowledged a feeling of national pride. Among those who claimed to be "left-wing" in political orientation, national pride was expressed by only 45 percent.[87] These percentages reflect the historically troubled relation between the German nation and the German political Left.

The rush toward national unity during 1989 and 1990 reaffirmed and/or reawakened all-German national sentiment across the German political-ideological spectrum in a dramatic (and to some observers, at times unsettling) fashion. At the same time, it was by no means clear throughout this process what weight such all-German feelings might ultimately carry vis-à-vis more specifically FRG- and GDR-oriented identities. One clear distinguishing factor was the vastly different economic condition in East and West Germany, a factor that appeared to have measurable political consequences. On the one hand, West Germans showed (on balance) considerably less excitement over unification and more worry over unity's financial and economic consequences for their affluent part of the "new" Germany. On the other hand, many East Germans eagerly supported unification with the prosperous FRG with an unmistakable mixture of genuine emotion and pragmatic material calculation. We return to this issue in Chapters 7 and 8.

Notes

1. In connection with the discussion that follows, the reader may wish to turn to John Ardagh, *Germany and the Germans: An Anatomy of Society Today* (New York: Harper & Row, 1988), for a much more extensive treatment than can be provided in the context of the present study.

2. Paul Schallück, ed., *Germany: Cultural Developments since 1945* (München: Max Hüber Verlag, 1971), pp. 9, 10, 11, 20, 21, 22, 24. For some conservative Germans, many of

the changes that were forced upon their country by the postwar occupying powers amounted to something like "brain-washing." See, for example, Caspar Schrenck-Notzing, *Charakterwäsche: Die amerikanische Besatzung in Deutschland und ihre Folgen* (Stuttgart-Degerloch: Seewald Verlag, 1965). For an attempt to compare the impacts of World Wars I and II on German politics, society, and diplomacy, see Gottfried Niedhart and Dieter Riesenberger, eds., *Lernen aus dem Krieg? Deutsche Nachkriegszeiten 1918–1945* (Munich: Verlag C. H. Beck, 1992). They place particular emphasis on the wars' impact on German attitudes and mentalities.

3. Ralf Dahrendorf, *Society and Democracy in Germany* (New York: W. W. Norton & Co., 1979), Chapter 25.

4. Dahrendorf, *Society and Democracy in Germany*, pp. 412, 413–414, 419, 422. See also Johannes Gross, *De Duitsers* (Baarn: Uitgeverij In den Toren, 1968), pp. 261, 263–264, 266, 268; Ardagh, *Germany and the Germans*, Chapter 4.

5. Russell J. Dalton, "A Changing Social Consciousness," in Peter H. Merkl, ed., *The Federal Republic of Germany at Forty* (New York/London: New York University Press, 1989), pp. 58–59, 73.

6. Dalton, "A Changing Social Consciousness," pp. 59–61.

7. Dalton, "A Changing Social Consciousness," pp. 63–64.

8. See especially Ronald Inglehart, *The Silent Revolution* (Princeton: Princeton University Press, 1977).

9. Dalton, "A Changing Social Consciousness," pp. 64–65.

10. Luigi Barzini, *The Europeans* (New York: Penguin Books, 1984), p. 69.

11. Gordon A. Craig, *The Germans* (New York: G. P. Putnam's Sons, 1982), pp. 10–11.

12. Hans W. Gatzke, in *Germany and the United States* (Cambridge, MA: Harvard University Press, 1980, pp. 22–23), notes the persistence of "a deeply rooted belief in human inequality."

13. Andrei S. Markovits, "Anti-Americanism and the Struggle for a West German Identity," in Merkl, ed., *The Federal Republic of Germany at Forty*, p. 53.

14. Leo Moulin, "Anti-Americanism in Europe: A Psychoanalysis," *Orbis*, vol. 1, nr. 4, Winter 1958, pp. 450–451. In this context, see my essay "Beyond Cowboys and Euro-wimps: European-American Imagery in Historical Context," *Orbis*, vol. 31, nr. 1, Spring 1987, and the sources cited therein. See also A. W. DePorte, *Europe Between the Superpowers* (New Haven/London: Yale University Press, 1979).

15. Attention to such enduring traditional German political traits characterizes (among others) the work of Martin Greiffenhagen, *Die Aktualität Preußens* (Frankfurt: Fischer Taschenbuch Verlag, 1981); Martin and Sylvia Greiffenhagen, *Ein schwieriges Vaterland* (Frankfurt: Fischer Taschenbuch Verlag, 1981); Alfred Grosser, *Geschichte Deutschlands seit 1945* (München: Deutscher Taschenbuch Verlag, 1974); Dahrendorf, *Society and Democracy in Germany*; Gross, *De Duitsers*; Heinz Rausch, *Politische Kultur in der Bundesrepublik Deutschland* (Berlin: Colloquium Verlag Otto H. Hess, 1980); and Hagen Schulze, "Die Versuchung des Absoluten," *Aus Politik und Zeitgeschichte*, 18 February 1984.

16. On the West German potential for ideological absolutism, see Greiffenhagen, *Ein schwieriges Vaterland*, pp. 132–137, 272–273. See also Schulze, "Die Versuchung des Absoluten."

17. In this context, see Erwin Curdt, "Wie demokratisch ist unsere Verwaltung?" *Aus Politik und Zeitgeschichte*, 9 February 1990.

18. Greiffenhagen, *Die Aktualität Preußens*. Michael Stürmer sees the Prussian legacy for postwar West Germany more in geopolitical terms: "Prussia was situated at the crossroads of all peninsulas that make up Europe, and the Federal Republic has inherited some of the problems [that result] from this position" ("Preussens Erbe an die Bundesrepublik: Entscheidung in Deutschland," in his *Dissonanzen des Fortschritts: Essays über Geschichte und Politik in Deutschland*, München/Zürich: Piper, 1986, p. 253).

19. Karl D. Bracher, *The German Dilemma* (London: Weidenfeld and Nicolson, 1974), p. 22.

20. This development can be especially traced by means of public opinion poll data. Most works cited in these pages contain such data, especially those by Greiffenhagen, Rausch, and Almond and Verba. For an overview of the evolution of attitudes in the areas of tolerance, political parties, and politics in general, see the material gathered by the Institut für Demoskopie Allensbach and published in Elisabeth Noelle and Erich P. Neumann, eds., *The Germans: Public Opinion Polls 1947–1966* (Westport, CT: Greenwood Press, 1981), pp. 179–194, 209–217, 395. For a record of public opinion concerning general German problems, the political system, political participation, and law and justice, see Elisabeth Noelle-Neumann, ed., *The Germans: Public Opinion Polls 1967–1980* (Westport, CT: Greenwood Press, 1981), pp. 115–127, 128–143, 150–155, and 156–171.

21. David P. Conradt, *The German Polity* (New York/London: Longman, 1982), pp. 81–82.

22. Rudolf Wassermann, "8. Mai 1945: Die Katastrophe als Chance zum Neubeginn," *Aus Politik und Zeitgeschichte*, 20 April 1985, p. 4.

23. On West German political arrangements as a political reaction to past experiences, see Gross, *De Duitsers*, Chapters 7–12.

24. Gross, *De Duitsers*, p. 68.

25. The inherent, mutual tension between the two kinds of fear is obvious, and was quite noticeable in the political controversy surrounding the *Notstandsgesetze* (legislation on emergency situations) in the late 1960s and the *Radikalenerlaß* (legislation on political radicals in public administration) of the early 1970s. See the discussion in Greg O. Kvistad, "Radicals and the State: The Political Demands on West German Civil Servants," *Comparative Political Studies*, vol. 21, nr. 1, April 1988.

26. See Grosser, *Geschichte Deutschlands seit 1945*, pp. 126–127.

27. An excellent source on the persistence of an extreme-right fringe in West German political life is Richard Stöss, *Die extreme Rechte in der Bundesrepublik* (Opladen: Westdeutscher Verlag, 1989). In Chapter 2, he stresses the continuation of such elements in the FRG's political culture due to a complex process of psychological *Verdrängung* (repression) and *Verharmlosung* (roughly translatable as a tendency to pretend the "harmlessness" of the Nazi legacy).

28. See, for example, Rausch, *Politische Kultur in der Bundesrepublik Deutschland*, Chapter 4. See also the survey of developments in postwar West German political culture furnished by Dirk Berg-Schlosser, "Entwicklung der politischen Kultur in der Bundesrepublik Deutschland," *Aus Politik und Zeitgeschichte*, 9 February 1990; Jürgen Turek, "Demokratie und Staatsbewusstsein: Entwicklung der Politischen Kultur in der Bundesrepublik Deutschland," in Werner Weidenfeld, ed., *Politische Kultur und deutsche Frage: Materialien zum Staats- und Nationalbewusstsein in der Bundesrepublik Deutschland* (Köln: Verlag Wissenschaft und Politik, 1989); Russell J. Dalton, *Politics in West Germany* (Glenview, IL/Boston, MA: Scott, Foresman and Co., 1989), Chapter IV.

29. For a good portrait of the postwar *Zeitgeist* in Germany, see Karl Dietrich Bracher, "Nachkriegserfahrung und Denkstrukturen des Wiederaufbaus" in his *Zeit der Ideologien* (Stuttgart: Deutsche Verlags-Anstalt, 1982), pp. 271–290.

30. For further discussion, see Hermann Eich, *The Germans* (New York: Stein and Day, 1980), Chapter 9; Craig, *The Germans*, Chapter 2.

31. Helmut Schelsky, *Die skeptische Generation* (Düsseldorf: E. Diederich, 1963).

32. Eich, *The Germans*, pp. 226, 228.

33. Gabriel Almond and Sidney Verba, *The Civic Culture* (Boston: Little, Brown & Co., 1965). See also Sidney Verba, "Germany: The Remaking of Political Culture," in Lucian Pye and Sidney Verba, eds., *Political Culture and Political Development* (Princeton, NJ: Princeton University Press, 1965).

34. Almond and Verba, *The Civic Culture*, p. 312.

35. Almond and Verba, *The Civic Culture*, pp. 312, 313.

36. Almond and Verba, *The Civic Culture*, p. 363.

37. On the *Zeitgeist* of the 1960s, see Bracher, *Zeit der Ideologien*, pp. 291–313.

38. On the ideology of the 1960s countercultural "New Left," see Erwin K. Scheuch, ed., *Die Wiedertäufer der Wohlstandsgesellschaft* (Köln: Markus Verlag, 1968), especially the essay by Peter Christian Ludz.

39. On the legacy of the protest movement, see Greiffenhagen, *Ein schwieriges Vaterland*, pp. 138–152.

40. On the *Zeitgeist* of the 1970s, see Bracher, *Zeit der Ideologien*, pp. 314–330.

41. In addition, sectarian forms of terrorism became a major issue in West German political life during the 1970s and 1980s, with the notorious Baader-Meinhof gang playing a particularly prominent role. For an interesting discussion, see "Hamburg: Terrorism in Germany," in Jane Kramer, *Europeans* (New York: Penguin Books, 1988), pp. 125–147. On the rise of citizen action in West German political life, see Dalton, *Politics in West Germany*, Chapter VI.

42. For further discussion, the reader may wish to consult the following: Rausch, *Politische Kultur in der Bundesrepublik Deutschland*; Rausch, "Politisches Bewußtsein und politische Einstellungen im Wandel," in Werner Weidenfeld, ed., *Die Identität der Deutschen* (Bonn: Schriftenreihe der Bundeszentrale für Politische Bildung, 1983); Kurt Sontheimer, *Grundzüge des politischen Systems der Bundesrepublik* (München: Piper, 1971); Sontheimer, *Die verunsicherte Republik* (München: Piper, 1979), pp. 119–126; Peter Reichel, *Politische Kultur der Bundesrepublik* (Opladen: Leske & Budrich, 1981); Conradt, *The German Polity*, Chapter 3; Conradt, "Changing German Political Culture," in Gabriel Almond and Sidney Verba, eds., *The Civic Culture Revisited* (Boston: Little, Brown & Co., 1980); Greiffenhagen, *Ein schwieriges Vaterland* (esp. pp. 65–115); Greiffenhagen, *Die Aktualität Preußens*; and Greiffenhagen, "Vom Obrigkeitsstaat zur Demokratie: Die politische Kultur in der Bundesrepublik Deutschland," in Peter Reichel, ed., *Politische Kultur in Westeuropa* (Bonn: Schriftenreihe der Bundeszentrale für politische Bildung, 1984). The importance of generational change in German political culture and the distinction between New and Old Politics (resulting from what Inglehart has called the "silent revolution"), and the emergence of the Greens, are the subject of *Germany Transformed* by Kendall L. Baker, Russell J. Dalton, and Kai Hildebrandt (Cambridge, MA: Harvard University Press, 1981).

43. The following discussion draws especially on Peter H. Merkl, "West Germany," in Peter H. Merkl, ed., *Western European Party Systems* (New York: Free Press, 1980); Grosser, *Geschichte Deutschlands seit 1945*, pp. 212–252; Greiffenhagen, *Ein schwieriges Vaterland*,

pp. 153–164. See also Ludwig Bergsträsser, *Geschichte der politischen Parteien in Deutschland* (München: G. Olzog Verlag, 1965); Dietrich Orlow, "West German Parties since 1945: Continuity and Change," *Central European History*, vol. 18, nr. 2, June 1985; Alf Mintzel and Heinrich Oberreuter, eds., *Parteien in der Bundesrepublik Deutschland* (Bonn: Schriftenreihe der Bundeszentrale für Politische Bildung, 1990). Probably the most comprehensive preunification survey of West Germany's political parties can be found in Richard Stöss, ed., *Parteien Handbuch: Die Parteien der Bundesrepublik Deutschland, 1945–1980*, 2 vols. (Opladen: Westdeutscher Verlag, 1983/1984).

44. See Erich Matthias, *Sozialdemokratie und Nation* (Stuttgart: Deutsche Verlags-Anstalt, 1952).

45. Kurt Klotzbach, *Der Weg zur Staatspartei* (Berlin/Bonn: Verlag J.H.W. Dietz Nachf., 1982). See also Susanne Miller, *Die SPD vor und nach Godesberg* (Bonn-Bad Godesberg: Verlag Neue Gesellschaft, 1974); Gerard Braunthal, "The Social Democratic Party: Reformism in Theory and Practice," in Merkl, ed., *The Federal Republic of Germany at Forty*.

46. Greiffenhagen, *Ein schwieriges Vaterland*, pp. 162–163.

47. On the Greens, see William E. Paterson, "The Greens: From Yesterday to Tomorrow," in Merkl, ed., *The Federal Republic of Germany at Forty*. See also Hans-Georg Betz, "Value Change and Postmaterialist Politics: The Case of West Germany," *Comparative Political Studies*, vol. 23, nr. 2, July 1990.

48. For a general historical overview, see Günther Rüther, ed., *Geschichte der christlich-demokratischen und christlich-sozialen Bewegungen in Deutschland* (Bonn: Schriftenreihe der Bundeszentrale für politische Bildung, 1987/1989).

49. See "Östlicher und protestantischer," *Der Spiegel*, nr. 25, 1990, p. 40ff.

50. Further information on the CDU's general ideology can, of course, be obtained from the party's programs and platforms. See also Helmut Kohl, "Freiheit und Gerechtigkeit—Perspektiven christlich-demokratischer Politik," in Gerhard Mayer-Vorfelder and Hubertus Zuber, eds., *Union alternativ* (Stuttgart: Seewald Verlag, 1976); William M. Chandler, "The Christian Democrats," in Merkl, ed., *The Federal Republic of Germany at Forty*.

51. When free elections were held in the GDR in March 1990, the East German SPD initially refused to join a coalition including the CSU's East German sister-party (DSU), but subsequently changed its mind.

52. See Abraham Ashkenasi, *Modern German Nationalism* (New York: John Wiley and Sons, 1976), Chapter 6.

53. On the FDP in West German political life, see Christian Søe, "'Not Without Us!' The FDP's Survival, Position, and Influence," in Merkl, ed., *The Federal Republic of Germany at Forty*.

54. According to Harold James, the development of German political identity between 1770 and 1990 was fundamentally shaped by "generational revolts against previous generations' assumptions about nationality"—hence the importance of "youth revolts" in Germany's political history. See his *A German Identity, 1770–1990* (London: Weidenfeld and Nicolson, 1990), pp. 215, 216. The focus on generational differences is central to Joyce Marie Mushaben's argument in *From Post-War to Post-Wall Generations: Changing Attitudes Toward the National Question and NATO in the Federal Republic of Germany* (Boulder, CO: Westview Press, 1998).

55. See Helmut Fogt, *Politische Generationen* (Opladen: Westdeutscher Verlag, 1982), pp. 126–137; Greiffenhagen, *Ein schwieriges Vaterland*, pp. 18–33.

56. David P. Conradt, "German Unification and the Remade Political Culture," paper prepared for delivery at the annual meeting of the American Political Science Association, 30 August–2 September 1990, San Francisco.

57. Conradt, "German Unification and the Remade Political Culture," pp. 3–6.

58. Conradt, "German Unification and the Remade Political Culture," p. 6.

59. Conradt, "German Unification and the Remade Political Culture," p. 20.

60. Wolfgang J. Mommsen, "Die Vergangenheit, die nicht vergehen will," in his *Nation und Geschichte: Über die Deutschen und die deutsche Frage* (München/Zürich: Piper, 1990), p. 107. According to Karl-Ernst Jeismann, the dispute among Germans about the meaning of their national history often results in a debate between those who emphasize the feasibility of continued identification with the past and those who call for the need to "emancipate" the German nation from its troubled history and move in new (and obviously more positive) directions. These two schools of thought are often to be found on the conservative versus liberal side of the political-ideological spectrum, respectively. See his essay "'Identität' statt 'Emanzipation'? Zum Geschichtsbewußtsein in der Bundesrepublik," *Aus Politik und Zeitgeschichte*, 17 May 1986.

61. On the enduring burden of Hitlerism and related questions, see, for example, Craig, *The Germans*, Chapter 3; Hans Mommsen, "The Burden of the Past," in Jürgen Habermas, ed., *Observations on 'The Spiritual Situation of the Age'* (Cambridge, MA: MIT Press, 1984); Ralph Giordano, *Die zweite Schuld oder Von der Last Deutscher zu sein* (Hamburg: Rasch und Röhring Verlag, 1987). For Giordano, the "first guilt" refers to "the guilt of the Germans during the Hitler era." The "second guilt" involves "the denial and repression [of guilt] by [these same Germans] after 1945" (p. 11). The ways in which Germany's traumatic history has complicated the search for a workable national identity are explored by Michael Stürmer in "Deutsche Identität: Auf der Suche nach der verlorenen Nationalgeschichte," in his *Dissonanzen des Fortschritts*, pp. 201–209. See also Barbara Heimannsberg and Christoph J. Schmidt, eds., *The Collective Silence: German Identity and the Legacy of Shame* (San Francisco: Jossey-Bass Publishers, 1993; originally published as *Kollektive Schweigen* by Roland Asanger Verlag in 1988), which heavily emphasizes psychological and psychoanalytical perspectives; and Thomas M. Gauly, ed., *Die Last der Geschichte. Kontroversen zur deutschen Identität* (Köln: Verlag Wissenschaft und Politik, 1988). An interesting comparative study of German and Japanese attitudes and approaches regarding the memory of World War II is Ian Buruma, *The Wages of Guilt: Memories of War in Germany and Japan* (New York: Farrar, Straus, Giroux, 1994).

62. Other occasions during the 1980s when Germany's traumatic past resurfaced prominently in the national consciousness were the television showings of the series "Holocaust" and "Heimat" during the early 1980s, and the fiftieth anniversary in January 1983 of Hitler's accession to power. Regarding the latter event, see the essays by Heinrich August Winkler and Hans-Ulrich Wehler in *Aus Politik und Zeitgeschichte*, 29 January 1983.

63. Good sources on the *Historikerstreit* that the reader may wish to pursue include the excellent collection of articles and essays published by Piper in München in 1987 under the title *Historikerstreit. Die Dokumentation der Kontroverse um die Einzigartigkeit der national-sozialistischen Judenvernichtung* (the essay "Zum Historiker-Streit" by Imanuel Geiss on pp. 373–380 in this volume is particularly informative); Charles S. Maier, *The Unmasterable Past: History, Holocaust, and German National Identity* (Cambridge, MA: Harvard University Press, 1988); several essays (especially "Welche Vergangenheit hat unsere

Zukunft? Anmerkungen zum Historikerstreit") in Wolfgang J. Mommsen, *Nation und Geschichte*. See also Herbert A. Strauss, "Antisemitismus und Holocaust als Epochenproblem," *Aus Politik und Zeitgeschichte*, 14 March 1987.

64. See Grosser, *Geschichte Deutschlands seit 1945*, pp. 304–321. See also the discussion in Agnes Blänsdorf, "Zur Konfrontation mit der NS-Vergangenheit in der Bundesrepublik, der DDR und in Österreich," *Aus Politik und Zeitgeschichte*, nr. 16-17, 1987.

65. Greiffenhagen, *Ein schwieriges Vaterland*, p. 47.

66. For general analyses, see Mommsen, "The Burden of the Past"; Peter Reichel, "Vergangenheitsbewältigung als Problem unserer politischen Kultur," in Jürgen Weber and Peter Steinbach, eds., *Vergangenheitsbewältigung durch Strafverfahren?* (München: G. Olzog Verlag, 1984). In the view of Charles E. McClelland and Steven P. Scher, *Vergangenheitsbewältigung* has become "the most characteristic trait of recent German cultural history" (*Postwar German Culture*, New York: E. P. Dutton, 1974, p. 2). On this important question, see also Alexander and Margarete Mitscherlich, *Die Unfähigkeit zu trauern* (München: Piper, 1967).

67. Armin Mohler, *Vergangenheitsbewältigung, oder wie man den Krieg nochmals verliert* (Krefeld: Sinus-Verlag, 1980).

68. Reichel, "Vergangenheitsbewältigung als Problem unserer politischen Kultur," pp. 151–162. See also the review of trends in public opinion in the 1947–1966 and 1967–1980 periods (gathered by the Allensbach Institut für Demoskopie) in Noelle and Neumann, eds., *The Germans: Public Opinion Polls, 1947–1966*, pp. 195–206; Noelle-Neumann, ed., *The Germans: Public Opinion Polls, 1967–1980*, pp. 112–114.

69. Greiffenhagen, *Ein schwieriges Vaterland*, p. 49.

70. Mommsen, "Die Vergangenheit, die nicht vergehen will," p. 114.

71. See Louis L. Snyder, *Roots of German Nationalism* (Bloomington: Indiana University Press, 1978), Chapter 13. On postwar developments in this regard, see also Wolfgang Mommsen, "Auf der Suche nach nationaler Identität," in Robert Picht, ed., *Das Bündnis im Bündnis* (Berlin: Severin & Siedler, 1982), p. 49ff.

72. Bracher, *The German Dilemma*, p. 11.

73. See the discussion on what it has meant to be a German since World War II and how West Germans perceived the East Germans in Mushaben, *From Post-War to Post-Wall Generations*, Chapters 2 and 3.

74. On the question and need of German *Geschichtsbewußtsein* (historical consciousness) and national identity, see Greiffenhagen, *Die Aktualität Preußens*, pp. 130–147. In this context, see also Christian Graf von Krockow, "Tradition und Geschichtsbewußtsein im sozialen Wandel," *Aus Politik und Zeitgeschichte*, 25 April 1981; Stürmer, "Deutsche Identität: Auf der Suche nach der verlorenen Nationalgeschichte."

75. See Greiffenhagen, *Ein schwieriges Vaterland*, pp. 34–44. For further discussion, see Karl-Ernst Jeismann, ed., *Einheit—Freiheit—Selbstbestimmung: Die Deutsche Frage im historisch-politischen Bewußtsein* (Frankfurt/New York: Campus Verlag, 1988), especially the essays by Erich Kosthorst, Wolfgang Marienfeld, Karl-Ernst Jeismann/Bernd Schönemann, Günter C. Behrmann, and Karl Rohe.

76. See the argument made by M. Rainer Lepsius, "Die Teilung Deutschlands und die deutsche Nation," in Lothar Albertin and Werner Link, eds., *Politische Parteien auf dem Weg zur parlamentarischen Demokratie in Deutschland* (Düsseldorf: Droste Verlag, 1981). See also Karl Rohe, "Die deutsche Einheit als Problem der politischen Kultur in der Bundesrepublik Deutschland," in Jeismann, ed., *Einheit—Freiheit—Selbstbestimmung*.

77. See Alexander Schwan, "Verfassungspatriotismus und nationale Frage: Zum Verhältnis von deutschem Staats- und Nationalbewußtsein," in Weidenfeld, ed., *Politische Kultur und deutsche Frage*. The term was coined in 1979 by Dolf Sternberger. See his collection of essays and speeches entitled *Verfassungspatriotismus* (Frankfurt/Main: Insel Verlag, 1990), p. 13ff.

78. See Almond and Verba, *The Civic Culture*; Richard Rose, "National pride in cross-national perspective," *International Social Science Journal*, vol. 37, nr. 1, 1985. Pre-1990 research showed a continued, relatively low level of West German national pride when compared with other nations. See Berg-Schlosser, "Entwicklung der politischen Kultur in der Bundesrepublik Deutschland," p. 32ff. (esp. table on p. 33).

79. Gebhard Schweigler, *Nationalbewußtsein in der BRD und der DDR* (Düsseldorf: Bertelsmann Universitätsverlag, 1973), especially pp. 110–195.

80. Silke Jansen, "Zwei deutsche Staaten—zwei deutsche Nationen?" *Deutschland Archiv*, vol. 22, nr. 10, October 1989, p. 1139.

81. See Greiffenhagen, *Die Aktualität Preußens*; Rudolf von Thadden, "Preußen—Ein Weg in die Moderne?" *Aus Politik und Zeitgeschichte*, 26 December 1981.

82. Jansen, "Zwei deutsche Staaten—zwei deutsche Nationen?" p. 1134.

83. Jansen, "Zwei deutsche Staaten—zwei deutsche Nationen?" p. 1139.

84. A most central expression of this profound dependence was, of course, the fact that the former World War II victors retained a crucial veto power over any significant alteration of the postwar status quo of a divided Germany. See Andreas Hillgruber, "Die Forderung nach der Deutschen Einheit im Spannungsfeld der Weltpolitik nach 1949," in Jeismann, ed., *Einheit—Freiheit—Selbstbestimmung*.

85. On nationalism in the Federal Republic, see, for example, Ashkenasi, *Modern German Nationalism*, Chapter 3.

86. See Ashkenasi, *Modern German Nationalism*, Chapters 4 and 6.

87. Rose, "National pride in cross-national perspective," pp. 91, 93.

3

East Germany:
An Enduring Legacy?

The division of Germany that resulted from the East-West Cold War after 1945 seemed to recast the German Question. In a way, there appeared to be two German Questions now, as each German state went its separate way, in spite of continued aspects of inter-German connection. It became quite common to analyze the domestic developments in the two German states in relative isolation from one another. The FRG and the GDR increasingly undertook their own search for identity and developed distinctly separate roles within their respective "camps" during the Cold War, leading to speculation about a dwindling all-German national consciousness as new generations appeared on the scene on both sides of the Elbe river.

Consequently, as the years passed, the two-state "solution" to the German Question struck most as stable and increasingly accepted by the Germans themselves. One observer suggested that "[i]n spite of the objective limits to inner-German relations imposed by the division of Europe into rival military alliances and social systems, the crafting of an FRG-GDR 'business basis' which has thus far largely transcended party lines in the Federal Republic must be seen as a stabilizing influence on European politics."[1] As a result, there seemed to be growing consensus that "[t]he real issue today—the 'new German Question'—relates not to reunification but to the evolving modalities of inter-German detente and their implications for European security."[2] This might be a difficult issue at times, but it was altogether manageable nonetheless. A well-known West German analyst, Gebhard Schweigler, whose influential book during the 1970s had sought to document a declining all-German national consciousness (see Chapter 2), spoke of "normalcy in Germany."[3] It was clear that most states surrounding Germany treated the problem of *German power* as the essence of "their" German Question, and partition struck most as a perhaps sad but certainly not ineffective solution. Provided that basic stability could be ensured, the presence of the two Cold War blocs on European soil seemed to create a comfortably predictable policy environment. And within this overall context, the GDR was certainly seen as fundamentally stable.

Yet, some observers had begun to raise important questions about the degree of dissent and dissatisfaction inside East Germany well before the full crisis of late 1989 erupted. In fact, had not Ralf Dahrendorf remarked during the 1960s that "the history of the [GDR] may be a history of internal conflicts seeking modes of expression"?[4] And in 1987, West German analyst Volker Gransow, for example, wrote that East Germany was at a turning point. "It seems possible that the calm in the GDR is delusive, that is the calm before the storm."[5] Another observer, Adrian Hyde-Price, still concluded, however, that "the short-term prospects for reform are slight, given the economic and political stability of the country."[6]

In retrospect, it has nonetheless become clear now that a rather extensive "nascent civil society" did indeed develop in the GDR in the course of the 1980s, especially focused on the need for internal political and socioeconomic reform, and not on unification with the FRG. A large amount of Western research and official attention was disproportionately devoted to the established SED government, so that much of the emergence of key (underground) groups went rather unnoticed. The Evangelical Church, independent Marxists, peace groups, and various other groups of intellectuals played a prominent role in this gathering opposition movement. As we shall see in Chapter 7, these groups were very instrumental in bringing about the collapse of Communist rule in the fall and winter of 1989–1990, although their influence would not last.[7]

In addition to its shaky political legitimacy and an increasingly disaffected population, the GDR regime also faced worsening economic conditions. These were, of course, intricately connected to the growth in political discontent. According to W. R. Smyser, "[s]ome of the weaknesses of the GDR economy [could] be traced to its slow revival after World War II." In the final analysis, however, "the East German economy suffered not so much from its slow start as from the directions that the GDR government chose in the 1950s and never abandoned, despite several halfhearted efforts to introduce different principles and practices."[8] In his view, "[t]he twin economic directions of East Germany . . . were central control of virtually all economic activity and, under that control, a concentration of trade toward other socialist states and especially toward the Soviet Union." As a result, the East and West German economies developed major gaps in the areas of productivity and finance. Smyser also stresses, however, that the "economy of East Germany [was] not the total failure often portrayed."[9] The GDR tended to be placed fairly high on the list of international economic powers, although that ranking appeared in retrospect to have been unrealistically high.

In light of such widespread assumptions about the GDR's fundamental "stability," the spectacular events in East Germany in 1989 generated a surprise and a question. The surprise was that the likelihood of German reunification suddenly appeared on a not-so-distant horizon in a quite definitive way. Such reunification had been easiest to support during the Cold War, when it seemed at best a distant and perhaps even entirely far-fetched eventuality. In this sense, events in the GDR added up to a rather unpleasant turn of events for many of Germany's neighbors, who had had reservations about German unity all along but kept them conveniently hidden.

Yet, the dramatic developments in East Germany also raised a fundamental question: Might the population of the GDR, if given the chance, freely decide to perpetuate a separate, reformed and democratized, East German state?[10] In response to the November 1989 confederation plan offered by West German Chancellor Helmut Kohl, for example, a group of prominent GDR citizens declared: "We *still* have the chance to develop a socialist alternative to the Federal Republic on the basis of neighborliness and equality among all states in Europe. We can *still* reflect on the antifascist and humanist ideals that once were our point of departure."[11] Similarly, a leading figure in the East German opposition citizens' movement Democracy Now, Konrad Weiß, had insisted in September 1989:

> I believe that both German states need to change, that the GDR as well as the Federal Republic are in urgent need of reforms. Perhaps that is a means by which, based on reforms in the prevailing systems, a rapprochement between both states can be achieved. That is, I do not want a united Germany which is a GDR enlarged by three-fourths, and I also do not want a Germany which is a Federal Republic enlarged by one-fourth. We do not wish to become a *Land* of the Federal Republic of Germany; rather, we wish to follow our own path. We want to be able to find a shared path together with the Germans in the Federal Republic.[12]

If this scenario came to pass, everyone would be caught even more off-guard, including many (if not most) West Germans who had lived for forty years with very definite reunification assumptions. These assumptions, particularly prevalent among West German conservatives, amounted to what I would call an *Anschluß* syndrome: the notion that German unification would basically involve the "absorption" of the GDR by the FRG. Although the FRG had been intended as a provisional German state, the presupposition had grown that the West German socioeconomic, political, and constitutional framework would be more or less extended to incorporate a GDR "released" from the clutches of Soviet Cold War imperialism, if that ever came to pass. The FRG always saw itself as the only true Germany, inheriting the mantle of historical German nationhood. Moreover, unification had always been considered ultimately compatible with continued West German integration into Western economic (EC) and security (NATO) systems, again encouraging *Anschluß* thinking. Could these assumptions survive the turbulence of 1989 and beyond? Needless to say, this question did not become intriguing only for the Germans.

These West German assumptions, and the more widespread surprise at the GDR's unexpected changes, also point to the rather "orphan" status that was commonly allotted to East Germany in much, though certainly not all, of what tended to be called "German studies," throughout the Cold War. At least four reasons seemed to account for the relative neglect of the GDR in research on Germany, especially in non-German, Western circles. First, the FRG was so much bigger that most would regard it as more important, even in a context of reunification. Considerations of power would always attract attention in the direction of West Germany. Second, the GDR was not as accessible to every type of research as the FRG, in view of the former's largely "closed" system between 1949 and 1989. Third, there was a widespread tendency to treat the GDR as the "so-called GDR," a basically illegitimate puppet state set up by the Soviets. In other words, why bother studying an artificial façade?[13] This was the kind of perspective that encouraged *Anschluß* thinking, of course. And fourth, a widespread expectation of continued political "stability" and increased "normalcy" inside the GDR may ironically have led many to ignore the potential for genuine upheaval in East Germany. This latter tendency would be connected with a more normatively based "satisfaction" with an apparently stable two-state solution to the thorny German Question.

Political Culture and National Identity in the GDR Before 1989

The upshot of all this was the emergence, in 1989 and 1990 and perhaps beyond, of an unexpected rendition of the German Question: *the East German Question.* We must consider the issues of German identity, German unity, Germany's international role, and Germany's power in more explicit reference to the GDR and its possible legacy. Particular questions arise. Was and/or is there a specific "East German" (or "eastern German") identity? What were the GDR's official attitudes with regard to German unity? What attitudes might we expect on the part of the population in former GDR territory? What role did the GDR play in European affairs? And how does the fate of the GDR fit into the larger context of German power? Although we may not be able to transcend the level of speculation in some cases, these questions nonetheless demand close attention. We examine them in the remainder of this chapter and again in Chapters 7 and 8.[14]

When we consider the notion of a separate East German identity and political culture, we may fruitfully explore the matter in two directions.[15] First, there is the possibility of an identity and a culture specifically linked to the GDR as a socialist state on German soil. The second tack includes aspects of an East German identity and culture that (could) build upon older German traditions peculiar to the territory on which the GDR was created in 1949. Here we shall encounter the legacy of Prussia as a major factor.

If a specific GDR or "eastern German" identity and culture can be shown to exist, then clearly the forty years between 1949 and 1989 have not been without their consequences. In such a case, an admittedly dictatorial regime may have been able to impart a noticeable ideological legacy, the elements of a possibly enduring "East" Germany. Back in the 1960s, Dahrendorf believed this to be already the case, writing that "while the two Germanies may still debate the academic or, rather, diplomatic question of whether they are two states, they have already become two societies." He saw East Germany as a socialist continuation of the "National Socialist revolution of modernity" in Germany and added that "[b]y contrast to National Socialist Germany, there are hardly any islands of tradition left in the [GDR]." The ongoing social transformation was felt to have political implications, insofar as "the inclusive process of social co-ordination in East Germany has involved the realization of that equality that is a precondition of effective citizenship rights . . . . [I]t probably constitutes the hard core of East German social changes, which can never be undone." He came to the conclusion that "the [GDR] is the first modern society on German soil," but it remained a totalitarian modernity.[16]

Writing some two decades later, however, C. Bradley Scharf sounded a note of much greater caution and pointed to the complexity of identity in the GDR:

> When outsiders first endeavor to comprehend a nation such as the German Democratic Republic, it is tempting to isolate a single attribute as the most essential defining element. English-speaking peoples, much affected by their government's involvement in East-West confrontations, have long tended to see the GDR as simply a Soviet "satellite," an unredeemable renegade from its Western past. But reality is far more complex. The GDR is a nation at a crossroads in a very profound sense. It is pulled in four directions simultaneously. It is intensely aware of its German past, while aspiring vigorously to a socialist future. It is a West European nation because of its shared popular culture, its shared problems of advanced urban-industrial ecology, and the highly visible presence of the Federal Republic as a point of interest and comparison. It is also an East European nation because of its military dependence on the Soviet Union and its more or less compulsory adoption of Soviet forms of political organization and public values.[17]

He concluded that "[i]t is no exaggeration to say that the GDR is in the midst of an identity crisis. Contrary to expectations, the passage of time has not brought much relief. As old riddles remain, new forms of change have only added new dimensions to the problem."[18]

The creation of a separate GDR identity was a persistent objective of the Communist regime after 1949. Hermann Rudolph described this official East German identity as a *verordnete Identität* ("imposed identity").[19] He suggested that, although the definition of that identity underwent particular modifications over time, the basic delineation of a specific GDR identity was nothing less than a matter of *Staatsräson* for the East German regime. The definition of the East German identity became part of the consolidation and perpetuation of the regime's power. On the one hand, the regime defined a GDR identity in the context of general German history. On the other hand, it asserted an identity vis-à-vis an FRG seen as hostile and reactionary.

Controlled by the SED (German Socialist Unity Party), the regime presented the GDR as the logical culmination of all progressive and revolutionary strands in German national history, such as the peasant revolts of the Reformation era, the Prussian Enlightenment, the war of liberation against Napoleon, the attempted 1848 revolution, the Weimar Republic, and the anti-Hitler resistance.[20] The day of the German surrender at the end of World War II (May 8, 1945) was turned into a holiday (*Tag der Befreiung*). The perspective on German history (*Geschichtsbild*) thus became noticeably selective, often serving the regime's consolidation and legitimation interests. As Rudolph put it, "[the GDR's leadership] attempted again and again to interpret [German] national history in such a way that [the GDR's existence] would appear to be [that history's] necessary and correct outcome."[21] In contrast to a West Germany allegedly controlled by ex-Nazis, nationalist revanchists, and capitalist reactionaries, the GDR was defined as the vanguard of a future socialist and democratic Germany. As we shall see later in this chapter, attitudes about a united Germany versus an enduring GDR shifted over time.[22]

Although this "imposed identity" may never have been a living reality among the bulk of the East German population, Rudolph pointed out that it left identifiable sociocultural and psychological traces because it influenced the contours of everyday life in East Germany for four decades.[23] GDR citizens had to cope with a socioeconomic and political environment shaped by the power monopoly of the Communist state-party apparatus. Social and political norms, centered on discipline, conformity, and passivity, if not outright docility, suffused one's daily existence. Rudolph noted the prevalence of "bureaucratic regulation," "social homogenisation," and "social control," and identified the impact of processes of constant indoctrination and mobilization expressed through propaganda campaigns and political ritualism. Nonconformism became relegated to the private realm.[24] Aspects of Germany's traditional, illiberal culture and political legacy were, if not consciously exploited, at least unintentionally reinforced. Dissent ended up underground or in exile, and resentment and cynicism spread.[25]

The result, according to Scharf, was a mixture of sentiments and orientations:

Western journalists and others who have lived in the GDR for extended periods report that most citizens are reflective and expressive on the subject of national identity. Most display considerable awareness of the virtues and defects of their own political system and a reasonably informed comprehension of the outside world. Some are implacable and cynical, and a few even undertake overt opposition to the current regime. Many pretend indifference to all political questions and simply focus their attention on the minimum requirements of work and the greater rewards of family and leisure pursuits. And there are others, generally younger adults, who persist in seeing some reasons for optimism, who believe that—since they are Germans, after all—there must be some way to make this system work.[26]

These remarks by Scharf point to the importance of elements of heterogeneity in any country's political culture, including the former East Germany. On the one hand, there is "an official culture, or public myth, which depicts government purposes and citizen aspirations in the most noble, idealistic light." In the case of the GDR, "Marxism-Leninism as the foundation for an officially propagated myth" constituted the obvious core of this official political culture,[27] with additional emphasis on achievement in work, the primacy of societal and collective over private and individualized needs and goals, and the supremacy of the state in all aspects of life (guided, of course, by the SED).[28] On the other hand, there are manifestations of political culture in a more informal sense, both public and private, on a mass level, shaped by everyday political realities.

In a 1989 analysis, Ralf Rytlewski suggested that many features of mass political culture in the GDR were not primarily shaped by the impact of official Marxist-Leninist dogma, and that there were limits to the ideological influence of the Soviets. Instead, he stressed the significance of persisting traditional German working-class and petty-bourgeois (Spießbürger) values. He also pointed to the existence of a popular mentality, focused on work and achievement, that is shaped by the contours of industrial society (industriegesellschaftliche Mentalität) and that is at least in part comparable to trends observable in other industrialized countries. In addition, he noted that cultural orientations and tastes were heavily influenced by "the proletarian and petty-bourgeois/idealist tradition of the German labor movement." The Lutheran tradition, with its simultaneous emphasis on obedience to official authority (Untertan der Obrigkeit) and its privatized introspection (private Innerlichkeit), resulting in a "loyalty-protection-relationship" (Treue-Schutz-Verhältnis) between citizens and government, also remained a fundamental reality among the vast majority of the population.[29]

Rytlewski concluded by stressing the perceptible emergence of an "alternative political [sub]culture" among many East Germans, alienated from official SED dogmas, focused on a mixture of ecological concerns, pacifism, and a desire for a more "open" and reformed version of socialism. He contrasted this dissent-oriented subculture (Konflikt-Kultur) among especially younger generations of East Germans with the adjustment- and reconciliation-oriented political culture (Anpassungskultur) prevalent among the older generations.[30]

There can be little doubt now, using the benefit of hindsight, that the imposed and enforced nature of much of the East German identity and way of life over time clearly undermined the legitimacy of the East German government.[31] A stable democratic political culture, like the one prevailing in the FRG, did not and could not develop, which some feared might have troublesome consequences when the former GDR's population moved into the new and uncharted waters of unification with the FRG, although others argued that many East Germans had "learned" democracy by means of indirect (media) or direct (travel) exposure to West German political life.[32]

In his analysis, Rudolph also suggested that the GDR's specific postwar experience had been a defining influence on the evolving East German identity.[33] Throughout the post-1949 era, this experience involved FRG-GDR comparisons and a sense of mutual competition and actual *Abgrenzung* ("isolation" or "separation"), inducing a heightened GDR assertiveness connected with an enduring, though not officially admitted, inferiority complex. Until the 1960s, the GDR was seen by many as a barely surviving artificial entity, denied the benefits of the sense of "normalization" experienced by the FRG as far back as the 1950s. After the 1960s, a sense of recovery and achievement began to affect the East German psychology. The GDR seemed to have found a more comfortably prominent place among its socialist sister-states in the Soviet bloc. Rudolph interpreted this as evidence of an East German "consolidation."

This consolidation was expressed quite vividly by the reality and the symbolism of the Berlin Wall, and the paradoxical though tragic stability it appeared to provide. The official policy of *Abgrenzung*, in spite of the continuing impact of West German radio and television, forced the population to come to terms with the GDR's own domestic existential realities and possibilities. The lack of alternatives, in view of rigid travel restrictions, was bound to generate at least a certain degree of attachment to East Germany's own way of life, especially its more palatable or successful aspects. Rudolph suggested that a certain GDR *Staatsbewußtsein* ("state consciousness") might indeed exist among the East German population, but that it was not primarily a positive political consciousness, rooted in a fundamental sense of ideological regime legitimacy. Instead, it was an acceptance of a basic framework (*Rahmen*) within which one's everyday existence evolved.[34] A widespread feeling of basic fulfillment and at least bearable normalcy would be crucial in this regard, as Rytlewski suggested with his notion of *Anpassungskultur*. The breaching of the Wall in November 1989 dramatically marked the end of the old *Abgrenzung* policy, and set in motion some major shifts in East German political life. In the course of the 1990s, many observers wondered whether attachment to life in "East" Germany was still strong enough among the population there to generate distinct manifestations of resistance to a full-fledged "takeover" by "West" Germany. We will return more fully to this issue in Chapter 8.

Although the GDR and FRG had led separate existences for more than forty years by 1989, it was undeniable that both had somehow remained connected, if only on a psychological level, to a joint, all-German past.[35] For the GDR, this linkage meant that this newly created socialist state had to define itself in a larger German historical context. Prewar German traditions and experiences retained their relevance in both German states, whether in the form of continuity or conscious reaction. We have already noted how the regime sought to tie a GDR identity to selected aspects of the German historical experience. Other aspects, such as a sense of responsibility for the crimes of Nazi Germany, were deliberately excluded, since the founders of the state considered themselves equally victimized by the National Socialists' tyranny and hence not liable for the deeds of the Third Reich.[36]

Both the FRG and the GDR had to confront a shared German history, however, and they generally did so unwillingly "together," in an atmosphere of contention and mutual ostracism. In Rudolph's view, both German states thus shared in Germany's historical fate (*Schicksal*). In this sense, the GDR was not an entirely new construction, but rather a mixture of historical inheritance and ideological innovation. We have seen that very much the same can be said about the Federal Republic, although one might add Rudolph's observation that the GDR did not experience the kind of postwar modernization (and Westernization) that had affected West Germany.[37]

The last point again draws our attention to the fact that the development of an East German identity and self-consciousness was inextricably connected with developments in the FRG. Both states led a "comparative existence" for more than four decades. Moreover, it was frequently suggested that the GDR appeared to be more "traditional" and therefore more "German" in direct proportion to the far-reaching "modernization" of life and society in the Federal Republic.[38] Furthermore, a case could be made that the West German acceptance of the de facto reality of two German states, in the context of the *Ostpolitik* of the 1970s and the *Deutschlandpolitik* of the 1980s, imparted a greater sense of legitimacy to the GDR and may in the long run have aided in the development of a clearer East German identity.

Yet, when all is said and done, in spite of all of the regime's ideological efforts, plus a forty-year existence, it is undeniable that the GDR continued to struggle with an "identity deficit." Rudolph described it as a "fragmented identity" and referred to East Germany as a *Reststaat*, roughly translatable as "rump state."[39] The GDR, only a small part of the larger historical German nation, tended to languish in the shadow of its larger, wealthier competitor to the West. Moreover, unlike other Eastern European states, the GDR could not truly claim to constitute a full-fledged nation. In addition, the GDR did not seem to occupy a territorial space coincident with a clearly definable historical part of Germany. All these factors heightened the degree of artificiality that many observed.

The Prussian Factor

Yet, if it is true that East Germany had to struggle mightily in the development of a true "GDR identity" after 1949, does this mean that it was a *completely* artificial façade? Perhaps not. There is an important historical factor to consider: Prussia. Rudolph pointed to this when he wrote:

> The GDR represents not just the predominance of Prussian and Saxon advantages and disadvantages, but it involves Prussians and Saxons [living] among themselves, stewing in the juices of their sober mentality, their discipline, their work-ethic, and their narrowness for three decades—without the influences of the easy-going Rhenish spirit or Bavaria's self-confidence to which they were exposed in the past.[40]

The relationship between the GDR and the Prussian legacy was and is, of course, embedded in the larger theme of East Germany's relationship with and treatment of all-German history. It is a facet of "GDR identity" that is well worth examining.[41]

Some eighty years ago, Oswald Spengler wrote an essay entitled *Preußentum und Sozialismus*,[42] which explored the connection or similarity between the Prussian worldview and socialist ideology in Germany's illiberal, authoritarian tradition. Was the GDR as we knew it since 1949 the realization of Spengler's analysis? How did regime and population in East Germany, a territory that once was a central part of Prussia, deal with the history of this so often controversial state? Was (and is) the Prussian legacy a living component of a possible "East" German identity?

The connection between East Germany and Prussia has two dimensions. On the one hand, there is the (usually official) pre-1989 East German perspective on Prussia in the general context of German history. Here we are interested in those aspects of Prussia that were ideologically rejected, and those that were "appropriated" in an effort to enhance a GDR identity and legitimacy. On the other hand, there is the more informal, and thus more unofficial, way in which the Prussian legacy remained detectable in East German social and political life.

As noted earlier, the SED regime consistently sought to present East Germany as the heir of all that was progressive in the history of the German people. The separation of "progressive" and "reactionary" traditions was always crucial to officially sanctioned East German historiography. The task thus became one of deciding what, if anything, in the Prussian legacy was to be considered acceptable as part of the GDR's historical-philosophical foundation.

As Jörg Bernhard Bilke has noted, the GDR regime inherited a rather explicit Marxist interpretation of the role of Prussia in the German historical experience, an interpretation that dates back to 1848.[43] The essence of the Marxist perspective was that Prussia represented all that was disastrous and ruinous in German history: militarism, illiberalism, nationalism, and *Junker* feudalism. The Prussian legacy was connected directly with the cancer of Nazism. A fairly prominent GDR historian like Alexander Abusch, writing in the Marxist tradition, even suggested in 1960 that the Prussian legacy was in fact fundamentally "anti-German."[44] He argued that Prussia increased and consolidated its power at the expense of the rest of Germany. The Prussian interest in German unity was, in the final analysis, purely selfish.

The traditional Marxist view of Prussia remained predominant until well into the 1950s. Nothing worthwhile could be salvaged from the Prussian legacy. In fact, most of German history was deemed irrelevant, as the GDR embarked on the road to a "construction of socialism." Yet in the course of the 1950s, interest in the links between the new GDR and Germany's national history began to grow. The regime decided to place the GDR in the context of the "progressive" aspects of German history. And among the elements of that history that were now "retrieved" for the benefit of a "new," socialist Germany were some with unmistakable Prussian aspects: the war of liberation against Napoleon, Russian-German alliance during that war, and the Prussian military reforms of those years, involving new, sudden heroes like Stein, Hardenberg, Gneisenau, and Scharnhorst. German patriotism seemed acceptable again, as long as it had "progressive" connotations. Bilke notes the irony of the fact that the Prussian-Russian "war of liberation" against Napoleon was in a fundamental sense a war of two reactionary regimes against the progressive implications of the French Revolution.[45]

The new outlook on Prussia was quite relevant to the development of the GDR's *Nationale Volksarmee* (National People's Army).[46] The legacy of the Prussian army reforms of 1807–1808, along with a variety of Prussian military traditions, was incorporated in East German military policy, practice, and symbolism. And references to Prussia's allegedly "Slavic" aspects were deemed helpful in the legitimation of the alliance with, if not hyperdependence on, a fraternally socialist Soviet Union.

Until the 1970s, the official East German perspective on German national history, emphasizing the GDR as the true and progressive Germany and the FRG as an imperialist construction, remained connected with the goal of ultimate German unification on a socialist basis. In other words, the notion was one of two competing German states within one persisting German nation. But in 1971, as the Ulbricht era drew to a close and the mantle of SED leadership passed to Erich Honecker, an emphasis on two German *nations*, one reactionary and the other progressive, became noticeable.[47] The goal of German unification was officially abandoned. The GDR would become a separate German nation, with a "socialist, national culture."[48] The change in emphasis and identity was captured in a fundamental revision of Article 1 of the GDR constitution in 1974. The old text read: "The German Democratic Republic is a socialist state of [within] the German nation." The revised text read: "The German Democratic Republic is a socialist state of workers and farmers."[49]

While this fundamental effort at transformation in the official GDR identity was occurring, the prominent East German historian Ingrid Mittenzwei led the way in the direction of a revisionist interpretation of the Prussian legacy.[50] This revision involved a basic rejection of a selective historiography that stressed only "progressive" traditions. By East German standards, such a revision would involve a good deal of *Vergangenheitsbewältigung* ("coming to terms with the past"), although not quite along the same lines as what had occurred in West Germany. For these revisionist historians, Prussia was an inescapable part of East Germany's (and West Germany's) historical legacy, the positive *and* negative aspects of which must be interpreted honestly and objectively. The traditional Marxist one-dimensionality clearly began to crumble.[51]

As some historians in the GDR went their revisionist way, official and popular interest in Prussia grew in both East and West Germany during the 1970s and 1980s. In the wake of *Ostpolitik*, detente between the two German states triggered an apparently renewed sense of all-German connectedness, in spite of Honecker's attempts at continued *Abgrenzung*. A Prussia Year was celebrated in East Germany in 1981. Commemorations of Frederick the Great and Bismarck occurred. The Prussian legacy became an important component in the Museum of German

History in East Berlin. And 1983 witnessed a joint German celebration of the 500th anniversary of the birth of Luther.[52]

Yet while the Prussian legacy might bind East and West Germany in terms of a shared history, Bilke shows how Prussia also played an important role in the GDR regime's *Abgrenzung* policy. He wrote in 1981 that

> Prussia was what the GDR is and will remain: a *Kunststaat* [artificial state] . . . , not the product of its own [internal] strength, but of the whim or the calculation of a victorious power. If the reference to Prussia in the West [that is, in the FRG] is aimed at the promotion of the idea of reunification, in the East [that is, in the GDR] the claim could be made (though perhaps not explicitly) that Prussia was a *Separatstaat* [a separate state], . . . a competitor of and then heir of the Habsburg dynasty. The result of such a political scenario would be the rejection of any idea of *Gesamtdeutschland* [unified Germany]. In a more solemn sense it would mean that the SED-State without a sense of real tradition and "separatist" Prussia extend one another the hand, across centuries and class barriers, in a fraternal renunciation of any notion of an [all-German] nation-state.[53]

Such a Prussianized East Germany would not be entirely inconceivable, insofar as much of the core of traditional Prussia was to be found within GDR territory. What is more, we noted earlier that observers often suggested possible sociocultural connections between *Altpreußen* (traditional Prussia) and *Rotpreußen* ("socialist GDR-Prussia"). According to Bilke, "[t]he authoritarian state structures of old Prussia and SED-Prussia share some basic traits: discipline, diligence, thrift, obedience, modesty, a desire for order, and an acceptance of the fact that the state takes actions that are in fact incomprehensible—all these virtues are deemed desirable [by the SED regime] between the Baltic Sea and the forests of Thuringia. It is not the people who rule, but the enlightened [Prussian] monarch or the unenlightened [SED] Politburo."[54]

This discussion of the GDR's basic search for identity suggests that the issues of identity, German unity, and East Germany's international role have in fact been crucially interconnected. At first, the GDR saw itself, at least officially, as a separate, "vanguard" state within a persisting German nation, striving to bring about a reunified, socialist Germany. Then came the shift to a conception of a separate "GDR nation" and a complete rejection of any kind of "national" reunification. Throughout, the SED regime defined the GDR's role as that of a loyal Warsaw Pact alliance partner. Internationally, the GDR would be a demonstration of a "new" Germany, revolutionary, progressive, and "peace-loving," all this in contrast with a revanchist, capitalist FRG. These principles were spelled out clearly in the revised constitution of 1974:

Article 6:

The German Democratic Republic has wiped out German militarism and Nazism on its territory, in accordance with the interests of the people and [its] international obligations. [The GDR] conducts a foreign policy that serves socialism and peace, understanding among peoples and security. . . . The German Democratic Republic supports those states and peoples that fight for freedom and independence against imperialism and its colonial rule in their struggle for social progress. The German Democratic Republic supports the realization of the principles of peaceful coexistence among states with divergent social orders and pursues cooperation with all states on the basis of equality and mutual respect.

Article 8:
The German Democratic Republic will never undertake a war of conquest or deploy its forces against the freedom of another people.[55]

This wording was a prominent attempt at self-definition by a regime that had to come to grips with the consequences of the detente era for its more militant self-image of the Cold War era. Yet each German state in many ways continued to maintain an image of the other as an illegitimate *Reststaat*.

In sum, the search for a solid GDR identity was reflected very clearly in East German *foreign policy*, and was tied to the GDR's search for a stable, emancipated role in the socialist "camp," based upon global recognition of full-fledged East German sovereignty.[56] During the early postwar years, the vision of a reunited but socialist Germany, perhaps even based on neutrality, persisted, but was fully abandoned after the creation of the Berlin Wall in 1961. From then on, domestic consolidation went hand in hand with efforts at *Abgrenzung*. Increased emphasis was placed on the development of a clearer East German *Staatsbewußtsein*. As we shall see in the next chapter, the FRG had pursued a *Westpolitik* focused on NATO and the European Community in an effort to regain sovereignty and international rehabilitation. In somewhat similar fashion, the GDR conducted a strict "*Ostpolitik*" aimed at finding a suitable role as reliable ally in the Warsaw Pact and Comecon. Throughout those years, the FRG's *Ostpolitik* remained either negative or nonexistent, centered on an unwillingness to interact in any formal sense with the "so-called GDR." Similarly, the GDR sought to isolate itself from what it perceived to be a revanchist and threatening FRG. The ways in which both German states mirrored one another's foreign policy orientations, amid manifold international constraints, is definitely striking.

With the advent of increased East-West detente efforts during and after the 1960s, the two German states risked growing international isolation if they persisted on their path of mutual ostracism. The FRG made the necessary adjustments after 1969 by embarking on a more active *Ostpolitik* and *Deutschlandpolitik*, but the East German predicament turned out to be more complicated.[57] Whereas West Germans increasingly accepted the notion of two states within one enduring German nation, with unification as a long-range dream, attempts were made in the GDR from the early 1970s onward to create an explicit sense of separate East German *nationhood*. In view of this rather vigorous attempt to sever any basic sense of all-German national linkage with the FRG, the pursuit of a

Janus-like diplomacy, involving an adequately balanced policy toward both East and West, would be at best a complex affair. As time passed, this became more and more obvious, since the East German preoccupation with a special GDR-FRG "security partnership" in Central Europe under circumstances of both detente and renewed Cold War, in addition to extensive and deepening FRG-GDR *economic* interaction,[58] served to demonstrate and reinforce a continued shared political consciousness between two purportedly "separate" German "nations" that no effort at *Abgrenzung* could obviate.[59] Also, Moscow's growing interest in the expansion of closer Soviet-FRG relations proved highly uncomfortable to an insecure GDR, inasmuch as it appeared to call into question East Berlin's special ties with the USSR, upon which East Germany had always been rather uniquely dependent for support and legitimacy. Thus, future historians may well conclude that the era of detente spelled the beginning of the end for a separate GDR.

Notes

1. Ernest D. Plock, *The Basic Treaty and the Evolution of East-West German Relations* (Boulder, CO: Westview Press, 1986), p. 234.

2. F. Stephen Larrabee, "From Reunification to Reassociation: New Dimensions of the German Question," in F. Stephen Larrabee, ed., *The Two German States and European Security* (New York: St. Martin's Press, 1989), p. 3. Writing about the "gradual liquidation of the German Question," Reinhard Meier had suggested in 1984 that "true normalization [of relations between the FRG and the GDR] means a softening and a reduction of the German division, which is not the same as reunification into one state, for which there is no realistic prospect [anyway]." Meier, "Die allmähliche Auflösung der deutschen Frage," *Europa-Archiv*, nr. 21, 1984, p. 654.

3. Gebhard Schweigler, "Normalität in Deutschland," *Europa-Archiv*, nr. 6, 1989.

4. Ralf Dahrendorf, *Society and Democracy in Germany* (New York: W. W. Norton, 1979), p. 402.

5. Volker Gransow, "East German Society at the Turning-Point?" *Studies in Comparative Communism*, vol. XX, nr. 1, Spring 1987, p. 109.

6. Adrian Hyde-Price, "East Germany: calm before the storm?" *The World Today*, vol. 44, nr. 8-9, August-September 1988, p. 147. See also Pedro Ramet, "Disaffection and Dissent in East Germany," *World Politics*, vol. 37, nr. 1, October 1984.

7. For an excellent discussion of this often underground opposition movement, see Vladimir Tismaneanu, "Nascent Civil Society in the German Democratic Republic," *Problems of Communism*, March-June 1989. See also Jan Wielgohs and Marianne Schulz, "Reformbewegung und Volksbewegung," *Aus Politik und Zeitgeschichte*, 13 April 1990; Hubertus Knabe, "Politische Opposition in der DDR," *Aus Politik und Zeitgeschichte*, 5 January 1990; B. Welling Hall, "The Church and the Independent Peace Movement in Eastern Europe," *Journal of Peace Research*, vol. 23, nr. 2, 1986, p. 200ff.; Daniel Hamilton, "Dateline East Germany: The Wall Behind the Wall," *Foreign Policy*, nr. 76, Fall 1989, especially p. 192ff.; Vladimir Tismaneanu, "Eastern Europe: The Story the Media Missed," *The Bulletin of the Atomic Scientists*, March 1990.

8. W. R. Smyser, "United Germany: A New Economic Miracle?" *The Washington Quarterly*, vol. 13, nr. 4, Autumn 1990, p. 160.

9. Smyser, "United Germany: A New Economic Miracle?" pp. 161, 162.

10. There were many expectations along these lines, especially during the last months of 1989, when the East German public still appeared more focused on the idea of a reformed GDR than on a merger with the FRG. Much of the thinking in East and West during those months was cast in terms of "confederation" ideas, a GDR-FRG "treaty-based community" (*Vertragsgemeinschaft*), and so on. A continuing exodus of GDR citizens to the FRG forced a different pace and scenario, however. See the discussion in "Ein Staatenbund? Ein Bundesstaat?" *Der Spiegel*, nr. 49, 1989, p. 24ff.

11. Quoted in "Ein Staatenbund? Ein Bundesstaat?" p. 25 (emphasis in original).

12. Konrad Weiß, "Wir möchten kein Land der Bundesrepublik werden," in Gerhard Rein, ed., *Die Opposition in der DDR* (Berlin: Wichern-Verlag, 1989), p. 72.

13. See Alfred Grosser, *Geschichte Deutschlands seit 1945* (München: Deutscher Taschenbuch Verlag, 1979), p. 370. See also the interesting essay by Wilhelm Bleek, "Zur Entwicklung der vergleichenden Deutschlandforschung," *Aus Politik und Zeitgeschichte*, nr. 38, 1984.

14. It is not the purpose of this chapter to provide any kind of comprehensive history of the former GDR. For material along these lines, the interested reader may wish to turn to sources like the following: Dierk Hoffmann, Karl-Heinz Schmidt, and Peter Skyba, eds., *Die DDR vor dem Mauerbau. Dokumente zur Geschichte des anderen deutschen Staates, 1949–1961* (Munich/Zürich: Piper Verlag, 1993); Hermann Weber, *DDR. Grundriß der Geschichte, 1945–1990* (Hannover: Fackelträger-Verlag, 1991); David Childs, *The GDR: Moscow's German Ally* (London: Unwin Hyman Ltd., 1988).

15. The following discussion of the East German identity question is particularly indebted to the excellent essay by Hermann Rudolph, "Wie sieht das Selbstverständnis der DDR-Gesellschaft aus?" in Werner Weidenfeld, ed., *Die Identität der Deutschen* (Bonn: Schriftenreihe der Bundeszentrale für politische Bildung, 1983), pp. 193–209. See also Harold James, *A German Identity, 1770–1990* (London: Weidenfeld and Nicolson, 1990), Chapter 8; and the essays by Ralf Rytlewski, Manfred Opp de Hipt, and Irma Hanke in Hans Georg Wehling, ed., *Politische Kultur in der DDR* (Stuttgart/Berlin/Köln: Verlag W. Kohlhammer, 1989). For more basic historical treatments of the GDR, see the works by Thilo Vogelsang (1980, Chapters 3, 6, and 9), Alfred Grosser (1979, Chapter 10), Christoph Klessmann (1982), Hermann Weber (1986 and 1987), Martin McCauley (1983), and Henry Krisch (1985), all listed in the Selected Bibliography of this book. See also Dietrich Staritz, "Auf dem Wege zur DDR (1948/1949)," *Aus Politik und Zeitgeschichte*, nr. 18, 1985.

16. Dahrendorf, *Society and Democracy in Germany*, pp. 398, 399, 400, 401.

17. C. Bradley Scharf, *Politics and Change in East Germany* (Boulder, CO/London: Westview Press and Frances Pinter Publishers, 1984), p. 18.

18. Scharf, *Politics and Change in East Germany*, p. 18.

19. Hermann Rudolph, "Wie sieht das Selbstverständnis . . . ," p. 197ff.

20. In this context, see Andreas Dorpalen, "Weimar Republic and Nazi Era in East German Perspective," *Central European History*, vol. 11, nr. 3, September 1978; Hans-Ulrich Thamer, "Nationalsozialismus und Faschismus in der DDR-Historiographie," *Aus Politik und Zeitgeschichte*, 28 March 1987; Agnes Blänsdorf, "Zur Konfrontation mit der NS-Vergangenheit in der Bundesrepublik, der DDR und in Osterreich," *Aus Politik und Zeitgeschichte*, nr. 16-17, 1987. In addition, see Hermann Weber, "'Weisse Flecken' in der DDR-Geschichtsschreibung," and Georgi Verbeeck, "Kontinuität und Wandel im DDR-Geschichtsbild," both in *Aus Politik und Zeitgeschichte*, 9 March 1990; Günther Hey-

demann, "Geschichtswissenschaft und Geschichtsverständnis in der DDR seit 1945," *Aus Politik und Zeitgeschichte*, 28 March 1987.

21. Rudolph, "Wie sieht das Selbstverständnis . . . ," pp. 197–198. See also Ronald Asmus, "The GDR and the German nation: sole heir or socialist sibling?" *International Affairs*, vol. 60, nr. 3, Summer 1984, pp. 403–418.

22. An excellent overview of evolving East German perspectives on the question of German national unity after 1949 is provided by Gottfried Zieger, *Die Haltung von SED und DDR zur Einheit Deutschlands 1949–1987* (Köln: Verlag Wissenschaft und Politik, 1988). Zieger concludes that "the . . . population in the GDR did not participate in [the government's] attempt to escape from the [all-]German nation" in favor of a separate GDR-based German socialist nation (p. 235).

23. Rudolph, "Wie sieht das Selbstverständnis . . . ," pp. 198–199. See also the discussion in Dahrendorf, *Society and Democracy in Germany*, Chapter 26. In early 1985, Timothy Garton Ash wrote: "In my experience, many GDR citizens truly appreciate the modest security of life in an efficient police welfare state." Ash, *The Uses of Adversity: Essays on the Fate of Central Europe* (New York: Random House, 1989), p. 78.

24. Rudolph, "Wie sieht das Selbstverständnis . . . ," p. 199.

25. Although the GDR projected an image of stability after the creation of the Berlin Wall in 1961, discontent and conflict were always present behind this façade of normalcy. Among intellectuals, this included a tendency (well rooted in German history) toward "internal emigration," i.e., withdrawal from the public sphere. See Ash, *The Uses of Adversity*, p. 11ff.

26. Scharf, *Politics and Change in East Germany*, p. 202.

27. Scharf, *Politics and Change in East Germany*, pp. 20–21.

28. See Ralf Rytlewski, "Ein neues Deutschland?" in Wehling, ed., *Politische Kultur in der DDR*, p. 23.

29. Rytlewski, "Ein neues Deutschland?" pp. 13–14, 15–16, 17, 18, 19.

30. Rytlewski, "Ein neues Deutschland?" p. 26.

31. For a review of some of the literature about the GDR, focused on the legitimacy question, see Angela Stent, "East German Quest for Legitimacy," *Problems of Communism*, March-April 1986. She concluded that "the GDR will face an uphill struggle in its efforts to secure full sovereignty and establish legitimacy both in the eyes of its own people and the eyes of other nations" (p. 85). She puts special emphasis on the impact of detente on the East German quest for both identity and legitimacy.

32. See Frederick D. Weil, "Cohorts, Regimes, and the Legitimation of Democracy: West Germany Since 1945," *American Sociological Review*, vol. 52, nr. 3, June 1987, pp. 308–324. For an alternative view, focused on FRG-GDR differences in political culture, see Karl-Rudolf Korte, "Die Folgen der Einheit. Zur politisch-kulturellen Lage der Nation," *Aus Politik und Zeitgeschichte*, 29 June 1990.

33. Rudolph, "Wie sieht das Selbstverständnis . . . ," pp. 200–201.

34. Rudolph, "Wie sieht das Selbstverständnis . . . ," p. 206.

35. The ways in which a shared German past remained a vital reality for both the FRG and GDR, despite ideologically based efforts to delineate two separate "national" histories, is discussed by Michael Stürmer in "Zwei Staaten in Deutschland—zwei deutsche Geschichten?" in his *Dissonanzen des Fortschritts: Essays über Geschichte und Politik in Deutschland* (München/Zürich: Piper, 1986).

36. See Grosser, *Geschichte Deutschlands seit 1945*, p. 401. Significantly, the SED caretaker government sought to reverse this long-standing GDR claim of nonculpability, but it was the democratically elected government after the March 1990 elections that issued a formal apology and expressed a willingness to pay reparations in connection with the Holocaust. See "The East Germans Issue an Apology for Nazis' Crimes," *The New York Times*, 13 April 1990. On the role of the Nazi past in GDR literature, see Marc Silberman, "Writing What—for Whom? 'Vergangenheitsbewältigung' in GDR Literature," *German Studies Review*, vol. 10, nr. 3, October 1987.

37. Rudolph, "Wie sieht das Selbstverständnis . . . ," pp. 202–203.

38. Rudolph, "Wie sieht das Selbstverständnis . . . ," p. 208.

39. Rudolph, "Wie sieht das Selbstverständnis . . . ," p. 205ff.

40. Rudolph, "Wie sieht das Selbstverständnis . . . ," p. 201.

41. The following discussion on the "Prussia factor" is especially indebted to Jörg Bernhard Bilke, "Preußentum und DDR-Sozialismus," *Aus Politik und Zeitgeschichte*, 26 December 1981. See also, in the same issue, Rudolf von Thadden, "Preußen—Ein Weg in die Moderne?" and Wolfgang Wippermann, "Nationalsozialismus und Preußentum." In addition, see Johannes Kuppe, "Kontinuität und Wandel in der Geschichtsschreibung der DDR," *Aus Politik und Zeitgeschichte*, 17 May 1986.

42. Oswald Spengler, *Preußentum und Sozialismus* (München: Beck Verlag, 1920).

43. Bilke, "Preußentum und DDR-Sozialismus," p. 25ff. For a brief overview of the evolution of the East German conception of the Prussian past, see *Das Preußenbild der DDR im Wandel*, published in 1981 in Bonn (Verlag Neue Gesellschaft) by the West German SPD's Friedrich-Ebert-Stiftung.

44. Quoted in Bilke, "Preußentum und DDR-Sozialismus," p. 28.

45. Bilke, "Preußentum und DDR-Sozialismus," p. 32.

46. Bilke, "Preußentum und DDR-Sozialismus," p. 31. See also Grosser, *Geschichte Deutschlands seit 1945*, pp. 402–403.

47. Bilke, "Preußentum und DDR-Sozialismus," p. 33. See also Grosser, *Geschichte Deutschlands seit 1945*, p. 416; M. Rainer Lepsius, "Die Teilung Deutschlands und die deutsche Nation," in Lothar Albertin and Werner Link, eds., *Politische Parteien auf dem Weg zur parlamentarischen Demokratie in Deutschland* (Düsseldorf: Droste Verlag, 1981), p. 429ff. For a discussion of the role played by considerations of national unity in the evolving GDR interpretation of German history and its own identity, see Karl-Ernst Jeismann, "Die Einheit der Nation im Geschichtsbild der DDR," *Aus Politik und Zeitgeschichte*, 13 August 1983. See also Roland W. Schweizer, "Die DDR und die Nationale Frage," *Aus Politik und Zeitgeschichte*, 21 December 1985.

48. Erich Honecker, quoted in Bilke, "Preußentum und DDR-Sozialismus," p. 33.

49. Hermann Weber, ed., *DDR: Dokumente zur Geschichte der Deutschen Demokratischen Republik, 1945–1985* (München: Deutscher Taschenbuch Verlag, 1987), p. 345.

50. Bilke, "Preußentum und DDR-Sozialismus," p. 34ff.

51. See the discussion in Georgi Verbeeck, "Kontinuität und Wandel im DDR-Geschichtsbild."

52. See Robert F. Goeckel, "The Luther Anniversary in East Germany," *World Politics*, vol. 37, nr. 1, October 1984. Goeckel focuses especially on the relationship between the East German Evangelical Church and the SED regime, as well as the impact of inter-German relations on the celebration (and vice versa).

53. Bilke, "Preußentum und DDR-Sozialismus," p. 37. In this context, see also Bernd Schick, "Preußisches Interregnum? Anmerkungen zum kleindeutschen Patriotismus der Reformbewegung in der DDR," *Deutschland Archiv*, vol. 23, nr. 6, June 1990.

54. Bilke, "Preußentum und DDR-Sozialismus," p. 37. For additional discussion on the general connections between GDR political culture and the German political-cultural heritage, see Gert-Joachim Glaeßner, "Politische Kultur und nationales Erbe in der DDR," in Karl-Ernst Jeismann, ed., *Einheit—Freiheit—Selbstbestimmung: Die Deutsche Frage im historisch-politischen Bewußtsein* (Frankfurt/New York: Campus Verlag, 1988).

55. Weber, ed., *DDR: Dokumente zur Geschichte der Deutschen Demokratischen Republik, 1945–1985*, pp. 345–346.

56. For more extensive discussion of the evolution of the GDR's foreign policy after 1949, see Martin McCauley, *The German Democratic Republic Since 1945* (New York: St. Martin's Press, 1983); Thilo Vogelsang, *Das geteilte Deutschland* (München: Deutscher Taschenbuch Verlag, 1980), pp. 199–202, 329–348; Grosser, *Geschichte Deutschlands seit 1945*, p. 411ff.; Joachim Nawrocki, *Relations Between the Two States in Germany* (Bonn: Press and Information Office of the Federal Government, n.d.); Hermann Weber, *Geschichte der DDR* (München: Deutscher Taschenbuch Verlag, 1986); Plock, *The Basic Treaty and the Evolution of East-West German Relations*; Scharf, *Politics and Change in East Germany*, Chapter 8; Wilhelm Bruns, *Die Außenpolitik der DDR* (Berlin: Colloquium Verlag, 1985).

57. For a discussion of the role played by diplomatic problems in the at first gradual and then precipitous collapse of the GDR, see Gerhard Basler, "Die 'Herbstrevolution' und die Ost-West-Beziehungen der DDR," *Europa-Archiv*, nr. 1, 1990. Basler stresses the consequences of the GDR's increased diplomatic and ideological isolation during the 1980s, culminating in a crisis of the long-standing orientation of *Abgrenzung*.

58. See Dietmar Petzina, "Deutsch-deutsche Wirtschaftsbeziehungen nach dem Zweiten Weltkrieg—eine Bilanz," in Jeismann, ed., *Einheit—Freiheit—Selbstbestimmung*; Gert Leptin, "Economic Relations Between the Two German States," and Juergen Nitz, "GDR-FRG Economic Relations: Determinants, Trends and Problems," both in Larrabee, ed., *The Two German States and European Security*. See also some of the discussion on pre-1989 FRG-GDR economic and financial relations in Jerzy Lisiecki, "Financial and Material Transfers Between East and West Germany," *Soviet Studies*, vol. 42, nr. 3, July 1990.

59. Although the detente era began to undermine East German efforts at *Abgrenzung*, it also made possible an enlarged room for diplomatic maneuver for the GDR within the Soviet bloc, just as the same detente era "loosened" the FRG's Cold War ties to the West. This increased room for maneuver for *both* German states was particularly visible in the context of the *Deutschlandpolitik* of the 1980s, especially in an atmosphere of renewed Cold War during the Reagan years. For further discussion of the GDR's diplomatic options during the early 1980s, see Peter Danylow, "Der außenpolitische Spielraum der DDR," *Europa-Archiv*, nr. 14, 1985. See also Bernard von Plate, "Deutsch-deutsche Beziehungen und Ost-West-Konflikt," *Aus Politik und Zeitgeschichte*, nr. 15, 1984.

4

Shifting Traditions and Lessons in Foreign Policy

The objective of this chapter and the next is to examine additional dimensions of the German Question by showing how the German historical experience, reflected in culture and political tradition, helped shape particular traditions and orientations in German foreign policy.[1] We shall encounter again questions of historical continuity and discontinuity, the sense of failure and its consequences, a problematic identity (reflected in a preoccupation with Germany's role and status in international affairs), and the foreign policy implications of an illiberal political tradition. As in earlier chapters, however, we shall focus on the profound changes wrought in the foreign policy of the Federal Republic by the shocks of National Socialism and World War II. Yet an explicitly historical perspective on the matter is vital, since postwar West German foreign policy can in many ways be best understood as a (usually conscious) *reaction* to the German past.

Additional aspects of pre-1990 West German foreign policy culture are to be explained against the background of Germany's utter defeat in World War II, resulting in foreign occupation, loss of sovereignty and national unity, a condition of general (initial) helplessness, and the development of new foreign controls through structures of dependency, especially in the area of security. From this context resulted some of what I shall refer to as the "emancipatory" aspects of West German foreign policy culture. They are connected with the question of nationalist assertiveness in postwar FRG foreign policy. At the same time, dependency and elements of helplessness or vulnerability also tend to give rise to attitudes that contrast sharply with emancipatory assertiveness: complacency and docility. These could be encountered in West German foreign policy as well.

In Chapter 5, we shall look at a variety of "-isms" as a way of acquiring a sense of the orientations that have guided German foreign policy, both in the pre– and post–World War II periods: Liberalism, Conservatism, and Socialism, national-

93

ism and supranationalism (or internationalism), and militarism and antimilitarism. They will give us important insights into the ideological and philosophical context of the general German Question. In the present chapter, our focus will be (1) the formative and the normative aspects of traditional German foreign policy; (2) the interaction of questions of identity, position, and role in German foreign policy before and after World War II; and (3) the impact of the Nazi legacy on West German foreign policy after 1945.

Normative Aspects of Traditional German Foreign Policy

Post-1871 German foreign policy shared in many of the diplomatic perspectives that prevailed elsewhere in Europe at that time. The German focus on *Realpolitik*, *Staatsräson*, and *Machtpolitik* were certainly not altogether uncommon. The idea of a *Primat der Außenpolitik* (primacy of foreign policy) found widespread acceptance among the other leading powers of the day. The legitimacy of warfare as an instrument of foreign policy enjoyed virtually unanimous diplomatic consent.

The specific aspects of the German condition and experience as presented in Chapter 1 imparted to German foreign policy a series of characteristics, however, that set the country apart from most other European states, even if only in relative terms. In a revealing passage that suggestively connects the Germans' past with much of their more recent predicament, Karl Deutsch and Lewis Edinger wrote in 1959:

> Throughout much of her history, Germany has been a country without equals. One or more of her Western neighbors have usually appeared to her as wealthier, more powerful, and more highly respected in the world. Her Eastern neighbors, on the other hand, the Poles, Czechs, Hungarians, Russians, and Baltic peoples, have usually been looked down upon by Germans as inferior—in wealth, technology, civilization, or military power. . . . [A]fter the thirteenth century, the German people never had a state quite large enough or advanced enough to dominate all their neighbors, or to sustain a bid for world leadership. Yet Germany never seemed to them quite small enough to accept the role of a small country.[2]

They concluded by suggesting that "[t]he German people cannot see themselves as a small nation, but just now [1959] they cannot act as a great one, and they have no clear image as to how a middle power should behave."[3]

As a modern great power, Germany was a latecomer. It entered an international arena in which established powers had already staked out dominant positions, and in which the new forces of nationalism were adding dynamic vigor and emotion to classical interstate competition. Consequently, German foreign policy after 1871 was frequently characterized by what may be called a "compensatory" style or mentality, especially during the Wilhelmine era. A desire to conquer Germany's "place in the sun" led to *Selbstüberschätzung* (self-overestimation), excessive *Großmachtvorstellungen* (great-power dreams), and a constant preoccupation with German prestige and status.

The stylistic dimensions of German diplomacy after 1871 have frequently been of analytical interest. For example, Gerhard Weinberg writes:

> There does appear to have been an adolescent assertiveness accompanied by a preference for bullying and drama, a preference so deep and abiding as to be unaffected by the weakness or strength of Germany's position in the world at any given moment. This proclivity for the abrasive touch may well grow out of a—largely if not entirely unwarranted—concern over not being taken seriously enough by others, especially as a new arrival on the international scene. It almost invariably led to Germany's being perceived by the outside world as threatening and as following diabolical plans, regardless of whether such fears did or did not have a realistic basis.[4]

Gordon Craig has similarly noted a tendency toward diplomatic maladroitness, amateurism, and parvenuism.[5] The role played by warfare in Germany's unification, together with the militancy of German nationalism and the rather aggressive ethos of a powerful German military elite, produced unmistakable militarism in German foreign policy culture.

It is frequently suggested that Bismarck, whose policies were so decisive for the *Reichsgründung* (creation of the empire) of 1871, turned into the leading representative of and role model for modern German diplomacy. In many ways, this is true, but it should also be remembered that Bismarck's successors, and even some contemporaries, acted with considerably less restraint and wisdom than he did. In his emphasis on *Realpolitik, Macht,* and *Staatsräson,* his devotion to what was felt to be the divinely ordained traditional, monarchical order, his Lutheran sense of duty, and his dedication to the prestige of the *Reich* in general and Prussia in particular, Bismarck was clearly a product of his class, culture, and age, and a powerful role model. In his politics and diplomacy, he was animated by the conservative, antiliberal, nationalist ethos that pervaded much of German political culture until at least the end of World War II.[6]

The more general argument can certainly be made that facets of Germany's illiberal political culture were closely related to characteristics of this traditional German foreign policy. The antidemocratic and intolerant ethos that frequently prevailed in German domestic politics spilled over into the conduct of foreign policy. Accusations of domestic and foreign *Reichsfeindschaft* (enmity toward the empire) constantly loomed. Traditional elites reigned supreme in domestic politics and foreign policy, behind a modern democratic façade.

The works of Heinrich von Treitschke and Carl Schmitt, whose lives and writings span different times in modern German history, show quite clearly this relation between political culture and foreign policy in traditional Germany. Writing

during the latter part of the nineteenth century, von Treitschke stressed the supremacy of the state in political life. Power is the state's vital principle. States are
the supreme actors in international politics, and foreign policy is defined as
Staatspolitik pure and simple. Domestic politics and foreign policy are reduced to
a struggle for power. The state stands above history, society, and individual interests. The preservation and augmentation of state power constitute the central
question in international political life. Since conflict is an inherent consequence
of international anarchy, the state's right and duty to conduct wars are beyond
ethical questioning. In fact, warfare is seen as integral, even beneficial, to the life
of state and society, and Liberal views of limited state power and peaceful international relations are rejected as misguided, harmful, and illusionary.[7]

The well-known distinction between "friend" and "enemy" in politics, made by
the twentieth-century theorist Carl Schmitt, is illustrative of the combative, con-
flictive conception of politics in traditional, illiberal German political culture.
Domestic and international politics are interpreted along similar lines. Human
existence acquires a profoundly polemical quality, a spirit of struggle and intense
antagonism. War is an existential reality and could never be "outlawed." The will
to survive is decisive in international politics. Neither one's friends nor one's enemies are ever permanent. Liberalism is denounced as a philosophy that misper-
ceives the true nature of politics and in effect seeks to "depoliticize" political life.[8]

An additional formative element in German foreign policy of which virtually
all German diplomats and politicians have been acutely conscious is Germany's
Central European location. As noted in Chapter 1, geographic factors have played
a crucial role in the problem of German identity: Cultural and political boundaries have never really coincided, and a sense of fluidity and inherent political revisionism, if not outright irredentism, has characterized the traditional German
sense of nationhood. Throughout modern history, this central continental location has given feelings of vulnerability, insecurity, and a lack of foreign policy
choice a constant prominence in German foreign affairs. There has been a persistent fear of diplomatic isolation, a Bismarckian *cauchemar des coalitions* (nightmare of coalitions). Aside from the military methods used to bring about German unification, this perceived security predicament did much to enhance a
continuous German focus on military issues. It also served to strengthen the position of the military establishment in German society.

The sense of geographic weakness and comparative disadvantage, the fear of
isolation and encirclement, combined with mounting political ambitions and often romanticized *Reichsvorstellungen* ("imperial dreams") over time led to the increasing popularity of *geopolitical* perspectives in German foreign policy culture.
As an outlook on political life animated by a profound sense of environmental
determinism, geopolitics emerged in the darwinistic and imperialist *Zeitgeist* of
late nineteenth-century Europe. (It is thus important to remember that geopolitical thinking was not a German philosophical monopoly.) To many Germans, the
geopolitical perspective seemed particularly suited to their country's political and

economic predicament, and also compatible with the organic-biological and an-
thropomorphic conceptions of the state that had been popular in Germany ever
since the days of Herder and Hegel.

According to Geoffrey Parker, German geopoliticians, such as Friedrich Ratzel
and Karl Haushofer, saw their trade as a mixture of science and art, aimed at the
development of a "spatial *Weltanschauung*." Any state that hoped to survive and
flourish needed *Lebensraum* (living space), leading to the acquisition of
Großraum (enlarged space) whereby "the dissemination of the national *Kultur*"
would play a decisive role. Effective geopolitical expansion would ensure economic autarky and defensible borders, both of which were seen as essential to effective great-power status.[9]

The political and ideological prominence of *Geopolitik* increased after World
War I in an atmosphere of revisionist anger and dreams during the Weimar years.
Particularly popular became the vision of a German-dominated *Großraum* in
central Europe (the so-called *Mitteleuropa* idea), which mixed geographic considerations with economic, political, and cultural factors. Eastern Europe, seen as
a *Teufelsgürtel* (devil's belt) of unstable states that separated Germany from the
crucial Eurasian heartland, was increasingly considered to be Germany's *Schick-
salsraum* (area alotted by fate)—hence the legendary German *Drang nach Osten*
(push toward the East). Such anti-Slavic and later anti-Soviet imperialist *Lebensraum* ideas, mixed with explicitly racial elements, played a central role in Nazi
foreign policy culture. In the conclusion of Parker,

> *Geopolitik* was . . . founded on environmental determinism since it was sustained by
> the belief that the power to which any state can attain is dependent upon its geo-
> graphical circumstances. The people of a dynamic state are in a sense "chosen" for
> their conquering mission, but more by the character of their physical space environ-
> ment than by the particular race to which they happen to belong. Despite this, it was
> inevitable that with the coming to power of the Nazis, racialism would creep in.[10]

As was true for many facets of German foreign policy culture, realist and romantic ingredients were combined in most geopolitical visions: *Macht* and military hardheadedness went hand in hand with dreams about German *Kultur* and
the old Holy Roman Empire. Defeat in World War II and the subsequent division
of Germany, plus the rise of the two superpowers, eliminated any and all ideas of
Mitteleuropa in West or East German foreign policy. This does not mean, however, that geopolitically based revisionism was absent from the Federal Republic's
foreign policy culture after 1949. The possibility of a revived geopolitical revisionism in the foreign policy of a reunited Germany, especially focused on former German territory now under Polish control, played a major role in the
course of 1990, as we shall see in Chapter 7.

There can be no question that World War II turned into a watershed event in
the development of Germany's foreign policy culture. It ended the militarization

of foreign policy and the illiberal ideological aspects of the *Realpolitik* tradition, while giving rise to supranational visions that would have been unthinkable in the golden age of Germany's nationalist foreign policy.

Although most observers would agree that fundamental foreign policy cultural changes have occurred in Germany as a result of World War II and its aftermath, debate concerning the question of continuity versus discontinuity in pre-1945 German foreign policy persists. While noting the major changes of the postwar period, Hans-Adolf Jacobsen also argues that prewar German foreign policy is characterized by greater discontinuity than is usually recognized.[11] German foreign policy between 1871 and 1945 cannot be described as simply *Großmachtpolitik* (great-power politics) in his view. Particularly the Nazi era, with its mixture of power politics, ideology, and racism, would need to be seen as qualitatively different.

In Jacobsen's opinion, there are at least four areas in which important elements of discontinuity are to be noted. First, the diplomatic setting in which German foreign policy has been conducted since 1871 has not been constant. As a result, Germany's *Spielraum* (room for maneuver) has varied considerably. Second, he stresses the important degree of discontinuity in Germany's foreign policymaking elites and structures, particularly between the imperial and National Socialist eras, and the postwar Federal Republic.[12] Third, the ideological elements in German foreign policy have not been constant. Nazi ideology was more than just an outgrowth of German political and philosophical (especially nationalist) traditions, according to Jacobsen. Additionally, the decline of nationalism and "statism" in postwar German foreign policy is to be noted, along with the rise of internationalist ideological perspectives. And fourth, relations between ends and means have varied significantly in modern German diplomatic history. Although the Weimar Republic, the Third Reich, and the FRG have all conducted a *Revisionspolitik* (revisionist foreign policy), a *Sicherheitspolitik* (security policy), and an *Ostpolitik*, for example, they have done so not only in different international settings and with different ideological outlooks, but also with very different means, ranging from aggression, reconciliation, and legalism to a variety of economic instruments. Jacobsen focuses largely on environmental and behavioral factors, and stresses the differences between the imperial, Weimar, Nazi, and postwar epochs.

Historian Andreas Hillgruber, however, deals more explicitly with aspects of foreign policy "culture" and emphasizes the historical degree of continuity in German foreign policy thinking.[13] He sees this thinking as consistently preoccupied with questions of German *Macht* and prestige, often in an extremist way. Aided by the powerful influence of the military on foreign policy, the ambitions of power in a rather fluid and unstable Central European environment induced an often militant and imperialist behavior, aimed at the creation of a German *Großraum* and an economic *Mitteleuropa*. There was a constant tendency to overcompensate for feelings of insecurity. Failure of these *Großmacht* ambitions produced repeated instances of revisionism. The main sources of philosophical continuity in German foreign policy were the foreign office and the military, influences that extended into the Nazi period as well.

According to Hillgruber, settings and strategies may change, but the key to continuity in German foreign policy has resided in nationalist, power-oriented ways of thinking. He summarizes his basic thesis as follows:

> The greater the chronological distance and above all the personal sense of distance from the watershed year 1945 in national and world history becomes, the stronger does the roughly 80-year history of the Prussian-German great power . . . strike one (particularly an historian of the younger generation) in terms of its basic unity, in spite of all its diversity. The lines and patterns of development across the Bismarckian, Wilhelminian, Weimar, and Third Reich eras strike this historian much more as defining [and constant] elements in this now concluded and thus surveyable [80-year] stretch of history than those watersheds and new beginnings which appear to the historian of an older generation (based on direct personal experience) as the most characteristic feature of the recent German past.[14]

A comparison of Jacobsen's and Hillgruber's observations reveals the dynamic interplay of cultural, environmental, and behavioral factors in foreign policy analysis: The relative presence of continuity or discontinuity in a country's foreign policy constitutes a question whose answer often depends on the angle or aspect the analyst emphasizes. In the German case, environmental and behavioral discontinuity might thus be contrasted with foreign policy cultural continuity.

The differences between the analyses offered by Jacobsen and Hillgruber point to a more fundamental controversy, however, because the debate about the nature and sources of traditional German foreign policy is very much connected with the larger debate about a purportedly negative German *Sonderweg* that we examined at some length in Chapter 1. In the case of German diplomatic history, one of the most controversial and pathbreaking studies was without doubt Fritz Fischer's *Griff nach der Weltmacht*, published in English translation in 1967 under the title *Germany's Aims in the First World War*. Writing on the causes of the Great War, Fischer argued that "[t]he July crisis [of 1914] must not be regarded in isolation. It appears in its true light only when seen as a link between Germany's 'world policy,' as followed since the mid-1890s, and her war aims policy after August, 1914."[15] His unmistakable indictment of Germany's pre-1914 diplomacy as a major cause of the outbreak of war has been hotly debated ever since.[16] The different interpretations of German diplomatic history offered by Jacobsen and Hillgruber are merely a recent illustration of this ongoing dispute.

Germany in International Politics: Identity, Position, and Role

Factors of power, geography, identity, and developmental timing have historically combined to turn the question of Germany's place in the international arena into a fundamental problem for German foreign policy and a basic feature in the development of German foreign policy culture. In terms of its power, Germany has tended to be either too weak to alleviate the perennial security fears that permeate German foreign policy culture, or too strong to leave wary neighbors reassured about their own safety. As noted earlier, the factor of geographic location induced a sense of fluidity, vulnerability, and encirclement.

As far as German foreign policy is concerned, therefore, the identity problem historically combines cultural-ideological, geographic, and political elements. Highly Germanocentric attitudes promoted a profound alienation from the West and invidiously anti-Slavic feelings toward the East, and were combined with a hypernationalist imperialism fed by glorified visions of German *Kultur*, particularly during the Wilhelmine era. Explicitly racist elements were added during the National Socialist era. The result was a comprehensive and extremely damaging degree of German international isolation.

In addition, we have noted that the timing of Germany's development and unification was highly unfortunate. The consolidation of German power in the center of Europe had a profoundly destabilizing effect on the nineteenth-century balance of power, and served to enhance the risk of conflict on the continent. According to Paul Kennedy,

> [t]wo factors ensured that the rise of imperial Germany would have a more immediate and substantial impact upon the Great Power balances than either of its fellow "newcomer" states [Italy and Japan]. The first was that, far from emerging in geopolitical isolation, like Japan, Germany had arisen right in the center of the old European states system; its very creation had directly impinged upon the interests of Austria-Hungary and France, and its existence had altered the relative position of *all* of the existing Great Powers in Europe. The second factor was the sheer speed and extent of Germany's further growth, in industrial, commercial, and military/naval terms. By the eve of the First World War its national power was not only three or four times Italy's and Japan's, it was well ahead of either France or Russia and had probably overtaken Britain as well.[17]

A fragmented Germany had served as a useful buffer zone among various powers, but now that "vacuum" was turned into a new competitor with compensatory ambitions. Consequently, David Calleo has argued that "[t]he German Problem ought properly to be seen within the context of [the] broad evolution of the Western national states and the international issues which that evolution inevitably posed." He points out that

> Germany was the last of the great European national states to be formed. . . . A good part of the Germans' ill fortune came from having failed to consolidate a national state before their neighbors. . . . [D]ynamic Germany was found to appear an aggressor, challenging the arrangements that had grown up in its absence and that presumed its continuing weakness. . . . To analyze Germany's ambitions and fears as essentially the product of its own unusual political culture subtly distorts history in

favor of Germany's victors. For Britain, France, Russia, and the United States were great powers with appetites no less ravenous than Germany's. . . . In short, Germany's "aggressiveness" against international order may be explained as plausibly by the nature of that order as by any peculiar characteristics of the Germans.[18]

Calleo's thesis stresses the significance of developmental timing and international geopolitical context in any consideration of the problem of Germany's role and position in international affairs, thereby clearly rejecting an oversimplified cultural reductionism. This problem runs as a red thread through German diplomatic history and foreign policy culture and makes up much of the core of what tends be called the German Question or Problem, particularly among Germany's wary neighbors.

From a historical perspective, German foreign policy culture has contained a variety of strategic visions aimed at dealing with this problem of Germany's power, role, and position in international affairs.[19] A consideration of these visions points up some interesting elements of continuity and change in German foreign policy.

One vision, especially associated with Bismarck, had as its point of departure the realization that Germany is first and foremost a Central European state (*Land in der Mitte,* or land in the middle) in many ways located between East and West.[20] From this vantage point, Germany was seen at times as a "bridge" between East and West, an entity with a balancing and mediating role. Close attention was paid to the maintenance of a European balance of power and the legitimate interests of other powers. Insofar as revisionist intentions entered German foreign policy, they were pursued with caution and considerable respect for the status quo. Germany tended to avoid overly rigid alliances, and aimed at keeping diplomatic options open.[21] According to Waldemar Besson,

[i]n the Central European tradition . . . there is, beginning with Bismarck, a school of thought which regards any German activity, however self-confidently conducted, as meaningful only if it does not threaten to alter the international constellation. This required of German policy a consideration for the interests of the other participants. In this school of thought of the Central European tradition, changes in the status-quo were only possible in so far as they did not fundamentally change the system and its equilibria. Anything else would have led to the endangering of one's own position, and to discord in the European Concert. . . . The latter, however, is precisely what Bismarck's followers brought about.[22]

While much of the Bismarck vision of Germany's position and role in international politics was rendered obsolete in the context of the Cold War and Germany's division, its influence could still be noted in the postwar era, and was very much expected to resurface in the diplomacy of a unified Germany beyond 1990. The idea of Germany as "bridge" between East and West, as developed by politicians like Jakob Kaiser (CDU) in the late 1940s, comes to mind.[23] So, too, do the various plans that were developed by the SPD and FDP in the course of the 1950s, aimed at the reunification of Germany based on German military neutrality, European military disengagement zones, and the creation of an all-European collective security system,[24] some of which were interestingly enough resurrected by GDR Communist caretaker prime minister Hans Modrow in early 1990. Or one might consider the idea of a special German *Sicherheits-* or *Friedenspartnerschaft* (partnership for security and peace) involving the FRG and the GDR, in the shadow of superpower bipolarity, as it emerged in the context of *Ostpolitik* during the 1970s.[25] These visions were largely at odds with the Federal Republic's dominant foreign policy orientations, however. They were frequently denounced as a dangerous revival of an obsolete German tradition of *Schaukelpolitik* ("switching policy") between East and West, based on the illusion of some positive German *Sonderweg* in international affairs.

Another foreign policy vision, associated with the militant *Großmachtpolitik* of Kaiser Wilhelm II and his entourage and the much more extreme racial-geopolitical imperialism of Hitler, shared with the first vision an essentially nationalist focus on Germany's position and role in international politics. But the problems of Germany's international situation were not solved by cautious revisionism, an avoidance of diplomatic isolation, and due regard for the balance of power and the proper interests of others. Instead, there were aggressive revisionism, reckless power politics, and expansionist behavior, all of these aimed at breaking the fetters imposed on Germany by geopolitical encirclement and disadvantage. The German *Sonderweg* led directly to imperialism and war. Hitler stood outside the German diplomatic tradition insofar as the racial elements in his policies were of an entirely new kind and different magnitude from anything that had existed in German foreign policy before. Fundamental philosophical rejection and lack of opportunity rendered obsolete all these militant, imperialist perspectives, in spite of repeated charges of "revanchism" leveled at the FRG by its various neighbors to the East during the Cold War. A slight revival might have occurred by means of some more extremist "rollback" and "liberation" ideas at the height of the Cold War, but these were never a realistic option.

A third vision for German foreign policy developed after World War II, and is particularly associated with the Adenauer legacy in FRG foreign policy.[26] The emergence of this vision cannot be separated from the international setting in which West German foreign policy had to be pursued. This was a setting characterized by defeat and occupation, national division, integration of the two German states into Cold War alliances, West German security dependence on the West (especially the United States), and revisionism regarding the East European status quo. The fact that the FRG could only be understood as a product of the Cold War and as the rehabilitated opponent of a not-so-distant past served to circumscribe Bonn's foreign policy *Spielraum* (room for maneuver) in many decisive ways, often forestalling choices and imposing particular needs. In addition, defeat, occupation, and subsequent security dependence in the Cold War made the FRG into a uniquely "penetrated" political system,[27] susceptible and sensitive to outside influences that deeply affected policy conceptions and directions.

Any consideration of West Germany's role and position in postwar international relations, while dependent on an understanding of *Germany's* historical predicament and fate, cannot be separated from the fate and destiny of *Europe* either. World War II and the eruption of the Cold War had at least five fundamental effects on virtually all (Western) European states.

First, there was the "displacement of the world power center from Europe," leading to the rise of the two superpowers and the development of Cold War bipolarity. Second, there was the "dismantling of the European empires," which became highly symbolic of Europe's reduced international role. Third, there was "European[s'] incapacity to guarantee their own national security," which led to the development of more Europeanist and/or Atlanticist perspectives on national defense, the creation of NATO, and a profound dependence on the U.S. security guarantee. Fourth, there was "European[s'] incapacity to promote their own national prosperity," which was conducive to the development of visions, plans, processes, and institutions aimed at increased European economic cooperation and integration. Fifth, there was a "European 'crisis of confidence,'" which was the cumulative result of the other four developments.[28]

Although these five effects were strongest in the immediate postwar period and were to some extent "softened" by subsequent recovery and integration successes and by a mitigation of the Cold War, the fundamental changes in Europe's international role and position to which they point were quite decisive. The sense that the traditional European nation-state is no longer an adequate framework for security, economic prosperity, and effective prestige and identity persists, despite a partial resurgence of nationalism since the Gaullist 1960s and Thatcherite 1980s. At most there has resulted a vacillation in policy between more Atlanticist and/or Europeanist, and nationalist frames of orientation.

On the positive side, the development of more supranational perspectives in European foreign policy cultures went hand in hand with a "modernization," democratization, and relative deideologization of European political life. In many countries, including West Germany, pragmatic modes of thinking and areas of political consensus expanded, while earlier forms of Left-Right polarization seemed to have been reduced or eliminated.[29] This in turn produced greater stability and consistency in the conduct of foreign policy, although developments in the 1980s would raise some new questions.

It is against this German and European postwar background that one must evaluate two key facets of Adenauer's *Westpolitik*: the "supranationalization" and the "Westernization" (*Verwestlichung*) of West Germany's foreign policy.[30] Supranationalization implied a basic abandonment of the almost exclusively nationalist thinking in earlier German foreign policy. The new West German state became a leading champion of schemes for European and Atlantic integration. In the context of the Cold War, these integration visions, the pursuit of which was the result of a mixture of choice and necessity, were in unmistakable tension with the simultaneous pursuit of reunification, a fact that led to bitter debate between the CDU and SPD during the 1950s. The interplay of national and supranational perspectives became a central theme in West Germany's postwar foreign policy culture.

"Westernization" aimed at a basic reconciliation of the historical alienation between Germany and the West. The *Verwestlichung* of German foreign policy was aided by a number of important factors, rooted in ideology and environmental compulsion.[31] Among West German political parties, the CDU in particular was animated by what may be called an *Abendland* ("Western civilization") ideology, stressing the political, philosophical, and religious beliefs and values that Germany was felt to share with the West.[32] There was a strong Catholic and even Carolingian component in the thinking of Adenauer and many of his supporters.

The Cold War division of Germany led to the creation of a *Weststaat* that contained regionally based traditions of Liberalism and moderate antinationalism, both of which were crucial for the supranationalization and Westernization of German foreign policy culture. In a Cold War environment marked by international ideological polarization, the FRG's security dependence on Western allies was complemented by strong anti-Communism, pro-Europeanism, and pro-Atlanticism. Although West German options were limited as a result of defeat and subsequent Cold War, Waldemar Besson is certainly correct when he stresses that "Adenauer did not merely make a virtue of necessity; he saw the future of the Germans as lying only in Western Europe."[33] According to Hans-Peter Schwarz, Adenauer's "basic point of departure was simple: the Federal Republic, but also a reunited Germany, is only secure, both for the Germans and their neighbors, if it is irrevocably connected . . . with the Western democracies." This was nothing less than a "new foreign policy tradition."[34]

Just as the supranationalism of Adenauer's *Westpolitik* constituted a sharp break with past nationalist traditions in German foreign policy culture, so did the reorientation effected by Germany's Westernization imply an abandonment of older Central European geopolitical perspectives. In the context of the Cold War, Germany became the divided heart of Europe, whereby each German state turned into the outer rampart of its respective alliance system. Adenauer's *Westpolitik* was at least in part animated by a persistent Potsdam complex, based on the fear of great-power agreements at Germany's expense. Only Western integration would prevent Germany from becoming or remaining a mere pawn or object in international politics.

Ideological inclinations and environmental constraints combined to lead to the failure of reunification ideas, offered by the SPD and the FDP, based on some form of German neutrality, during the early postwar years. Growing numbers of West Germans backed Adenauer in his rejection of new attempts at a German *Schaukelpolitik* between East and West.[35] There was certainly in many Western states a distinct "Rapallo complex," fed by fears regarding Germany's diplomatic and ideological reliability, although, as Fritz R. Allemann pointed out during the 1960s, the Cold War setting differed so strongly from the 1920s that a new "Rapallo" was never a real option in FRG foreign policy.[36]

The divided Germany was not able, however, to escape the geopolitical logic of its Central European location or the older, national framework of thinking. The decisive problem here was, of course, the issue of reunification. Both supranationalism and Westernization appeared to be conditional to the extent that they had to be reconciled with unavoidable nationalist, Central European West German revisionism. In the era of the Cold War and successful Western integration, the inherent contradiction was "solved" through the assumption that reunification would result from a *Westpolitik* based on strength, although that assumption was attacked by many critics.

This assumption of "reunification through strength" during the Cold War years also implied a particular West German perspective on a possible detente. This took the form of a concept of *Junktim,* or "linkage," whereby any kind of meaningful detente would depend on clear progress toward German reunification. Taken to an extreme, this notion could mean that the German reunification issue might block detente opportunities, in case the Soviets proved unwilling to accept this linkage. According to Josef Joffe,

> [i]n the 1950s, as long as conflict constituted the dominant feature of East-West relations, the solidarity between the Western powers and the Federal Republic, crucial both as pre-requisite and instrumentality of German policy, remained assured on most issues. Since the German problem was largely coterminous with, or at least symbolic of, the more comprehensive problem of a global confrontation, the *Junktim* not only joined together the Federal Republic's Eastern and Western policy, but also became the nexus of the Alliance's relations with the East. . . . [A]lthough there was no progress on the reunification issue, the *Junktim* served to fuse the Federal Republic's exclusive preoccupation in the West with her inactivity in the East and to undergird the assumption that her amalgamation in the Atlantic structure would ultimately lead to German unity.[37]

But Joffe points out that "[t]he advent of the Kennedy Administration in 1961 was accompanied by perceptible shifts in the priorities of American foreign policy."[38] Increased detente efforts between East and West, unconnected to firm progress on German reunification, and a lack of progress (even backsliding) in Western integration undermined earlier orientations and increased the FRG's role uncertainty. A resurgence of West German consciousness with respect to Germany's Central European fate combined with fears of increased West German international isolation to generate a considerably more active *Ostpolitik* as a counterweight to the passive and rather negative *Ostpolitik* that had accompanied the previous *Westpolitik*.[39] At the same time, these new openings in the East greatly helped to expand the FRG's foreign policy *Spielraum*. The framework of thought in this new *Ostpolitik* was inherently more nationalist than was officially acknowledged, but its recognition of the European status quo also meant a mitigation of the more explicitly revisionist nationalism of the Cold War era. Both *Westpolitik* and *Ostpolitik* came to symbolize the inevitably Janus-like nature of German foreign policy.[40] As policies and as foreign policy cultural orientations, they reflected the imperatives that continued to be generated by Germany's geopolitical location.[41]

Against this general background, West German foreign policy culture tended to contain some distinct *role* conceptions, largely reflective of roles the FRG actually played.[42] The traditional role conception of Germany as *Großmacht* lost virtually all cultural legitimacy,[43] but the development of new role conceptions became hampered by Germany's defeat and division, the purported provisionality of the FRG, and continued international sensitivities concerning German power. West Germany played not just the role of a modern, medium-sized power in international relations, but rather a multiplicity of roles, some freely chosen and some "assigned" as a result of environmental constraints. In many instances, these roles involved a conscious downplaying of German power, although a greater West German power-consciousness emerged during the 1970s and 1980s, and will no doubt be evident in the unified Germany.[44]

As Schwarz has pointed out, the Federal Republic's favorite international role tended to be not political or military, but economic.

> [T]here is much evidence for saying that the role the West Germans play most assiduously and with the greatest success is that of an efficiently and pragmatically operating economic power with world connections—even though until quite recently they liked most to *talk* about their role as a divided and very frustrated nation. [Note: This was written in 1971.] Both German and foreign observers have characterized the retreat from politics and public life into the private sphere and towards a materialistic maximization of welfare as a dominant feature of West German postwar society. It is not difficult to look at the economic orientation of postwar foreign policy as the product of the hangover of a madman who, having slept off his intoxication with power, devotes himself to quietly raking in money by the barrel.[45]

The events of 1989–1990 certainly made many analysts wonder whether the hangover would pass and the risk of intoxication might return. We will speculate on that issue in Chapters 7 and 9.

The German predilection for the economic role appeared to result from the idea that economic power is presumably more benign and less likely to arouse the wrath or suspicion of Germany's neighbors. It was felt to permit an avoidance of overt power politics and fit well with Germany's newly developed self-image as a country dedicated to international peace. By stressing the realities of interdependence and the values of integration and internationalism in well-nigh ritualistic fashion, West German policymakers aimed at a further sublimation or dilution of the FRG's power profile. Hence they stressed Germany's role as a progressive international economic power, dedicated to constructive *Partnerschaft* with all. A certain similarity between postwar Japan and West Germany in this respect was unmistakable.[46]

Toward both the East and the West, the FRG was guided by two role conceptions.[47] During the Cold War years, relations with the Soviet Union were characterized by varying degrees of hostility, whereby West Germany would be placed in the role of victim and the USSR would be seen as a persistent security threat and the ultimate cause of Germany's division. With regard to the GDR, the Federal Republic tended to see itself as the ideologically, politically, and legally superior protagonist in a "German civil war" in the context of the East-West Cold War. It may be suggested, however, that these rather negative roles vis-à-vis the Soviet Union and East Germany were considerably mitigated in the era of *Ostpolitik*, leading to a somewhat uncertain search for new role conceptions, possibly along the lines of a detente-based *Sicherheitspartnerschaft*.

In its relations with the West, the FRG was guided both by a self-conception as partner in a Free World alliance, with all the identity, equality, and security that such membership entailed, and as special ally of the United States within that broader, integrated context. The Federal Republic's postwar dependence on the United States was profound, implying a West German role as virtual "vassal" in the eyes of some critics. This dependence tended to be softened and diluted, however, by the multilateral, integrated framework in which it became embedded, as well as by the FRG's resurgence as a key international power with diplomatic maneuverability after the 1960s. The extent to which the United States played the role of *model* in postwar West German politics and society is perhaps the best evidence of the psychocultural significance of this dependence.

Since these Western role conceptions in FRG foreign policy culture were in many ways the product of the Cold War, the international changes of the post–Cold War era have resulted in a good deal of role uncertainty in German foreign policy, reflecting elements of incongruence between environmental changes and lingering foreign policy orientations.[48] Over time, foreign policy thinking adjusts itself, and it can be argued that the postwar West German predicament repeatedly imposed the need for such *Anpassung* (adjustment) on the FRG's diplomacy.[49] The unification of the FRG and the GDR in a changing Europe is posing even more fundamental (and fateful) questions about the identity, role, and position of the new Germany in world affairs, as we shall see in Chapters 7 and 9.

Shadows of the Past

Every country is the product of cumulative historical experiences. A consideration of the importance of historical experience for postwar West German foreign policy is particularly useful, however, since that foreign policy (like West German domestic politics) could in many ways be best understood as a conscious *response* and *reaction* to past German foreign policy.

Broadly speaking, there are three major ways in which West German foreign policy culture could be seen as a reaction to past experiences.[50] First, there was an explicit rejection of Germany's previous *Großmachtpolitik*, and especially the aggressive *Weltmachtpolitik* of the Nazi era. Much of German diplomatic history took on the quality of a negative model and a bitter lesson. There was a new sobriety in diplomacy, and a considerable deideologization of foreign policy. Traditional, illiberal nationalism lost much of its appeal, and war and force as instruments of foreign policy were increasingly rejected. Instead, there appeared new manifestations of internationalism, an emphasis on international cooperation and tolerance, evidence of pacifism, and a constantly reaffirmed dedication to *Gewaltverzicht* (nonuse of force) in the solution of the German Question during the Cold War. There continued to be great sensitivity to all facets of military power. A rejection of an older tradition of illiberal, often militant *Realpolitik* was accompanied by increased interest in the relation between morality and foreign policy.[51] In view of past misdeeds, there was a deep desire for German international rehabilitation, a persistent pursuit of various forms of reconciliation (especially with France and Israel, and more recently with Eastern Europe), and a profound interest in enhancing international trust toward Germany.

Second, West German thinking regarding foreign policy turned away sharply from what is now labeled pejoratively as Germany's traditional tendency toward *Schaukelpolitik*. This involved rejection of a more nationalist German *Sonderweg*, and opposition by most West Germans during the Cold War era to any idea of German reunification based on neutralization. With almost ritualistic precision, West German leaders time and again stressed the FRG's allegiance to the Western camp during the years of East-West confrontation.

Third, West German leaders, especially the FRG's "Founding Fathers," and most of the West German public shared with the rest of the Western world a deep concern about any repetition during the Cold War of the West's disastrous appeasement of totalitarian aggression in the 1930s. This is what is generally referred to as the "Munich syndrome." The result was a strong emphasis on deterrence and a *Politik der Stärke* (policy of strength) in West Germany's Cold War foreign policy.[52] The advent of detente mitigated this element to some extent, although West German wariness persisted. From an ideological point of view, concerns about appeasement were accompanied by considerable anti-Communism, expressive of a psychological sense of *Abgrenzung* (insulation) with respect to the East, and occasionally heightening the possibility of a revival of illiberal intolerance at home.

It is important to note that there were some generational differences in the impact of historical lessons on West German foreign policy culture. There were definite distinctions between the FRG's so-called *Gründergeneration* ("founding generation"), whose roots reached back to the Second Empire and/or the Weimar era and for whom many facets of Germany's traditional foreign policy culture were very significant, and those who were socialized by the experience of National Socialism and World War II, thereby developing a greater sense of reaction to Germany's past orientations. Those who were socialized by the Cold War experience have lacked a direct pre–World War II psychocultural frame of reference. They have generally been dedicated Europeanists with a reduced national focus, and were especially supportive of a search for detente and reconciliation with the East. For the youngest generation, the FRG's historical experience has become the almost exclusive source of meaning. The potential for a new German nationalism among generations that have neither experienced the German past nor fully learned its lessons is a topic of frequent research and debate.[53] This is especially so in the context of German reunification, of course.

Writing at the end of the 1970s, Schwarz evaluated the contemporary significance of historical lessons in West German foreign policy as follows:

> If one asks today which historical lessons shape foreign policy thinking, the answer is not hard to come by: no longer the experiences of the interwar period, certainly no longer the experiences of the times before World War I, and only as a distant negative image the experiences of the Third Reich. Rather, it is the historical experiences of the Federal Republic itself that provide the West Germans today with a conscious or unconscious source of orientation. Among these experiences one finds the conviction that national security is not to be pursued by a self-reliant military policy but in the context of the Western alliance. A further experience is that multidimensional cooperation in the system of European integration, which precludes an autonomous economic or foreign policy, also increasingly affects domestic politics. Among these experiences is also to be found the East-West conflict with its permanent dangers and its chances for partial normalization, along with the realization that a promising development of East-West relations cannot be achieved through isolated action but only as a result of a joint Western policy. The experiences of the Cold War are just as much a living historical reality as the detente experiences, and the successful internationalism is just as consequential for [the West German consciousness] as the frustration of the all-German sense of nationhood.[54]

It ought to be emphasized here that from a different angle, Germany's past continued to haunt West German foreign policy as well, namely in international attitudes toward Germany.[55] It is only by recognizing the persistent shadows of the past, both in German attitudes and in international images of Germany, that we can grasp the full meaning of the mixture of docility and assertiveness, reorientation and frustration, and protestations of reliability and good faith that characterized West German foreign policy culture during the postwar, Cold War era.

Notes

1. Most discussions of (West) German foreign policy are chronological and/or thematic: They focus on developments over time and/or on particular issue-areas. A consid-

erable number of them have been used for both this chapter and the next. Aside from the sources cited in the different endnotes, the reader may wish to consult the Selected Bibliography for a listing of books on German foreign affairs.

2. Karl Deutsch and Lewis Edinger, *Germany Rejoins the Powers* (Stanford: Stanford University Press, 1959), p. 19.

3. Deutsch and Edinger, *Germany Rejoins the Powers*, p. 19.

4. Gerhard Weinberg, "National Style in Diplomacy: Germany," in Erich Angermann and Marie-Luise Frings, eds., *Oceans Apart?* (Stuttgart: Klett-Cotta, 1981), p. 149.

5. Gordon Craig, "Germany and the United States: Some Historical Parallels and Differences and Their Reflection in Attitudes Toward Foreign Policy," in James A. Cooney, Gordon A. Craig, Hans-Peter Schwarz, and Fritz Stern, eds., *The Federal Republic of Germany and the United States* (Boulder, CO: Westview Press, 1984).

6. For brief discussions of Bismarck's diplomatic style and ethos, see Gordon A. Craig, *From Bismarck to Adenauer: Aspects of German Statecraft* (Baltimore: Johns Hopkins University Press, 1958), Chapter 1; Hajo Holborn, "Bismarck's Realpolitik," in his *Germany and Europe* (Garden City, NY: Doubleday, 1970). One of the most able biographies of Bismarck remains A.J.P. Taylor, *Bismarck: The Man and the Statesman* (New York: Vintage Books, 1967). In the course of 1998, the centennial of Bismarck's death was the occasion for frequent debate about the Prussian statesman's legacy in German history. See, for example, Jürgen Kocka, "Otto von Bismarcks zweites Leben," *Der Tagesspiegel*, 26 July 1998, p. W3.

7. Heinrich von Treitschke, *Politics* (published in the United States by the Macmillan Company in 1916; republished in 1963 by Harcourt, Brace & World Inc., New York), vol. I.

8. Carl Schmitt, *The Concept of the Political* (New Brunswick, NJ: Rutgers University Press, 1976). Schmitt's antiliberal reputation has been the subject of scholarly controversy. See Paul Silverman's book review in *The Journal of Modern History*, vol. 62, nr. 1, March 1990, pp. 101–105.

9. Geoffrey Parker, *Western Geopolitical Thought in the 20th Century* (London: Croom Helm, 1985), pp. 58, 60.

10. Parker, *Western Geopolitical Thought in the 20th Century*, pp. 62–63.

11. Hans-Adolf Jacobsen, "Zur Kontinuität und Diskontinuität in der deutschen Außenpolitik im 20. Jahrhundert," in his *Von der Strategie der Gewalt zur Politik der Friedenssicherung* (Düsseldorf: Droste Verlag, 1977).

12. For a discussion of post-1949 changes in West Germany's foreign policy elite, see Heino Kaack and Reinhold Roth, "Die Außenpolitische Führungselite der Bundesrepublik Deutschland," *Aus Politik und Zeitgeschichte*, 15 January 1972. They detect four main developmental phases: a 1949–1957 phase of centralized foreign policy making, centered around Adenauer; a development of pluralistic decentralization in the years 1957–1966, caused in large part by intra-CDU fragmentation; polarization around Kiesinger (CDU) and Brandt (SPD) in the 1966–1969 period; and renewed centralization (around Brandt) during the years 1969–1972. They are particularly interested in the structural distribution of power and consensus/dissensus within the larger West German foreign policy making elite.

13. Andreas Hillgruber, "Kontinuität und Diskontinuität in der deutschen Außenpolitik von Bismarck bis Hitler," in his *Großmachtpolitik und Militarismus im 20. Jahrhundert* (Düsseldorf: Droste Verlag, 1974). Even after World War II, there were still some lingering

Großmacht ideas and illusions, especially in a revisionist Cold War context and sometimes along the lines of German power in an integrated Western European *Großmacht.*

14. Hillgruber, "Kontinuität und Diskontinuität in der deutschen Außenpolitik von Bismarck bis Hitler," p. 11. See also Andreas Hillgruber, *Germany and the Two World Wars* (Cambridge, MA/London: Harvard University Press, 1981), which is the English translation of his *Deutschlands Rolle in der Vorgeschichte der beiden Weltkriege* (Göttingen: Vandenhoeck & Ruprecht, 1967/1979).

15. Fritz Fischer, *Germany's Aims in the First World War* (New York: W. W. Norton, 1967), p. 92. (The original German version of the book was published in 1961 by Droste Verlag in Düsseldorf under the title *Griff nach der Weltmacht.*) See also Imanuel Geiss, ed., *July 1914: The Outbreak of the First World War. Selected Documents* (New York: Charles Scribner's Sons, 1967). Geiss suggests that "German *Weltpolitik,* the containment policy of the Entente and Germany's refusal to be contained made war inevitable" (p. 35).

16. See Ulrich Heinemann, "Kriegsschuld 1914. Nach wie vor ein publizistischer Dauerbrenner. Neue Literatur zur Kriegsschulddiskussion," in Wolfgang Michalka, ed., *Die Deutsche Frage in der Weltpolitik* (Stuttgart: Franz Steiner Verlag Wiesbaden, 1986).

17. Paul Kennedy, *The Rise and Fall of the Great Powers* (New York: Random House, 1987), pp. 209–210.

18. David Calleo, *The German Problem Reconsidered* (Cambridge: Cambridge University Press, 1978), pp. 3–6.

19. See Renata Fritsch-Bournazel, "La permanente quête d'une identité," in Renata Fritsch-Bournazel, André Brigot, and Jim Cloos, *Les Allemands au Coeur de l'Europe* (Paris: Fondation pour les Études de Défense Nationale, 1983); Waldemar Besson, "The Conflict of Traditions: The Historical Basis of West German Foreign Policy," in Karl Kaiser and Roger Morgan, eds., *Britain and West Germany* (London: Oxford University Press, 1971); Walter F. Hahn, *Between Westpolitik and Ostpolitik* (Beverly Hills/London: Sage Publications, 1975), Chapter 1.

20. Besson, "The Conflict of Traditions," pp. 63–70.

21. Gustav Stresemann can also be associated with this vision. His Western-oriented Locarno policy was balanced by the Soviet-German understanding reached at Rapallo, even though Stresemann did exhibit a more explicit ideological allegiance to the West than had been the case before the Weimar Republic.

22. Besson, "The Conflict of Traditions," pp. 64–65.

23. See Kaiser's 1946 speech on pp. 76–80 in Peter Brandt and Herbert Ammon, eds., *Die Linke und die nationale Frage* (Reinbek bei Hamburg: Rowohlt Taschenbuch Verlag, 1981).

24. For illustrations, see, in Hans-Adolf Jacobsen and Otto Stenzl, eds., *Deutschland und die Welt* (München: Deutscher Taschenbuch Verlag, 1964), pp. 116–125 (Sethe), 132–137 (Mende), 144–157 (Erler); in Brandt and Ammon, eds., *Die Linke und die nationale Frage,* see pp. 132–134 (Hiller), 161–165 (Erler), 177–178 (Schmid/Erler).

25. See Brandt and Ammon, eds., *Die Linke und die nationale Frage,* pp. 280–287 ("Diskussionsbeitrag zur sozialdemokratischen Politik. . . .").

26. See Besson, "The Conflict of Traditions," p. 70ff.

27. See Karl Kaiser, "Interdependence and Autonomy: Britain and the Federal Republic in their Multinational Environment," in Kaiser and Morgan, eds., *Britain and West Germany.*

28. See Daniel Lerner and Morton Gorden, *Euratlantica* (Cambridge, MA: MIT Press, 1969), p. 50, and Chapters 1, 2, and 10 in general for the following discussion.

29. Lerner and Gorden, *Euratlantica*, Chapter 10.

30. For useful general discussions and illustrations of *Westpolitik*, see, in Jacobsen and Stenzl, eds., *Deutschland und die Welt*, pp. 46–54 (Adenauer), 284–291 (Brentano), 304–310 (Schröder); Alfred Grosser, *Geschichte Deutschlands seit 1945* (München: Deutscher Taschenbuch Verlag, 1979), pp. 436–455; Jim Cloos, "La R.F.A. et l'intégration européenne," in Fritsch-Bournazel, Brigot, and Cloos, *Les Allemands au Coeur de l'Europe*; Josef Joffe, "Von Adenauer bis Schmidt: Grundzüge der Außenpolitik," in Eckhard Jesse, ed., *Bundesrepublik Deutschland und Deutsche Demokratische Republik* (Berlin: Colloquium Verlag, 1980/1985); Walter Hallstein, "Germany's Dual Aim: Unity and Integration," *Foreign Affairs*, vol. 31, nr. 1, October 1952; Klaus Epstein, "The Adenauer Era in German History," in Stephen R. Graubard, ed., *A New Europe?* (Boston: Houghton Mifflin, 1964); Besson, "The Conflict of Traditions," p. 70ff.; Helga Haftendorn, *Security and Detente* (New York: Praeger Publishers, 1985), pp. 36–47; Helga Haftendorn, Lothar Wilker, and Claudia Wörmann, eds., *Die Außenpolitik der Bundesrepublik Deutschland* (Berlin: Wissenschaftlicher Autoren-Verlag, 1982), pp. 136–151 (Ziebura), 101–102 (Adenauer), and pp. 91–93.

31. On the "Westernization" of German foreign policy culture, see Frank R. Pfetsch, *Die Außenpolitik der Bundesrepublik, 1949–1980* (München: Wilhelm Fink Verlag, 1981), p. 43ff. The profound Franco-German reconciliation became perhaps the greatest symbol of the end of Germany's alienation from the West.

32. See Hans-Peter Schwarz, "Die westdeutsche Außenpolitik—Historische Lektionen und politische Generationen," in Walter Scheel, ed., *Nach Dreissig Jahren* (Stuttgart: Klett-Cotta Verlag, 1979), p. 164ff.

33. Besson, "The Conflict of Traditions," pp. 73–74.

34. Schwarz, "Die westdeutsche Außenpolitik—Historische Lektionen und politische Generationen," p. 155. See also the essay by Christian Hacke, "Traditionen und Stationen der Außenpolitik der Bundesrepublik Deutschland," *Aus Politik und Zeitgeschichte*, 15 January 1988. For critical perspectives on Adenauer's *Westpolitik* and the accompanying "Westernization" of the Federal Republic, see the essays in parts 2 and 3 of Rainer Zitelmann, Karlheinz Weißmann, and Michael Großheim, eds., *Westbindung. Chancen und Risiken für Deutschland* (Frankfurt: Verlag Ullstein/Propyläen Verlag, 1993).

35. See W. Phillips Davison, "Trends in West German Public Opinion, 1946–1956," in Hans Speier and W. Phillips Davison, eds., *West German Leadership and Foreign Policy* (Evanston, IL: Row, Peterson, 1957); Anna J. and Richard L. Merritt, eds., *Public Opinion in Semisovereign Germany* (Urbana: University of Illinois Press, 1980).

36. Fritz R. Allemann, "Rapallo: Myth and Reality," in Walter Stahl, ed., *The Politics of Postwar Germany* (New York: Praeger Publishers, 1963).

37. Josef Joffe, "Germany and the Atlantic Alliance: The Politics of Dependence, 1961–1968," in William C. Cromwell, N. Forman, and Josef Joffe, *Political Problems of Atlantic Partnership* (Bruges: College of Europe, 1969), p. 348.

38. Joffe, "Germany and the Atlantic Alliance: The Politics of Dependence, 1961–1968," p. 348.

39. For discussion and illustrative documents concerning the impact of Western detente efforts on West German *Westpolitik*, the question of reunification, and demands for a more active *Ostpolitik*, see parts III and IV in Jacobsen and Stenzl, eds., *Deutschland und die Welt*; pp. 224–302 in Brandt and Ammon, eds., *Die Linke und die nationale Frage*.

40. See Peter H. Merkl, "The German Janus: From Westpolitik to Ostpolitik," *Political Science Quarterly*, vol. 89, nr. 4, Winter 1974–75; Josef Joffe, "Westverträge, Ostverträge und die Kontinuität der deutschen Außenpolitik," *Europa-Archiv*, nr. 3, 1973. Joffe saw many parallels between *Westpolitik* and *Ostpolitik*, especially their similar relevance to the FRG's diplomatic emancipation and the definition of its international role and self-image. Both involved an attempted reconciliation of national dreams and international realities.

41. This is not to suggest any kind of complete geopolitical "determinism," however. As Christian Hacke has pointed out, for example, the individual personalities of West German chancellors since 1949 left a considerable mark on the FRG's conception and pursuit of *Ostpolitik* and *Deutschlandpolitik*. See his essay "Von Adenauer bis Kohl: Zur Ost- und Deutschlandpolitik der Bundesrepublik 1949–1985," *Aus Politik und Zeitgeschichte*, 21 December 1985.

42. The following discussion is particularly indebted to Hans-Peter Schwarz, "The Roles of the Federal Republic in the Community of States," in Kaiser and Morgan, eds., *Britain and West Germany*. See also Hans-Adolf Jacobsen, "The Role of the Federal Republic of Germany in the World, 1949–1982," in Charles Burdick, Hans-Adolf Jacobsen, and Winfried Kudszus, eds., *Contemporary Germany: Politics and Culture* (Boulder, CO: Westview Press, 1984).

43. Debate about Germany's role as a reunited great power was visibly triggered by the crisis in the Persian Gulf in 1990 and the question about possible German military participation. See "With Aid Pledge, Kohl Tries to Show Germany Is Dependable," *Los Angeles Times*, 17 September 1990, p. A6.

44. See the discussion in Volker Rittberger, "Die Bundesrepublik Deutschland—eine Weltmacht?" *Aus Politik und Zeitgeschichte*, 19 January 1990.

45. Schwarz, "The Roles of the Federal Republic," p. 233. See also Elke Thiel, "West Germany's Role in the International Economy: Prospects for Economic Policy Coordination," *Journal of International Affairs*, vol. 42, nr. 1, Fall 1988.

46. As far as German and Japanese approaches to their nations' troubled pasts are concerned, there are some interesting differences, however. See "The Axis: Odd Twins on Ascent," *Los Angeles Times*, 13 August 1990. More generally, see the fascinating study by Ian Buruma, *The Wages of Guilt: Memories of War in Germany and Japan* (New York: Farrar, Straus, Giroux, 1994).

47. Schwarz, "The Roles of the Federal Republic," p. 235ff.

48. See Fritsch-Bournazel, "La permanente quête d'une identité"; Waldemar Besson, "Prinzipiennfragen der westdeutschen Außenpolitik," in Gilbert Ziebura, ed., *Grundfragen der deutschen Außenpolitik seit 1871* (Darmstadt: Wissenschaftliche Buchgesellschaft, 1975).

49. According to Josef Joffe, West German tendencies of *Anpassung* were especially directed toward relations with Western allies. He has seen the FRG's tendency to adapt to Western policies as part of an important "syndrome of psychological elements," involving a good deal of "diplomatic ritual." West German attitudes toward the West were (and still are in many ways) essentially informed by a desire to "gain friendship, trust, solidarity, and redemption." Needless to say, *Anpassung* as a "mental habit" introduced a substantial degree of "immobility" in FRG foreign policy. Joffe, "Germany and the Atlantic Alliance," pp. 323–327. See also Joffe, "Westverträge, Ostverträge."

50. The following discussion is particularly indebted to the analysis of historical lessons in FRG foreign policy in Schwarz, "Die westdeutsche Außenpolitik—Historische Lektionen und politische Generationen," especially pp. 147–158.

51. During the last years of the Cold War, Hans-Peter Schwarz perceptively discussed the German legacy of *Machtpolitik* and argued that German diplomatic style in the twentieth century had swung from a disastrous *Machtbesessenheit* (obsession with power) to an equally objectionable *Machtvergessenheit* (a state of oblivion when it comes to the realities of power in world politics). He called for a more *verantwortliche Machtpolitik* ("policy based upon responsible power considerations"). See Schwarz, *Die gezähmten Deutschen. Von der Machtbesessenheit zur Machtvergessenheit* (Stuttgart: Deutsche Verlags-Anstalt, 1985). For an analysis of the interaction among state power, democratic consensus, and policymaking in postwar Germany, see Rudolf Wildenmann, *Macht und Konsens als Problem der Innen- und Außenpolitik* (Köln/Opladen: Westdeutscher Verlag, 1967).

52. On the "policy of strength," see Jacobsen and Stenzl, eds., *Deutschland und die Welt*, pp. 46–54 (Adenauer), 263–271 (Guttenberg), 407–414 (Strauß); Haftendorn, Wilker, and Wörmann, eds., *Die Außenpolitik der Bundesrepublik Deutschland*, pp. 283–289 (Schwarz); Manfred Wörner, "Das sicherheitspolitische Konzept der Union," and Franz-Josef Strauß, "Die Bundesrepublik Deutschland im Kräftefeld der Weltpolitik," both in Gerhard Mayer-Vorfelder and Hubertus Zuber, eds., *Union alternativ* (Stuttgart: Seewald Verlag, 1976); Klaus von Schubert, ed., *Sicherheitspolitik der Bundesrepublik Deutschland: Dokumentation 1945–1977* (Köln: Verlag Wissenschaft & Politik, 1978/1979), vol. I, pp. 117–123 (Adenauer), and vol. II, pp. 504–511 (Adenauer).

53. For further discussion of generational aspects of West German foreign policy culture, see Pfetsch, *Die Außenpolitik der Bundesrepublik*, pp. 25–28; Schwarz, "Die westdeutsche Außenpolitik—Historische Lektionen und politische Generationen," p. 168ff; Johannes R. Gascard, "Junge Generation und Außenpolitik," *Europa-Archiv*, nr. 6, 1972; Dietmar Schössler and Erich Weede, *West German Elite Views on National Security and Foreign Policy Issues* (Königstein: Athenäum-Verlag, 1978), pp. 63–65.

54. Schwarz, "Die westdeutsche Außenpolitik—Historische Lektionen und politische Generationen," p. 168.

55. See Alfred Grosser, *Das Deutschland im Westen* (München/Wien: Carl Hanser Verlag, 1985), pp. 313–320. See also Karl-Rudolf Korte, "Deutschlandbilder—Akzentverlagerungen der deutschen Frage seit den siebziger Jahren," *Aus Politik und Zeitgeschichte*, 15 January 1988.

5

Philosophical and Ideological Orientations in West German Foreign Policy, 1945–1990

In Chapter 4 we saw that the context of German diplomatic traditions, perennial questions of Germany's identity and role in world politics, and the burdens of a troubled past in international behavior are themes that are essential for any analysis of the German Question. We now embark on the next step: a more explicitly philosophical and ideological survey, focused primarily on developments in the Federal Republic after 1949. We shall see that the connected themes of national unity and German political identity constitute an important element in the various philosophical and ideological currents.

Conservatism, Liberalism, and Socialism

In the German historical experience, ideological conflict and polarization have been severe and common. Throughout the pre–World War II period, Conservatism was the dominant ideology, reaching a radical extreme in Nazism during the 1930s and 1940s. Both Liberalism and Socialism (or Social Democracy) were either weak on an official political and diplomatic level, or, if gradually ascendant (as in the Weimar era), subject to attacks in a highly polarized political climate. World War II turned into a watershed in German ideological development. The destruction of traditional elites, the loss of Prussia, and the rise of a more explicitly bourgeois culture in the new *Weststaat* brought about a distinct liberalization and democratization of political culture. Liberalism and Socialism came to play decisive roles in the new West German politics. Conservatism did not disappear, but it had to adjust itself to a new domestic and international environment. This was true in both domestic politics and foreign policy.

As a decisive ideological factor in traditional German foreign policy, Conservatism contained four major elements that were central to its philosophical makeup: a *Realpolitik*-based conception of international politics and foreign policy, an illiberal political ethos, a nationalist frame of reference, and a focus on military power. During the postwar era, elements of this set of ideological orientations were visible in the CDU's right wing, the Bavarian CSU, the FDP (during the FRG's early years), the Deutsche Partei (DP), Sozialistische Reichspartei (SRP), and the Bund der Heimatvertriebenen und Entrechteten (BHE, often referred to as "expellees" from former eastern German territory) during the 1950s, the Nationaldemokratische Partei Deutschlands (NPD) in the 1960s and 1970s, and the Republikaner in the 1980s and 1990s (despite all the other differences among these various parties and organizations). In addition, they were relatively more prevalent among West German Protestants than Catholics.[1]

Postwar Conservative West German views on international affairs largely matched those of philosophical "realism."[2] At the same time, the Cold War environment imparted to them a strongly polarized view of international relations, with the Free World engaged in an existential struggle against world Communist totalitarianism. A sometimes virulent anti-Communism tended to lead for some, at least indirectly, to a post-facto legitimation of the anti-Bolshevism of the Third Reich and Germany's campaign against the Soviet Union during World War II. In this profoundly Cold War–oriented perspective, detente in general and West Germany's *Ostpolitik* in particular came to be viewed with deep suspicion, concern, or even alarm. Nightmares of German national impotence and encirclement generated nationalist assertiveness directed at the surrounding powers, and an illiberal fear of change. The primary emphasis was placed on security and freedom, not necessarily on peace. But at times even freedom would seem to take a backseat to national unity, although only among a maverick minority of Conservatives. There was, therefore, an unmistakable tension in Conservative West German thinking between freedom and reunification during most of the postwar era: the former resulting from Cold War anti-Communism, the latter from a continued nationalist frame of reference.

Despite this frame of reference, however, the bulk of West German Conservatives were quite supportive of Western integration schemes, although it was a support from which calculations of national interest were by no means absent. Integration was especially favored to the extent that it promoted German emancipation after defeat and occupation. From the Conservative vantage point, the pursuit of rearmament was particularly crucial, in view of Cold War Soviet threats and the "civil war" between the FRG and the ("so-called") GDR.

This pragmatic willingness regarding integration for emancipatory purposes was matched by a philosophical conviction among many Conservatives that the age of superpower Cold War had rendered the Western European states individually too weak for security self-sufficiency. Hence occasionally emerged "Euro-Gaullist" visions of a Western European "third power" in international politics, in partnership with the United States and equipped with both conventional and nuclear capability. Any future European *Weltgeltung* ("global relevance") was seen to be dependent on a pooling of economic and military resources.[3] Back in 1952, for example, conservative CSU leader Franz-Josef Strauß said:

> The [free] remnant of Europe, split up into 17 states in between the Bolshevist colossus and superpower America, must be transformed into a Europe united on a basis of freedom and equality. Otherwise Europe will soon be no more than a geographic term on the map. . . . We want to regain German unity on a basis of freedom; but we also know that the solution to all these questions cannot be achieved through our own good will, but only by a united Europe that knows what it wants.[4]

And in 1968, he argued that "Europe only has to unite its material and spiritual means in order to exist alongside America as equal partner."[5]

In general, it could be argued that many West German Conservatives, Germanocentrically preoccupied with the German national question, tended to be quite instrumental and conditional in their support of the FRG's *Westpolitik*. Euro-Atlantic forms of cooperation would be accepted only as long as they did not violate or jeopardize fundamental German interests. As a result, Conservatives faced a major philosophical crisis when the West's increased interest in detente from the late 1950s onward seemed to go at the expense of the old *Junktim* (linkage) that had made such detente dependent on progress with respect to the reunification question. Yet West Germany's need for Western security guarantees precluded any real foreign policy alternatives. In addition, the ideological attachment of West German Conservatives to basic facets of the *Abendland*-based *Weltanschauung* of the Cold War era guaranteed their ultimate allegiance to the West. Detente frustrations did not really generate *Schaukelpolitik* illusions.

Conservative West German foreign policy culture contained a noticeably legalistic perspective on the German Question. Its central feature was, at least until Brandt's post-1969 *Ostpolitik*, the so-called Hallstein Doctrine, aimed at a prevention of international recognition of the GDR. Underlying this doctrine were some fundamental *Rechtsbehauptungen* (legal claims).[6] First, it was claimed that World War II and Cold War division had not caused the prewar German state to disappear in a legal sense. Second, it was argued that, under international law, the German nation continued to exist in its 1937 boundaries. Third, no juridical equality between the FRG and the GDR could be accepted. The result of these legalistic criteria was the West German claim of *Alleinvertretung*, that is, the idea that only the FRG legally represented all of Germany. One consequence of this posture was a fundamental insistence that there was only one "German" nationality, not separate West and East German nationalities.[7] Furthermore, no final peace treaty could be accepted unless and until a reunited, free Germany could participate in the peacemaking process. Reunification would basically imply the absorption by the FRG of a GDR abandoned by the Soviet Union, a perspective not altogether absent from West German government policy on the 1989–1990 "takeover" of East Germany by the Federal Republic. The demand for reunification was often put to the USSR in fairly all-or-nothing terms.

A last important feature of West German Conservative thinking reflected the significant interplay of elements of domestic politics and foreign policy in the FRG's political life. The Conservative conception of democracy was greatly influenced by the militant ideological climate of the Cold War. The result was a simultaneous stress on freedom and domestic security in the face of the totalitarian challenge from the East, a dual focus that contained obvious sources of tension.[8] Conservative elements were stressed in the *Abendland* ideology that was seen as the basis of Western Cold War solidarity: freedom, strength, anti-Communism, private enterprise, and state security interests.

The (unintended) bourgeoisification of German political life caused by National Socialism and World War II, followed by German division and an ideological Cold War between Liberalism and Marxism-Leninism, helped give greatly increased prominence to Liberal perspectives in West German political culture and foreign policy culture. The participation of the new *Weststaat* in the Western European integration process further strengthened Liberal political and economic thinking.

A distinction between "Cold War," conservative, and "post–Cold War" (or "detente") liberal internationalism can be observed in West German Liberal thought with respect to foreign policy and international politics in the decades after 1949. In fact, one might even argue that, with the passing of time, there were two areas of considerable ideological convergence in the FRG's foreign policy culture: on the one hand, between older German Conservatism and "conservative," Cold War–oriented Liberalism; on the other hand, between a more pragmatic (centrist) and less dogmatic form of Social Democracy (as opposed to doctrinaire Socialism or left-wing "alternative" ideology) and "liberal," detente-oriented Liberalism.

As far as West German Liberalism as a whole is concerned, there was an important developmental aspect to this dual process of convergence, insofar as a Cold War–oriented posture was gradually but perceptibly abandoned in favor of a more detente-oriented posture. The evolution of the FDP showed this most clearly, with the decline of the older, more conservative, nationalist leadership of Erich Mende and Thomas Dehler, and the subsequent rise of "younger," new Liberals like Walter Scheel, Hans-Dietrich Genscher, and others, whose outlook was more "liberal" and internationalist.

We should also note the growth of a more "liberal," detente-oriented perspective in the CDU in the course of the 1960s (Gerhard Schröder, Kurt Georg Kiesinger, Walther Leisler Kiep, and others) and a more pragmatic realism on the "right wing" of the SPD during the late 1950s and the 1960s (Willy Brandt, Fritz Erler, Helmut Schmidt, and so on).[9] These developments appeared to signal the consolidation of a considerable foreign policy cultural consensus, balancing security needs with detente perspectives, and continued revisionism regarding the national question with a realistic accommodation to postwar European conditions. The impact of West Germany's foreign minister, Hans-Dietrich Genscher (who served in this position from 1974 until 1992), was especially important here.

By and large, the ascendant, new West German Liberalism was consistently internationalist, whether for more realist or idealist reasons. Even nationally oriented Liberal thinking was greatly supportive of a *Westpolitik* aimed at the promotion of European and Atlantic integration schemes.[10] Consider the mixture of realist and idealist internationalism in this 1976 Genscher speech as an example that could be multiplied numerous times:

> A politically united Europe is as vital for its members as an economically integrated Europe. The present world is a world of continental powers—USA, USSR, China—and a world of large negotiation blocs—oil countries, developing countries. In such a world the *individual* European state can no longer pursue its vital interests effectively. Acting on its own such a state is instead more or less an object, not a subject, of world politics. Only in unity can Europe be the master of its own fate. Only in unity can it realize *internally* its ideals of freedom and human dignity. Only in unity can Europe defend freedom *externally*. . . . There is no alternative to European unity.[11]

There was also strong backing for Liberal international trade practices and a domestic West German *soziale Marktwirtschaft* (welfare state on a capitalist basis) that guaranteed free enterprise. Furthermore, the new West German Liberalism was predominantly Atlanticist. Liberals fully shared in an *Abendland* ideology that stressed common Western democratic values. The Liberals were also ardent supporters of the consolidation of West German democracy. Their conception of freedom was often broader and more tolerant than that of West German Conservatives, and they were not as constantly preoccupied with domestic security issues. They fully shared the legalistic approach to the German national question, although Liberal legalism was somewhat more flexible and pragmatic. The main emphasis tended to be on a Liberally defined German right of national self-determination, often tied to an active interest in general human rights issues in world affairs.

West German Liberal foreign policy orientations were very much shaped by the kinds of reactions to the German political and diplomatic past that were outlined earlier. There was a frequent sense that the defeat in World War II also contained a good deal of liberation, a view with which many German Conservatives would much less readily agree. Liberals were consistently anti-Communist, although there was a noticeable decline in intensity after the height of the Cold War.

The Liberal perspectives that prevailed during the first ten to fifteen years after World War II contained a considerable affinity with West German Conservative thinking during the Cold War. Older German Conservatives, faced with a new domestic and international environment, and conservative Liberals, ascendant in the new German *Weststaat* and connected with similar ideological perspectives elsewhere in the Western world during the Cold War, experienced considerable ideological convergence.

Yet, as noted, during the late 1950s and the 1960s a more detente-oriented thinking began to emerge among West German Liberals, particularly on the FDP's "left wing." Faced with a growing East-West stalemate and the dangers of nuclear confrontation, there was increased realization that reunification-through-*Westpolitik* might be an illusionary vision and that the key to a solution of the German Question might lie in a mixture of general detente and international arms control, including possibly Central European military disengagement and the military neutrality of a reunified Germany.[12] As Genscher put it in 1975: "We could and we can, especially as Germans, derive no gain from confrontation in Europe. But we can achieve gains if we encourage the process of detente as we understand it." He also added, however, as a good Atlanticist, that "detente policy requires security as its foundation, and without the alliance and its (and our) commitment to defense there is no security for us. Whoever believes that he could achieve security only on the basis of attention to detente is a dangerous dreamer."[13]

Continued Cold War prevented the (full) realization of all these visions until the 1970s, but there were clear changes in Liberal thinking, involving an emphasis on peace as well as freedom, negotiations as well as strength, and a much more flexible legalism regarding the German Question. Superpower stalemate, post-Stalin changes in the Soviet Union and Eastern Europe, and the rise of the Third World were among the developments that were felt to have profoundly affected the international environment. Interdependence among nations became a key concept in this Liberal foreign policy culture.[14] Again, Genscher provides a good illustration of this line of thinking:

> Problems have become global in scope. The unstoppable trend towards ever closer mutual dependence among states is the dominant characteristic of the new age, the driving force of world history. For the first time humanity is approaching a common future together: common survival or common demise, common prosperity or common decline. For the entire world there is an unshakeable law of interdependence: the parts cannot prosper if the whole does not. . . . The only alternatives we have are common progress or common chaos.[15]

From a foreign policy cultural point of view, the Social Democrats carried a double legacy into the postwar period: on the one hand, a tradition of socialist internationalism, focused on international working-class solidarity and transnational contacts with sister-parties and among labor unions; on the other hand, a historically problematic relation with the German nation and German nationalism. According to Peter Brandt and Herbert Ammon,

> [t]he trauma of the German Left consists in the fact that the workers' movement, treated as *Reichsfeind* by the dominant [political] power bloc [during the Second Reich], could not develop its own national-democratic identity in opposition to the imperialist nationalism [of that power bloc]. Instead, [the workers' movement] gravitated increasingly toward an abstract internationalism which in the final analysis could not resist the pull of mass nationalistic enthusiasm in August of 1914. The majority of the SPD responded by adjusting to the bourgeois state.[16]

SPD foreign policy orientations after 1945 can only be understood if both of these elements are kept in view.[17]

The first legacy (socialist internationalism) was connected with a variety of SPD perspectives. Among these was a strong anti-Communism as a result of a basic dispute on the Left during the Cold War with respect to the nature of and relationship between socialism and democracy. The SPD tended to see the Cold War as an ideological as much as a political-military conflict. There was much support for a socialist-democratic version of the *Abendland* ideology, and a constant confidence that a Western world animated by the values of freedom, social justice, progress, and solidarity would win the ideological Cold War. But such a victory could be achieved without military means, as West Berlin's mayor Willy Brandt suggested in 1962, a year after the creation of the Berlin Wall: "Berlin has proved convincingly that true coexistence is a competition that Communism is bound to lose." He described the Wall as "the most brutal means to stem the flow of refugees but also the most obvious propaganda against Communism since 1917."[18] The SPD was strongly in favor of Western integration ideas but criticized Adenauer's *Westpolitik* during the 1950s as overly motivated by conservative, capitalist, and Catholic/Carolingian considerations. The traditional emphasis on solidarity, peace, and negotiations in socialist internationalism, together with a rejection of many facets of *Realpolitik*, ambivalence toward military power, and an at least partial element of pacifism, stimulated a persistent SPD interest in East-West reconciliation and detente. These factors led to the Social Democrats' support for disengagement ideas during the 1950s, for disarmament, and for a more forthcoming *Ostpolitik* throughout the postwar era.

A major resolution adopted by the SPD party conference in Munich in 1956 summed up many of the ideas on detente and reunification that had begun to crystallize in previous years:

> The reunification of Germany in secure freedom is part of a lasting "peace order" [*Friedensordnung*] in Europe. The foreign policy of the Federal Republic must promote all efforts which help create such a lasting "peace order" in Europe. . . . The di-

vision of Germany can only be overcome when East and West give up the objective of integrating a reunified Germany in such a way into their own military-political system that the other side would perceive it as a threat. . . . A new foreign policy for the Federal Republic must make all efforts to move toward the creation of a collective security system in Europe. . . . Normalization of relations between the Federal Republic and those states in Europe or Asia that belong to the Eastern bloc should be pursued as a contribution to the policy of detente.[19]

The potential link between East-West military disengagement in Europe and German reunification was suggested by SPD leaders like Erler, who wrote in 1959:

> Germany will certainly remain divided as long as both halves of Germany are integrated into mutually hostile military alliances. The presence of foreign troops from both alliance systems on German soil is an additional guarantee that the division will continue. . . . Germany will only be able to reunite when a united Germany has a different military status than do the two halves [of Germany] at the present time.[20]

The second legacy (ambivalence toward German nationalism) led the SPD to adopt what Alfred Grosser called a "preventive" nationalist posture during the first fifteen postwar years, aimed at demonstrating SPD national ideological reliability, forestalling a dangerously revisionist right-wing nationalism in the face of uncertain reunification prospects, and casting the SPD as the true representative of the German national interest. Many facets of Adenauer's *Westpolitik*, particularly West German rearmament and NATO membership, were strongly opposed as damaging to the chances for German reunification. Although the party supported most of the standard legal principles concerning the German Question during the Cold War, early doubts regarding the wisdom of the Hallstein Doctrine did develop.

The apparent hopelessness with respect to (early) reunification in the face of increased East-West stalemate and detente, and the construction of the Berlin Wall in 1961, produced two important changes in SPD foreign policy thinking. First, there was an acceptance of the results of Adenauer's *Westpolitik*, including West German rearmament and NATO membership. Second, there was a renewed interest in a more active *Ostpolitik*, but no longer predicated on a revision of the postwar European status quo. Germanocentric visions of detente were replaced by the idea of a general European *Friedensordnung* ("peace order"), in which the guiding principle would be *Wandel durch Annäherung* ("change through rapprochement") rather than dangerous confrontation.

The consequences of these changes for FRG-GDR relations were expressed by Brandt in the Erfurt Declaration of March 1970, upon the conclusion of an unprecedented East-West German meeting. Especially in view of its diplomatic significance at the time, the document deserves quoting at length:

Both states [the FRG and the GDR] have a duty to safeguard the unity of the German nation. They are not foreign countries to one another. . . . Otherwise the generally recognized principles of interstate law should be observed, particularly the prohibition against all forms of discrimination, respect for territorial integrity, the duty to pursue a peaceful resolution of all conflicts and disagreements, and a respect for one another's borders. To this should be added the responsibility not to seek the violent alteration of the social structure within the territory of one's treaty partner. . . . The existing rights and duties of the Four Powers with regard to Germany as a whole and Berlin must be respected. . . . For a normalization of relations formal documents are not sufficient; the population on both sides must gain from this normalization. . . . In my opinion a true normalization must contribute to overcoming intra-German barbed wire constructions and walls. They symbolize our deplorably special situation. This is probably a situation that cannot be changed overnight. Our efforts must have as their objective, however, to achieve progress in the area of liberalization in the relationship between people in both parts [of Germany] and to make room for human rights in both states. . . . The principles of non-discrimination and equal treatment [between the FRG and GDR] should not alter our goal one day to restore [the authority of] the actual sovereign, the German people.[21]

In comparison with the CDU/CSU, the SPD, seeing Germany's World War II fate not only as defeat but also as liberation, turned out to be more willing to accommodate itself to the realities of postwar Europe. In so doing, it incurred the hostility of West German conservatives who, in the tradition of the German *Reichsfeind* epithet, accused the SPD of practicing an anti-German *Verzichtpolitik*, a surrender of German rights.[22]

Insofar as West German foreign policy thinking developed in dynamic interaction with the FRG's environmental constraints and opportunities, there is an interesting similarity in the fate of Conservatism and Socialism in postwar West German orientations, centered on the idea of *Anpassung* (adjustment), as described earlier. Conservatism abandoned most of its illiberal ethos, Germanocentrism, and inclinations toward militarism in a setting in which Liberalism constituted the philosophical foundation of the new *Weststaat* and of the West's ideological position in the Cold War, in which integration sublimated an older nationalism and reunification prospects dimmed, and in which international as well as domestic sensitivity and control regarding West German military power made independent German revisionism all but impossible. As Conservatives adjusted, they "converged" philosophically with a conservative form of Liberalism.

Similarly, West German Socialism was forced to mitigate its dogmatic radicalism, socialist internationalism, and antimilitarism in an at least problematic setting. A setting, namely, in which U.S. occupation policies and ascendant Liberalism prevented the enactment of fully socialist plans, in which Cold War polarization undermined the chances for more all-encompassing international cooperation, in which the CDU's *Westpolitik* served to define a particular foreign policy environment for future West German governments, and in which Cold War needs produced an inescapable Western interest in some form of West German rearmament. Social Democratic *Anpassung* led to a convergence with a more "liberal" version of Liberalism.

As a result, there developed in the FRG's foreign policy culture a bifurcation involving conservative and liberal internationalism. It tended to line up the SPD against most of the CDU/CSU, with the FDP in a "balancing" position, in spite of persisting elements of an underlying consensus, particularly with respect to Atlantic security arrangements and the need for some basic *Ostpolitik*. West German foreign policy discussions frequently aimed at a reconciliation of liberal and conservative internationalist thinking and the creation of a broader consensus. During the last ten years of the Cold War, Schmidt, Genscher, and Kohl repeatedly made such attempts.

Nationalism, Internationalism, and Supranationalism

The two basic factors that served to guarantee continued national orientations in the FRG's foreign policy culture after 1949 were the Federal Republic's pursuit of increased sovereignty, emancipation, and leverage in international affairs, and the question of German reunification. In the postwar context, then, German nationalism tended to take the form of West German assertiveness rooted in a mixture of (FRG-oriented) emancipatory and (all-German) revisionist attitudes.

An examination of the national frame of reference in FRG foreign policy thinking during the years after 1949 reveals some important inner tensions and contradictions. Essentially, these involved a basic element of incompatibility between the goal of reunification and other foreign policy objectives, especially during the years of the Cold War. Alfred Grosser points to some of the inherent dilemmas when he writes:

> In 1949, acquiring the right and possibility of conducting foreign policy had to be the first priority of all German diplomacy. That is, to cease being the object and instead to become a subject in international politics: is it not the [German] starting position [in 1949] that determines which goal should be given highest priority? Yet the answer is less obvious than would seem to be the case at first sight. The bid for sovereignty was inevitable, but from the emergence of two German states in 1949 until the talks between the two German government leaders in 1970 this bid for sovereignty could never be unequivocally articulated or even understood. . . . The sovereignty of a [West] German state and the unity of Germany could not be pursued simultaneously and were in no way compatible. Should one not forgo this symbol or that reality of freedom of action [resulting from regained West German sovereignty] in order to preserve the possibility of even an unlikely reunification?[23]

The preservation of West German freedom, the consolidation of the new *Weststaat* and its security, the maintenance of international peace, and the recovery of

(West) German sovereignty after occupation—each of these goals was in some fundamental way at odds with a simultaneous pursuit of reunification. West German foreign policy debates at numerous points in time revolved around attempts to reconcile these inherent contradictions. Cold War constraints prevented a reconciliation of West German freedom and security with German national unity. Dangers of East-West conflict imparted a higher priority to the maintenance of peace than a perilously revisionist insistence on German reunification. And the vital reacquisition of West German sovereignty could not be left waiting, in view of the growing uncertainty with respect to reunification.

Looking at the matter from a somewhat different angle, we can note the presence of two types of nationalism or nationally oriented thinking in West German foreign policy culture in the decades after 1949. On the one hand, the legacy of German national unity (*Reichseinheit*) and the dream of national reunification helped preserve important all-German perspectives in foreign policy culture. On the other hand, as noted in Chapter 2, a growing FRG *Staatsbewußtsein* ("state consciousness") also developed, raising the question of the extent to which a more *Weststaat*-oriented "national" German thinking was emerging. Again, it is obvious that there would be a basic tension between these two types of nationalism. Any emancipation and consolidation of the FRG, leading to an increasingly explicit West German *Staatsräson*, would risk being at odds with a preservation of a sense of all-German identity and *raison de nation*.[24] The inherent contradiction was greatest between the goal of reunification and West German security policy during the Cold War.

One of the often quite explicit goals in West German *Ostpolitik* during the 1970s and 1980s was to preserve and strengthen a basis of common German nationhood despite a seemingly finalized national German division. Thus, one Social Democrat might write:

> The *Deutschlandpolitik* of the 1970s can no longer be focused on the reconstruction of unity in a national state. One can only prudently attempt, recognizing the facts created by World War II, to achieve a kind of cooperation [between the FRG and the GDR] which serves the peace in Europe.[25]

Yet the official SPD perspective remained closer to more traditional national perspectives:

> The concept of nationhood contains both historical reality and political will. The idea of nationhood entails and means more than common language and culture, more than common state and social order. A nation rests upon the continuing sense of belonging together [*Zusammengehörigkeitsgefühl*] of the members of a people. Nobody can deny that in this sense there is and will be *one* German nation, as far as we can foresee. The GDR also claims to be a part of this German nation in its constitution. . . . Patriotism requires a recognition of that which is and an attempt to achieve that which is possible. It requires the *courage to recognize reality* [*Mut zum Erkennen der Wirklichkeit*].[26]

There was a general tendency in postwar West German foreign policy thinking away from an explicit preoccupation with all-German reunification, toward a more primary focus on specifically West German interests, however. Until the sudden events in the GDR in 1989, the reunification question gradually ceased to be a leading item on the foreign policy agenda. Rather, short of reunification, there was considerable interest in various forms of intra-German rapprochement, involving such issues as improvements in East German political and socioeconomic conditions, intra-German travel and communication, the idea of a common German *Friedenspartnerschaft* in Central Europe, and the maintenance of German identity despite political and ideological division.[27] In short, the nature of West German *Deutschlandpolitik* seemed to change over time. This development in West German attitudes reflected a good deal of *Anpassung* to the apparently inexorable solidification of the postwar European status quo.

As a result, a prominent analyst of German affairs could be essentially correct as late as early 1989 in making the following observation:

> The old German question, as understood in the early postwar period, centered around the question of reunification. Yet changes in international politics, as well as in public attitudes in both the Federal Republic and the GDR, suggest that this issue has lost much, though not all, of its former relevance. The real issue today—the "new German Question"—relates not to reunification but to the evolving modalities of inter-German *detente* and their implications for European security. . . . [I]t is on this problem, rather than the highly theoretical and less politically relevant issue of reunification, that scholars and politicians should focus in the 1990s.[28]

Whether one looks at postwar manifestations of all-German or of FRG-oriented nationalism, both contained some common psychological denominators. They expressed a spirit of assertiveness, which was in turn rooted in various mental attitudes. Among these would be an increased West German political self-confidence, a self-consciousness about Germany's importance in international politics, an anti-Americanism in some quarters fueled by dependency frustrations, a morally less apologetic and repentant outlook among many younger West Germans, a survival or resurgence of an older nationalist spirit among some, resentment regarding continued international scrutiny of German reliability, and so forth. In this sense, reduced reunification hopes, together with heightened West German assertiveness, came to reflect a basic process of emancipation and maturation in FRG foreign policy attitudes, and a relative "normalization" of West Germany's international status and position. More and more, the Germanocentric element in West German foreign policy culture shifted from an FRG focus tied to all-German visions, to a clearer conception of a West German *Staatsräson* independent of the all-German destiny, even though this was rarely officially admitted.

Although there were overarching aspects to nationalism in West German foreign policy thinking after 1949, such as those discussed thus far, it is necessary to grasp the differences between the nationalist perspectives that animated West German Conservatives and conservative Liberals on one side, and Social Democrats and left-Liberals on the other side.

The more conservative type of West German nationalism was essentially Cold War–oriented and influenced by many traditional German perspectives. Informed by a strong anti-Communism, a militant revisionism, and a rigid legalism, its posture was frequently confrontational. Consider the flavor of the following statement by CSU member of parliament Karl Theodor Freiherr zu Guttenberg in the fall of 1961, after the construction of the Berlin Wall:

> The essential point, both now and in the coming years, is to keep one's cool and to resist any attempt to purchase peace based on concessions. Firmness, not flexible compliance, is the price to be paid for peace. Negotiations that are conducted only because one side fears a war inevitably bring on a catastrophe. This does not suggest a refusal to engage in negotiations altogether. But the West should conduct such negotiations courageously; that is, the West must demand from the other side [a willingness] to accept the fulfillment of inalienable Western rights as a basis for negotiations. The wall in Berlin exists; to conduct negotiations on the basis of the wall's continued existence would already imply a concession. Only an offensive Western negotiating strategy can convince Moscow of the uselessness of its threats. If Moscow persisted with these threats, then it would one day face the necessity of having to pull its own head out of the noose, because Moscow . . . also does not want war.[29]

Conservative all-German nationalism was accompanied by an assertive perspective on *West German* rights of *Alleinvertretung* ("sole representation") regarding Germany as a whole. The ("so-called") GDR was to be treated as an illegitimate pariah "state."[30] Reunification was envisioned as the result of a combination of West German ideological and economic "magnetism" and military strength, for some extremists even involving explicit demonstrations of force.

A basic division developed within the conservative camp, however. For some, the pursuit of reunification became militant and unilateralist to the point that it began to hark back to the spectre of a possibly aggressive German international *Sonderweg*. But for most, German reunification was to be achieved on the basis of *Westpolitik*, integration, and West German international reliability. During the Cold War, the FRG's *Westpolitik* could count on fairly broad conservative support, inasmuch as it was seen as compatible with a militantly revisionist pursuit of reunification. The mitigation of the Cold War, however, along with the relative stabilization of the European status quo and the increased decoupling of detente and German reunification in Western policy, led to fundamental disagreement between hard-line conservatives, who continued to adhere to Cold War–oriented revisionism, and more moderate conservatives, who began to urge careful adjustment to new circumstances.

The more liberal type of West German nationalism came to be represented especially by the SPD, although it was also in evidence on the CDU and FDP "left" (more moderate) wings. It was a type of nationalism that most clearly represented a sense of reaction to the German past. Although dedicated to the restoration of national unity and the defense of the German right of self-determination, it turned into a nationalism that differed considerably from its conservative opposite. This more "liberal" nationalism in the FRG was tied to visions of a radically, or at least quite substantially, new type of German nationhood and society, generally along liberal-democratic or democratic-socialist lines. Thus the 1956 SPD party conference declared: "The German Social-Democratic Party stands for a socialistic reorganization of Germany, of which democracy will be an inalienable component. The SPD refuses to make the internal order of a reunified Germany subservient to foreign interests and commands."[31]

SPD nationalism, whether focused on German reunification or the FRG's international emancipation, was part of a persistent Social Democratic internationalism. Throughout the postwar era, the pursuit of German interests was not seen as incompatible with far-reaching forms of integration, provided that such integration was not defined in conservative terms and did not hinder peace, detente, and possible reunification. The national assertiveness of the SPD, particularly during the Cold War, gave expression to the party's ideological self-image as a truly national democratic alternative to both the far Left, including the East German Socialist Unity Party (SED), and the Right, and as a representative of a new Europe that would surmount old nationalist divisions. Some of these sentiments were well expressed by SPD member of parliament Horst Ehmke in a 1979 essay:

> We must start from the assumption, shared by our compatriots in the GDR, that progress on the German Question can only be achieved in conjunction with a pursuit of a policy of peace and detente. It was a policy of small steps instead of big words which has made the boundary running through Germany and Europe more permeable, a boundary that not so long ago was called the "Iron Curtain." It was the policy of detente that has brought the Germans in East and West back together. . . . After the collapse of the Nazi regime German Social Democracy, based on its democratic tradition, has become a decisive political force in the Federal Republic, even though the restoration-oriented policy of the allies and of Konrad Adenauer in a context of Cold War made it difficult for the SPD to carry through [successfully]. Today democratic socialism is gaining increased weight and influence in Europe and in the world, because this democratic socialism has sought to pose and answer most decisively the central political question of our [human] community, . . . namely the economic liberation of the moral and political person.[32]

Compared with German conservatives, whose nationalism was part of a hardline Cold War posture, Social Democrats proved more able to reconcile national dreams with the realities of international detente and European "normalization." This was partly the result of a compatible tradition of socialist internationalism, which helped reduce nationalist emotions, and partly the consequence of a sense of resignation regarding Germany's historical failure and fate that is not uncommon to the German Left.[33]

Nevertheless, national German perspectives were quite prominent in evolving SPD conceptions regarding *Ostpolitik*. A leading SPD politician could say without hesitation in 1967:

> Let me say this openly: It is no expression of a reactionary nationalism, more than twenty years after the end of the war, when we speak out with self-confidence and dignity in order to advocate our [German] interests. This is our right and our duty. If we did not, we would endanger the process of recovery of the [German] people.[34]

But a dedication to peace and freedom led the SPD, since at least the early 1960s, to deemphasize a revisionist nationalism and focus on conceptions of coexistence and a European *Friedensordnung* (peace order), involving a degree of intra-German reconciliation and rapprochement based on current realities that went far beyond what conservative West German nationalism would permit.

The German Question was essentially redefined as a European Question.[35] Detente was considered to be the best way in which a sense of German nationhood could be preserved, and perhaps even restored at some point in the more distant future. As a result, the distinction between the SPD and the CDU in this respect was quite noticeable. Whereas the traditional CDU *Junktim* (linkage) held that detente in Europe would depend on progress regarding the solution of the German reunification question, the SPD and most of the FDP began to reverse this in the 1960s: the German Question could only be solved within a framework of detente. Thus, in 1967, Brandt suggested that

> [t]he fate of Germany is affected in a very special way by the division of Europe. We, who are responsible for German policy at this point in time, wish to dedicate ourselves with all our energy to a policy which aims at overcoming the division of Europe and which lays the foundations for a lasting European "peace order." A lasting European peace order will also contain a united Germany. It is a matter of historical experience that an enforced division does not break a people's will to national unity. . . . Statesmanlike wisdom will be attuned to the fact that it is impossible in the long run to keep a great people in the heart of Europe divided when we wish to remove tensions, heal unhealthy conditions, and achieve constructive cooperation among European peoples through peaceful coexistence.[36]

A desire to overcome a Cold War–oriented Germanocentric foreign policy induced visions of a shared East-West German interest as detente-bridge between East and West. As Brandt put it in 1966: "For centuries Germany was a bridge between Western and Eastern Europe. We would like to take up that role again."[37] Alliance loyalty and acceptance of established Western integration were supplemented with an active policy of reconciliation with Eastern Europe.

SPD attitudes with respect to detente thus began to involve a negative and positive national perspective. On the one hand, there was a desire to eliminate a Germanocentric foreign policy controlled by revisionist, peace-endangering nationalism. On the other hand, there was a search for a detente framework that would permit a continued sense of German identity and nationhood in the face of dim reunification prospects.

As far as FRG-oriented assertiveness is concerned, the more liberal type of West German nationalism shared with conservatives a deep interest in the Federal Republic's international emancipation and a restoration of sovereignty. SPD nationalist assertiveness was informed by a good deal of "egalitarian" internationalism: German equality was to be a prerequisite for any West German participation in integration schemes.[38] This assertiveness was noticeable in a 1950 speech by SPD leader Kurt Schumacher amid the controversy over West German rearmament within a Western alliance context:

> Equal treatment is still a goal that we must achieve. . . . No country can serve as defense for other countries. Military defense is only possible on the basis of mutuality. Yet what is being expected of us [West Germans] thus far in the conception [of rearmament] is [acceptance of] inequality, the practical inequality of the victim, an inequality in the area of risk, an inequality of chance for our people vis-à-vis other peoples. But for the Germans only a factual equality and an insolubility of ties and interdependence with other nations constitutes the positive precondition [for rearmament].[39]

We have already had occasion to note, however, that West German foreign policy culture experienced a profound development away from an older Germanocentric nationalism in the direction of increased internationalism.[40] Some public opinion data show this trend quite dramatically. In 1965, poll data showed that 69 percent of the West German population considered unification with the GDR "very important," while only 24 percent declared European integration to be "very important" and 7 percent had no opinion or did not want to answer. By 1973, the percentage of those who felt that unification with the GDR was very important had dropped significantly, to 23 percent, while 65 percent emphasized the importance of European integration and 12 percent had no opinion. And by 1983, the importance of unification had grown again in public opinion, now reaching 36 percent, but a very solid majority of 60 percent still placed greater importance on issues of European integration, while a much smaller percentage than before (3 percent) had no opinion.[41]

An important fact that must be kept in mind in this context is that this German development was part of a broader European transformation in foreign policy thinking after World War II. The experience of utter defeat, occupation, and national fragmentation gave particular expression in West Germany to tendencies that could also be encountered elsewhere. The upheaval of World War II undermined European self-confidence and international prestige and power. After two devastating world wars, and in the context of new aggregates of international power, nationalism as an ideology and the nation-state as a frame of reference and political action appeared to have lost a great deal of their former legitimacy and adequacy.

It was in this political and psychological climate that internationalist orientations became increasingly salient. These orientations were generally of two basic kinds. On the one hand, there was a greater dedication to various forms of international communication and cooperation, both within Europe and between Europe and the rest of the world, tied to a growing sense of interdependence among nations, but without major reductions in the prerogatives of national sovereignty. On the other hand, there were visions of supranational cooperation based on a considerable degree of integration, implying a notable diminution of national sovereignty. In order to distinguish between these two kinds of internationalism, one might refer to them as general internationalism (or intergovernmentalism) and supranationalism, respectively.

Incidentally, it should be stressed that a frequent emphasis on "interdependence" in West German foreign policy culture coexisted with the inescapable reality of security dependence (especially on the United States, of course). Insofar as the latter was an inherently undesirable condition, reference to the former could at times amount to a mental escapism. In that case, emphasis on the idea of "interdependence" was meant (1) to enhance West Germany's equality in its quest for international rehabilitation, (2) to emphasize equality between (U.S.) patron and (West German) client despite obvious dimensions of inequality, and (3) to reduce the need for and obscure the reality of independent foreign policy initiatives by a state whose recent history had left its political leadership and mass public with a profound sensitivity to the independent exercise of national power. The coexistence of the ideals of interdependence and the constraints of real dependence was responsible for a persistent tension in West German foreign policy culture.

In the postwar European environment of which the FRG formed a part, three conceptions for the ordering of transatlantic relations existed, two of which had explicit supranational implications.[42] First, there was the idea of *Atlantica*, based on a vision of Free World solidarity and involving close European-U.S. cooperation and even partial integration. This conception was most clearly visible in NATO and to a lesser extent in the Marshall Plan. Second, there was the dream of *Europa*, based on far-reaching Western European union, preferably leading to a European position as independent Atlantic partner of the United States. Third, there was a tendency of *Euro-nationalism*, often associated with conservatives (especially Gaullists), which combined European assertiveness directed at both the United States and the Soviet Union with a basic rejection of many forms of integration and a continued attachment to a more exclusively national policy focus. In reality, Western European internationalist thinking and supranational institutions consistently reflected a combination and interaction of these three basic conceptions. Moreover, the postwar period witnessed a notable decline over time of supranational idealism, with an attendant resurgence of more "neonational" perspectives.[43]

Aside from international constraints on a new German *Machtpolitik*, there was a clear German philosophical reaction against the nationalist excesses of the past, coupled with a desire to embed a new Germany in a more internationalist network of relations.[44] Throughout the postwar period, West Germany became one of the most ardent supporters of a great variety of international integration and organization schemes.

It should also be stressed that the new FRG did not enjoy full choice as far as Western integration was concerned. Given the prevalence of Europeanist and Atlanticist idealism elsewhere in Western Europe, and the consequences of allied control and planning, West German cooperation in integration processes was at times more a matter of necessity and *Anpassung* than of choice and opportunity.[45] The basic realities were well captured by Adenauer in 1952, as debate continued in the new Federal Republic about the various diplomatic options:

> At the present time, the Federal Republic is situated between two great colossi, on one side the Eastern [colossus], on the other side the United States and its [allies], and we are caught in the middle; we are subject to an Occupation Statute that can be completely reinstated at any moment, [we are] completely disarmed, completely defenseless and unfree. And if you think of Germany's situation along these lines and ask yourselves what the Federal Republic ought to do under these circumstances, three possibilities present themselves: 1. we stay where we are—that is, we allow ourselves to be neutralized; second possibility: we join the Eastern camp—and, my friends, I do not have to explain in these [CDU] circles what that would mean. It may suffice for me to point out that, in my view, this would mean the demise of the German people, insofar as we conceive of this people. If, then, we refuse to go this route, we are left with no other option but to join the West. And we have succeeded in making the West interested in joining its efforts with ours in order to bring about a reunification of Germany in freedom.[46]

In addition, it is significant to note that Western integration turned out to be highly beneficial to the FRG, inasmuch as it had four crucial *functions*: It provided a framework for successful economic reconstruction and resurgence; it opened possibilities for political emancipation and rehabilitation; it helped give the new state a sense of identity; and it provided the Federal Republic with basic security guarantees.[47] Insofar as the value of these benefits was realized, supranationalism became a key facet of West German foreign policy culture.

A related issue in this context is the extent to which postwar West German supranationalism was genuine or merely instrumental, that is, subservient to basically national priorities. This in turn raised the general question of the interplay of nationalist and supranationalist motivations in West German foreign policy postures. To what extent could integrated European frameworks, especially in the security area, be considered vehicles by certain German groups (for example, some of the expellee organizations) for the recovery of German power and the pursuit of revisionist West German claims against the East? Throughout the postwar era, however, prominent West German politicians warned against the temptation of subordinating international cooperation and supranational integration to narrower national objectives. In 1963, for example, Foreign Minister Gerhard Schröder said:

> Europe has only one choice: either it remains stuck in patterns of thought oriented toward national states . . . or it pools national forces [and resources]. . . . This is not to suggest that national interests and national characteristics should be neglected or destroyed. Nations will not vanish without a trace in a united Europe, but instead they will serve transcendent ideas, namely freedom, peace, and a just order of peoples with equal rights.[48]

The moral had remained very much the same for a fully resurgent West Germany in 1976, when Foreign Minister Genscher suggested that

> [a]n increased [West German] responsibility, especially for European unification, corresponds with the increased [international] weight of the Federal Republic. We take on this responsibility—without "self-overestimation" [*Selbstüberschätzung*] but also without an inferiority complex. We see ourselves as a country that is embedded in the European Community and in the Atlantic Alliance.[49]

The issue was clearly of enduring importance, since it resurfaced during 1989 and 1990 in the form of Western concern about a possible West German preoccupation with national reunification at the expense of further European integration.

A survey of postwar West German diplomacy yields striking evidence of various types of internationalism, some with notable supranational features, that were present in West German foreign policy culture. According to Hans-Peter Schwarz, these three types crystallized quite clearly by the 1950s:

> [F]irst, a European internationalism, oriented toward the goal of integration. Second, a liberal, free enterprise oriented "internationalism" with strong Atlanticist components. Third, a left-liberal and social-democratic kind of internationalism with its traditional support for global international organizations, collective security systems, global disarmament and detente policies, humanitarian development assistance, and decolonization.[50]

Perhaps the most consistently dominant type was a supranationalist focus on Western European integration.[51] This was the central component in Adenauer's *Westpolitik*, and was especially supported by the CDU/CSU. In the context of the Cold War and uncertain reunification prospects, it was particularly this type of integration that fulfilled most directly the four functions mentioned above. West German participation was aimed at securing a restoration of German sovereignty and (at least formal) Western support for German reunification, and was promoted by a mixed Liberal-Conservative *Abendland* ideology. Insofar as European integration was clearly beneficial to West German economic, political, and security interests, there were obvious instrumental, not just philosophical, considerations at the root of German attitudes. National and supranational orientations mixed.[52]

A related type of internationalism centered on a more neo-Liberal Atlantic vision, equally anti-Communist and animated by a conception of a Free World of which a uniting Europe would be part. There was also a heavy emphasis on the importance of free trade. Where ideas of a united Europe were placed in an Atlantic context, the European and Atlantic visions were quite compatible. Such compatibility did not exist, however, whenever the notion of European unity was tied to ambitions for an independent European superpower alongside the United States and the Soviet Union.

Another source of tension emerged in the 1960s. The Euro-Atlantic focus of Adenauer's *Westpolitik* was essentially dependent on the political and ideological environment of the Cold War, whereby integration was made serviceable to West German interests, especially reunification. Increased detente and declining European supranationalism exposed the illusions with respect to reunification that had been part of earlier *Westpolitik*. Conservative West German Europeanists became entangled in a neonationalist Gaullism, while Liberal Atlanticists and Social Democratic internationalists experienced a considerable convergence in pursuit of a new, post–Cold War *Ostpolitik*. The Cold War flavor of previous *Westpolitik* clearly slipped into the background.[53]

A rather different kind of internationalism existed on the German Left, rooted in traditions of socialist internationalist solidarity and a notable degree of pacifism. The Cold War prevented realization of the idea of a confederal, socialist pan-Europe in which nations would have retained a good deal of sovereignty, and which was meant to be a third force between U.S. capitalism and Soviet Communism.[54] Instead, the foreign policy cultural convergence of Social Democrats and "left-wing" Free Democrats gave rise to a "social-liberal" internationalism focused on disarmament and arms control, Third World development, East-West detente (based on Western security arrangements), and international organization. Some went further and advocated some form of collective security for all of Europe.[55] This social-liberal internationalism still contained a clear Atlantic component, based on a mixture of ideological conviction and pragmatic necessity. In this perspective, *Westpolitik* and *Ostpolitik* would be fully complementary.[56]

As far as Western integration is concerned, the SPD was at first critical with regard to its apparently damaging impact on the chances for German reunification. In addition, Social Democrats tended to reject the capitalist, small-European, "militarist," Cold War–oriented aspects of CDU *Westpolitik*. To some extent, visions of a fully integrated European Community tended to fade in SPD foreign policy thinking as the years went by, in favor of ideas for a broader European "peace order" based on detente and joint East-West security arrangements.[57]

Over time, the SPD and the CDU developed a considerable degree of consensus with respect to the importance of European integration and Atlantic community building, despite almost constant interparty rhetoric, but the exact relation between *Westpolitik* and *Ostpolitik* continued to lead to clearly different perspectives. The SPD tended to see greater compatibility than the CDU. It should also be remembered that attitudes in both parties were by no means homogeneous. The CDU appeared to split into a prodetente, pro-Atlantic liberal wing and an antidetente, pro-Atlantic conservative wing, with many mixtures and shades in between.[58] The SPD became fragmented due to a moderate branch oriented to a detente-plus-security approach, and a more radical prodetente and prodisarmament left wing, part of which split off to help create the Green Party. West German supranationalism and internationalism thus constituted a complex phenomenon: both constant and changing over time, fragmented among and within parties and sectors of West German society, and in persistent interplay with nationally oriented attitudes and interests.

The various forms of West German internationalism were significantly shaped and affected by external developments and constraints. The relative drifting apart of Western Europe and the United States, the seeming decline of supranational sentiment in Western Europe, the reemergence of nationalist attitudes, and the buildup of detente contacts between Western and Eastern Europe, all after the latter part of the 1960s, served to pose anew the perennial question of Germany's position, role, and status in international affairs. As the forces of Europeanist and Atlanticist supranationalism waned in strength, West Germany began to face once again the thorny problem of its identity.

In a Europe of self-conscious nations, the FRG could not (yet) be a "normal" nation. One of the key functions that Western integration had had for the Federal Republic, namely the development of a clearer identity and role, was thus partially undermined. In the context of the new *Ostpolitik* of the 1970s, these developments were conducive to uneasy attempts by West Germany to find elements of common German interest and identity in its relations with the GDR. Those attempts in turn at times heightened a Rapallo-like concern among the FRG's partners about possible deals between the Federal Republic and the Soviet Union, as well as a resurgence of German nationalism, in spite of assertions by government leaders like Brandt that "[i]n the Federal Republic of Germany there is not a single question of any importance that could be treated outside the context of American-European relations."[59]

Yet altogether the established Europeanist and Atlanticist foreign policy ortho-
doxies remained dominant. West German dependence on the Atlantic security
framework in many ways persisted undiminished. Most West Germans continued to favor further European integration in conjunction with an active *Ostpolitik.* Supranational institutions remained crucial for FRG foreign policy as a guarantee of West German international political emancipation and status, as a
means to prevent renewed German international isolation, and as a shield behind
which increased West German power could be unobtrusively and effectively
wielded. With regard to the latter point, Jim Cloos pointed to "the exacerbated
susceptibility [that is, sensitivity] of certain countries with respect to every even
slightly controversial German position." As a consequence, he suggested, "the
FRG takes voluntary refuge behind the European façade when a position must be
taken on an international problem that is of direct interest to the FRG."[60]

Security and the Military

We conclude this chapter with an exploration of the importance of military security issues in West German foreign policy thinking after 1949. According to
Walter F. Hahn,

> more than any other European people (with the possible exception of the Russians)
> the Germans are captives of history and geography. Situated in the vulnerable trough
> of Europe, they have always grappled with the question of how to cope with insecu-
> rity: whether to turn to the East, to the West or go it alone, whether to achieve secu-
> rity through passive accommodation or assertive power.[61]

In order to understand post-1949 West German attitudes in the area of national
security, military affairs, and war and peace generally, we must consider Germany's past experience *and* postwar international setting.[62] Broadly speaking,
two issue-areas can be distinguished. The first is the problem of the legacy of
German militarism in the relation between the military establishment and the
political system in West German democracy. The second is the definition of
proper security policies in the face of past failures and present needs and possibilities.

There is little doubt that a powerful militarist ethos pervaded German diplomacy and national life after 1871, but also earlier, in the case of Prussia. From a
cultural point of view, German militarism was partially rooted in the glorifica-
tion of struggle, war, and heroism that could be encountered during the Romantic era, very much in contrast with the antimilitarist rationalism of the Enlightenment.[63] As far as German foreign policy was concerned, this ethos expressed
itself in the assertive, nationalistic style and aggressive impulses that characterized German international behavior, especially during the Wilhelmine and Nazi
eras.

The connections between militarism, nationalism, and darwinism were by no means unique to Germany, and could be found elsewhere in Europe as well. Yet German militarism acquired its particular character and vigor as a result of the Prussian martial tradition, the military way in which German unity was achieved, compensatory assertiveness generated by international parvenu status, and the survival of traditional, illiberal elites in the industrializing *Reich*. Nationalism, illiberalism, and militarism formed a closely related ideological triangle in traditional Germany. The failure of German Liberalism extended to the military establishment: Military reforms of the Gneisenau/Scharnhorst/Hardenberg period in the early nineteenth century were not sustained, and the military remained the bulwark of an antidemocratic and often antimodern Conservatism.

Within German society, militarism constituted a pattern of orientations in which many values centered on war, violence, conflict, heroism, duty, order, and sacrifice. According to Emilio Willems,

> [i]n order to understand the nature of militarism, one might conceive of it as a *Kulturkomplex*, that is, as an aggregate of inter-connected elements that derive their meaning and function from a dominant core element. The core or focal point of militarism is war and the application of organized violence, respectively, as the best or only means to solve international and certain types of domestic conflicts and thereby to realize specific political goals.[64]

Military prestige was in many ways dependent on civilian admiration and promotion of martial values. The military establishment tended to see itself as the *Schule der Nation* ("school of the nation"), thus becoming a key pillar in the traditional sociopolitical order. The role of the military extended from foreign policy to domestic politics, where it had a prominent social function as *Ordnungsfaktor* ("guarantor of order") in Germany's polarized political life.[65]

Due to its social pervasiveness, historical German militarism should be seen, perhaps, as both a military and civilian phenomenon. According to Wolfgang Sauer, the political consequences were both "peculiar" and fateful:

> The peculiarity of the German system of government consisted therefore—both in the [Second] Empire as well as in the [Weimar] Republic—of two clearly separated elements, namely, the then existing institutions based on law and order but politically weak, and under or behind these, a concealed military "State within the State," as a hard core or stabilizing factor of the whole system. It is without doubt a proof of the cautiousness and intelligence of the German generals that they renounced making forthright bids for power. Only thus was it possible for the dual system to survive for such a long time. But undoubtedly this created a society too full of pretense and illusion to overcome the German crises; the reaffirmation of this system at all turning points of modern German history slowly undermined both the civil as well as the military institutions and made them ready for Hitler's coming to power.[66]

In view of this troubled, antidemocratic military legacy, coupled with total defeat in World War II, it is not surprising that a considerably antimilitary, and at times even explicitly pacifist, reaction ensued in Germany after 1945. Domestic German sensitivity concerning military power and its possible impact on a fledgling West German democracy, with Weimar memories still fairly fresh, was amply matched by international concerns about potential German militarist revisionism in the face of a more or less lasting national division.[67] Yet the exigencies of the Cold War also made some form of West German rearmament inevitable. This led to major controversy in West German society, with the CDU/CSU and the SPD as key political protagonists.

For the CDU/CSU, rearmament was both a matter of no-choice realism and a vital aspect of a Cold War–oriented *Politik der Stärke* aimed at forcing the Soviet Union into a pro-Western solution of the German Question. Thus Adenauer could argue in 1950 that "the reunification with our German brothers and sisters in the Soviet zone [GDR] could be achieved by means of the creation of [a] defensive front [*Abwehrfront*] [of the West against the USSR]."[68] It was also seen as an ideal way to enhance West German sovereignty and international status, by making the FRG an indispensable partner in the Western alliance. Adenauer concluded:

> The Federal government believes that the German Federal Republic, when requested by the Western powers, should be willing to make a fitting contribution to the creation of this [anti-Communist] defensive front, in order to guarantee [the FRG's] survival, the freedom of its citizens, and the continued vitality of Western cultural ideals. Precondition for such a contribution [by the FRG] is the completely equal status of Germany in this defensive front compared with the other participating powers, and also [the creation of] a defensive front with sufficient strength to make any Russian aggression impossible.[69]

Hence, for the CDU/CSU the issue of rearmament was not so much a matter of "if" but "how," focused on the creation of a new, democratic military and the insurance of adequate political control.

SPD attitudes were considerably more ambivalent, to say the least. For one thing, the SPD had to come to terms with a historically deeply rooted German Social Democratic distaste for and alienation from the military establishment. In addition, for the SPD rearmament represented a threat to Germany's new democracy ("If Germany embarks on the road to rearmament, the entire political and social life in the Federal Republic would be fundamentally altered"[70]), to German reunification, and to international peace. Rather than enhancing West German sovereignty, rearmament was seen as a reinforcement of West German international inequality, by turning the Germans into the foot soldiers of the Cold War and a possible World War III. Or, as SPD leader Schumacher put it in 1950, "Europe cannot be the forward-based defense-belt for America, and Germany cannot be the forward-based defense-belt for other European states."[71] He concluded:

> The consequences of a [West German] participation in the military rearmament of the Western world must under present circumstances and conditions be seen as unequivocally negative. Contrary to a widespread illusion a German military contribution within the framework of what is currently possible and what is desired by the Allies can in no way guard Germany against its fate of becoming a "war-zone."[72]

Throughout the 1950s, the Social Democrats resisted the security policy pursued by the CDU government. At a national party conference in Berlin in 1954, the SPD defined its position in a very prominent way:

> The Social Democratic Party calls for energetic efforts by the Western world to strive for negotiations with the current Soviet sphere of influence concerning the creation of regional security systems within the framework of the UN Charter. Within a comprehensive system of collective security a reunified Germany should also make its contribution to the maintenance of peace on a basis of equal rights and equal risks. Therefore, the Social Democrats urge the [government of the] Federal Republic to champion steadfastly the conduct of further negotiations by the great powers, whereby European security and German reunification should be treated as interconnected tasks. The tight integration of the [two] parts of Germany, divided by the occupation powers, into western and eastern alliance systems would make the continuation of the Cold War inevitable and increase the threat to peace.[73]

This strong declaration was followed, however, by an enumeration of those conditions under which the SPD might yet assent to a West German rearmament: continued focus on reunification, continued pursuit of a collective security system, invalidity of treaty obligations that might block reunification, equal treatment, and democratic-parliamentary control over the new military. Indeed, in the course of time, the SPD resigned itself to the reality of rearmament, and joined other West German parties in ensuring the democratic reliability of the new *Bundeswehr*.

Beginning in the 1950s, there was a double focus in efforts to create a new, democratic military establishment.[74] On the one hand, there was persistent attention to questions of civil-military relations. In view of the German past, extensive arrangements were made to guarantee democratic political control over the military and prevent the reemergence of a military *Staat im Staate* ("state within the state").[75] Domestic political control was matched by controls generated by the FRG's military integration into NATO. On the other hand, there was a focus on the ideological orientation and democratic reliability of the individual soldier.[76] This effort centered on the notions of *Staatsbürger in Uniform* (citizen in uniform) and *Innere Führung* ("inner, personal leadership"), whereby military loyalty to democratic values and the democratic political order was to be accompanied by civilian support for the military contribution in the ideological Cold War between the Soviet Union and the Free World. The German soldier was no longer to be an apolitical tool in the hands of the state.

The creation of a new military in West Germany after 1949 was burdened not only by the need for democratization but also by the related problem of an effective military tradition. German history is marred by discontinuity and tragedy, and by Liberal failures and militarist excesses, all of which have rendered more difficult the task of deciding on the appropriate content of an acceptable military tradition.[77] The problem of military tradition in West Germany tended to be focused more on the reconciliation of an illiberal military past with present democratic requirements than on those specifically martial virtues, such as duty, loyalty, and courage, that have existed throughout modern German history. Seen from this angle, the question of German military tradition was merely one more aspect of the broader political transformation in Germany after World War II. German history was reevaluated in a context of new needs and realities.

It is against the background of this historical legacy that post-1949 West German security policy must be analyzed. At the same time, we must see such policy as a reflection of West Germany's postwar geostrategic and political predicament, involving an exposed location, national division, dependence on Western security guarantees, lingering foreign controls of various kinds, and so forth. There are probably few countries in the world that have been more preoccupied with security questions than the FRG. In fact, Alfred Grosser pointed to the West German "desire for security" during the Cold War and suggested that, "in spite of all appearances, from the beginning it is not European unity and not German reunification, but security that has absolute priority in German foreign policy."[78] Yet this constant pursuit of security confronted West Germany with a variety of inner contradictions, the intractability of which formed an important part of West German foreign policy culture.

Thus we encounter tensions between antimilitary sentiment and the need for rearmament and an active security policy in the 1950s, the enhancement of West German security at the expense of national reunification throughout the Cold War era, dependence on the U.S. security guarantee at the expense of more independent European defense options, and a conflict between Western integration and reunification-through-disengagement. Europeanist and Atlanticist security visions were at times clearly incompatible.

West German ambivalence and anxiety regarding the relation between defense, deterrence, and detente was particularly noteworthy. In this respect, the Federal Republic joined the other European NATO allies in a set of orientations that were frequently quite distinct from prevailing U.S. strategic thinking, particularly with respect to the role of nuclear weapons in NATO defense policy. Hahn pointed to some of these differences and tensions when he wrote in 1975:

Almost from the inception of NATO, Americans and Europeans (the West Germans included) reached basic agreement on the two principal pillars of alliance strategy: deterrence and "forward defense." Deterrence implied that the potential enemy was to be dissuaded from aggression by a NATO posture that would make it clear that the risks entailed by attack outweighed any foreseeable advantages to be gained. "Forward defense" meant that if deterrence crumbled, the enemy's attacking armies were to be met and contained as far to the east on NATO territory as possible. . . . United States policy in NATO generally has leaned on a concept in which effective deterrence is more or less equated with effective defense. . . . The West German view, which evolved after 1950, has been markedly different. Apprehensive of the new and formidable danger from the East, the West Germans eagerly entered into the alliance offered by the United States. Almost from the beginning, however, deterrence was equated with the American commitment to Europe, particularly with the nuclear commitment. . . . The ups and downs in U.S.–West German relations since 1955 [when the FRG entered NATO] can be correlated in a meaningful way with vacillating West German faith in the credibility of the American guarantee and of the U.S. strategic nuclear deterrent.[79]

Hahn argued that the end result of these nuclear dilemmas had been a notable West German ambiguity regarding nuclear weapons over the years, especially short-range or battlefield nuclear weapons that would primarily affect German territory:

For purposes of deterrence, West German planners . . . would like a reasonably low nuclear threshold, at least as seen from the vantage point of the potential adversary. For purposes of actual warfare, however, they would like a much higher threshold. They know that they cannot have it both ways. The only answer, therefore, is to keep the weapons but to remain as ambiguous as possible with regard to their use in a conflict contingency.[80]

The dramatic 1989–1991 transformation of East-Central Europe brought about a significant alteration of the FRG's Cold War security environment, of course, permitting a striking diminution of traditional West German anxieties. The collapse of Communism and the Warsaw Pact in Eastern Europe, the disappearance of the Soviet military threat, coupled with successful East-West conventional arms control agreements, and the unification of the two German states necessitated profound adjustment in NATO doctrine and strategy. Throughout 1990, the Western alliance tried to come to grips with the implications of these revolutionary European changes. As the months passed, a reduced emphasis on the (first) use of nuclear weapons in NATO's flexible response strategy, a considerable reduction of conventional forces in Europe (including a numerical ceiling on the all-German army), and an increased interest in utilizing the Conference on Security and Cooperation in Europe (CSCE) became the hallmarks of a rapidly changing security environment. Even more far-reaching changes soon followed. We return to these issues in Chapters 7 and 9.

Throughout the postwar period, additional tensions existed between a West German pursuit of sovereignty and international equality on the one hand, and security needs and continued forms of allied control on the other hand. West German security policy had to be formulated in full awareness of persisting international sensitivity regarding German power and intentions. The need for West German realism and *Anpassung* was repeatedly at odds with a variety of ideals and illusions that were simply beyond realization. The FRG underwent a major role change, from defeated enemy to key ally, but the shadows of the past continued to affect its alliance status. The realities of security dependence produced attitudes of clientelistic loyalty *and* emancipatory assertiveness that could be repeatedly detected in West German national security debates. Additional problems were caused by the fact that West German security policy became essentially dependent on, or was made to be a function of, East-West relations in general, and Soviet-U.S. relations in particular.

Policies formulated on the basis of this kind of dependence also tended to take on a life and momentum of their own, however. Thus the FRG's initial diplomatic posture, dependent on East-West Cold War, persisted even when international detente efforts were under way. And West German diplomatic dependence on detente continued undiminished in the "postdetente" era of the early 1980s, leading some analysts to point to a "new German Question," namely, a special interest on the part of the FRG (and the GDR) in preserving the benefits of the *Deutschlandpolitik* of the 1970s in an internationally less favorable climate. Richard Löwenthal, for example, concluded:

> For the first time in modern history, then, what appears as the German Question has taken the form of an almost desperate desire for peace by the German people in West and East—a desire strong enough to exert major pressure on the foreign policies of both governments. It is *not* a pressure for leaving their respective alliances, but rather for attempting to influence the superpowers that lead them.[81]

Thus, circumstances of dependence, expressive of multiple forms of vulnerability, tended to induce a constant element of uncertainty, fear, and even paranoia in West German security orientations.

The security predicament and corresponding attitudes, as sketched in this chapter, characterized West Germany throughout its forty-year history. In one way or another, the major West German political parties had to deal with the same predicament, thereby sometimes developing very similar attitudes. Yet, we have seen repeatedly that major differences existed between the two largest parties, the CDU/CSU and the SPD. Each of these parties also experienced an evolution in orientations over time, and neither was free of intraparty disagreements.

In general, it can be argued that the security attitudes of the CDU/CSU, especially its powerful conservative wing, were most Cold War–oriented.[82] The pursuit of *Westpolitik*, as conceived by the CDU, entailed a fundamental Atlanticist orthodoxy, involving loyalty to the alliance, dependence on the United States, strong anti-Communism, a *Politik der Stärke* vis-à-vis the East, fear of West German political-military isolation, a rejection of neutralist ideas, a vigorous promotion of European integration, and an emphasis on security before reunification. Thus, Strauß spoke for many CDU/CSU conservatives in 1976 when he denounced the "anti-Western nationalism" of the SPD, pointed to both a continued "expansion of Communist imperialism" in spite of detente efforts and the dangers of a "detente policy pursued unilaterally by the West," emphasized that "only strength can guarantee the peace," and concluded by suggesting that "our country and free Europe as a whole find themselves in a condition of continuing internal and external danger" leading to the "dramatic alternative of a demise with a loss of freedom or survival in liberty"—a choice between "freedom or socialism."[83]

In contrast, SPD national security attitudes were more frequently detente-oriented, as we have noted before. The Social Democrats favored policy initiatives that would help overcome the division of Germany and Europe, such as disengagement zones, nuclear-free zones, possible German military neutrality, a European collective security system, and various other disarmament schemes. The SPD's anti-Communism had more ideological than military connotations. Although by no means fully pacifist, the SPD was wary of a potential revival of German militarism and very sensitive with respect to nuclear weapons and the arms race. At various times the SPD tended to see NATO as essentially a Cold War institution, and as an instrument aimed at the international control, and thus unequal treatment, of (West) Germany. Although the focus on reunification had all but disappeared by the 1980s, if not earlier, the emphasis on security based on a mixture of deterrence and detente remained.[84]

There were clear intraparty differences within the SPD, however. Schumacher's more Cold War–oriented views were replaced by a greater focus on detente and increased pacifist sentiment regarding rearmament around 1952–1955 and regarding nuclear weapons in the late 1950s and particularly in the 1980s. The late 1950s and the 1960s witnessed the rise of the SPD's "right wing," with politicians like Fritz Erler and Helmut Schmidt as leading proponents of a greater realism, focused on NATO loyalty, balance-of-power and deterrence factors, and pragmatic detente efforts. They helped prepare the way for SPD *Anpassung* to the CDU's *Westpolitik* and a considerable philosophical convergence between the two parties with respect to basic national security questions, even though great differences remained regarding *Ostpolitik*. But a more radically pacifist left wing continued to exist, especially centered around Brandt, in conjunction with the rise of the Green party and the renewed appearance of various protest movements.

*   *   *

These reflections on developments in postwar West German thinking in the area of security matters and military tradition bring to a conclusion our survey of those factors that must lie at the core of any exploration of the German Question as it existed at least until the 1980s, if not beyond. Among these would be Germany's experience of historical discontinuity, the illiberal aspects of its sociopolitical tradition, its enduring identity problem, the Nazi legacy, and the new orientations of post-1949 West (and East) Germany.

Prior to the astounding events of 1989–1990, however, a number of additional developments occurred in West Germany, and in its increasingly close relations with the GDR amid a renewed atmosphere of Cold War, that necessitate closer examination. Many observers spoke of a new German Question, and raised "new questions" about the course of West German domestic politics and foreign policy. It is to these issues that we now turn.

Notes

1. On Conservative attitudes in the new FRG, see Wolfram F. Hanrieder, *The Stable Crisis* (New York: Harper & Row, 1970), p. 129ff.

2. The following discussion of Conservative thinking in postwar West German foreign policy is particularly illustrated by Franz-Josef Strauß, "Die Bundesrepublik Deutschland im Kräftefeld der Weltpolitik," and Manfred Wörner, "Das sicherheitspolitische Konzept der Union," both in Gerhard Mayer-Vorfelder and Hubertus Zuber, eds., *Union alternativ* (Stuttgart: Seewald Verlag, 1976); Klaus von Schubert, ed., *Sicherheitspolitik der Bundesrepublik Deutschland: Dokumentation 1945–1977* (Köln: Verlag Wissenschaft & Politik, 1978/1979), vol. I, pp. 79–83 (Adenauer), 117–123 (Adenauer), vol. II, pp. 546–550 (Strauß); Helga Haftendorn, Lothar Wilker, and Claudia Wörmann, eds., *Die Außenpolitik der Bundesrepublik Deutschland* (Berlin: Wissenschaftlicher Autoren-Verlag, 1982), pp. 367–378 (Guttenberg), 336–337 ("Antrag der CDU/CSU. . . ."); Hans-Adolf Jacobsen and Otto Stenzl, eds., *Deutschland und die Welt* (München: Deutscher Taschenbuch Verlag, 1964), pp. 263–271 (Guttenberg), 344–354 (Thedieck), 368–374 (Grewe), 379–383 (Guttenberg); Erich Eisner, *Das europäische Konzept von Franz Josef Strauß* (Meisenheim am Glan: Verlag Anton Hain, 1975).

3. Here again nationalist German calculations played a notable role, inasmuch as German power was expected to be of decisive significance in such a united Western European superpower. The weight of European power could then be made to serve the interests of the only European state (FRG) with a major revisionist foreign policy goal (reunification). Western Europe's position in the Cold War would be enhanced, and intensified Soviet-European competition in Eastern Europe would open the possibility of a revision of the outcome of World War II and the Yalta and Potsdam conferences. Older ideas of *Mitteleuropa* could partially return in a new guise.

4. Quoted in Eisner, *Das europäische Konzept von Franz Josef Strauß*, p. 45.

5. Eisner, *Das europäische Konzept von Franz Josef Strauß*, p. 46.

6. See Rudolf Schuster, "Die 'Hallstein-Doktrin,'" *Europa-Archiv*, nr. 18, 1963.

7. For a useful discussion of this issue, see Wilhelm A. Kewenig, "Die deutsche Staatsangehörigkeit—Klammer der Nation?" *Europa-Archiv*, nr. 18, 1987.

8. A good example is the infamous 1962 "Spiegel affair," which pitted Strauß (then minister of defense) against the left-liberal weekly *Der Spiegel* in a battle over national security versus freedom of the press. The issue also surfaced in the late 1960s in the context of parliamentary debate about "emergency legislation" and in the early 1970s with the promulgation of the so-called *Extremisten-Beschluß*.

9. On the rise of the SPD's "right wing," and its impact on SPD foreign policy orientations, see Abraham Ashkenasi, *Reformpartei und Außenpolitik* (Köln: Westdeutscher Verlag, 1968), especially Chapter 7.

10. Early postwar Liberal leaders often were not so supportive, or at most were purely superficial in their support. See, in Jacobsen and Stenzl, eds., *Deutschland und die Welt*, pp. 96–108 (Pfleiderer), 132–137 (Mende), 219–224 (Dehler).

11. Hans-Dietrich Genscher, *Deutsche Außenpolitik* (Stuttgart: Verlag Bonn Aktuell, 1981), p. 119.

12. On disengagement and German neutrality plans in the FDP and SPD, see Kurt Hirsch, ed., *Deutschlandpläne* (München: Rütten & Löning Verlag, 1967), pp. 261–269 (Pfleiderer) and 279–283 (the SPD's 1959 *Deutschlandplan*); Jacobsen and Stenzl, eds., *Deutschland und die Welt*, pp. 132–137 (Mende), 389–400 (Schmidt), 144–157 (Erler); Peter Brandt and Herbert Ammon, eds., *Die Linke und die nationale Frage* (Reinbek bei Hamburg: Rowohlt Taschenbuch Verlag, 1981), pp. 134–138 ("Entschließung des SPD-Parteitags . . . ") and 161–165 (Erler); Rudolf Hrbek, *Die SPD—Deutschland und Europa* (Bonn: Europa Union Verlag, 1972), Chapter 13; Kurt Klotzbach, *Der Weg zur Staatspartei* (Berlin/Bonn: Verlag J.H.W. Dietz Nachf., 1982), pp. 326–355; von Schubert, ed., *Sicherheitspolitik der Bundesrepublik Deutschland*, vol. I, pp. 515–520 (Erler).

13. Genscher, *Deutsche Außenpolitik*, p. 46.

14. See especially the speeches by Genscher in his *Deutsche Außenpolitik*, pp. 43–62, 87–104, 165–180, 207–226, 227–240, 290–305, 306–332. These developments led to growing discord between CDU conservatives and the FDP during the 1960s, since the former continued to be exponents of a Cold War–oriented foreign policy culture. It also produced the well-known split within the CDU between conservative "Gaullists," who resisted various Western detente plans, and more liberal Atlanticists, who were more supportive of Western diplomacy toward the Soviet Union.

15. Genscher, *Deutsche Außenpolitik*, p. 89.

16. Brandt and Ammon, eds., *Die Linke und die nationale Frage*, pp. 15–16.

17. The following discussion of the evolution of thinking in the SPD on issues of West German foreign and security policy is especially based upon material and commentary provided in Jacobsen and Stenzl, eds., *Deutschland und die Welt*; Brandt and Ammon, eds., *Die Linke und die nationale Frage*; Susanne Miller, *Die SPD vor und nach Godesberg* (Bonn-Bad Godesberg: Verlag Neue Gesellschaft, 1974); Willy Brandt, *Brandt—Reden 1961–65* (Köln: Verlag Wissenschaft & Politik, 1965); Haftendorn, Wilker, and Wörmann, eds., *Die Außenpolitik der Bundesrepublik Deutschland*; Ashkenasi, *Reformpartei und Außenpolitik*; Hrbek, *Die SPD—Deutschland und Europa*; Klotzbach, *Der Weg zur Staatspartei*; von Schubert, ed., *Sicherheitspolitik der Bundesrepublik Deutschland* (vols. I and II); Helga Haftendorn, *Security and Detente* (New York: Praeger Publishers, 1985); Udo Löwke, *Für den Fall, daß . . . : SPD und Wehrfrage, 1949–1955* (Hannover: Verlag für Literatur & Zeitgeschehen, 1969); Walter F. Hahn, *Between Westpolitik and Ostpolitik* (Beverly Hills/Lon-

don: Sage Publications, 1975); Alfred Grosser, *Geschichte Deutschlands seit 1945* (München: Deutscher Taschenbuch Verlag, 1979), esp. pp. 455–472; Dietmar Schössler and Erich Weede, *West German Elite Views on National Security and Foreign Policy Issues* (Königstein: Athenäum-Verlag, 1978); Willy Brandt, *Plädoyer für die Zukunft* (Frankfurt: Europäische Verlagsanstalt, 1972); Willy Brandt, *Außenpolitik, Deutschlandpolitik, Europapolitik* (Berlin: Berlin-Verlag, 1968); Helmut Schmidt, *Kontinuität und Konzentration* (Bonn-Bad Godesberg: Verlag Neue Gesellschaft, 1975).

18. Brandt, "Die Mauer als Eingeständnis der Schwäche," in Jacobsen and Stenzl, eds., *Deutschland und die Welt*, p. 273.

19. "Entschließung des SPD-Parteitags in München zur deutschen Wiedervereinigungspolitik vom 14.7.1956," in Brandt and Ammon, eds., *Die Linke und die nationale Frage*, pp. 134, 135, 136.

20. Erler, "Disengagement und Wiedervereinigung," in Jacobsen and Stenzl, eds., *Deutschland und die Welt*, pp. 145, 146. These ideas played a central role in the so-called *Deutschlandplan* presented by the SPD in 1959.

21. Brandt, "Erklärung in Erfurt am 19.3.1970 (Auszug)," in Brandt and Ammon, eds., *Die Linke und die nationale Frage*, pp. 311, 312, 313, 314.

22. See the discussion in Grosser, *Geschichte Deutschlands seit 1945*, pp. 455–472.

23. Grosser, *Geschichte Deutschlands seit 1945*, pp. 417, 418.

24. This terminology is used by Renata Fritsch-Bournazel, "La permanente quête d'une identité," in Renata Fritsch-Bournazel, André Brigot, and Jim Cloos, *Les Allemands au Coeur de l'Europe* (Paris: Fondation pour les Études de Défense Nationale, 1983).

25. Helmut Lindemann, "Überlegungen zur Bonner Deutschlandpolitik 1945 bis 1970," in Brandt and Ammon, eds., *Die Linke und die nationale Frage*, p. 302.

26. Brandt, "Bericht zur Lage der Nation vor dem Bundestag am 14.1.1970," in Brandt and Ammon, eds., *Die Linke und die nationale Frage*, pp. 302–303, 304 (emphasis in original).

27. Regarding these newer forms of *Deutschlandpolitik*, see Brandt and Ammon, eds., *Die Linke und die nationale Frage*, pp. 302–305 (Brandt), 348–350 (Bahr); some elements in Genscher, *Deutsche Außenpolitik*, pp. 290–305. Various links between a new *Ostpolitik* and a new *Deutschlandpolitik* are made by Brandt, in his *Plädoyer für die Zukunft*, pp. 30–43, 52–63, his *Brandt—Reden 1961–65*, pp. 42–66, 70–94, 98–137, and his *Außenpolitik, Deutschlandpolitik, Europapolitik*, pp. 12–19, 20–27, 40–50, 80–89, 102–118. See also Schmidt, *Kontinuität und Konzentration*, pp. 9, 15–17, 243–255; von Schubert, ed., *Sicherheitspolitik der Bundesrepublik Deutschland*, vol. II, pp. 550–553 (Bahr), 555–569 (Brandt), vol. I, pp. 273–286 (Schmidt); Jacobsen and Stenzl, eds., *Deutschland und die Welt*, pp. 189–197 (Jaspers), 197–203 (Mann).

28. F. Stephen Larrabee, "From Reunification to Reassociation: New Dimensions of the German Question," in F. Stephen Larrabee, ed., *The Two German States and European Security* (New York: St. Martin's Press, 1989), pp. 3, 29.

29. Karl Theodor Freiherr zu Guttenberg, "Keine Politik der Konzessionen," in Jacobsen and Stenzl, eds., *Deutschland und die Welt*, p. 271.

30. The SPD and CDU/CSU tended to differ about the FRG's exact legal status with respect to Germany as a whole. Whereas the CDU/CSU saw the Federal Republic as the western part of Germany, with the full right to represent all of Germany, the SPD saw the FRG as a mere *Weststaat*, with a more circumscribed claim regarding *Alleinvertretung*. See Schuster, "Die 'Hallstein-Doktrin,'" pp. 680–681. Whereas both liberal and conservative West German nationalism stressed the provisionality of the FRG, the SPD was much more willing to accept the de facto existence of two juridically equal German states as the in-

escapable reality for the foreseeable future. See, for example, Brandt and Ammon, eds., *Die Linke und die nationale Frage*, pp. 224–226 (Abendroth), 252–255 (Augstein), 258–263 ("Katechismus . . . "), 301–302 (Lindemann), 302–305 (Brandt); Haftendorn, Wilker, and Wörmann, eds., *Die Außenpolitik der Bundesrepublik Deutschland*, pp. 330–332 ("Bahr-Papier"); Schmidt, *Kontinuität und Konzentration*, p. 243ff.

31. "Entschließung des SPD-Parteitags in München zur deutschen Wiedervereinigungspolitik vom 14.7.1956," in Brandt and Ammon, eds., *Die Linke und die nationale Frage*, p. 137.

32. Horst Ehmke, "Was ist des Deutschen Vaterland?" in Brandt and Ammon, eds., *Die Linke und die nationale Frage*, pp. 355, 356.

33. In this context, see Brandt and Ammon, eds., *Die Linke und die nationale Frage*, p. 13ff. See also their essay "Patriotismus von Links," in Wolfgang Venohr, ed., *Die deutsche Einheit kommt bestimmt* (Bergisch Gladbach: Gustav Lübbe Verlag, 1982).

34. Brandt, *Außenpolitik, Deutschlandpolitik, Europapolitik*, p. 26.

35. Linking the German question with the larger European context was not an SPD invention, of course. It had been a basic element in West German foreign policy since 1949. But it is the conception of that linkage that led to political and philosophical differences between the CDU and the SPD, for example. Within the SPD itself, the linkage between Germany's fate and the larger European context was not exactly new either. In 1945, early postwar SPD leader Kurt Schumacher had said: "One cannot take care of the German problem only from a German perspective and angle. There is no German question which is not at the same time a European question." Schumacher, "Konsequenzen deutscher Politik," in Brandt and Ammon, eds., *Die Linke und die nationale Frage*, p. 66.

36. Brandt, *Außenpolitik, Deutschlandpolitik, Europapolitik*, p. 25.

37. Brandt, *Außenpolitik, Deutschlandpolitik, Europapolitik*, p. 13.

38. On SPD "egalitarian" internationalism, see, for example, Jacobsen and Stenzl, eds., *Deutschland und die Welt*, pp. 90–96 (Schumacher); Brandt and Ammon, eds., *Die Linke und die nationale Frage*, pp. 63–67 (Schumacher); Miller, *Die SPD vor und nach Godesberg*, pp. 95–100 ("Aktionsprogramm . . . "); Carlo Schmid, "Germany and Europe: The German Social Democratic Program," *Foreign Affairs*, vol. 30, nr. 4, July 1952.

39. Kurt Schumacher, "Erst Gleichberechtigung—dann Aufrüstung," in Jacobsen and Stenzl, eds., *Deutschland und die Welt*, pp. 90, 93–94.

40. Already in the 1950s, observers noted increasingly internationalist attitudes among elites and the general public, alongside lingering elements of nationalism. See Karl Deutsch and Lewis Edinger, *Germany Rejoins the Powers* (Stanford: Stanford University Press, 1959), pp. 208–212, 215–216; W. Phillips Davison, "Trends in West German Public Opinion, 1946–1956," in Hans Speier and W. Phillips Davison, eds., *West German Leadership and Foreign Policy* (Evanston, IL: Row, Peterson, 1957).

41. Poll data provided in *Die Deutsche Frage*, Heft Nr. 203 in the series "Informationen zur politischen Bildung" of the Federal Republic's Bundeszentrale für politische Bildung in Bonn, 1984, p. 2ff. Cited in Jürgen C. Hess, "Westdeutsche Suche nach nationaler Identität," in Wolfgang Michalka, ed., *Die Deutsche Frage in der Weltpolitik* (Stuttgart: Franz Steiner Verlag Wiesbaden, 1986), p. 50 (note 74).

42. See Daniel Lerner and Morton Gorden, *Euratlantica* (Cambridge, MA: MIT Press, 1969), Chapter 2. See also David Calleo, *Europe's Future: The Grand Alternatives* (New York: W. W. Norton, 1965/1967).

43. See Fritz Stern, "Germany in a Semi-Gaullist Europe," *Foreign Affairs*, vol. 58, nr. 4, Spring 1980.

44. See Hans-Peter Schwarz, "Die neuen außenpolitischen Denkschulen der fünfziger Jahre," in Hermann Kunst, Helmut Kohl, and Peter Egen, eds., *Dem Staate verpflichtet* (Stuttgart/Berlin: Kreuz Verlag, 1980), p. 91f.

45. On the issue of choice versus compulsion in FRG foreign policy with respect to Western integration, see Jacobsen and Stenzl, eds., *Deutschland und die Welt*, pp. 304–310 (Schröder); Walther Leisler Kiep, *Good-Bye Amerika—Was Dann?* (Stuttgart-Degerloch: Seewald Verlag, 1972), p. 106ff., p. 137ff.; Grosser, *Geschichte Deutschlands seit 1945*, p. 417ff.; von Schubert, ed., *Sicherheitspolitik der Bundesrepublik Deutschland*, vol. II, pp. 504–511 (Adenauer).

46. Adenauer, "Rede des Bundeskanzlers Konrad Adenauer zur Perspektive seiner Außen-und Sicherheitspolitik auf einer Sitzung des Bundesparteiausschusses der CDU in Bonn am 14.6.1952," in von Schubert, ed., *Sicherheitspolitik der Bundesrepublik Deutschland*, vol. II, p. 509.

47. See Grosser, *Geschichte Deutschlands seit 1945*, p. 436ff.; Alfred Grosser, *Das Deutschland im Westen* (München/Wien: Carl Hanser Verlag, 1985), p. 299.

48. Gerhard Schröder, "Die deutsche Europa-politik," in Jacobsen and Stenzl, eds., *Deutschland und die Welt*, pp. 304, 305.

49. Genscher, *Deutsche Außenpolitik*, p. 137.

50. Schwarz, "Die neuen außenpolitischen Denkschulen der fünfziger Jahre," p. 92. The following discussion is particularly indebted to this insightful essay.

51. For a very good general discussion, focused on underlying philosophical facets, see Haftendorn, Wilker, and Wörmann, eds., *Die Außenpolitik der Bundesrepublik Deutschland*, pp. 136–151 (Ziebura).

52. For general overviews of the evolution of West German *Europapolitik*, see Herbert Müller-Roschach, *Die deutsche Europapolitik* (Baden-Baden: Nomos Verlagsgesellschaft, 1974; second edition was published in 1980 in Bonn by Europa Union Verlag), which covers the period 1949–1977; and Jim Cloos, "La R.F.A. et l'intégration européenne," in Fritsch-Bournazel, Brigot, and Cloos, eds., *Les Allemands au Coeur de l'Europe*, which deals with the years 1949–1983. For a discussion of Adenauer's basic philosophical *Westorientierung*, see Anneliese Poppinga, *Konrad Adenauer: Geschichtsverständnis, Weltanschauung und politische Praxis* (Stuttgart: Deutsche Verlags-Anstalt, 1975), especially Part III, Chapters 2 and 3.

53. On West German *Europapolitik* in the era of detente, see Cloos, "La R.F.A. et l'intégration européenne," p. 51ff., p. 79ff.; Müller-Roschach, *Die deutsche Europapolitik*, pp. 217–293 (1969–1972 period), 295–358 (1972–1974 period), 359–448 (1974–1976 period), and especially p. 418ff. with respect to the 1975 Conference on Security and Cooperation in Europe (CSCE) and the development of a "European" foreign policy posture in the detente era.

54. On socialist ideas regarding Europe and international affairs in general, see Miller, *Die SPD vor und nach Godesberg*, pp. 88–94 ("Ziele und Aufgaben des Demokratischen Sozialismus").

55. Most of these perspectives can be found in speeches and essays by leading Social Democrats, such as Brandt, Schmidt, Erler, and the like. Many liberal Free Democrats also emphasize these themes. See, for example, Genscher, *Deutsche Außenpolitik*, passim; and Walter Scheel, "Transnationale Orientierung deutscher Politik," in Walter Scheel, ed., *Perspektiven deutscher Politik* (Düsseldorf/Köln: Diederichs, 1969).

56. See Willy Brandt, "Germany's 'Westpolitik,'" *Foreign Affairs*, vol. 50, nr. 3, April 1972.

57. For discussions and illustrations of the development of the SPD's *Europapolitik*, see Jacobsen and Stenzl, eds., *Deutschland und die Welt*, pp. 338–344 (Jaksch); Brandt and Ammon, eds., *Die Linke und die nationale Frage*, pp. 134–138 ("Entschließung des SPD-Parteitags . . ."), 280–293 ("Diskussionsbeitrag . . ."), 345–346 (Bahr), 359–362 (Schmidt); Miller, *Die SPD vor und nach Godesberg*, pp. 95–100 ("Aktionsprogramm . . ."), 117–131 ("Grundsatzprogramm . . ."); William E. Paterson, *The SPD and European Integration* (Lexington, MA: Lexington Books, 1974), Chapter 6; Brandt, *Brandt—Reden 1961–65*, pp. 70–94; Brandt, *Außenpolitik, Deutschlandpolitik, Europapolitik*, pp. 20–27; von Schubert, ed., *Sicherheitspolitik der Bundesrepublik Deutschland*, vol. I, pp. 273–286 (Schmidt); Helmut Schmidt, *Der Kurs heißt Frieden* (Düsseldorf/Wien: Econ-Verlag, 1979), pp. 57–84. See also Willy Brandt, "Europa und die Vereinigten Staaten—ein neuer Anfang," in Peter Raina, ed., *Internationale Politik in den siebziger Jahren* (Frankfurt: S. Fischer Verlag, 1973).

58. On the evolution of CDU/CSU attitudes in the crucial area of *Ostpolitik*, from antagonism and opposition to resignation and cooperation, see Clay Clemens, *Reluctant Realists: The Christian Democrats and West German Ostpolitik* (Durham, NC: Duke University Press, 1989).

59. Brandt, "Germany's 'Westpolitik,'" p. 416. The SPD, main architect of the *Ostpolitik* of the 1970s, for years sought to placate Western Rapallo fears. See, for example, Jacobsen and Stenzl, eds., *Deutschland und die Welt*, pp. 65–71 (Schmid); Miller, *Die SPD vor und nach Godesberg*, pp. 139–151 (Brandt). Accusations by conservatives of alleged SPD unreliability in the area of foreign policy were a persistent feature of West German internal political debate.

60. Cloos, "La R.F.A. et l'intégration européenne," p. 91.

61. Hahn, *Between Westpolitik and Ostpolitik*, p. 3.

62. See Joyce Marie Mushaben, *From Post-War to Post-Wall Generations: Changing Attitudes Toward the National Question and NATO in the Federal Republic of Germany* (Boulder, CO: Westview Press, 1998), Chapter 4.

63. For general discussions of German militarism, see Emilio Willems, *Der preußisch-deutsche Militarismus* (Köln: Verlag Wissenschaft & Politik, 1984); Gerhard Ritter, "Das Problem des Militarismus in Deutschland," in Volker Berghahn, ed., *Militarismus* (Köln: Kiepenheuer & Witsch, 1975); Gordon A. Craig, *The Germans* (New York: G. P. Putnam's Sons, 1982), Chapter 11.

64. Willems, *Der preußisch-deutsche Militarismus*, p. 14.

65. See Wolfgang Sauer, "Militarism in the Federal Republic?" in Walter Stahl, ed., *The Politics of Postwar Germany* (New York: Praeger Publishers, 1963), pp. 249–252.

66. Sauer, "Militarism in the Federal Republic?" p. 252.

67. On the issue of domestic and international sensitivity regarding German (military) power, see Martin and Sylvia Greiffenhagen, *Ein schwieriges Vaterland* (Frankfurt: Fischer Taschenbuch Verlag, 1981), pp. 280–297; Grosser, *Geschichte Deutschlands seit 1945*, p. 430ff.; Grosser, *Das Deutschland im Westen*, p. 313ff.

68. Konrad Adenauer, *Bundestagsreden* (Bonn: Verlag AZ-Studio, 1967), p. 75 nn.

69. Adenauer, *Bundestagsreden*, p. 77.

70. Schumacher, in Löwke, *Für den Fall, daß . . .*, p. 245.

71. "Für die deutsche Gleichberechtigung—Ein verklausuliertes Ja," in Löwke, *Für den Fall, daß . . .*, p. 243.

72. Schumacher, in Löwke, *Für den Fall, daß . . .*, p. 247.

73. Löwke, *Für den Fall, daß . . .* , p. 252.

74. For relevant discussions, see Greiffenhagen, *Ein schwieriges Vaterland*, pp. 280–297; Johannes Gross, *De Duitsers* (Baarn, Netherlands: Uitgeverij In den Toren, 1968), Chapter 20; Craig, *The Germans*, Chapter 11; Sauer, "Militarism in the Federal Republic?" p. 252ff.

75. These efforts were not free of inner contradiction, insofar as a desire to connect the military with civil society coexisted with considerable military isolation as a result of civilian dominance and fear of military influence. See the discussion in Sauer, "Militarism in the Federal Republic?" p. 260ff.

76. See the discussion by one of the "founding fathers" of the *Bundeswehr*, Count Wolf Baudissin, "The New German Army," *Foreign Affairs*, vol. 34, nr. 1, October 1955.

77. Peter Balke and Gerhard Wuthe suggested that a useful German military tradition must contain a mixture of lessons, warnings, models, and guidelines, whereby democratic criteria would generally be decisive. See Balke, "Tradition als Last? Militär und Gesellschaft in Deutschland," and Wuthe, "Militärische Tradition im Spannungsfeld demokratischer Politischer Kultur," both in *Aus Politik und Zeitgeschichte*, 25 April 1981. The early nineteenth-century Prussian military reform period, the 1848 era, and the 1944 anti-Hitler plot have usually been felt to generate the most positive elements.

78. Grosser, *Geschichte Deutschlands seit 1945*, p. 437.

79. Hahn, *Between Westpolitik and Ostpolitik*, pp. 45, 46, 47.

80. Hahn, *Between Westpolitik and Ostpolitik*, p. 63. See also Uwe Nerlich, "Die nuklearen Dilemmas der Bundesrepublik Deutschland," *Europa-Archiv*, nr. 17, 1965; Joseph I. Coffey, Klaus von Schubert, et al., *Defense and Detente: U.S. and West German Perspectives on Defense Policy* (Boulder, CO: Westview Press, 1989).

81. Richard Löwenthal, "The German Question Transformed," *Foreign Affairs*, vol. 63, nr. 2, Winter 1984–85, p. 314.

82. See, for example, Strauß, "Die Bundesrepublik Deutschland im Kräftefeld der Weltpolitik;" Manfred Wörner, "Das sicherheitspolitische Konzept der Union;" Schössler and Weede, *West German Elite Views*, especially p. 41ff.

83. Strauß, "Die Bundesrepublik Deutschland im Kräftefeld der Weltpolitik," pp. 41, 43, 44, 45, 47.

84. On the SPD's evolving national security views, see the sources cited above in note 17. See also Erich P. Neumann, *Die Deutschen und die NATO* (Allensbach: Verlag für Demoskopie, 1969), pp. 18–21; Helmut Schmidt, "Die Bundesrepublik Deutschland im Gleichgewicht der Kräfte," in Raina, ed., *Internationale Politik in den siebziger Jahren;* Lloyd Free, *Six Allies and a Neutral* (Glencoe, IL: Free Press, 1959), p. 143ff.

6

The Last Cold War Decade: A New German Question?

The spectacular events of 1989–1990 came as the conclusion of a decade that had led most observers to assume that the German Question had been "solved," at least for the time being, in view of an increasing degree of desirable "normalization" between the Federal Republic and the GDR as two definitively separate states. This international relaxation of concern about Germany followed upon a turbulent period of renewed East-West Cold War, however, during which this closeness of the FRG and the GDR struck many as an undesirable "neutralist" revival of German nationalism, a new German *Sonderweg* based on equidistance between the two Cold War "camps." It is essential, therefore, to take a closer look at developments regarding the German Question during a decade that swung from international tension to relaxation, for they partially set the stage for the surprising turn of events that followed. In addition, they deserve closer scrutiny insofar as they contained potential implications for the political and diplomatic course that the reunited Germany might pursue in the years ahead.

Developments in West German Foreign Policy Attitudes in the 1980s

In Chapter 5 we saw that a relatively workable foreign policy consensus, focused on continued *Westpolitik* and the increased need for a more active *Ostpolitik*, appeared to develop in West Germany in the course of the 1960s. After 1969, however, this consensus rapidly disintegrated as a result of profound dispute between the CDU/CSU and the SPD-FDP coalition concerning the latter's new *Ostpolitik* and *Deutschlandpolitik*, policies that essentially terminated West Germany's previous Cold War foreign policy posture and reconciled West German diplomacy with the advent of general detente efforts in East-West relations. Yet at the same time, a fair amount of NATO-oriented consensus continued to exist among the CDU/CSU, the FDP, and the moderate wing of the SPD, both as a result of necessity based on security dependence and a general recognition of the validity of NATO's so-called Harmel formula, which was officially adopted in 1967 and which called for the simultaneous pursuit of defense/deterrence and detente.

The collapse of East-West detente in the early 1980s led to renewed foreign policy cultural fragmentation, but with a more peculiar twist. Despite occasionally polarized rhetoric and clear differences of emphasis, the SPD, the FDP, *and* the CDU were all largely committed to a continuation of the *Ostpolitik* and *Deutschlandpolitik* of the 1970s, although there were some critical nuances based on each party's evaluation of the original policies, its definition of West Germany's ultimate interests, and its perceptions of Soviet foreign policy intentions.[1] What was even more clearly shaken was the previous consensus with respect to national security policy.[2] Thus Christoph Bertram commented almost wistfully in 1982, amid the public debate over NATO's decision to deploy new medium-range missiles in Western Europe:

> Security policy has become controversial again, and its central feature, the nuclear question, is precisely the symbol of polarization in Western societies. The idyll during which the experts had only to point to the defense effort of the East in order to be credible and convincing, has ended.[3]

In this area of security policy, one could witness a clear fragmentation of the SPD, a burgeoning peace movement, an occasionally drifting public opinion, and the emergence of the Greens. The overall consequence appeared to be a revival of the German Question in a particular way. At this point, let us survey the general foreign policy orientations across the West German political spectrum in the 1980s, *prior* to the upheavals of 1989.

The Federal Republic entered the 1980s with a continued coalition of the SPD and the FDP. These two parties had experienced a considerable foreign policy cultural convergence in the course of the 1960s. The more pragmatic Helmut Schmidt, who did not subscribe to the lingering ideological dogmatism present in some SPD quarters, had succeeded the more idealistic Willy Brandt as federal chancellor in 1974. And his main coalition partner, the FDP's Hans-Dietrich Genscher, shared Schmidt's pragmatic internationalism and himself stood clearly to the left of the FDP's former nationalist conservatism. Both men, and those who supported them, attempted to reconcile a realist focus on the East-West balance of power with the idealist, but equally vital, pursuit of increased detente.

For Schmidt, realism and the maintenance of a stable East-West balance of (deterrent) power were preconditions for any successful detente policy. In 1982, he suggested that

> in the part of the world, namely Europe, where we Germans live, there cannot be security without an approximate balance of military power. No responsible govern-

ment can accept that its country is threatened by an excessive arms build-up by one side, or even that its country is exposed to the possibility of political blackmail.[4]

Consequently, he asserted that the conduct of a "realistic policy of peace" (*realistische Friedenspolitik*) required that "[w]hoever wants peace should not limit himself to a declaration of his convictions and should not close his eyes against reality, and against the real conditions under which we must pursue a policy of peace."[5] His emphasis on Atlantic alliance harmony and the need for military strength was far more explicit than Brandt's. Although the maintenance of peace was seen as the most fundamental goal of West German foreign policy, Schmidt rejected any kind of moral absolutism in diplomacy, be it radical pacifism on the left or anti-Communist zeal on the right.

At the same time, however, his affinity with the SPD's idealist tradition in foreign policy led him to stress the profound importance of East-West detente, based on dialogue, trust, and *Gewaltverzicht* (renunciation of the use of force). He underlined the necessity for international arms control, even though he might see full disarmament as a *fata morgana*. Schmidt envisioned the gradual development of an East-West *Sicherheitspartnerschaft* ("security partnership"). In light of Germany's historical record, he stressed West Germany's "duty" to promote peace and good-neighborliness throughout Europe: "We Germans must do everything within our means for the cause of peace, since so much was done against peace and for war in Germany's name in the past."[6] This realization was (and still is) often connected with a basic declaration: "Never again should war originate from German soil."[7]

Schmidt directed relatively little explicit attention to the German Question in its traditional postwar form, that is, national reunification. Instead, he anticipated a true solution only in the context of an all-European "peace order" that would overcome the division of the continent. In 1980, he declared to the West German parliament:

> As far as the future of the German nation is concerned, we must soberly conclude that the political constellations in the world and in Europe at the present time do not offer possibilities to overcome the division of Germany into two states. . . . The division of Germany is at the same time the division of Europe. In a concrete sense, this means that the German problem is only accessible [soluble] in a European context. Everything that Europeans on both sides can do in order to smooth the trenches between us and create greater solidarity is at the same time of service to the German cause.[8]

Despite his occasionally assertive stances vis-à-vis the United States and his inclination to gain more independence for West German foreign policy, Schmidt rejected suggestions, especially within his own party, that an SPD-FDP coalition might need to consider resurrecting a latter-day version of Germany's tradition of (unpredictable) *Schaukelpolitik*. "It is quite clear: German foreign policy must not and can never be made on a basis of equal distance between Washington and Moscow. Our place is on this side, on the side of free peoples enjoying equal rights."9 He remained firmly committed to West German diplomatic reliability and Atlantic partnership. Western firmness and East-West detente were seen as fully complementary.

In addition, Schmidt tended to devote considerable attention to international economic issues, emphasizing the need for stability and free trade. Traumatic German historical experience led him to stress the importance of West German domestic economic security and stability. He was fully supportive of expanded *Osthandel* (trade with the East bloc) as a way of increasing East-West interdependence, which in turn would promote detente. North-South issues were also high on his political and philosophical agenda, and he combined encouragement of Third World *Blockfreiheit* (nonalignment) with a clear resistance to the transfer of East-West competition and confrontation into the North-South realm.

Genscher essentially matched the foreign policy orientations of Schmidt. We find a similar emphasis on detente based on a stable balance of power, East-West arms control and confidence building, a European peace order linked to continued West German Atlantic loyalty, the realities of global interdependence, Germany's "peace duty," Germany's "interests" in the new East-West context, Third World nonalignment, East-West economic interdependence, and increased Western European self-consciousness. Genscher warned against illusions with respect to German reunification, since the German Question could only be solved in a larger European context. The following quotes, taken from a 1982 article, are illustrative of his basic orientations:

> Europe's historic task in the present era is an active policy for peace [*Friedenspolitik*]—for the European continent and for the world as a whole. In that context peace and freedom are indivisibly connected for us. . . . A Europe that wished to take its position in value-free equidistance between the United States and the Soviet Union would ultimately lose its weight in international politics and particularly vis-à-vis the East, thereby [undermining] the basis for an effective policy of peace. . . . Whoever in Europe complains about the dependence on America, complains in reality about insufficient progress toward European unity. . . . The supreme "peace task" [*Friedensaufgabe*] for Europe and for the world today, as yesterday, concerns the pursuit of as constructive an East-West relationship as possible, by means of a realistic policy of detente based on dialogue, arms control, and cooperation. The maintenance of world peace is at stake here, and also the solution of the great global problems that face humanity.10

However, in the wake of the apparent collapse of East-West detente by the early 1980s, and NATO's two-track INF ("Euromissile") decision, the SPD clearly began to shift in a leftward direction, led by Brandt, Egon Bahr, and others, as it experienced the growing clout of a more radically pro-detente left wing. The SPD's always problematic image in the area of national security and Atlantic reliability appeared to deteriorate further, and observers wondered whether the previous balance be-tween *Westpolitik* and *Ostpolitik* in the SPD's foreign policy conceptions had now dangerously shifted in a less Atlanticist, more neutralist, direction. The Left's pre-occupation with peace (at all cost?), tied to a renewed search for a German "iden-tity," seemed to signify the emergence of a potent neutralist-nationalist brew in West German foreign policy culture. People like Bahr appeared to downplay East-West ideological differences while advocating nuclear-free zones, European collec-tive security, and an East-West security partnership. At the same time, they at-tempted to preserve a link with the West German political center by emphasizing the need for a realistic balance of power, West German Atlantic reliability, and the impossibility of full East-West disengagement in Europe.[11]

The main tendency of the SPD left wing, however, was clearly in a radical di-rection, undermining the long-standing (tacit) West German political consensus on security questions, and quite directly leading to the increased isolation of the Schmidt faction within the SPD, the desertion from the coalition by the FDP, and the demise of Schmidt as federal chancellor in 1982.[12] The main facets of the SPD Left's foreign policy culture entailed a downplaying of the Soviet threat to West-ern Europe, a deep ambivalence regarding balance-of-power questions, a rejec-tion of nuclear deterrence, opposition to the division of Europe between NATO and the Warsaw Pact, an interest in an all-European peace order (including nu-clear-free zones), visions of "alternative defense" (including "social defense"), and a possibly neutral Europe and/or Germany between East and West, all of it tied to a socialistically reconstructed domestic order.[13] Not surprisingly, the SPD Left became a key pillar in West Germany's peace movement of the early 1980s.

According to Jeffrey Herf, who provided a conservative evaluation of these de-velopments, "[b]oth the break in the consensus over Western security and the emergence of the peace movement in the early 1980s [were] inexplicable without taking into account the hopes—and illusions—raised during the preceding decade of detente."[14] In his view,

> East-West detente continued the delegitimation of anti-communism begun during the war in Vietnam among large segments of public opinion while fostering the view that the East-West conflict itself was either over or in a state of permanent latency. Hence the need for a strong Western military defense appeared anachronistic if the Soviet Union was, in Egon Bahr's term, in a relationship of *Sicherheitspartnerschaft* with Western Europe.[15]

He pointed to a "dialectic between *Ostpolitik*, the emergence of the peace move-ments, and West German neutralism," and concluded that, as far as West Ger-many was concerned,

> the moral order of liberal democracy was fractured under the combined impact of a return of political romanticism and the national question, the legacies of the radical

Left from the 1960s, and the erosion of complexity in foreign policy in the era of détente. Neutralist sentiment and the illusions of a third way grew on confusion over the moral foundations of the Western alliance.[16]

Some argued that West German intellectuals, especially peace researchers, were a major catalyst in the SPD's leftward drift, inspired by radical visions of international relations and utopian solutions to West Germany's security dilemmas. Herf, for example, suggested that "the members of recent peace movements in Western Europe are drawn almost exclusively from one group: young, university-educated, left-leaning intellectuals and people who have passed through West German universities in the 1960s and after."[17]

Beyond the SPD's left wing, the emergence of the Greens and various other groups holding alternative views constituted a new development in postwar West German electoral politics. They were not without roots in German history, however. There were clear areas of affinity, for example, between the Greens of the 1980s and some of the romantic, antimodern, anticapitalist, anti-Western, antiliberal, and antiindustrial idealism in the German cultural and political heritage. The Greens at times shared in forms of cultural nationalism, cultural pessimism, and ecological conservatism that have definite precedents in German history. In 1983, Kim Holmes argued that "the broad themes which run through the Green movement are suspiciously familiar, for the Greens are, despite their statements to the contrary, carriers of historical traditions whose origins reach as far back as the end of the eighteenth century."[18] In some cases, there were also links with some of the populist anarchism and utopian socialism that could be found in nineteenth-century Europe.

In addition, the Greens could be philosophically connected with the leftist opposition to Adenauer in the 1950s, the APO (extraparliamentary opposition) and New Left of the 1960s, and the postindustrial values of new generations, as evidenced by the so-called *Bürgerinitiativen* (citizens' initiatives), *Ökopax* ("eco-peace") ideas, and communalist idealism of the 1970s. It should be stressed that the West German Greens were also an expression of a "silent revolution" that could be observed in other Western countries. Although they did not "found" it, the mostly young, middle-class Greens became a key element in the peace movement of the 1980s. Their general antiestablishment orientation encouraged the aggregation of often remarkably divergent political interests and philosophical perspectives within the general Green movement.[19]

Josef Joffe pointed to an important generational dimension of the emergence of the Greens, rooted in the discontinuity in historical experience that continues to be so central to an understanding of modern Germany:

Given the catastrophic end of the ultranationalist orgy of the Third Reich, the Federal Republic became a half-nation without national symbols—bereft of identity, patriotism, or any other underpinning of legitimacy. Its main source of legitimacy was economic performance. And the remains of nationhood were submerged in Europe and the Atlantic Alliance. Instead of minimal ("healthy"?) nationalism, there was only the multinational ersatz of Europeanism and anti-Communism. This proved enough for the shell-shocked parents. A generation later, however, the stage had changed. The old trans-Atlantic order that had provided the West Germans with a role and a raison d'être was crumbling. And the United States was reeling under the blows of Vietnam and Watergate, Afghanistan and the Ayatollah. Into that vacuum stepped a new generation which knew nothing of the War and the Cold War—seeing only the burdens of bipolarity and none of its blessings, instinctively searching for an identity their elders had denied them, and eager to shake off the burden of collective moral inferiority the founding fathers had bequeathed to them instead.[20]

In the area of foreign policy, the Greens tended to be guided by a set of principles that put them clearly outside the general postwar West German foreign policy consensus. Writing in the early 1980s, Clay Clemens suggested that

[t]he Greens charge that the unecological, antisocial and undemocratic way of thinking and the obsession with force which they claim dominate modern German society also characterize the conduct of global affairs by the industrialized world—above all the West. This mentality is said to result in policies that sustain confrontation between the blocs, particularly the rivalry of a deadly nuclear arms race, while perpetuating and exploiting the Third World's underdevelopment—circumstances which give rise to repression, conflict and impending Armageddon.[21]

Hence the Greens advocated strong opposition to nuclear weapons, deterrence, NATO, and in many cases also the *Bundeswehr*.[22] They frequently downplayed the ideological differences between East and West, seeing the Soviet Union as a basically conservative great power threatened by U.S. Cold War imperialism. They opposed emotional anti-Communism and desired to neutralize Europe in order to remove it from the Cold War. They tended to be antimilitarist, favored (unilateral) disarmament, and envisioned a reliance on "social defense" against foreign invaders. They continued to place a high priority on North-South issues and a campaign against Western imperialism. Altogether, there was a profoundly moralist, idealist, escapist, pessimist (or alarmist) and absolutist flavor in the foreign policy culture of many of the Greens during the last decade of the Cold War.

In light of their assertive agitation for "German interests," the Greens were increasingly linked to the notion of an emerging German neutralist nationalism.[23] Clemens, for example, concluded that

[t]o help blur distinctions between the blocs, Green programs stir up a sense of national victimization among fellow Germans. Ignoring their country's own past and overlooking its very brief period as a completely unified state (1871–1945), they declare that Germany has been divided unnaturally by the superpowers, which are in-

tent solely on carrying out their power struggle. This notion is reinforced by para-
noid charges of "backstabbing" and "betrayal" aimed at the Western allies. The Federal Republic and Berlin are "exploited" by America, which continues to "prolong its
occupation" of both. Washington plans to use the country as "a staging area" and a
"battlefield" and—like the Soviet Union—"will never give away" its half of Germany,
but will instead reserve it for use in the "power struggle."[24]

It is important to note that such thinking had always held a certain attraction for
the West German extreme right as well.[25]

After the fall of the SPD-FDP coalition, a CDU/CSU-FDP coalition led by Helmut Kohl came to power in 1982. The CDU/CSU had vigorously opposed the
Ostpolitik and *Deutschlandpolitik* of the 1970s, but had also learned to live with
their necessity and at least partial benefits. Yet the right wing of the CDU, particularly the refugee groups from former eastern territories, continued to be highly
critical and often unabashedly nationalist (*and* Atlanticist) in its outlook. In addition, the CSU, especially when led by the late Franz-Josef Strauß, persisted in
an anti-Communist hard line, focusing on the failures and illusions of detente
and *Ostpolitik*, the need for Atlantic orthodoxy, the growing global Soviet threat,
the importance of Western ideological vigilance with regard to the Soviet Union,
the supremacy of freedom over peace, the necessity of continued containment,
and the dangers of a neutralist peace movement.[26] To the West German Right, the
Ostpolitik of the 1970s was essentially a sellout of West German "rights."

Many of these themes were widely shared in the CDU. The Christian Democrats' foreign policy culture continued to stress the importance of Atlantic partnership, the necessity of a stable balance of power, peace based on strength, the
avoidance of a German *Schaukelpolitik* between East and West, and the preservation of German diplomatic reliability.[27] As Kohl summarized it in 1983:

> [T]he Federal Republic of Germany is and remains a reliable and predictable partner
> in the European Community and in the Atlantic Alliance. We do not see ourselves as
> mediator between West and East. We shall not pursue a path or permit a develop-
> ment which removes us from the friendship of the West and leads us into depen-
> dence on a hegemonic East. We will not seek an understanding with the Soviet
> Union at the expense of our friendship and partnership with our allies and [at the
> expense of] our friends in the United States or our friends in France. The solid
> mooring and position of the Federal Republic of Germany in the West is an indis-
> pensable foundation for a policy of detente, of mutual understanding, and of the co-
> operation with the peoples of Central and Eastern Europe which we desire so much.
> In short: we, the Germans in the free part of our fatherland, in the Federal Republic
> of Germany, we are no wanderers between two worlds [East and West].[28]

The world tended to be seen in clearly ideological terms, pitting freedom against
totalitarianism. The need for Western "rearmament" was recognized, tied to increased "realism" in the realm of arms control.[29]

A nationalist assertion that the German nation continued to exist and that the German Question was still "open" was linked to demands for German self-determination, warnings against neutralism, and reaffirmations of the integral relation among German unity, security, and freedom. The adamant orientation of West German conservatives on the national question was captured well by the following statements of Kohl in the early 1980s:

> Historical experience shows: the current situation is not unchangeable. Realpolitik: yes; resignation: no! . . . We insist on the right of self-determination for the Germans, and we insist on the unity of the nation. . . . We Germans do not accept the division of our fatherland. . . . There are two states in Germany, but there is only one German nation. The existence of that nation is not a matter of government decree and majority decisions. That nation is the product of history, part of Christian, European culture, shaped by its location in the center of the continent. . . . We cling to the right of self-determination for our people and to the unity of our nation. We do not resign ourselves [to the current situation]. We have been obligated by our constitution to aim at a condition of peace in Europe in which the German people achieves its unity in free self-determination.[30]

Together with continued support for Western European integration, CDU foreign policy culture remained loyal to Adenauer's earlier "Christian realism."[31] As Kohl stressed in 1983: "I insist that the road that the CDU/CSU and FDP took under [the leadership of] Konrad Adenauer not be deserted."[32]

Yet the CDU's recognition of Germany's historical ties with the East, the Central European responsibilities of the two German states, the need for continued *Deutschlandpolitik* (albeit along more conservative, purely humanitarian lines), the importance of (West) German interests in international affairs, and NATO's commitment to both defense and detente were evidence of an additional dimension in CDU foreign policy culture, one that could be more clearly at odds with purely hard-line orientations. Thus Kohl argued that

> based on our situation and our history, we Germans are required to maintain good relations with West and East. We Germans have countless historical ties with the East. We have a deep appreciation for the cultural unity of Europe in all its diversity and variety. We consider our neighboring peoples in Central and Eastern Europe as part of Europe, and not merely in this cultural sense.[33]

The Christian Democrats' (rhetorical) support for a European "peace order," insofar as it was predicated on a fundamental degree of intra-European reconciliation, could not permit an all-out East-West Cold War, especially in view of the sensitive human dimension of FRG-GDR relations. West Germany could simply not afford to be part of an uncontrolled East-West arms race, given its vulnerable geostrategic location. Nor could a CDU-led government be expected to jeopardize the economically lucrative benefits of increased trade with the East in an era of detente, considering the Christian Democrats' close political connections with and dependence upon West Germany's business community.[34] Kohl captured the various strands of thought when he said:

> Before all else, . . . German foreign policy is focused on the preservation of freedom and the solidification of peace in Europe and in the world. For us an active policy of peace is a political necessity and a moral obligation. . . . We live on the fault-line between East and West. This imposes special security burdens upon us and requires of us in a special way an intellectual-political face-off with the Communist social system, but it also obligates us to pursue [greater] understanding [with the East].[35]

In addition, the maintenance of a coalition with the less conservative FDP obviously required a certain amount of foreign policy moderation. The evidence of profound differences between the CDU/CSU and the SPD in the 1980s, however, despite areas of continued consensus, was undeniable and highly significant.

The advent of Gorbachev and the resurgence of detente after 1985 in East-West relations somewhat reduced the impact of the conservative foreign policy views of the CDU, giving a boost to the liberal internationalism of the FDP, and providing the opposition SPD with a new opportunity to press its *Ostpolitik* agenda. The INF (intermediate-range nuclear forces) treaty in 1987 helped rid the Federal Republic of a deeply controversial security issue.[36] In spite of significant areas of consensus, philosophical fragmentation in West German attitudes on foreign policy persisted, and took on new dimensions during and after the turbulent changes in the GDR in 1989 and 1990, as we shall see in Chapters 7 and 9.

Revival of the German Question During the Reagan Years

In the course of the 1980s, Western Europe and the United States experienced a relationship marked by considerable mutual assertiveness and friction.[37] Both sides of the Atlantic clashed with regard to East-West relations, crises in the Third World, and the fight against terrorism. West Germany had its full share in these alliance disputes. The 1980s also witnessed the waxing and waning of powerful peace movements in Western Europe and the United States. And again, West Germany was no exception.

Yet in contrast with other countries, conditions in the Federal Republic, as sketched above, attracted special interest and not infrequently concern. There was a widespread belief among a considerable number of Western observers in official circles, academia, and the media that developments in the 1980s amounted to a revival of the German Question in a new international context. Thus Walther Leisler Kiep argued in 1984 that

> [t]he Ostpolitik of the 1970s has given way to the Deutschlandpolitik of the 1980s. The former, with then Chancellor Willy Brandt as its leading champion, focused pre-

dominantly on detente. It coincided with a weakening of the desire for reunification among Germans, and as a consequence there was a tendency in many countries to misunderstand Ostpolitik as being in itself a settlement of the German Question. Deutschlandpolitik is a reflection of changing West German attitudes. The quest for new ideals and opportunities for personal identification is leading Germans back to their own history and into public discussion of "national awareness," "homeland," "fatherland" and "nation." These "national" tendencies can be observed in the peace movement and elsewhere on the left. Even the neutralist Greens are actively pursuing their own Deutschlandpolitik. The "ice age" between East and West Germany that was predicted by many critics of the current West German government led by Helmut Kohl has not occurred. . . . [T]he quest for a "German identity" that has been taken up in West Germany is also emerging to an increasing extent in East Germany.[38]

During the first half of the decade, the impression spread that the old problem of German identity and Germany's role and position in international affairs, together with the lingering revisionist objective of national reunification, had become increasingly linked to nuclear *Angst,* pacifist neutralism, a resurgence of cultural anti-Westernism, and a continued West German devotion to *Ostpolitik* in spite of renewed East-West tension.[39] Fritz Stern saw this as "the reappearance of the German soul in world politics," and suggested that

[t]his time the German soul combines a universalist appeal—against war, against nuclear lightheartedness—with a nationalist note that speaks to the division of the country. German preoccupation with self may be the contemporary analogue to nationalism, and the world is leery of anything that resembles German nationalism because of its aggressive past, its unsatisfied present, and its unpredictable future. History would suggest that an FRG that feels itself isolated abroad and beset at home is most likely to be volatile or unpredictable.[40]

The context of East-West tension gave way to one of renewed detente after the mid-1980s, but international preoccupation with the revived German Question continued. And just when this "new" German Question appeared to lose some of its prominence toward the end of the decade, the collapse of the Communist regime in the GDR posed again the "original" German Question—namely, unification and its implications.

As far as the pre-1989 "new" German Question was concerned, many of the West German orientations were reflections of geostrategic necessity and historical legacy. Thus Joffe pointed out (in 1981) that

[t]here are few nations whose security policies have fluctuated as widely and wildly as Germany's. Throughout history, Germany has been either too weak or too strong, either a prey of its neighbors or a threat to European and, ultimately, global stability. The experience of impotence, however, has been the abiding one.[41]

But he also emphasized that "[i]n stark contrast to past German history, the course of postwar German defense policy has remained incredibly steady."[42] Although this steady policy was predicated on close association with the West, the *Ostpolitik* of the 1970s was clearly a natural development, given Germany's Central European location and its historically close ties with Eastern Europe. Joffe noted that "the FRG's exclusive post–World War II alignment with the West appears almost as a freak exception to a rule that had Germany looking East for two centuries." He stressed the importance of some "abiding realities—notably those of geographic propinquity and relative power—that impose the need for accommodation between West Germany and its Soviet neighbor. These realities have repeatedly claimed their due, and, no matter how strident the rhetorical exorcism, they will not go away."[43]

Thus Germany has never been able to escape the need to be on good diplomatic terms with both East and West. The Federal Republic continued to face this dilemma to a significant extent, in spite of its multiple postwar ties to the West. The necessity to deal with both East and West in order to enhance the prospects of unification and preserve at least a semblance of German nationhood was an additional reason for the Federal Republic to pursue a vigorous *Ostpolitik*. Germany's position as a divided nation between East and West regularly led some in the FRG to express increased interest in serving as a "bridge" or "honest broker" between East and West and as a zone of stability and continued detente in periods of tension. German military vulnerability tended to induce *both* German states to focus on the preservation of intra-German detente during the 1970s and 1980s to an extent that from time to time clearly conflicted with the prevailing interests of their respective superpower patrons.[44]

The West German achievement of a greater balance between *Westpolitik* and *Ostpolitik* increased the room for maneuver in West German foreign policy, partially transformed the FRG's interests, and thus encouraged a greater German diplomatic independence and assertiveness.[45] In the words of a prominent West German foreign policy analyst, written in 1980, "[t]o an increasing extent, German *Ostpolitik* reflects the growing responsibilities and problems of West Germany's reemerging status as a European great power," although he also highlighted "the intricate web of dependence on the outside world that heavily circumscribes the margin of maneuver of the Federal Republic."[46] For another observer, however, these developments pointed to a potentially new German *Größenwahn* (megalomania), resulting from "the dreamy self-overestimation with which we [Germans] assume that we could, by ourselves and without any risks, develop an orientation toward the East of the same intensive and positive character [as our] orientation toward the West, without damage to or removal of the American foundation upon which the Federal Republic rests."[47] Needless to say, all these developments were watched warily by Western observers accustomed to West German Atlanticist orthodoxy and docility. In this sense, increased West German political assertiveness actually appeared to be a reflection of the end of the postwar era and a process of "normalization."

In addition, the resurgence of the German Question was a specific manifestation of broader transatlantic phenomena.[48] The earlier Atlanticist idealism, which had also dominated West German foreign policy, seemed to have worn off in an era of increased nationalist self-centeredness on both sides of the Atlantic. Joffe went so far as to conclude in 1981 that "it is clear that perceptions and beliefs on both shores of the Atlantic are drastically out of phase. The few premises that are still shared by Europeans and Americans are dwarfed by the many disputes where they clash not only over tactics but over *Weltanschauung*."[49] On the U.S. side, Irving Kristol emphasized "the different conceptions the United States and Western Europe have of their own roles in the world," with the United States dedicated to a "world power" role and Western Europe slipping into a "regional-isolationist phase."[50]

There also seemed to be a definite erosion of Europeanist idealism in Western Europe, although there was undoubtedly a partial resurgence of "Europhoria" as a result of the EC'92 program.[51] But in 1982, at least, Alexander Boguslawski could conclude that

[s]ince the mid-1960s, under the important but not causal influence of de Gaulle's intransigence, a development was accelerated by which national governments strengthened their role in the decision-making processes of the EC, "infiltrated" the [EC executive] machinery in Brussels, and undermined the Commission's competence in the area of directives. The vision of a *supranational* European government evaporated steadily, and the coordination among sovereign states practically displaced the principle of supranational fusion. This change, although occurring only gradually and largely unnoticed by the public at large, did register among the German population, albeit in a delayed fashion. While the supranational dream still echoes in answers [to opinion polls], it is undeniable that the population is increasingly oriented toward [the prevailing] reality when defining its image of Europe: away from a supranational and toward a looser federal structure.[52]

The FRG's intensified relations with the East, the relative erosion of European supranationalism, and the weakening of Atlanticist idealism seemed to have undermined to some extent the Federal Republic's earlier, supranationally cast sense of identity, prompting a shift in focus either to a specifically West German identity or to a search for continued all-German consciousness and meaning. Related to these developments appeared to be a reduced West German confidence in the United States (including its deterrent reliability), tied to an interest in additional security reassurance with France, with all of Western Europe, with East Germany, and/or with the Soviet Union. It seemed that the result might at some point be a greater West German willingness to maneuver between East and West, despite official denials of a revived German *Schaukelpolitik*. Needless to say, such a development would have had profound implications for the FRG's role and position in Western Europe in particular and in the Western alliance in general.

A further factor behind the resurgence of the German Question appeared to lie in the increased prominence in the Federal Republic (and elsewhere) of a new "successor" generation whose foreign policy orientations were shaped less by the experiences of the 1930s, World War II, and the Cold War than by the detente efforts of the 1960s and 1970s.[53] A former official at the U.S. Embassy in Bonn suggested in 1981 that

> [i]n the Federal Republic of Germany experts guess that the German Successor Generation (born in 1943 or thereafter) roughly divides into thirds. In the first are those who support the present establishment or at least go along with it. The second is apathetic and wants to be left alone. The last lies in a spectrum which begins with a pronounced negative view of the establishment and its policies and ends with out-right hostility. Whether the last group comprises thirty-three percent or twenty-five percent is relatively unimportant as it includes the most activist and engaged elements of West German society. Another point is that the groupings are not static; there is shifting around and suspicion that the last third in Germany may soon reach 40 percent.[54]

One of the resulting concerns was that "the next generation of German leaders [would] be less supportive of NATO and ties to the United States."[55]

It was argued that an important segment of this new generation, which emerged in the course of the 1960s and 1970s, was attracted to the cultural protest, psychological traumas, and radical foreign policy ideas of the Greens, to the peace movement, and to the SPD's left wing. These new forces would be more prepared to question key aspects of West Germany's overall political and foreign policy consensus, in large part because they shared in a widespread popular perception that the Soviet threat had greatly diminished. Opinion polls reflected this notion: "Surveys of German opinion conducted between 1950 and 1979 have indicated a steadily diminishing belief in the probability of war."[56] All this led to considerable Western worry about a "new" German neutralism. But Stephen Szabo examined the polling data and concluded in 1983:

> [A] review of survey data collected over a period of nearly 30 years reveals no perceptible increase in neutralist sympathies. Indeed, support for the neutralization of Germany was higher in the early 1950s than it was in the early 1980s. Nevertheless, although a substantial proportion (30–40%) of West Germans remain receptive to neutralist appeals, the intensity of neutralist feelings is probably low. . . . While support for neutralism has been stable, preference for a German foreign policy increasingly independent of the United States has probably grown in the last five years and is more substantial than the support for neutralism.[57]

Conclusions drawn by Szabo and Hans-Peter Schwarz suggested a mixture of continuity and change in West German attitudes, with the *generational* factor as a crucial criterion. Szabo maintained that

> [w]hat is happening in West Germany is the convergence of old themes with the emergence of a new generation in an altered international environment. Concerns of pre-

war German historical experience, particularly the debate about the "Westernness" of German culture and the general struggle for identity, have merged within a postwar historical milieu in which the issue of national identity has become even more dramatic. Adenauer's policy of integration within a Western framework has become modified by the *Ostpolitik* and the result is a distancing from the United States.[58]

He argued that "[p]ostwar Germans are facing these traditional German questions from a different historical frame of reference. They are more distant from America and more sceptical of American intentions and policies. Although they harbour few positive feelings toward either the Soviet Union or the German Democratic Republic, they nevertheless have a lower perception of military threat from the East than their parents or grandparents."[59]

Writing in 1984, Schwarz cautioned against an overly dramatic anxiety about alleged *incertitudes allemandes* when he suggested that an "in-depth analysis of currently prevalent attitudes produces no sharp breach in long-term, relatively stable opinions." Thus, "[t]he vast majority of West Germans see their democratic constitutional government as natural." He noted that "[t]he political ties to the West have become a living, new tradition, just as with democratic constitutional government," and added that "[p]robably the most encouraging development in the decades since 1949 was the withering away of German nationalism." As a result, "the change brought about by the experience of Hitler's nationalism and the sufferings of the war is as deep-reaching and as permanent as the conversion to the value system of Western democracy." As far as the spectre of a German neutralism was concerned, Schwarz concluded that "[t]his neutralism may reflect a yearning for a reunified, neutral Germany (as in the '50s), or it may be concerned exclusively with the Federal Republic (as in the 1970s and early '80s). In either case it indicates uneasiness about East-West tensions and signals a tendency to shy away from the unpleasant realities of power politics. To most of those who confess a certain neutralism, this is much more a vague mood than a determination to abandon the NATO camp."[60]

In spite of suggestions of a broad-based new "neutralist-nationalist" sentiment in the FRG during the 1980s (generationally based or not), evidence of *ideological variety* must be noted.[61] It is true that the apparent revival in the 1980s of a German Question that was widely felt to be at least dormant—even if not "solved," in view of the Federal Republic's seemingly stable democracy and firm *Westpolitik*, plus an *Ostpolitik* that was predicated on an "acceptance" by the West Germans of the reality of two German states—centered on an assertion of "German interests" by both Left and Right in West Germany. David Gress even argued that "[t]here is . . . a symmetry of outlook on the Left and Right, or at least among certain influential elements in both the Left and Right, that is supportive of nationalist neutralism."[62] Yet the two sides of the political spectrum tended to differ in their approach to and definition of these German interests. A comparison of these perspectives is essential for a proper understanding of West German foreign policy culture in the 1980s.

As far as their thinking on "Germany" is concerned, the principal frame of reference of both moderate and more revisionist West German conservatives tended to be "national" in the conventional sense. Their focus was on the ultimate reunification of Germany through German self-determination and the defense of West German "rights" and "responsibilities" with regard to the German Question. More explicitly revisionist conservatives like Bernard Willms even defined reunification as West Germany's "national imperative," and saw it as an obligation to "desire to restore a united nation at any moment in history and in every context and situation; to treat [nationhood] with a sense of assertiveness, to consider the realization [of the nation] as a constant task; to create and renew [the nation] consistently in its living totality."[63] The only true Germany would be a reunited Germany.

The conservatives' attitude toward the Soviet Union was generally hard-line, and they consistently had difficulty in accepting a Communist-run GDR as a legitimate negotiating partner, stressing the latter's "lack of legitimation" and "lack of national identity."[64] The SPD's *Ostpolitik* of the 1970s was seen as severely damaging to West Germany's legal position, especially because it appeared to accept a moral equivalence between the FRG and the GDR, and because it was (at least implicitly) predicated upon an acceptance of two sovereign German states. For the conservatives, the German Question tended to be linked to anti-Communism and was thus in part a matter of ideological confrontation between East and West, whereby the Soviet Union was felt to bear virtually sole guilt for the division of Germany. As Willms put it, "[t]he Soviet Union is the actual enemy of the German nation [and German nationhood]."[65] Prior to the emergence of new possibilities for actual reunification in 1989, most conservatives favored an inevitable but highly competitive coexistence with East Germany. They stressed the continued reality of one German nation, asserted that the German Question was still "open," and called (like Willms) for a persistent focus on the preservation of an all-German consciousness and sense of shared history.

These conservatives tended to side with the West in the Cold War but were also highly suspicious and critical of the widespread willingness in East and West to see the division of Germany as essential to international stability. Willms, for example, could suggest quite confidently that "except for the Germans nobody is interested in the restoration of [the Germans'] national identity."[66] Yet most would envision a reunified Germany as a reliable Western alliance partner. For the vast majority of West German conservatives, neutralism between East and West (what Willms referred to as a corrupting, left-wing "neutralization-nationalism")[67] was simply not a realistic option, given prevailing international conditions, foreign distrust of Germany, and Germany's vulnerable geostrategic location.[68] It should be stressed again that the majority of West German conservatives followed the Adenauer tradition in placing the FRG's Atlantic commitments above the dream of national reunification. For them, Atlanticism and reunification did not constitute an "either/or" proposition. Only a maverick conservative fringe would contemplate a more risky "go-it-alone" option.

In contrast, the assertiveness of the West German Left in the course of the 1980s was not really the result of a traditional nationalist perspective linked to Cold War anti-Communism. Instead, it was primarily the outgrowth of security fears and an attempt to maintain East-West detente in Europe whenever Cold War and perceived U.S. diplomatic and military recklessness would heighten the sense of threat. Pierre Hassner suggested that a "concern with nuclear weapons and peace has been generalized into a deeper, existential feeling of angst and self-pity that has become a positive, moral, and metaphysical value in itself."[69] It was nuclear *Angst* that led the Left to focus increasingly on a shared West German–East German "peace interest" between East and West during the 1980s, prompting one commentator to argue that "the peace movement is today the strongest link between the two Germanies."[70] The new all-German consciousness during the decade leading up to unification was generated by a desire to "escape" from a Cold War that increased the chances of a conflict in which Germany would be the foremost casualty.[71] As Fritz Stern put it:

In the FRG, as elsewhere, the peace movement is a response to the new cold war and the new arms race, though the fear of nuclear power in any of its guises is real enough. But in the FRG there is the added fear that the two Germanys would of necessity become the battleground of the two superpowers. Germany would be devastated first, perhaps Germany would be sacrificed while the superpowers protected themselves from the ravages of nuclear war.[72]

Even much of the more moderate German assertiveness was directed at the irrationalities and dilemmas inherent in NATO strategy (both nuclear and conventional) or what might be seen by some as unwise U.S. strategic proposals, ideas, or initiatives, such as a vision of strategic defense (SDI) that might decouple Europe from the United States, or a NATO no-first-use policy regarding nuclear weapons that would eat away at the alliance's deterrent credibility.[73] The INF deployment question provided an especially relevant focus and symbol for this nationally oriented German fear and resentment. A peace movement emerged in which pacifism and nationalism were linked. Security fears became the basis for a "new" sense of German identity.

This mixture of fear and assertiveness encouraged the formulation of a variety of left-wing visions for a different German future.[74] Guided by security fears, most of these visions did not have German reunification as their primary objective. Rather, Germany's division was seen as the result of Cold War security arrangements between East and West. Hence these visions emphasized German neutrality, and perhaps even European neutrality, as a precondition for German reunification. Some proponents spoke of military neutrality, others implied an ideological neutrality as well. One could not fail to see a definite, even if unintended, affinity with the old *Sonderweg* tradition in German foreign policy. For some left-wing nationalists, like Rudolf Bahro, the new German consciousness,

rooted in fear and resistance to continued dependence, might lead to a neutralized, reunified Germany with a socialist domestic order. It was this combination
of a peace movement's rejection of West Germany's basic security orientation
and a nationalist revisionism regarding the German Question by both Left and
Right that especially fueled foreign worries about the new West German assertiveness.[75]

Once again, however, we should examine realistically the state of *mass public
opinion* in the Federal Republic during the 1980s, and not merely the impact of
highly visible but numerically small groups of intellectuals and politicians. In doing so, we can also avoid an excessive focus on a single, and inevitably diverse,
"successor generation." Survey research in fact tended to suggest that many of the
worries were quite unfounded, at least as far as the general West German public
was concerned.[76]

The vast majority of West Germans remained committed to NATO, rejecting a
Schaukelpolitik between East and West. Although the U.S. image by and large
tended to be more positive than the Soviet image, the impact of "Gorby-mania"
after 1985 became unmistakable, coupled with a clear "erosion in America's image in Europe" that was already visible during the 1970s.[77] Support for national
reunification combined with more sober expectations regarding its rapid
achievement. Observers detected a growing *West German* consciousness. West
Germans seemed to desire both a Western alliance *and* East-West detente, while
neutralism in the sense of equidistance between East and West would appear to
gain appeal only in times of international crisis. Most continued to support a balanced pursuit of *Westpolitik* and *Ostpolitik* and were willing to have the FRG play
the role of "detente broker" between East and West. Traditional German nationalism seemed clearly no longer in vogue, with West Germans more interested in
the total European picture. There might be evidence of emancipatory assertiveness, but true anti-Americanism did not appear to be really widespread. The Soviet Union tended no longer to be seen as an immediate threat by most West Germans, especially not in an age of infatuation with "Gorby."

The Left and Right might be influential (or at least vocal), but there continued
to be a large and vital center in the West German political spectrum. The majority recognized inevitable foreign policy constraints and vulnerabilities, and dis-
played considerable realism with regard to the enduring dilemmas of West German foreign policy, such as reunification versus security, detente versus
deterrence, and deterrence versus defense.[78] Neutralist sentiment reached a high
point in about 1983 but clearly declined thereafter. Confidence in U.S. foreign
policy tended to fluctuate, in part reflecting the West German predicament of
high dependence. A great majority continued to stand behind the *Bundeswehr*,
willing actively to defend the Federal Republic. Most tended to perceive a rough
East-West balance of power. In sum, this sketch of public opinion trends would
suggest that one could clearly exaggerate *les incertitudes allemandes* in an analysis
of conditions in the FRG during the 1980s.[79]

One additional aspect of the German Question that generated concern during the 1980s should be mentioned here: the Germans' attitudes toward their past.[80] We have examined this issue of forgetfulness and remembrance, of guilt and responsibility, of reconciliation and "mastering" the past in previous chapters. Throughout the 1980s, West German political leaders stressed the need for remembrance and the learning of basic lessons. Speaking on the fiftieth anniversary of Hitler's 1933 accession to power, Kohl reiterated some basic principles:

> We are moved by sorrow for the victims: those who were murdered, tortured, or fell in battle; tormented cities and countries; sorrow for the [destruction of the] peace of Europe; sorrow for the divided German nation. We focus on the remembrance of the immediate and more distant causes of the dictatorship, as well as its evolution and consequences. For the present and for the future, we accept responsibility. We are moved by this trinity of sorrow, remembrance, and responsibility. No one can absolve himself of the responsibility which ensues from the past and which shapes the present so decisively. . . . In the name of Germany the face of humanity was desecrated. From that bitter experience grows for us Germans today a high responsibility for right [justice] and peace at home and in the world.[81]

Yet the fortieth anniversary in June 1984 of D-Day, and especially the fortieth anniversary of Germany's May 1945 surrender, marked highly uneasy episodes in the FRG's relations with its new allies in the West. An unidentified West German government official even lamented that it would take only

> [o]ne false step and our 40 years of democratic history are wiped out. It is instructive. We have learned how thin the protective layer is that shields us from condemnation by our allies and friends. The Satan image of the German is back and everything will be more difficult in the future, at home as well as in our relations with our neighbors.[82]

There were painful reminders of the past when the West German government was not invited to participate in the commemoration in Normandy. Perhaps more important, the West German government's sensitivity toward the German past was questioned when Kohl insisted on a highly controversial visit by President Reagan to a military cemetery at Bitburg, which contains a number of SS graves, as an act of reconciliation. And the past continued to haunt the Germans, as the international fallout over Kohl's clumsy handling of the German-Polish border issue showed all too clearly in early 1990.

The foregoing discussion suggests that the issue of a revived German Question burdened the psychological climate of West Germany's relations with the East and especially the West during the last decade of the Cold War. Even before the spectacular events of 1989–1990, this German Question had taken on many guises, depending on the positions, perceptions, and interests of foreign observers. Was it a fear, prevalent in the West, of a reckless West German *Ostpolitik* that might lead to German (self-)Finlandization? Or was it the Eastern fear of a renewed German revisionism and revanchism? Or perhaps a joint concern of East and West concerning an FRG-GDR rapprochement leading to a revival of an unpredictable German *Schaukelpolitik*? Or an anxiety in East and West generated by the potential consequences of German reunification? Or fear of a new German aggressiveness? Or German economic competition and hegemony (especially within Western Europe)? Or West German democratic instability? Or a Western unease at being forced to admit the hollowness of one's rhetorical support for German reunification? Was it a concern regarding West German alliance disloyalty? Was not the control over Germany the grand shared interest between East and West? All these questions were crucial, and some will continue to be quite significant even beyond Germany's unification. They show the many faces of the German Question and reveal as much about German as about U.S., British, French, Polish, or Soviet/Russian foreign policy.[83]

Yet few (if any) could have surmised amid the ebb and flow of world affairs during the 1980s that all these questions would pose themselves so suddenly and so dramatically after the fall of 1989. Even a decade or more later, the world is still attempting to come to grips with the far-reaching implications of the events that have unfolded since the breaching of the Berlin Wall on November 9, 1989.

Notes

1. An excellent study of the period between 1961 (the construction of the Wall) and 1989 (its collapse) in inter-German relations, including the evolution of West German policy on the national question, is A. James McAdams, *Germany Divided: From the Wall to Reunification* (Princeton, NJ: Princeton University Press, 1993).

2. See Gebhard Schweigler, *West German Foreign Policy: the domestic setting* (New York: Praeger Publishers, 1984; Washington Papers nr. 106), Chapter 6; Joyce Marie Mushaben, *From Post-War to Post-Wall Generations: Changing Attitudes Toward the National Question and NATO in the Federal Republic of Germany* (Boulder, CO: Westview Press, 1998), Chapter 5.

3. Christoph Bertram, "Der Kampf um den Konsens," in Helga Haftendorn, Lothar Wilker, and Claudia Wörmann, eds., *Die Außenpolitik der Bundesrepublik Deutschland* (Berlin: Wissenschaftlicher Autoren-Verlag, 1982), p. 224.

4. Helmut Schmidt, *Freiheit Verantworten* (Düsseldorf: Econ-Verlag, 1983), p. 106.

5. Schmidt, *Freiheit Verantworten*, p. 67.

6. Schmidt, *Freiheit Verantworten*, p. 67.

7. Schmidt, *Freiheit Verantworten*, p. 127.

8. Schmidt, "Bericht zur Lage der Nation vor dem Bundestag am 20.3.1980," in Peter Brandt and Herbert Ammon, eds., *Die Linke und die nationale Frage* (Reinbek bei Hamburg: Rowohlt Taschenbuch Verlag, 1981), p. 362. See also his comments in Helmut Schmidt, *Der Kurs heißt Frieden* (Düsseldorf/Wien: Econ-Verlag, 1979), p. 79ff.

9. Schmidt, *Freiheit Verantworten*, p. 269. See also his "A Policy of Reliable Partnership," *Foreign Affairs*, vol. 59, nr. 4, Spring 1981.

10. Hans-Dietrich Genscher, "Europas Rolle in der Weltpolitik," *Europa-Archiv*, nr. 4, 1982, pp. 86–87. See also Hans-Dietrich Genscher, *Deutsche Außenpolitik* (Stuttgart: Verlag Bonn Aktuell, 1981), pp. 306–332 and passim.

11. See, for example, Egon Bahr, "Gemeinsame Sicherheit," *Europa-Archiv*, nr. 14, 1982. Many prominent SPD politicians were acutely affected by what they saw as a fundamental U.S.-European divergence on key issues in security and foreign policy, leading to a desire to have Europe assert more fully its own interests. See, for example, Horst Ehmke, "Eine Politik zur Selbstbehauptung Europas," *Europa-Archiv*, nr. 7, 1984. Ehmke's essay is illustrative of what might be called an SPD posture of "critical alliance partner," in contrast with the more orthodox CDU positions.

12. For further discussion of the SPD's drift in the 1980s, see David M. Keithly, "Whither German Social Democracy?" *Strategic Review*, Summer 1985.

13. Some of these ideas were not new, of course, as can be seen in the material presented in Chapters 4 and 5. See also Walter Möller and Fritz Vilmar, *Sozialistische Friedenspolitik für Europa: Kein Frieden ohne Gesellschaftsreform in West und Ost* (Reinbek bei Hamburg: Rowohlt Taschenbuch Verlag, 1972); and the "political and military security models" discussed in Part D of Wolfgang Heisenberg and Dieter S. Lutz, eds., *Sicherheitspolitik kontrovers: Auf dem Weg in die neunziger Jahre* (Bonn: Schriftenreihe der Bundeszentrale für politische Bildung, 1987).

14. Jeffrey Herf, "Neutralism and the Moral Order in West Germany," in Walter Laqueur and Robert Hunter, eds., *European Peace Movements and the Future of the Western Alliance* (New Brunswick, NJ: Transaction Books, 1985), p. 384. See also Jeffrey Boutwell, "Politics and the Peace Movement in West Germany," *International Security*, vol. 7, nr. 4, Spring 1983.

15. Herf, "Neutralism and the Moral Order in West Germany," p. 385.

16. Herf, "Neutralism and the Moral Order in West Germany," p. 392. See also his *War by Other Means: Soviet Power, West German Resistance, and the Battle of the Euromissiles* (New York: Free Press, 1991), in which he employs a rather restrictive (highly conservative) conception of democracy and equates visions of security neutrality with antidemocratic consequences. His presentation mixes analysis with ideologically debatable positions.

17. Jeffrey Herf, "War, Peace, and the Intellectuals," *International Security*, vol. 10, nr. 4, Spring 1986, p. 172. See also the critical responses to this article in the Fall 1986 issue of the same journal.

18. Kim Holmes, "The Origins, Development, and Composition of the Green Movement," in Robert L. Pfaltzgraff, Kim Holmes, Clay Clemens, and Werner Kaltefleiter, *The Greens of West Germany* (Cambridge, MA/Washington, DC: Institute for Foreign Policy Analysis, 1983), p. 15, and pp. 15–25 generally.

19. See Holmes, "The Origins, Development, and Composition of the Green Movement," pp. 25–46.

20. Josef Joffe, "The Greening of Germany," *The New Republic*, February 14, 1983, p. 20. See also Stephen F. Szabo, "West Germany: generations and changing security perspectives," in Stephen F. Szabo, ed., *The Successor Generation: International Perspectives of Postwar Europeans* (Boston: Butterworths, 1983).

21. See Clay Clemens, "The Green Program for German Society and International Affairs," in Pfaltzgraff, Holmes, Clemens, and Kaltefleiter, *The Greens of West Germany*, p. 68 and pp. 68–79 generally.

22. Hans-Georg Betz suggested, however, that "in regard to an important issue like the position on NATO there is hardly a consensus in the Green Party" (p. 500). He explored the

important differences between the "realist" and "fundamentalist" wings in the party. "Strange Love? How the Greens Began to Love NATO," *German Studies Review*, vol. XII, nr. 3, October 1989.

23. See David M. Keithly, "The German Fatherland—of the Left," *Orbis*, vol. 34, nr. 1, Winter 1990.

24. Clemens, "The Green Program for German Society and International Affairs," p. 75.

25. One can find this mixture of left-wing and conservative nationalism, with some clear neutralist elements, well reflected in the essays in Wolfgang Venohr, ed., *Die deutsche Einheit kommt bestimmt* (Bergisch Gladbach: Gustav Lübbe Verlag, 1982).

26. See Franz-Josef Strauß, "A New German Policy for Peace," *AEI Foreign Policy and Defense Review*, vol. 4, nr. 3/4, 1983. However, the same Franz-Josef Strauß also managed to arrange a massive financial aid package for a faltering GDR in the course of the 1980s.

27. See, for example, Volker Rühe, "Perspektiven der Friedenssicherung in Europa," *Europa-Archiv*, nr. 22, 1987.

28. Helmut Kohl, *Reden, 1982–1984* (Bonn: Presse- und Informationsamt der Bundesregierung, 1984), p. 102.

29. See especially Kohl, *Reden, 1982–1984*, p. 271ff. See also the 1982 policy statement by Kohl ("West German Foreign and Security Policy") in *Survival*, January-February 1983.

30. Kohl, *Reden, 1982–1984*, pp. 158, 177, 221, 222, 255. See also Wolfgang Schäuble, "Die deutsche Frage im europäischen und weltpolitischen Rahmen," *Europa-Archiv*, nr. 12, 1986.

31. See especially Kohl, *Reden, 1982–1984*, p. 376ff. See also Helmut Kohl, "Die Grundlagen unserer Außenpolitik," in Hermann Kunst, Helmut Kohl, and Peter Egen, eds., *Dem Staate verpflichtet* (Stuttgart/Berlin: Kreuz Verlag, 1980), p. 74ff.

32. Kohl, *Reden, 1982–1984*, p. 145.

33. Kohl, *Reden, 1982–1984*, p. 149.

34. On FRG-GDR economic relations during the 1980s, see Jürgen Nitz, "Wirtschaftsbeziehungen DDR-BRD: Bestimmungsfaktoren, Tendenzen, Probleme und Perspektiven," and Horst Lambrecht, "Die deutsch-deutschen Wirtschaftsbeziehungen zum Ende der achtziger Jahre," both in *Aus Politik und Zeitgeschichte*, 3 March 1989.

35. Kohl, *Reden, 1982–1984*, p. 144.

36. On the INF controversy, see Hans-Henrik Holm and Nikolaj Petersen, eds., *The European Missiles Crisis* (New York: St. Martin's Press, 1983), especially Chapter 1; Helga Haftendorn, "Germany and the Euromissile Debate," *International Journal*, vol. XL, Winter 1984–85; Thomas Risse-Kappen, *The Zero Option: INF, West Germany, and Arms Control* (Boulder, CO: Westview Press, 1988).

37. Stanley Hoffmann, "The Western Alliance: Drift or Harmony?" *International Security*, vol. 6, nr. 2, Fall 1981; Stanley Hoffmann, "Cries and whimpers: thoughts on West European–American relations in the 1980s," *Daedalus*, vol. 113, nr. 3, Summer 1984.

38. Walther Leisler Kiep, "The New Deutschlandpolitik," *Foreign Affairs*, vol. 63, nr. 2, Winter 1984/85, p. 316. See also the discussion in Dietrich Staritz, "Von der 'Befreiung' zur 'Verantwortungsgemeinschaft,'" *Aus Politik und Zeitgeschichte*, 4 April 1987. Staritz emphasized the increased acceptance of (or resignation to) the reality of two German states among the public in both the FRG and the GDR, with a shift from thinking about the German Question in terms of "liberation" and reunification to conceptions of a joint FRG-GDR "community of responsibility" in the center of Europe (with continued loyalty to the respective alliances).

39. For general discussions of these issues, in addition to the sources cited in the various notes below, see Eberhard Schulz and Peter Danylow, *Bewegung in der deutschen Frage?* (Bonn: Forschungsinstitut der Deutschen Gesellschaft für Auswärtige Politik, Arbeitspapiere zur Internationalen Politik, nr. 33, 1984); Martin J. Hillenbrand, *Germany in an Era of Transition* (Paris: Atlantic Institute for International Affairs, 1983), Chapters V and VI; Pierre Hassner, "The Shifting Foundation," *Foreign Policy*, nr. 48, Fall 1982; Joffe, "The Greening Of Germany;" Brigitte Sauzay, *Le Vertige allemand* (Paris: O. Orban, 1985); Jürgen C. Hess, "Westdeutsche Such nach nationaler Identität," in Wolfgang Michalka, ed., *Die Deutsche Frage in der Weltpolitik* (Stuttgart: Franz Steiner Verlag Wiesbaden, 1986); Arnulf Baring, *Unser neuer Größenwahn: Deutschland zwischen Ost und West* (Stuttgart: Deutsche Verlags-Anstalt, 1988).

40. Fritz Stern, "Conclusion: German-American Relations and 'The Return of the Repressed,'" in James A. Cooney, Gordon A. Craig, Hans-Peter Schwarz, and Fritz Stern, eds., *The Federal Republic of Germany and the United States* (Boulder, CO: Westview Press, 1984), p. 251. In an essay entitled "The German Question" in his *The Uses of Adversity: Essays on the Fate of Central Europe* (New York: Random House, 1989), Timothy Garton Ash argued (in early 1985) that this "question" "is really two questions": "[I]s the Federal Republic still a fully committed and reliable member of the Western alliance," and "is West Germany still a stable pillar of Western liberal democracy?" (p. 71ff.).

41. See Josef Joffe, "German Defense Policy: Novel Solutions and Enduring Dilemmas," in Gregory Flynn, ed., *The Internal Fabric of Western Security* (Totowa, NJ: Allanheld, 1981), p. 63.

42. Joffe, "German Defense Policy: Novel Solutions and Enduring Dilemmas," p. 89.

43. See Josef Joffe, "All Quiet On the Eastern Front," *Foreign Policy*, nr. 37, Winter 1979–80, pp. 162–163.

44. According to A. James McAdams ("Inter-German Detente: A New Balance," *Foreign Affairs*, vol. 65, nr. 1, Fall 1986), the detente relation between East and West Germany shifted in favor of the former, with the latter increasingly in a position of dependence or even vulnerability. In his view, the CDU had to adjust its hard-line foreign policy posture to the increased West German interest in and dependence on "inter-German" detente. On the ways in which all this affected West German–U.S. relations, see W. R. Smyser, *German-American Relations* (Beverly Hills: Sage Publications, Washington Papers nr. 74, 1980), especially Chapters I and II; George Carver, "Incompatible Crystals: US–West German Communication," *Washington Quarterly*, vol. 3, nr. 1, Winter 1980.

45. For further discussion, see Richard Löwenthal, "The German Question Transformed," *Foreign Affairs*, vol. 63, nr. 2, Winter 1984–85; Kiep, "The New Deutschlandpolitik;" Renata Fritsch-Bournazel, "La R.F.A. et l'Europe de l'Est," in Renata Fritsch-Bournazel, André Brigot, and Jim Cloos, *Les Allemands au Coeur de l'Europe* (Paris: Fondation pour les Études de Défense Nationale, 1983), especially pp. 227–245; Klaus Ritter, "Zum Handlungsspielraum der Bundesrepublik Deutschland im Ost-West-Verhältnis," *Europa-Archiv*, nr. 18, 1984.

46. Karl Kaiser, "The New Ostpolitik," in Wolfram F. Hanrieder, ed., *West German Foreign Policy: 1949–1979* (Boulder, CO: Westview Press, 1980), pp. 145, 154.

47. Baring, *Unser neuer Größenwahn*, pp. 10–11.

48. See Fritz Stern, "Germany in a Semi-Gaullist Europe," *Foreign Affairs*, vol. 58, nr. 4, Spring 1980. See also Helene Seppain, "The Divided West: Contrasting German and US Attitudes to Soviet Trade," *Political Quarterly*, vol. 61, nr. 1, January-March 1990. She con-

cluded: "The economic dominance of the United States, which has long been taken for granted, is being questioned; and the US exertion of extraterritorial power in Western export control policy toward the Soviet Union and Eastern Europe will increasingly be questioned too" (p. 63).

49. Josef Joffe, "European-American Relations: The Enduring Crisis," *Foreign Affairs*, vol. 59, nr. 4, Spring 1981, p. 842.

50. Irving Kristol, "Uncertain Future—NATO After 35 Years," in Laqueur and Hunter, eds., *European Peace Movements and the Future of the Western Alliance*, p. 37.

51. See Peter Reichel, "Was blieb von der Europa-Euphorie?" in Peter Reichel, ed., *Politische Kultur in Westeuropa* (Bonn: Schriftenreihe der Bundeszentrale für politische Bildung, 1984).

52. Alexander Boguslawski, "Rückzug aus Europa?" *Europa-Archiv*, nr. 1, 1982, p. 11.

53. See Stephen F. Szabo, "Conclusion," in Szabo, ed., *The Successor Generation*, especially pp. 168–170.

54. Alexander A. Klieforth, quoted in Szabo, ed., *The Successor Generation*, p. 44.

55. Szabo, "West Germany: generations and changing security perspectives," in Szabo, ed., *The Successor Generation*, p. 44.

56. Szabo, "West Germany: generations and changing security perspectives," p. 55.

57. Szabo, "West Germany: generations and changing security perspectives," p. 67. See the more worried analysis by David Gress, "What the West Should Know About German Neutralism," *Commentary*, vol. 75, nr. 1, January 1983, who concluded that "[n]ationalist neutralism is no longer in a political ghetto in Germany" (p. 31).

58. Szabo, "West Germany: generations and changing security perspectives," p. 70.

59. Szabo, "West Germany: generations and changing security perspectives," pp. 70–71.

60. Hans-Peter Schwarz, "The West Germans, Western Democracy, and Western Ties in the Light of Public Opinion Research," in Cooney, Craig, Schwarz, and Stern, eds., *The Federal Republic of Germany and the United States*, pp. 92, 93, 94.

61. See the interesting collection of essays in Dieter Blumenwitz and Gottfried Zieger, eds., *Die deutsche Frage im Spiegel der Parteien* (Köln: Verlag Wissenschaft und Politik, 1989).

62. Gress, "What the West Should Know About German Neutralism," p. 31.

63. Bernard Willms, *Die Deutsche Nation* (Köln-Lovenich: Edition Maschke Hohenheim, 1982), p. 281. See also Caspar von Schrenck-Notzing and Armin Mohler, eds., *Deutsche Identität* (Krefeld: Sinus Verlag, 1982); Wolfgang Venohr, ed., *Ohne Deutschland geht es nicht* (Krefeld: Sinus Verlag, 1985).

64. Willms, *Die Deutsche Nation*, p. 292.

65. Willms, *Die Deutsche Nation*, p. 288. See also Oswald Feiler, *Moskau und die Deutsche Frage* (Krefeld: Sinus Verlag, 1984).

66. Willms, *Die Deutsche Nation*, p. 284. In a similar vein, Jane Kramer argued that "[t]he West does not intend to unite Germany any more than the Russians do. Everyone knows this, but the working arrangement is that no one admits it. . . . [N]o one in Europe *is* really comfortable with German enthusiasm for 'Germany.'" Kramer, *Europeans* (New York: Penguin Books, 1988), pp. 497, 496.

67. Willms, *Die Deutsche Nation*, p. 257.

68. For additional conservative perspectives on the German Question, see Kiep, "The New Deutschlandpolitik" (a more moderate view); Kohl, *Reden, 1982–1984*, pp. 68–72, 158–163, 173–180, 221–239, 344–364.

69. Hassner, "The Shifting Foundation," p. 6.

70. Ernst Otto Mätzke, quoted in Hassner, "The Shifting Foundation," p. 8. See also Stern, "Conclusion: German-American Relations and 'The Return of the Repressed,'" p. 244.

71. See some of the views expressed by Günter Gaus in *Wo Deutschland liegt* (Hamburg: Hoffmann und Campe Verlag, 1983). Gaus was FRG representative in the GDR in the era of the SPD's *Ostpolitik*.

72. Stern, "Conclusion: German-American Relations and 'The Return of the Repressed,'" p. 242.

73. For further discussion on nuclear no-first-use, see Karl Kaiser, Georg Leber, Alois Mertes, and Franz-Josef Schulze, "Nuclear Weapons and the Preservation of Peace," *Foreign Affairs*, vol. 60, nr. 5, Summer 1982. On the SDI controversy during and after 1983, see Claus Richter, "Strategische Verteidigungsinitiative (SDI)," *Aus Politik und Zeitgeschichte*, 6 April 1985; Hans-Henrik Holm, "SDI and European Security: Does Dependence Assure Security?" *Alternatives*, vol. X, nr. 4, 1985; Michael Lucas, "SDI and Europe," *World Policy Journal*, vol. 3, nr. 2, Spring 1986; Manfred Wörner, "A Missile Defense for NATO Europe," *Strategic Review*, vol. XIV, nr. 1, Winter 1986; Werner Kaltefleiter, "Strategic Defense on the Broader Historical Stage," *Strategic Review*, vol. XIII, nr. 3, Summer 1985; Christoph Bertram, "Strategic Defense and the Western Alliance," *Daedalus*, vol. 114, nr. 3, Summer 1985; Karl Kaiser, "SDI und deutsche Politik," *Europa-Archiv*, nr. 19, 1986.

74. See Clemens, "The Green Program for German Society and International Affairs."

75. See Gress, "What the West Should Know About German Neutralism;" Herf, "Neutralism and the Moral Order in West Germany." Although such concerns diminished as the 1980s progressed, they remained prevalent. See, for example, the discussion in Keithly, "The German Fatherland—Of the Left." For "national" thinking on the West German Left during the 1980s, see Günter Gaus, *Texte zur deutschen Frage* (Darmstadt: Hermann Luchterhand Verlag, 1981); Egon Bahr, *Was wird aus den Deutschen? Fragen und Antworten* (Reinbek bei Hamburg: Rowohlt Taschenbuch Verlag, 1982).

76. See especially Schwarz, "The West Germans, Western Democracy, and Western Ties in the Light of Public Opinion Research." For an additional evaluation, see Wallace Thies, *The Atlantic Alliance, Nuclear Weapons and European Attitudes* (Berkeley: University of California, Institute of International Studies, 1983).

77. Alvin Richman, "The U.S. Image Under Stress: Trends and Structure of Foreign Attitudes Toward the United States," in Charles W. Kegley and Patrick J. McGowan, eds., *Challenges to America: United States Foreign Policy in the 1980's* (Beverly Hills: Sage Publications, 1979), p. 205.

78. See Joffe, "German Defense Policy: Novel Solutions and Enduring Dilemmas."

79. For further discussion and data, see Schweigler, *West German Foreign Policy*, Chapters 3, 4, 5, 6, and the opinion data presented in the Notes (pp. 90–124). See also Eckhard Jesse, "Die (Pseudo-)Aktualität der deutschen Frage—ein publizistisches, kein politisches Phänomen," in Michalka, ed., *Die Deutsche Frage in der Weltpolitik*.

80. An interesting way in which German attitudes about the past and about nationhood jointly surfaced during the 1980s occurred during the fall of 1984, when West German television aired a series entitled *Heimat* (a nearly untranslatable word that means at least "home" but actually a great deal more). Jane Kramer has described the widespread popularity of the series as "an escape from that exhausting, impossible enterprise called the German past—not so much an evasion as a surrender, a collapse into simplicities." She in-

terprets it as an "assertion of the German soul," a form of German Romanticized fundamentalism filled with backward-looking sentimentalism, uncomplicated by troubling political or historical questions, but focused instead on positive, traditional aspects of
"homeland." Kramer, "Being German," in her *Europeans*, pp. 493–508. The broadcasting of
a documentary series on the Holocaust triggered very different reactions, however. On
these matters, see also Ash, "The Life of Death," in his *The Uses of Adversity*, pp. 120–142.

81. Kohl, *Reden, 1982–1984*, pp. 106, 111. The speech given in early May 1985 by FRG
President Richard von Weizsäcker acquired particular fame in this context. It is reprinted
in Richard von Weizsäcker, *Von Deutschland aus* (München: Deutscher Taschenbuch Verlag, 1987), pp. 11–35.

82. Quoted in Dennison I. Rusinow, "Old Wounds: Reflections on the Storm over V-E
Day 1985," *UFSI* (Universities Field Staff International) *Reports*, nr. 15, 1985, p. 2.

83. On the West German response to these foreign concerns, see Schulz and Danylow,
Bewegung in der deutschen Frage? See also Beate Gödde-Baumanns, "Die deutsche Frage in
der französischen Geschichtsschreibung," and Krzysztof Baczkowski et al., "Deutschland
und die deutsche Frage in der polnischen Geschichtsschreibung," both in *Aus Politik und
Zeitgeschichte*, 4 April 1987. Shifts in international images and perceptions of Germany
and the Germans are analyzed by Karl-Rudolf Korte in "Deutschlandbilder—Akzentverlagerungen der deutschen Frage seit den siebziger Jahren," *Aus Politik und Zeitgeschichte*,
15 January 1988. More generally, see also Manfred Koch-Hillebrecht, ed., *Das Deutschenbild* (München: Beck Verlag, 1977).

7

The Unification of Germany and the Transformation of Europe

Winter of Turbulence and Discontent

The astounding events of fall 1989 completely shook just about all of the German "certainties" of the previous forty years. Events unfolded with a rapidity that left observers and policymakers alike breathless.[1] Amid spreading political protest, the true dimensions of the fundamental crisis of East Germany's socioeconomic and political system became fully manifest, as discussion and recrimination began about its causes and who was to blame.[2] The mass exodus of East Germans to the West led to the collapse of the Honecker regime in November and the breaching of the Berlin Wall. A brief SED interregnum followed, led first by Egon Krenz and then by Hans Modrow, with whom West German Chancellor Helmut Kohl clearly did not wish to deal in any serious longer-term way. As economic and political collapse became imminent, the days of Communist rule in the GDR were numbered. Free elections, the first in that area of Germany since 1932, were scheduled for May 1990 and then rescheduled for mid-March 1990, in view of a worsening crisis.

Meanwhile, events in the GDR began to have their international implications. Kohl offered a rather daring ten-point plan for German confederation, with continued NATO membership, in November 1989, without consulting his closest allies.[3] His go-it-alone assertiveness was a demonstration of West Germany's increased self-confidence in an environment of collapsing Communist rule in Eastern Europe. The Soviet Union was about to lose one of its closest allies in Eastern Europe and made suggestions regarding a possible German confederation outside both NATO and the Warsaw Pact in the hope of salvaging as much of its position as possible. GDR leader Modrow echoed this idea with a January 1990 proposal for a neutralized united Germany. Both ideas were clearly reminiscent of various (Soviet) ideas of the early 1950s, and were flatly rejected by a West German government that had increasingly worried Western allies to contend with.[4] The FRG's allies were concerned about the Federal Republic's future in both NATO and the EC, and it fell especially to FRG Foreign Minister Genscher to provide the needed assurances. It was also Genscher who sought to break a deadlock over possible NATO membership of a reunited Germany by suggesting that NATO forces should stay clear of GDR territory in a united Germany and that the USSR should be allowed to maintain a contingent of forces on East German territory for a prearranged period after unification.

By early 1990, it was clear that full German reunification was all but inevitable, and all confederation ideas, predicated on a continued existence in some form of two separate German states, found their end in history's dustbin. The rapidity of change rendered obsolete the ideas of analysts like Anne-Marie Burley, who wrote in late 1989: "Stability in Europe means the maintenance of the existing international structure: two superpowers and two Germanies. Stability in the G.D.R. means reform without the threat of reunification. . . . [R]ecognizing the German division as permanent could be the final step toward overcoming it."[5]

The human exodus from East to West Germany continued, economic conditions in the GDR worsened steadily, and East German opinion swung clearly in the direction of unification with the West. In a November 1989 survey, only 16 percent of GDR citizens had expressed strong support for unification, while 32 percent were moderately in favor, and 52 percent were either moderately or strongly opposed to the idea. By February/March 1990, however, 84 percent were moderately or strongly in favor of unification, while only 16 percent remained moderately or strongly opposed.[6] In addition, an interesting 60 percent of GDR citizens professed support for the notion of a militarily neutral united Germany.[7]

It is also worth noting, however, that opinion polling in March 1990 in East Germany detected a significant difference among generations as far as levels of identification with "Germany" and the "GDR" were concerned. Of those born before 1930, 74 percent professed a strong sense of being German, with only 22 percent stressing a more primary GDR identity. The respective percentages were as follows for the other generations: among those born between 1931 and 1945, 66 percent versus 28 percent; among those born between 1946 and 1960, 55 percent versus 39 percent; and among those born after 1960, 52 percent versus 37 percent. In other words, although a strong sense of being "German" characterized all generations, a significant identification with the GDR was quite pronounced among those who had been fully socialized by life in East Germany after 1949. In addition, supporters of the SED overwhelmingly continued to identify with the GDR, whereas clear majorities of the supporters of the other major (emerging) parties in East Germany professed a more primary "German" identity.[8]

A major breakthrough occurred in February 1990. Agreement was reached in Ottawa between FRG and GDR representatives and the former Allies of World War II (the United States, the USSR, Great Britain, and France) with their residual legal rights in Germany (including Berlin) on the so-called two-plus-four formula: The two German states would work out the internal modalities of unification, while they would join the Four Powers to make the necessary international security adjustments. As far as the internal German process was concerned, the key issue quickly became the cost of what was no less than a West German bailout of a collapsing GDR. East-West disagreement over a possible NATO membership of the new Germany, plus the sensitive issue of the German-Polish border, clearly topped the agenda on the international side of the bargaining process.

The internal German process was heavily colored by the fact that 1990 became a year of "Siamese" German elections (March elections in the GDR, December elections in the FRG). For the first time since the creation of the two German states in 1949, free elections were to take place on both sides of the intra-German dividing line. And, needless to say, reunification became the decisive campaign issue on both sides. An additional Siamese dimension of this joint German electoral process lay in the fact that in both German states, some of the principal parties in the political contest came to coexist (and be allied) as sister parties. Thus one encountered the phenomenon of Christian Democratic, Social Democratic, and Free Democratic parties on both sides, in addition to parties or movements with Green or ecological orientations.

The partially conflicting visions of West Germany's two key parties, the Social Democrats and Christian Democrats, in the area of foreign policy were discussed in previous chapters. It became obvious rather quickly that these differences would continue to play a significant role in Germany's political future. The dynamic of "competitive nationalism" between these two large parties, aimed at proving one's nationalist credentials to the electorate, tends to be particularly dangerous. Carried to an extreme, such a competition could be highly destabilizing for Germany's evolving democratic political culture, not to mention the country's image in the rest of the world.

Chancellor Kohl's West German Christian Democrats sought to position themselves as true guardians of the nation, but also as the representatives of the Adenauer *Westpolitik* legacy with its strong emphasis on both European integration and Atlantic partnership with the United States. We saw in Chapters 5 and 6 that the CDU's German nationalism has been primarily embedded in a Europeanist, Atlanticist, and procapitalist ideological framework, although older nationalist elements clearly survive in some sectors of the CDU and its Bavarian sister-party, the CSU, and among some of the groups of expellees from former eastern German territories. Yet the possibility also presented itself that if East-West negotiations over NATO membership of a future Germany encountered serious stalemate, the CDU's Atlanticism could become a political liability. Insofar as NATO's purpose had been not only the defense of Western Europe vis-à-vis the Warsaw Pact but also the control of German power, continued acceptance of NATO constraints (especially foreign troops on German soil) by a CDU-led government could well turn into a deeply emotional issue in a reuniting Germany, an issue with considerable nationalist explosive potential, which the SPD, among others, could be expected to exploit. This is why many argued that the transcendence of both NATO and the Warsaw Pact, legacies of a passing era, by means of the creation of a pan-European security order should receive urgent attention.

The West German Social Democrats had tended to be less strongly Atlanticist, and hinted at a willingness to reexamine Germany's role (and membership) in NATO in the context of the overall reunification process, a fact that led some to warn of a resurgence of SPD-led German neutralism. After the late 1950s, the SPD's support of European integration became quite genuine, although it showed sensitivity to domination of the European Community by big business at the expense of social needs. After initial, and electorally costly, hesitation in 1989 about the reunification issue, the SPD endorsed the broad outlines of Kohl's confederation plan, before seeking to move ahead to articulate its own policy preferences on the matter of national unity amid rapidly evolving inter-German conditions. For the SPD, long-standing contacts with the disgraced and disintegrated East German SED were likely to be a political liability in the time ahead. The same could be said of the SPD's historic alienation from German nationhood.[9]

The Free Democrats continued to be a crucial coalition partner for either the CDU or the SPD, despite the party's small size. Although more Atlanticist than the SPD, they did collaborate with the Social Democrats during the years after 1969 in formulating the basic reorientation of West German foreign policy known as *Ostpolitik*. For the foreseeable future, however, the Free Democrats were expected to continue their participation in the coalition with the CDU/CSU. The Greens on the Left and the *Republikaner* on the Right did not appear to be decisive players (yet).[10]

Needless to say, the East German political scene was much more turbulent. The Socialist Unity Party (SED), now renamed Party of Democratic Socialism (PDS), continued to disintegrate as 1990 progressed, facing both a basic political credibility problem and a noticeable fragmentation into more conservative and reformist camps. Initial SED attempts to retain influence (if not power) by playing up an alleged neo-Nazi threat clearly backfired. The various opposition groups (New Forum, Democratic Awakening, and Democracy Now) that emerged in the course of 1989 saw their political influence weaken considerably by the beginning of 1990, despite their participation in Round Table talks with the caretaker government and subsequent participation in that government. Some were heavily dominated by groups of intellectuals, and many had to struggle hard to define an electoral identity, to decide whether they wished to be a formal political party at all, and to delineate a position on the twin questions of German unity and the GDR's future.[11] Initially committed to the continued existence of a separate East German state, they were all soon confronted with a seemingly uncontrollable popular rush in the direction of reunification, and had to adjust their platforms accordingly. Many developed a clearly enduring resentment against what they saw as an East German "sellout" to West German bourgeois capitalism.[12]

The SED's former allies, "bloc parties"[13] like the East German CDU and FDP, appeared to be severely afflicted by a basic credibility problem in the eyes of the GDR's electorate. As a result, the West German CDU and FDP were at first far from eager to lend electoral support and endorsement to these sister parties. Faced with the rapid growth of the SPD in the GDR, however, Chancellor Kohl's CDU swung its support behind a small East German coalition of center-right opposition groups (*Allianz für Deutschland*) that did include the East German CDU.

By the early months of 1990, East Germany's newly reconstituted Social Democratic Party (SDP, subsequently renamed SPD) seemed to emerge clearly as the major new force in GDR politics. This party could not be tainted by the stigma of collaboration with the SED regime, and could tap the historical electoral strength of Social Democracy in the east of Germany. In addition, the party could present itself as a credible defender of those social programs that the average East German might not wish to see eliminated altogether after reunification with the more prosperous Federal Republic.

Yet the GDR elections on March 18 defied all earlier forecasts, turning into a triumph for the CDU-backed conservative Alliance. Unlike a still-hesitant SPD and PDS, the Alliance promised quick unification in the most unambiguous way, and clearly benefited from its closeness to a West German chancellor who would be expected to fulfill his promises of massive economic aid. The fact that the Alliance fell just short of an absolute majority (about 48 percent) necessitated the formation of a coalition. After a brief period of haggling, overshadowed by allegations concerning collaboration with the former state security police (*Stasi*) by many of the GDR's new politicians, a grand coalition was formed, including both the Alliance and the SPD, which had polled 22 percent of the vote. The PDS, which had scored a somewhat surprising 16 percent in the election, was excluded: Communist rule in East Germany had formally come to an end.

With a freely elected East German government in place, the two-plus-four process could now move forward in more decisive fashion. We examine first the internal German process, and then turn to the international ramifications of the creation of a united Germany.

Germany Reunites: Economics, Elections, and Emotions

The intra-German process of unification focused on some crucial constitutional, socioeconomic, financial, and political issues. As far as the constitutional modalities of unity were concerned, several possibilities existed.[14] Usage of Article 23 in

West Germany's Basic Law would necessitate a reconstitution of the original *Länder* (states) in East Germany, which could then vote one by one to accede to the Federal Republic.[15] This was the formula preferred by the Christian Democrats. Another possibility, favored by the Social Democrats, would be to take the route of Article 146, which would involve the drafting of an entirely new constitution by an all-German constituent assembly.[16] A third constitutional possibility, namely the continued existence of two German states in a confederation of some kind, quickly vanished from all official and scholarly discussion. Most observers came to see unification based on Article 23 as the best route, also because it would be the easiest way to bring the GDR into the European Community without elaborate negotiations.[17]

The socioeconomic and financial aspects of unification generated far more immediate controversy, particularly among the general public, than the more technical and even obscure constitutional modalities. The basic question quickly became evident: What would it cost and who would pay? Estimates of the total (long-term) cost of unification would soon range from 500 billion to 1 trillion D-mark (deutsche marks). As 1990 progressed, popular pressure in the FRG grew to put an end to West Germany's generous support of those who had left the GDR. It became clear that the emotional excitement of the fall of 1989 had been replaced by outright worry over the economic and financial consequences of a West German bailout of the GDR, in addition to widespread concern about the need to absorb and integrate a seemingly endless number of "immigrants" (*Übersiedler*) from the GDR.[18] As W. R. Smyser put it at the time, "[t]he unification of Germany is only superficially a merger between a capitalist and a socialist economy. It is really a merger between rich and poor."[19]

Predictions of increased inflation and higher taxes in the FRG created visible uneasiness among the West German public, which in turn was probably responsible for the CDU's loss in two important state elections in West Germany in May that resulted in SPD control of the *Bundesrat* (the upper house of the West German parliament). Clear popular majorities continued to support the objective of unification, but matters of speed and cost became a source of noticeable political divisiveness. The CDU/CSU-FDP coalition government favored a rapid pace and played down the possibility of adverse economic consequences, while the opposition SPD urged a slowing of the pace and hoped to benefit politically from public anxiety over the high cost.[20] Concern over trends in West German public sentiment even seemed to prompt Kohl to strive for earlier-than-planned all-German elections, clearly hoping to cash in on his party's popularity in the East and thereby offset possible voter losses in the West.[21]

·Anxiety was also easy to detect among the population in the GDR, focused on fear over increased unemployment, an inability to compete with the more powerful West Germans, the possibility of sudden property claims arising from past confiscations, and an elimination of numerous aspects of the GDR's relatively generous welfare-state provisions. Sadness among GDR citizens over the real prospect of a noticeable loss of identity also began to surface, as ironic as that may seem in light of the overwhelming anti-SED and prounification mood.[22] Yet the desire for rapid unity, coupled with the expectation of massive West German economic assistance, was sufficient to bring the CDU-dominated Alliance a ringing victory in the March elections, although the Alliance's electoral outlook for the longer term had to be considered uncertain at best.

Particular controversy was generated by Chancellor Kohl's desire to bring about a quick monetary union between the two German states, to be set up by means of a formal *Staatsvertrag* (state treaty). Initial opposition by the FRG's *Bundesbank* (Central Bank) subsided, but uneasiness over the monetary consequences clearly remained. East and West German negotiators haggled over the conversion rate that would be applied between the strong West German D-mark and the GDR's very weak Ostmark. Popular anxiety in the East rose dramatically, since an unfavorable rate could have a devastating impact on savings, pensions, and purchasing power.[23] In the end, a one-for-one rate was agreed upon, although a ceiling was set for the amounts that could be converted at that rate. Early July was selected as the target date for full monetary union, although concerns and disagreements on related economic matters, particularly in the area of market-oriented reform, continued to slow down the process.

But as the spring ended, considerable progress had been made. FRG-GDR negotiations had resulted in a draft state treaty on economic and monetary union that was signed in May. After some complex political maneuvering within the West German SPD, involving the (unsuccessful) demand by the party's chancellor-candidate, Oskar LaFontaine, that the SPD block the state treaty unless certain improvements were made in the text, the treaty was ratified by the parliaments of both German states in June. On July 1, 1990, amid uncertainty, anxiety, and anticipation, the FRG-GDR economic and monetary merger went into effect.[24] And now, more than ever before, the likelihood of all-German elections in December 1990 came clearly into view.

A $70 billion fund to finance the merger had meanwhile been created, coupled with a "no new taxes" promise from the Bonn government, although widespread skepticism persisted. The fund would cover a four-year period, with expenditures focused on the rebuilding of the GDR's old industries and infrastructure, adjustments in the tax system, and a much-needed cleanup of the heavily polluted environment in East Germany. Yet it was also significant that the state treaty did not address some highly sensitive issues that would have to be settled through separate negotiations, such as ownership of private property in a desocialized GDR and some of the basic aspects of reform of East German industry and agriculture, with a potential for a level of unemployment that some felt might reach well beyond 1, 2, or even 3 million (out of a population of 16 million).

Some, but by no means all, of these issues were decided in a second *Staatsvertrag* that was ratified by the parliaments of both German states on the eve of the formal unification date (October 3, 1990), after a turbulent negotiation process that saw continued political instability and friction in the GDR's shaky "grand coalition" of conservative Alliance, liberal FDP, and left-wing SPD. Yet property claims and divergencies in abortion legislation remained among the most important issues that promised continued controversy. The signing of the second treaty, and the at times clearly subdued and noticeably nonnationalistic celebration of unification, were followed by elections in the newly reconstituted *Länder* (states) in the GDR (and in Bavaria in the old FRG) on October 14. The Christian Democrats scored impressive victories in four of the eastern *Länder* (Saxony, Thuringia, Saxony-Anhalt, and Mecklenburg), whereas the SPD was successful in gaining a majority of the vote only in Brandenburg. The former Communist party managed to gain an average of about 10–12 percent of the vote in each GDR state. The election results also brought a restoration of the CDU/CSU-FDP majority in the *Bundesrat*.

Aside from the many economic difficulties faced by the new Germany in its internal affairs—such as unemployment, the risk of inflation, disputes over property claims, hesitation among potential investors, and instances of criminal financial corruption in a collapsing former GDR—political and basic social problems also came more strongly to the fore. A fundamental revamping of educational policy and curricular content in the primary- and secondary-school system of the former GDR was among the urgent questions to be addressed, in addition to much-needed reform of overstaffed academic institutions. Health care and other social services were on the brink of full-scale collapse. Instances of racism and/or violence by skinheads and other disaffected and alienated groups, including squatters and anarchists in Berlin, emerged as an additional challenge to a virtually disintegrated East German law-enforcement apparatus. Tensions between East Germans and the remaining groups of foreign "guest workers," as well as the thousands of Soviet soldiers, increased steadily.

Political debate over the appropriate policy to be pursued with respect to former GDR spies, *Stasi* (secret police) employees, border guards, and Communist officials, ranging from possible amnesty to full-scale persecution and partial incarceration, continued to flare up with predictable regularity. At the same time, controversy over *Stasi* files and their inherent potential for political embarrassment, if not blackmail, persisted undiminished. Furthermore, former East German political parties, especially the SED, were forced to surrender their extensive accumulations of capital and property.

Meanwhile, the campaign for Germany's first truly national elections since the end of the war had erupted in full force, with the governing CDU/CSU-FDP coalition in Bonn enjoying the clear status of virtually unbeatable favorite in the December 2 ballot-box contest. The polls left little doubt about the likely outcome, especially in light of the CDU's renewed successes in the October 14 GDR elections, and most in the SPD appeared resigned to the inevitable: Helmut Kohl would remain the new Germany's *Einheitskanzler* (chancellor of unity), a new Bismarck in a democratic Germany.[25] Despite widespread West German worry about the costs of unification, the SPD proved incapable of using this issue to greater political benefit. Its political message seemed to fall on deaf ears, especially in the East German area.

The SPD's prospects were further dampened by the decision of West Germany's Federal Constitutional Court in September that mandated the use of separate five-percent electoral thresholds in former East and West Germany in the December balloting. This would benefit smaller parties, especially in the East, that might not otherwise make it into the new German parliament, but it also deprived the SPD of potential crossover votes from small East German left-wing parties and citizens' movements.

The results of the December 2 all-German vote were largely as expected. Kohl's Christian Democrats, with their Bavarian CSU allies, captured 43.8 percent of the total national electorate, as opposed to the SPD's 33.5 percent, which amounted to the Social Democrats' worst showing in thirty years. The Free Democrats succeeded in reaching 11 percent of the vote and were widely expected to demand more ministerial posts in the new CDU/CSU-FDP coalition government. Parties on the extreme right or left generally fared badly. In the West, the Greens failed to surmount the five-percent electoral threshold and would therefore not return to the *Bundestag*. They had been alienated by the increasingly patriotic mood after the collapse of the Berlin Wall, and their ecological agenda had been in large part adopted by the major parties. Only in the East did a coalition of environmental and peace groups known as Bündnis90 capture enough votes to gain representation in the *Bundestag*. The PDS, successor of the discredited Communist SED, also gained a sufficient number of votes in the East (9.9 percent) to enter the national parliament (although nationally it received no more than 2.4 percent). The far-right *Republikaner* received only a meager 2.1 percent of the vote, well below the required five percent for *Bundestag* representation. Despite a rather low 77.8 percent voter turnout, the message of the election was fairly clear: no experiments, continuation of the current coalition, and a strengthening of the center of Germany's political spectrum.

Toward a Pax Germanica or a Pax Europaea?

It was in the international realm, however, rather than the internal FRG-GDR sphere with its focus on sometimes bitter electoral contests and the marks-and-pfennigs issues of socioeconomic merger, that the German Question with its four central dimensions of identity, unity, role, and power made itself felt most dramatically after November 1989.[26] One analyst captured the essence of international concern as follows:

> There are only two real certainties in European politics today: Eastern Europe has been effectively liberated from Soviet domination, and the reunification of Germany is approaching. For all their historic worth, these certainties, in turn, create new un-

certainties—after all, the postwar system of European stability, of deterrence and detente, was based on the permanence of the Soviet threat and of the division of Europe and of Germany. Now that history has turned the tables, it is the hitherto un-
questioned structures of European order that are entering a period of
unpredictability: in the East, all structures—from the Warsaw Pact to Comecon—set
up to camouflage Soviet centralized control; in the West, the NATO alliance and the
European Community (EC); in Europe as a whole the familiar ways in which East-
West relations are conducted. Germany is at the center of all these uncertainties, not
only geographically but politically.[27]

He added that "Europe's two new certainties are interdependent: had Eastern Europe not succeeded in slipping away from Soviet control, there would be no
chance for the reunification of Germany."[28]

One basic and decisive question concerned the diplomatic intentions of the
various players in this unfolding drama.[29] Perhaps most important, was Moscow
willing to abandon its East German ally and permit reunification without major
Western concessions? Soviet options were by no means clear, and neither were
the Kremlin's ultimate objectives.[30] After its unsuccessful attempt to bring about
an FRG-GDR confederation that would have preserved the Soviet position in
Central Europe to its maximum extent under already adverse circumstances,
Moscow appeared to accept full reunification as inevitable, but continued to op-
pose NATO membership of a united Germany, until a breakthrough was reached
in July 1990.

The Genscher proposal, discussed earlier, sought to break the stalemate,
whereupon the Soviets suggested a German membership in both NATO and the
Warsaw Pact. But this idea was quickly rejected by both Bonn and its allies. Serious limitations on German military power as part of an East-West compromise
remained likely, while Western leaders expected Moscow to abandon its opposition to German NATO membership. Such expectation was fueled by a variety of
considerations, such as Gorbachev's growing preoccupation with domestic troubles, the steady disintegration of the Warsaw Pact, and a widespread Eastern European preference for a NATO-bound rather than neutralized (read: unpredictable and uncontrolled) Germany.

In addition, polls showed that NATO membership for a united Germany remained clearly the preferred option among West Germans. A June 1990 poll, for
example, found that 51 percent of West Germans interviewed preferred a united
Germany in NATO, 34 percent would opt for neutrality, and 15 percent were undecided. In addition, 53 percent of the sample indicated willingness to "accept the
presence of foreign troops [on German soil] as part of [Germany's] NATO obligations," whereas 31 percent felt that "foreign troops should withdraw" (16 percent were undecided). Attitudes on nuclear weapons were also interesting. Of the
interview sample, 54 percent agreed that nuclear weapons should now be removed from German soil, but 37 percent argued that they should remain, while

9 percent were undecided. When asked whether nuclear weapons should be pulled out of Germany if "the Soviet Union made its agreement to German unity conditional on [such a removal of nuclear weapons]," however, only 25 percent agreed with such a scenario, while 65 percent felt that "we should not allow ourselves to be pressured in the matter of German unity," and 10 percent declared themselves undecided.[31]

As the months passed, the likelihood emerged that NATO membership of a united Germany would be tied to an overall East-West agreement on conventional forces in Europe (resulting from the CFE negotiations in Vienna) plus extensive Western economic and financial assistance to the struggling Soviet economy. This latter approach, extending beyond the newly created Bank for East European Development, was looked upon skeptically by the United States and Great Britain, but favored by the other Western allies, including especially the FRG, which had already promised Moscow to assume the GDR's trading obligations vis-à-vis the USSR.

For many, Kohl's exceedingly clumsy handling of the German-Polish border issue in early 1990 was unmistakable proof of the need to anchor the new Germany firmly in the Western alliance. Allegedly concerned over the potential loss of the West German bloc of expellee votes to the far right, Kohl hesitated badly when asked to declare the Oder-Neisse line as the definitive border between Germany and Poland. His argument that only a newly constituted German government and parliament could effectively make such a pledge was legally correct but politically extremely ill-timed and unwise. Declarations by both German parliaments, plus Allied assurances that Poland would be allowed to participate in discussions regarding its border with Germany in the context of the two-plus-four talks, subsequently defused the immediate controversy and anxiety, but the damage had been done. By July, the two German states and Poland reached a full understanding about the finality of the current German-Polish border, to be formalized in a treaty at the time of Germany's official reunification and tied to plans for extensive German-Polish economic cooperation. In November, agreement on the formal German-Polish treaty indeed became reality: The existing border was declared fixed once and for all, although the fundamental challenge of reconciliation and cooperation would require more long-term effort on both sides.

The Polish-German border issue was illustrative of more widespread anxiety among many of Germany's neighbors regarding the prospect of unification, however. A poll conducted in January 1990 in eight countries (Spain, Italy, FRG, Hungary, Britain, France, USSR, and Poland) detected mixed feelings. "Roughly two out of three Poles are opposed to the reunification of Germany, but a majority of Russians and Hungarians feel positively about the idea. . . . [W]hile a solid majority of those questioned in five Western European countries favored a single German state, a significant number of Britons and French—around one in four—were opposed." The poll revealed "continuing uncertainty throughout Europe." For example, "[a]mong the Western European countries polled, only Italy had a majority that thought lasting peace was within reach. Forty-nine percent of Britons and 50 percent of French said a serious European conflict was still possible."[32] As the months progressed, some of the international worries seemed to ease, particularly as a result of a variety of diplomatic assurances made by the Bonn government.[33] Jewish concerns frequently persisted, however, in part because no explicit all-German admission of guilt for the Holocaust was included in the final FRG-GDR unification treaty. The likelihood of claims made against a reunited Germany by Jews and others also continued to loom as a source of very probable controversy, as events in the 1990s have indeed confirmed.

As Christoph Bertram pointed out, the basic international agenda resulting from the inexorable drift toward German reunification involved "the security status of Germany, the cancellation of the remnants of Germany's now obsolete postwar legal regime, the special rights of the Four Powers, the status of the city of Berlin, and the finalization of Germany's external borders, particularly with Poland." In addition, the European Community would have to "define the modalities of permitting one of its member states to be enlarged."[34]

The exact ways in which this agenda would be managed, and the various issues settled, could only become clearer as the months and weeks passed, and some aspects might not be fully settled for at least several years after formal FRG-GDR unification. What became very obvious, however, was that this agenda reflected the basic dimensions of an enduring German Question with which Germans and non-Germans alike had to contend. It was clear that one aspect of that Question, namely national *unity*, was at least formally "solved," although lingering revisionism due to the loss of former Eastern territories might have to be watched carefully.

But it was also important to remember that territorial and legal German unification by itself did not by any means result in immediate, genuine East-West German cultural and psychological unity. Forty years of political-ideological and psychological separation could not and would not be undone overnight. What is more, the dismal economic picture in the former GDR all but guaranteed that the population in "East" Germany would for some years to come have to cope with a (perceived as well as real) status as "second-class" citizens in the new Germany, frequently subject to "West" German disdain, ridicule, and resentment.[35] In fact, Michael Meyer suggested that "[t]he German Question has . . . been reincarnated, in a new form," because "[t]he new Germany will be one nation, but two peoples."[36] Interesting in this context of continued "disunity" was also the discussion of what the "eastern" part of the new Germany ought to be called in political discourse: "the former GDR," "the new Federal *Länder*," "eastern Germany"? For many conservatives who continued to harbor revisionist dreams regarding the lost "eastern" territories in Poland and the Soviet Union, of course, the former GDR would always remain *Mitteldeutschland*.[37]

Furthermore, there was absolutely no doubt that the three remaining dimensions of the German Question—*identity*, *role*, and *power*—would also continue to preoccupy scholars and policymakers alike for at least the foreseeable future. Beyond the concrete military, political, and economic issues that the international community would face in striving to deal with the new Germany, the psychological aspects, particularly fear of a new German nationalism, would be equally significant.

Western and West German insistence on placing the new German giant firmly in the Western community was the clear outgrowth of perceived lessons of the German and European past. Throughout its history, Germany's geopolitical location in the heart of Europe, coupled with its growing power, have been the source of both trauma and temptation, of insecurity and instability. Germany's alienation from the West was further enhanced by at least partially diverging cultural values and political traditions. In this respect, Germany's reconciliation with the West and the FRG's membership in both NATO and the EC rank among the great success stories of postwar Western, and West German, diplomacy. The steady democratization of West German political culture became a source of reassurance to the country's traumatized neighbors.

In light of these considerations, Western and West German insistence on a Germany firmly tied to the West, militarily in NATO and economically through the EC, was necessary, inevitable, and under prevailing circumstances desirable. A reaffirmation of Germany's Western *identity*, coupled with a well-defined *role* in multilateral (even supranational) Western institutions and organizations, would provide the most appropriate basis for a solution to what has been perhaps the most crucial dimension of the German Question: *power*.[38] In fact, if this study has proved anything, it is that what has tended to be called the German Question is *not* necessarily the problem of German reunification but perhaps primarily the problem of German power. History has given us ample indication that the effective management of German power by the Germans themselves and by Germany's neighbors is crucial to the creation of a stable European order.[39] The Cold War "solution" to this problem, based on the division of Germany and the integration of both states into opposing alliance systems, came to an end in 1990. What would the future bring?

The management of the new Germany's power would be an international task, but, as Bertram stressed, the Germans themselves would now face perhaps the major responsibility:

Germany holds a pivotal role as a generator of policy. The ideas, initiatives and commitments to shape a stable European future will now largely have to come from the Germans themselves—not only because of their weight in Europe's politics and economy, but also because, with the notable and welcome exception of the United States, Germany's main partners in the West have largely retreated into attentive (France) or irritated (Britain) passivity. German politicians must thus display an immense degree of statesmanship, not only in order to manage the domestic process of reunification, but to pave the way for the international one as well. This is a tall order for any country. Germany must accommodate the concern of those worried about the German past as well as that of those troubled by its new power; it must reassure Soviet security interests without arousing suspicions in the West; it must strengthen its Western ties through participation in the reform of NATO and through promotion of political union in Western Europe. In short, Germany has to use its weight and power wisely, considerately as well as confidently.[40]

International concern over German military power was likely to persist, particularly the scenario of a future revisionist German superpower armed with nuclear weapons. Hence there was increased effort on all sides to examine various possible security arrangements, including arms control agreements, that might stabilize the emerging post–Cold War European continent.[41]

Major breakthroughs on the security status of a united Germany were finally achieved during the summer of 1990, after months of intense negotiations and posturing by the various parties.[42] In mid-July, the Soviet Union removed its objection to the NATO membership of a united Germany, in return for extensive Western (especially German) aid for the faltering Soviet economy; a limit of 345,000 on the troop strength of the all-German army; a German pledge not to acquire any nuclear, chemical, or biological weapons; and German agreement to help pay for the maintenance of Soviet troops on East German territory for a transitional period of three to four years as well as for their subsequent removal. The last obstacle to the rapid and successful conclusion of the two-plus-four talks had been definitively cleared, and on September 12, the four wartime allies and the two German states signed the agreement formally restoring full German sovereignty. The Soviet-German breakthrough culminated in a formal treaty of friendship and cooperation between the two continental European giants in November, whereupon a grand European–North American summit meeting of the Conference on Security and Cooperation in Europe gave its formal endorsement to German unity, a far-reaching conventional arms control agreement between East and West, and the construction of a new European order beyond the Cold War in what became known as the Charter of Paris.

Yet many of the more immediate and realistic considerations focused not on Germany's military power but on its inevitable political and economic clout in a changing Europe. The following (estimated) figures offered an indication of a united Germany's projected economic power as the decade of the 1990s began. Exports by the new united Germany were expected to total $354 billion a year, compared with $321 billion for the United States, $265 billion for Japan, and $110 billion for the USSR. The new Germany's balance of trade was projected to show a $74 billion surplus, compared with Japan's $77 billion surplus, the Soviets' meager $3 billion surplus, and a $138 billion deficit for the United States. Per capita GNP was calculated at $14,000 for a united Germany, nearly $20,000 for the United States, $14,000 for Japan, and less than $9,000 for the USSR.[43] Based on 1988 figures, the united Germany would have a GDP of about $1 trillion, compared with $4.8 trillion for the United States, $2.5 trillion for the Soviet Union, $1.7 trillion for Japan, $762 billion for France, $755 billion for the UK, and $754 billion for Italy.[44] Many suggested that Germany's geographic location could be expected to be a key asset in that country's economic future. Smyser, for example, suggested that "Germany [would] benefit from its central position in Europe, not only as a transportation hub but also as a production center."[45]

Some sought to place the economic power of a united Germany in Europe in context, however, attempting to counter undue concerns. Thus John Roper, pointing to the widespread "speculation of the role that a united Germany would play within the [European] Community," wrote:

> True, its population of some 78m [million] would be one-third greater than that of either Britain, France or Italy, and twice that of Spain. But the change would be quantitative rather than qualitative. West Germany is already the largest member of the EC with just under 20 per cent of the Community's population and 24 per cent of its economic output (gdp). A unified Germany would increase its share of the EC's population to 22.7 per cent and initially to around 26 per cent of the Community's economic output, but this could rise to 29 per cent if the labour productivity of the two Germanies was equated. On the other hand, if eventually the other five Eastern European countries were to join, the united Germany's proportion of the total EC population would be lower than that of West Germany—at present—only 17 per cent. Its economic share is more difficult to calculate, but it is probable that it would also be less than the present 24 per cent.[46]

He concluded that "the idea that, by unification, Germany would automatically leap from a non-dominant to a dominant role is clearly misplaced." Roper added that "[a]s to the political aspect, there are too many hands on the levers of the Community for any single member state to impose its will on the rest."[47]

Perhaps the hope that a German economic superpower would be effectively tamed in a context of progressive European integration would turn out to be justified, but the fact also remained that the new Germany would wield very significant influence in most areas of Central and Eastern Europe.[48] It would also be the European country most directly affected by any turbulence in East-Central Europe in the wake of the collapse of Communism and its socioeconomic as well as ethnonationalist consequences. For historical, geopolitical, and cultural reasons, it was inevitable that the united Germany would in the coming years and decades once again occupy its Janus-like position as a multifaceted "bridge" between the West and the East, with all the opportunities and liabilities that this might entail, including pressures from an economically troubled Eastern Europe and USSR/Russia for economic and financial assistance.

In addition, it was an unmistakable fact that the process of German unification had run ahead of the process of European integration, which could pose particularly difficult challenges for the entire EC in the time ahead.[49] In a changing world, where economic strength had increasingly become as important as military capability, Germany could be expected to be a truly decisive actor on the world stage. Yet, as Fritz Stern pointed out in 1989, "[f]or Germans more than for any other people in the Western world, both the past and the future are unsettled, uncertain, open."[50] Whether the reunited Germans would manage their power responsibly and play their new global as well as Central European roles effectively, with a solidly anchored Western identity, became the essence of a lingering German Question as the last decade of a turbulent century began.

Notes

1. In the course of the 1990s, a considerable number of books were published, ranging from memoirs by key players to edited volumes resulting from conferences, that provided a retrospective on the turbulent events of 1989–1990, as summarized in the following pages, and their implications. See, for example, Pekka Kalevi Hämäläinen, *Uniting Germany: Actions and Reactions* (Boulder, CO: Westview Press, 1994); Horst Teltschik, *329 Tage. Innenansichten der Einigung* (Berlin: Siedler Verlag, 1991); Peter H. Merkl, *German Unification in the European Context* (University Park: Pennsylvania State University Press, 1993); M. Donald Hancock and Helga A. Welsh, eds., *German Unification: Process and Outcomes* (Boulder, CO: Westview Press, 1994); Christopher Anderson, Karl Kaltenthaler, and Wolfgang Luthardt, eds., *The Domestic Politics of German Unification* (Boulder, CO/London: Lynne Rienner Publishers, 1993), especially Part 1; Charles S. Maier, *Dissolution: The Crisis of Communism and the End of East Germany* (Princeton, NJ: Princeton University Press, 1997); Helmut Kohl, *Ich wollte Deutschlands Einheit* (Berlin: Propyläen Verlag, 1996); Konrad Jarausch, *The Rush to German Unity* (New York: Oxford University Press, 1994); Manfred Görtemaker, *Unifying Germany, 1989–1990* (New York: St. Martin's Press, 1994); and Timothy Garton Ash, *In Europe's Name: Germany and the Divided Continent* (New York: Vintage Books, 1994), which focuses also on the years of West German *Deutschlandpolitik* leading up to the reunification drama.

2. See Gert-Joachim Gläßner, "Vom 'realen Sozialismus' zur Selbstbestimmung," *Aus Politik und Zeitgeschichte*, 5 January 1990.

3. See the discussion in "Ein Staatenbund? Ein Bundesstaat?" *Der Spiegel*, nr. 49, 1989, p. 24ff., on the visions and possibilities (including Kohl's ten-point plan), ranging from confederation to federation. For a more general discussion of "confederation" ideas in post-1945 German history, see Theodor Schweisfurth, "Die Deutsche Konföderation—der große nationale Kompromiß als tragendes Element einer neuen europäischen Friedensordnung," *Aus Politik und Zeitgeschichte*, 12 December 1987. See also Wolfgang Venohr, "Konföderation Deutschland," in Venohr, ed., *Die deutsche Einheit kommt bestimmt* (Bergisch Gladbach: Gustav Lübbe Verlag, 1982). Some subsequent research has emphasized the role played by luck and coincidence in Kohl's policy responses. See, for example, "Helmut im Glück," *Der Spiegel*, nr. 24, 8 June 1998, p. 54ff.

4. Two good collections of often worried foreign and domestic voices regarding the sudden disintegration of the GDR and the rush toward German unification are Ulrich Wickert, ed., *Angst vor Deutschland* (Hamburg: Hoffmann und Campe, 1990); and Harold James and Marla Stone, eds., *When the Wall Came Down: Reactions to German Unification* (New York/London: Routledge, Chapman and Hall, Inc., 1992).

5. Anne-Marie Burley, "The Once and Future German Question," *Foreign Affairs*, vol. 68, nr. 5, Winter 1989–90, pp. 82, 83.

6. For a discussion of the East Germans' unmistakably economic calculations in their opinions regarding unification, see the discussion and data provided in Manfred Kuechler, "Pocketbook Patriotism: Economic Expectations and the Pursuit of German Unity," paper presented at the annual meeting of the American Political Science Association, 30 August–2 September 1990, San Francisco.

7. See *Der Spiegel*, nr. 11, 1990, p. 40, for poll results.

8. Data gathered by the Institut für Demoskopie Allensbach 8–15 March 1990, and reported in David P. Conradt, "German Unification and the Remade Political Culture," paper prepared for delivery at the annual meeting of the American Political Science Association, 30 August–2 September 1990, San Francisco.

9. See the essay by Hellmuth Karasek, "Mit Kanonen auf Bananen?" *Der Spiegel*, nr. 13, 1990, pp. 56–57. Karasek pointed to the "new gap" that had opened up in Germany "between the Left and the national question." See also Michael Charlier, "Deutschland, schwierig Vaterland," *Blätter für deutsche und internationale Politik*, February 1990.

10. On the positions taken by West German left-wing groups (including the Greens) during the 1990 election campaign, see "Leere Hände, leere Hirne," *Der Spiegel*, nr. 8, 1990, p. 52ff. On the *Republikaner*, see Hans-Georg Betz, "Politics of Resentment: Right-Wing Radicalism in West Germany," *Comparative Politics*, vol. 23, nr. 1, October 1990.

11. On the various East German opposition groups that emerged in the course of 1989, see Hubertus Knabe, ed., *Aufbruch in eine andere DDR* (Reinbek bei Hamburg: Rowohlt Taschenbuch Verlag, 1989); Gerhard Rein, ed., *Die Opposition in der DDR* (Berlin: Wichern-Verlag, 1989); Hannes Bahrmann and Christoph Links, *Wir sind das Volk. Die DDR zwischen 7. Oktober und 17. Dezember 1989. Eine Chronik* (Berlin/Weimar: Aufbau-Verlag Berlin, 1990); Charles Schüddekopf, ed., *"Wir sind das Volk!" Flugschriften, Aufrufe und Texte einer deutschen Revolution* (Reinbek bei Hamburg: Rowohlt Taschenbuch Verlag, 1990); Michael Naumann, ed., *"Die Geschichte ist offen". DDR 1990: Hoffnung auf eine neue Republik* (Reinbek bei Hamburg: Rowohlt Taschenbuch Verlag, 1990); Detlef Pollack, "Außenseiter oder Repräsentanten? Zur Rolle der politisch alternativen Gruppen im gesellschaftlichen Umbruchprozeß der DDR," *Deutschland Archiv*, vol. 23, nr. 8, August 1990; Walter Süß, "Revolution und Öffentlichkeit in der DDR," *Deutschland Archiv*, vol. 23, nr. 6, June 1990; Ehrhart Neubert, "Eine protestantische Revolution," *Deutschland Archiv*, vol. 23, nr. 5, May 1990; Hubertus Knabe, "Was war die 'DDR-Opposition'?" *Deutschland Archiv*, vol. 29, nr. 2, March/April 1996; Karl-Dieter Opp, Peter Voss, and Christiane Gern, *Origins of a Spontaneous Revolution: East Germany, 1989* (Ann Arbor: University of Michigan Press, 1995).

12. See, for example, Jens Reich, "Germany—a Binary Poison," *New Left Review*, nr. 179, January/February 1990; "Die Krake müssen wir sezieren," *Der Spiegel*, nr. 37, 1990, p. 54ff.

13. The SED had always governed as part of what was presented as a truly democratic "coalition" of progressive parties. In reality, the SED had been essentially omnipotent, and the "coalition" was really more like a "monolith." See Wolfgang Mleczkowski, "Bewegung im Monolith," *Aus Politik und Zeitgeschichte*, 21 April 1984.

14. See the interesting analysis of the various possibilities by two FRG Federal Constitutional Court justices in "Nachdenken über Deutschland," *Der Spiegel*, nr. 10, 1990, p. 72ff.

15. The exact text in Article 23 read: "This Basic Law applies for the time being in the area of the *Länder* Baden, Bavaria, Bremen, Greater Berlin, Hamburg, Hessen, Lower Saxony, North-Rhine Westphalia, Rhineland-Pfalz, Schleswig-Holstein, Württemberg-Baden and Württemberg-Hohenzollern. It will enter into force in other parts of Germany upon their accession." Note that, given Germany's postwar fate and the loss of various territories, the phrase "other parts of Germany" is strikingly vague.

16. Article 146 read: "This Basic Law loses its legal validity on the day when a constitution enters into force which has been adopted by the German people in a free decision."

17. In this context, see the discussion by Werner Ungerer, "Die Europäische Gemeinschaft und die Einigung Deutschlands," *Blätter für deutsche und internationale Politik*, April 1990; Marc Beise, "Die DDR und die europäische Gemeinschaft," *Europa-Archiv*, nr. 4, 1990.

18. See Volker Ronge, "Die soziale Integration von DDR-Übersiedlern in der Bundesrepublik Deutschland," *Aus Politik und Zeitgeschichte*, 5 January 1990.

19. W. R. Smyser, "United Germany: A New Economic Miracle?" *The Washington Quarterly*, vol. 13, nr. 4, Autumn 1990, p. 173.

20. The frequent fluidity in West German public opinion throughout late 1989 and 1990 is ably discussed and illustrated in Hans-Joachim Veen, "German Unity: Public Opinion and Voting Trends," *The Washington Quarterly*, vol. 13, nr. 4, Autumn 1990.

21. Poll data also showed a continued CDU/CSU-FDP lead in the West German campaign, however. See "Kohls zweiter Sieg schon sicher?" *Der Spiegel*, nr. 14, 1990, p. 36ff.

22. "Der Heimatverlust schmerzt," *Der Spiegel*, nr. 8, 1990, pp. 27–28; Helmut Hanke, "Identität in der Krise," *Deutschland Archiv*, vol. 23, nr. 8, August 1990.

23. Polls also reflected a continued *West* German optimism about the unification process as a whole, however, although mixed opinion about the FRG-GDR state treaty was clearly evident (42 percent had a "good impression" of the treaty, 28 percent had "not a good impression," and a significant 30 percent were "undecided"). See Richard E. Meyer, "West Germans Optimistic About Reunification, Poll Finds," *Los Angeles Times*, 1 July 1990.

24. See the special report "Germany Toward Unity," in *Time*, 9 July 1990, especially pp. 76–78. For an excellent overview in English of the various financial, social, and economic aspects of the FRG-GDR monetary/economic union, see the special report ("Survey") entitled "The New Germany" in *The Economist*, 30 June 1990.

25. Poll data can be found in "Ist die Wahl schon entschieden?" *Der Spiegel*, nr. 26, 1990; "Nur jeder vierte glaubt an Wechsel," *Der Spiegel*, nr. 31, 1990; "Kohl dem Wahlsieg noch näher," *Der Spiegel*, nr. 35, 1990; "Sieg oder Triumph Kohls?" *Der Spiegel*, nr. 44, 1990; "Vor der Wahl noch eine Wende?" *Der Spiegel*, nr. 47, 1990.

26. Probably the best English-language scholarly analysis of the international dimensions and dynamics of the reunification process is Philip Zelikow and Condoleezza Rice, *Germany Unified and Europe Transformed: A Study in Statecraft* (Cambridge, MA/London: Harvard University Press, 1997). See also Stephen F. Szabo, *The Diplomacy of German Unification* (New York: St. Martin's Press, 1992).

27. Christoph Bertram, "The German Question," *Foreign Affairs*, vol. 69, nr. 2, Spring 1990, p. 45.

28. Bertram, "The German Question," p. 45.

29. Although Soviet objectives and interests were probably most affected by the rush toward German unity, the other great powers with continued legal rights in the divided Ger-

many were also challenged to review and, if necessary, adjust their basic positions. For further discussion, see Michael H. Haltzel, "Amerikanische Einstellungen zur deutschen Wiedervereinigung," Walter Schütze, "Frankreich angesichts der deutschen Einheit," and Richard Davy, "Großbritannien und die Deutsche Frage," all in *Europa-Archiv*, nr. 4, 1990.

30. For some speculation, see Wolfgang Seiffert, "Die Reformpolitik Gorbatschows und die Deutsche Frage," *Osteuropa*, vol. 39, nr. 4, April 1989; Fred Oldenburg, "Sowjetische Deutschland-Politik nach der Oktober-Revolution in der DDR," *Deutschland Archiv*, vol. 23, nr. 1, January 1990. A general discussion of the evolution of official Soviet attitudes regarding the question of German unification and security status is provided by Hans-Peter Riese, "Die Geschichte hat sich ans Werk gemacht," *Europa-Archiv*, nr. 4, 1990. See also Hannes Adomeit, "Gorbachev and German Unification: Revision of Thinking, Realignment of Power," *Problems of Communism*, July-August 1990.

31. For poll results and discussion, see *The Economist*, 30 June 1990, pp. 45–46.

32. "Survey Finds 2 in 3 Poles Opposed to German Unity," *The New York Times*, 20 February 1990, p. A8. Additional poll results were published in *The Economist*, 27 January 1990, pp. 29, 32. On foreign reactions and worries, see also Wickert, ed., *Angst vor Deutschland;* and James and Stone, eds., *When the Wall Came Down.*

33. "Europe's Fears of a United Germany Dissipate," *Los Angeles Times*, 5 May 1990; "From Germany's Neighbors, Respect and Then Acceptance," *The New York Times*, 27 September 1990. Evidence that worries nonetheless lingered just below the surface was probably at no recent time clearer than during July 1990, when a conservative British government minister resigned after inflammatory statements about the Germans and their alleged behavioral inclinations and intentions. The uproar gathered further momentum when a British government memo was subsequently leaked that contained very sharp and negative evocations of the Germans' purported "national character." An abridged version of the memo was published by *The New York Times* on 20 July 1990. See also Dominic Lawson, "Saying the Unsayable," *Orbis*, vol. 34, nr. 4, Fall 1990; David Wedgwood Benn, "Germany II: Britain and the 'enemy image,'" *The World Today*, vol. 46, nr. 10, October 1990, pp. 181–182.

34. Bertram, "The German Question," pp. 50–51.

35. See the interesting discussion in "Es ist ein anderes Leben," *Der Spiegel*, nr. 39, 1990, p. 34ff. See also the useful poll data on this issue in "Zwei Klassen im einig Vaterland," *Der Spiegel*, nr. 38, 1990, p. 28ff. Of East Germans polled, 78 percent expected to be second-class citizens for the foreseeable future, whereas only 21 percent anticipated equal treatment and equal rights.

36. Meyer, "The Myth of German Unity," *Newsweek*, 9 July 1990, p. 37. A fascinating portrait of differences between Germans in east and west was compiled by *Der Spiegel*, largely on the basis of opinion survey data. See "Den Neuen fehlt Selbstvertrauen," *Der Spiegel*, nr. 46, 1990, pp. 114–128; "Frauen zurück an den Herd?" *Der Spiegel*, nr. 47, 1990, pp. 113–127.

37. See the interesting discussion in "Aehm, also, sag doch mal," *Der Spiegel*, nr. 42, 1990, pp. 51, 54.

38. See "Germany Inc.: Awesome Power Might Be the Only Predictable Trait of a Unified Land," *The New York Times*, 18 February 1990, sect. 4; "The New Superpower," *Newsweek*, 26 February 1990, p. 16ff.

39. See the discussion in Michael Lind, "German Fate and Allied Fears," *The National Interest*, nr. 19, Spring 1990.

40. Bertram, "The German Question," pp. 61–62. As Bertram noted, the United States had indicated that it intended to remain fully engaged in the future of Europe. To some, the U.S. presence in Europe was in fact a key stabilizing factor. See Josef Joffe, "Europe's American Pacifier," *Survival*, July/August 1984; William E. Odom, "Only Ties to America Provide the Answer," *Orbis*, vol. 34, nr. 4, Fall 1990.

41. This crucial issue can only be touched upon in the context of this study. For discussion, see Manfred Müller, "Deutschlands Rolle in einem neugestalteten europäischen Sicherheitssystem," *Europa-Archiv*, nr. 6, 1990; Rupert Scholz, "Deutsche Frage und europäische Sicherheit," *Europa-Archiv*, nr. 7, 1990; Robert E. Hunter, "The Future of European Security," and Joachim Krause and Peter Schmidt, "The Evolving New European Architecture—Concepts, Problems, and Pitfalls," both in *The Washington Quarterly*, vol. 13, nr. 4, Autumn 1990; Pierre Hassner, "Europe beyond partition and unity: disintegration or reconstitution," *International Affairs*, vol. 66, nr. 3, 1990; Ian Davidson, "The search for a new order in Europe," *International Affairs*, vol. 66, nr. 2, 1990; Jack Snyder, "Averting Anarchy in the New Europe," *International Security*, vol. 14, nr. 4, Spring 1990; Roger Morgan, "Germany in Europe," *The Washington Quarterly*, vol. 13, nr. 4, Autumn 1990; Ole Waever, "Three competing Europes: German, French, Russian," *International Affairs*, vol. 66, nr. 3, 1990.

42. The important breakthrough was especially made possible by the results of the summit meetings of the EC, NATO, and the G-7 (leading Western industrial nations) that occurred in rapid succession during June and July 1990. West German success in getting allied support for (its own or joint) economic and financial aid to the USSR, plus subtle but significant shifts in NATO strategy and military/political posture, was particularly decisive.

43. Data adapted from *Newsweek*, 26 February 1990, pp. 18, 19, 21.

44. Figures in *Time*, 26 March 1990, p. 36.

45. Smyser, "United Germany: A New Economic Miracle?" p. 173.

46. John Roper, "Europe and the future of Germany—a British view," *The World Today*, vol. 46, nr. 3, March 1990, p. 48.

47. Roper, "Europe and the future of Germany—a British view," p. 48.

48. In this connection, see "East, West Economies Join, New German Reich Begins," *Los Angeles Times*, 1 July 1990; "A Unified Germany's Foreign-Policy Mantra Will Be: Go East, Young Germans," *Los Angeles Times*, 15 July 1990, explores the inevitably eastward orientation in the new Germany's diplomacy. See also the interview with historian Gordon A. Craig ("Zu groß für Europa?") in *Der Spiegel*, nr. 46, 1989, p. 183ff.

49. See Henry A. Kissinger, "Joining Two Germanys," *Los Angeles Times*, 14 January 1990, sec. M. Or as Roper has put it, "Germans and other Europeans may appear to be working on different timetables" ("Europe and the future of Germany—a British view," p. 48). See also Ungerer, "Die Europäische Gemeinschaft und die Einigung Deutschlands."

50. Fritz Stern, *Dreams and Delusions: National Socialism in the Drama of the German Past* (New York: Vintage Books, 1989), p. 20. See also the commentary by A. M. Rosenthal, "The German Question Remains Open," *The New York Times*, 26 April 1990, p. A23.

8

United But Not Yet Unified: Germany Between Past and Future

In the course of the 1990s, a series of postcards entitled "*Typisch Berlin!*" appeared on the market in the German capital that provided an often ironic commentary on the challenges faced by the newly unified Germany. One such card showed a reunited couple, he a *Jammerossi* (a constantly whining easterner), she a *Besserwessi* (a just as consistently arrogant westerner). The card used the image of an unexpectedly recovered relationship, involving five children representing the five new *Bundesländer* that once constituted the former GDR, to provide some food for thought about the state of German (dis)unity. The following text appeared alongside a picture of the arguing couple:

> They knew each other from a former life, and fate brought them unexpectedly together again. They celebrated three days and nights and fell into each other's arms, weeping for joy. Then they got married. They brought five children into the world with the names *Arbeitslos* (unemployed), *Pleite* (bankruptcy), *Solidaritätszuschlag* (solidarity surtax), *Ausländerfeindlichkeit* (hostility toward foreigners), and *Baustelle* (construction site). What then followed was awful everyday life with all its problems. She always knew everything better, and he did nothing but whine. Where does it go from here? The minister in church says: "Until death does you part."[1]

The card fits Berlin's well-established tradition of political irony and sarcasm, and the problems to which it alludes certainly manifest themselves in sharper outline there than in just about any other German location. Yet the card has been popular because its message transcends Berlin and points to important facets of life in the reunited Germany as a whole. After the heady days of 1989–1990, the euphoria that accompanied what was truly an unexpected "rush to unity"[2] was soon replaced by uncertainty, anxiety, irritation, and indifference.[3] Critics of the unification process, such as Wolfgang Dümcke and Fritz Vilmar, even spoke of the "colonization of the GDR" by a western German power elite and pointed to a range of missed opportunities that might have produced a more positive outcome.[4] As the 1990s unfolded, the total cost of unification far exceeded initial estimates, prompting the Kohl government to create a *Solidaritätszuschlag* ("solidarity surtax") that was increasingly disliked in the "old" Federal Republic.

A poll conducted in 1990 indicated that only 21 percent of West Germans felt a general willingness to make sacrifices, as opposed to 65 percent who expressed the opposite attitude (while a further 14 percent was uncertain about the issue). At the same time, only 27 percent of the West Germans agreed that they should share in the burdens faced by former GDR citizens, while some 78 percent of the East Germans felt that the *Wessis* should do so.[5] Such attitudes are in part a reflection of the easily overlooked fact that, especially in the "old" FRG, "Germans perceive unification less as a return to normality, the end of an exceptional state of affairs, than as a *departure* from normality."[6] The process of privatization and overall economic transformation in the former GDR was accompanied by considerable controversy and anxiety, as many people lost jobs that had once seemed all but guaranteed. From the modernization of a decaying infrastructure and the cleanup of ecological damage to the extension of the western German welfare state and the renovation of poorly built housing projects, the new federal government faced the likelihood of annual transfers of roughly 100–150 billion deutsche marks for the foreseeable future to "complete national unity" (*Vollendung der Einheit*) and bring about an "upswing in the east" (*Aufschwung Ost*). Much of the federal effort at financing unification was integrated into a broad-based Solidarity Pact that was adopted by a large *Bundestag* majority in 1992.

In addition to the tremendous economic challenges generated by unification, accompanied by often heated political debate that has seen parties as well as regions pitted against one another, the social and psychological aspects of life in the reunited Germany have become the object of considerable attention. In this context, the creation of a secure, new sense of identity is a particularly dramatic challenge for eastern Germans and is connected with the socioeconomic and physical transformation of the former GDR. In the words of Mary Fulbrook, "[a]lthough it is very difficult to define precisely, a sense of identity—personal, social, and national—is very closely tied in with the landscape in which one lives and moves. The outward and visible changes in the appearance of East Germany are the external correlate of the dramatic reshaping of the contours, rules, and symbols of the less tangible social landscape in which citizens of the new Germany have to learn to live."[7] Much research has been carried out on questions of east-west divergence in identity, values, socialization, mental orientation, and sociopolitical behavior.[8] Speaking of eastern and western Germany, respectively, Anne-Marie LeGloannec has suggested that "[u]nification is a merging of a community whose sole aim is to become a modern society, economically and politically, with a society which believed, to some extent, at least, that it was postindustrial and post-modern."[9] These facets have, in turn, been central to much of the discussion about the current state of German political culture and the prospects for German democracy. It is these issues and questions that constitute the focus of this chapter.[10]

In Chapters 1, 2 and 3, we examined the elements of "identity" and "unity" in the German Question in historical perspective by analyzing such matters as the failure of the country's 1848–1849 liberal-democratic unity project and its subsequently delayed national unification; its illiberal political tradition and post-Napoleonic alienation from the West; its imperial, nationalist, and militarist legacies; the democratization of West German political culture after 1949; the juxtaposition of an official Communist political culture and a set of more private semitraditional and semimodern orientations in the GDR; and the constant reminders of the tragedies and terrors of a receding Nazi past. At the end of Chapter 7, we reviewed some early speculations about the likely issues and challenges faced by a reuniting Germany.

We now turn to this theme more fully once again, in order to ascertain the state of Germany's political culture in general and the country's identity and unity in particular. First, we examine the twin issues of identity and unity by considering to what extent today's Germany is faced by the problem of two political cultures in one nation. Has Germany in the 1990s been characterized by *civic* disunity, despite a sense of *ethnic* unity? What is more decisive in the country's political culture, to be a German or to be a *Wessi* versus *Ossi*? Do political attitudes in east and west differ, and if so, are there trends that suggest a widening or narrowing of such a gap? What are the implications of what Martin and Sylvia Greiffenhagen have referred to as the "40 years of double-headedness" (*Doppelköpfigkeit*) of Germany and the corresponding "twin-track" nature (*Doppelgleisigkeit*) of its recent history?[11]

Second, we analyze the overall state of Germany's political culture in comparison with the country's illiberal prewar past. Has a democratic political culture solidified itself in Germany as a whole, and where can older elements still be detected? In addition to east-west differences, distinctions between generations, political parties, and other sources of subculture will be important again, as was the case in previous chapters.

Third, we consider the thorny question of "mastering the past" (*Vergangenheitsbewältigung*), not only regarding the Nazi era but at least as importantly vis-à-vis the GDR's legacy (and aspects of the Cold War as a whole). Here the unified Germany (especially its eastern part) confronts the dilemmas and controversies of "trials and files." Throughout this overview of various dimensions of postunification German political culture, evidence gathered by means of survey research and compiled by several institutes will serve as a source of some key insights.

Germany in the 1990s has been, perhaps more than at any other time in the twentieth century, a country in search of "normalcy." It is not clear, however, what this "normalcy" ought to entail.[12] As Stephen R. Graubard has argued, "Germany may or may not be a 'normal' nation. One wonders whether such is an adequate description of any state in the world today. However, it is a society seeking desperately to perpetuate certain goods realized in the decades after the end of World War II, all the while quieting fears about the future, common to many both inside and outside the country."[13] He points to the connection between a "wary Germany's" domestic political condition and its international role and conduct, an issue that has informed much of this book as well and that links this chapter to the next.

The Enduring Question of National Identity

One of the most frequently told jokes in Germany in the 1990s involves an encounter between an eastern and a western German. The *Ossi*, invoking one of the key slogans used in demonstrations in the course of 1989–1990, tells the *Wessi* that "We are one people," whereupon the latter replies: "So are we." This not-so-subtle piece of postunification humor sums up the basic theme that underlies much of the analysis of German politics, economics, society, and culture today: To what extent does the German population share an effective, single, overarching national identity and political culture? Or are east-west divergences more significant and influential?[14]

As we shall see, many analysts have emphasized aspects of east-west divergence. Yet what are the sources of these differences between *Wessis* and *Ossis*? Is it the outcome of political and societal divergence after World War II, imparting to each German state a distinct legacy that now complicates the challenge of "bringing together what belongs together," to paraphrase former West German chancellor Willy Brandt? Or is eastern Germany simply lagging behind western German developments, by belatedly undergoing a societal modernization process that occurred in the old FRG in the course of the 1950s and 1960s and led to a postnational, postindustrial society characterized by the spread of increasingly postmaterialist values?[15] If so, then the political culture prevailing in eastern Germany today would resemble what existed in western Germany prior to the significant postwar value-shifts. Martin and Sylvia Greiffenhagen, for example, have concluded that "[p]olitical consciousness and social attitudes among eastern Germans often correspond with analogous conditions among western Germans of 30 or 40 years ago."[16] Another possibility would be that more traditional German attitudes and values were utilized by the Communist regime for the maintenance of its totalitarian system, on the one hand, and survived in the more privatized *Nischengesellschaft* (niche society) that evolved alongside the official culture, on the other hand.[17] Both developments would thus have facilitated the persistence of older, prewar aspects of German (political) culture in the east into the contemporary era.

A fourth and final explanation of east-west divergence in Germany might focus on the overall dynamic of the unification process into the 1990s and examine distinct eastern German attitudes (including evidence of *Ostalgie*, that is, a nostalgic "longing" for real or imagined aspects of life in the vanished GDR) that have resulted from what is subjectively experienced as a western German "takeover" (perhaps even *Kolonialisierung*) of the "new *Bundesländer*." In this latter scenario, east and west in Germany have diverged rather than converged with the passing of time during the 1990s, resulting in a possibly quite durable "eastern identity" in political, social, and cultural life. An interesting measure of this trend has been provided by survey research carried out by the EMNID institute. It asked eastern Germans to indicate whether they considered East Germany to have been inferior or superior to West Germany in nine areas: standard of living, protection against crime, equal treatment of women, science and technology, social security, education, vocational training, health care, and housing. Whereas in 1990 the respondents felt the GDR to have been superior in merely three areas, this number had risen to seven by 1995.[18] In a related finding, opinion researchers noted in 1992 that a majority of 63 percent of eastern Germans felt that "socialism was a good idea, yet poorly carried out," while the basic notion of socialism (including its GDR version) was considered a negative proposition by no more than 36 percent.[19]

In their analysis of "East and West German identities," Helga A. Welsh, Andreas Pickel, and Dorothy Rosenberg have raised the question whether divergences in these identities "undermine a sense of community and common national goals," whether "the differences are serious enough to affect the political stability of the Federal Republic or whether ethnic and civic identity coincide."[20] How strongly have the two parts of Germany been integrated into a "new" Federal Republic, and how does this affect the outlook for stable democracy in the country as a whole? These questions are, of course, closely related to the issue of *national* identity (and even nationalism) in the unified Germany.

As we saw in previous chapters, the two German states developed Cold War identities that never quite amounted to a workable national identity, in view of continued division. The unlikely prospect of reunification generated an identity structure in the FRG that mixed elements of economic pride and well-being (*Wirtschaftswunder* and *soziale Marktwirtschaft*), a smoothly functioning political system (*Verfassungspatriotismus*), postnational European integration ("a European Germany instead of a German Europe"), and increasingly tenuous aspects of an all-German past (in the form of dark shadows from the Nazi era as well as facets of a historical German *Kulturnation*). According to LeGloannec, "[a]s a new democratic state, the Federal Republic offered more than a guarantee against the past; it provided, in a new sense, an escape from it."[21] West German polling data in the latter part of the 1980s revealed a considerable intergenerational gap with respect to national identity. Whereas some 90 percent of FRG citizens over the age of sixty felt that they still belonged to a single German nation, only 65 percent of those fourteen to twenty-nine years old felt the same way. And while the GDR was considered to be a foreign country by only 15 percent of older West

Germans, a solid 50 percent of younger FRG inhabitants held this view.[22] In the GDR, a kind of "Red Prussia" emerged, which integrated older German elements into a Soviet-dominated Communist mold, denied a sense of direct responsibility for Nazi crimes by claiming an exclusive legacy of anti-Fascist (*Antifa*) resistance, and increasingly relinquished any (official) attachment to an all-German sense of nationhood.

Today, however, for the first time in history, a united and democratic German nation-state, no longer drifting between East and West but firmly integrated into Western political, economic, and security institutions, is confronted with the challenge of fashioning a commensurate national identity while at the same time preserving the international reorientation achieved during the Cold War. In the words of the historian Heinrich August Winkler,

> [u]nited Germany today stands before two challenges, which at first glance are not easy to reconcile with one another: On the one hand, it has to hurry along the inner, psychological unification process, which in view of four decades of mutual alienation means nothing less than working on the rebuilding of the German nation. On the other hand, the Europeanizing and Westernizing of Germany, probably the most effective insurance against a relapse into German nationalism, has to proceed. The first task demands, above all, great material and moral efforts from the West Germans. The second task will demand more of the East Germans.[23]

What do the notions of Germany and of being German mean in today's post–Cold War Europe? What do they mean in the aftermath of four decades of division and the accompanying east-west ideological divergence? As Konrad Jarausch has suggested, "Germans keep searching for a collective sense of themselves," particularly in light of "the unforeseen return of the nation-state through unification."[24] The issue is complicated by the fact that, as we saw in previous chapters, the German sense of national identity has, in political and psychocultural terms, been strikingly fluid throughout modern history. The drama of unification called into question the separate identities that the FRG and GDR had previously cultivated. Even in the "old" Federal Republic, although it was victorious in the Cold War contest with its smaller eastern neighbor, the aftermath of unification has generated increased awareness of the inevitability of change. According to Fulbrook, "the new Germany is not going to be simply an enlarged, dyspeptic version of the former Federal Republic, suffering a little bout of indigestion in the wake of swallowing its smaller, poorer neighbor. Although more is changing, and will continue to change, in the Eastern *Länder* than in the West, something new is emerging for all Germans."[25] Some of these changes in fact entail the reemergence of older elements from the past. "During the upheaval of 1989–90," Jarausch has written, "an older set of identities resurfaced with elemental strength and eventually superseded many of the newer postwar identifications," resulting in "a widespread sense of uncertainty in the old and new states of the FRG."[26]

Germany has experienced frequent and dramatic watershed episodes in its national historical development. In the words of the Greiffenhagens, "Germany has passed through turbulent historical changes [a *Wechselbad*] that are basically unequalled [anywhere else]."[27] Each point of transition represented a fundamental political and psychocultural break, although elements of continuity were and have always been present as well, as the shadows of the pre-1918 Empire or of the Third Reich cast over the Weimar Republic and the postwar German states, respectively, show all too clearly. Seen in this light, the turbulent process of unifying West and East Germany in the 1990s would appear to continue a well-established pattern. As Jarausch has suggested, "[a]fter every collapse, in 1918, 1933, and 1945, the new regime viciously criticized what had previously gone wrong in order to set itself off from its predecessor" and proceeded to "implement its ideological blueprint, which sought to transform not only the form of government but also the political beliefs of its citizens." Although contemporary developments in Germany in many ways fit this pattern, the crucial difference lies in the fact that "this time only one of two states collapsed and the other in effect took over the former's territory, imposing its own system on the loser. By being generally limited to the East, the latest rupture has created more asymmetrical conditions for redefining self-perceptions than did the broader upheavals of the past."[28]

Seen from this perspective, one of the crucial questions faced by the united Germany is the extent to which such an attempt at western political-constitutional and sociocultural "imposition" in the country's eastern half will succeed, or whether alternatively an older German tendency of separating *Kultur* and *Politik* will reemerge. This in turn could lead to a national identity constructed on the basis of an apolitical or depoliticized sense of German *Kulturnation*, risking a potential repetition of the fateful nineteenth-century divorce of unity, nationhood, and *Deutschtum* ("Germanness") on the one hand and democracy and civic constitutionalism on the other hand. Can the reunited Germany recast itself as a nation-state built upon stable democratic foundations? Insofar as today's Germany may constitute the first truly Western, democratic German nation-state in history, the answer to this question will be crucial indeed.[29]

Frequently contested conceptions of the prewar shared past are among the more decisive aspects of this ongoing process of identity construction in the united Germany. Yet from the perspective of active identification, prewar Germany is not only debatable as a model and troublesome due to its illiberal and in the end totalitarian legacy, but it is also increasingly removed from the life experiences of the vast majority of the population. As a result, for most German generations it is the question of identification with one of the two postwar German states that is most decisive. Yet how can a single national identity be constructed on the basis of decades of division and divergence? One way this might occur in a country in which the very notion of national identity and pride have become ambiguous and questionable is on the basis of confidence and pride in "system performance," both politically (through *Verfassungspatriotismus,* or "constitu-tional patriotism") and economically (through *Wirtschaftspatriotismus,* or "eco-nomic patriotism").[30] These were also the ways in which considerable popular identification with the "old" Federal Republic emerged after 1949. Yet Germany's economic difficulties and political drift in the 1990s have raised some questions about the continued viability of this type of system support and identification. Alternatively, as noted, the possibility of a more ethnic national identity (*Deutschtum*) looms, especially as a way of bridging east-west political estrange-ment and economic frustrations, with all the consequences that this might en-tail.[31]

The oft-discussed issues of xenophobia, immigration law, and definition of cit-izenship constitute a key example of the ways in which older impulses of *Deutschtum,* frequently with fairly illiberal implications, continue to affect the Germans' contemporary search for national identity.[32] The Greiffenhagens have suggested that this element is especially pronounced in eastern Germany. Com-pared with western Germany, they argue, "the eastern German view of history turns out to be the more traditional one. Instead of a socialist internationalism [left behind by the GDR], the East Germans give evidence of a stable sense of *Deutschtum.*"[33]

Postunification Germany has been the scene of a dramatically increased num-ber of violent assaults on foreign residents (especially guest workers and asylum seekers). Many observers have stressed the socioeconomic roots of such violence, particularly in the east: social dislocation, high unemployment, dilapidated hous-ing, existential anxiety, and so forth, especially among urban youth.[34] Others have sought to place German developments in a larger perspective by pointing to the occasional electoral success of the extreme right and the fairly widespread in-cidence of far-right violence in other European countries. Nonetheless, such elec-toral success (so far primarily at the *Land* or local level) or such violence in Ger-many is always considered inherently more troublesome in view of the horrendous Nazi legacy. Debate continues over the extent to which expressions of neo-Nazism are ideologically "genuine," thereby conjuring up the spectre of a "Fourth Reich" among worried commentators both inside and outside Germany, or "merely" symbolic gestures and efforts at attracting attention in the midst of social uncertainty and frustration. In the east in particular, neo-Nazism can be seen at least in part as a delayed rebellion against the more or less artificially im-posed anti-Fascist orthodoxy of the GDR era.[35]

Perhaps even more troublesome has been a series of neo-Nazi incidents in-volving members of the *Bundeswehr.* Such incidents have apparently been on the rise since unification, and in early 1998 Claire Marienfeld, in her capacity as spe-cial *Bundestag* commissioner for *Bundeswehr* affairs, reported that the number of cases known to the authorities had increased from 44 in 1996 to 177 in 1997.[36] One of the most controversial incidents involved the revelation that a convicted and rather prominent neo-Nazi had been permitted to make an official presentation at a key *Bundeswehr* training institute in 1995. Some suggested that the incidents were merely the result of poor training and a lack of historical knowledge among the recruits, yet the issue continued to haunt Defense Minister Volker Rühe (CDU). The idea of a formal ideological screening (*Gesinnungsprüfung*) of draftees was rejected, however.

A number of observers have raised the larger question of the degree to which such incidents, many involving violence, are also to some extent the destructive outgrowth of a lingering authoritarianism and a more deep-seated aversion to multicultural pluralism in German society.[37] Germany is a country of paradox in this regard. On the one hand, in the shadow of the horrors of the Nazi era, its political culture has become increasingly democratic, as we saw in Chapter 2, and its asylum laws continue to be more liberal than those of many, if not most, other European countries, despite a relative tightening of policy agreed to by both Christian Democrats and Social Democrats in 1993. With some 7 million foreign residents of various kinds, Germany is no longer an ethnically homogeneous society, if it ever was (prior to unification, 6.8 percent of the FRG's population and merely 0.3 percent of the GDR's population, not including Soviet military personnel, was foreign). On the other hand, some shadows of the past remain, and German citizenship laws, dating back to the first decades of this century, are rather severely restrictive, defining nationality on the basis of German ethnicity. This legality has enabled countless so-called *Aussiedler* (ethnic Germans from various parts of Eastern Europe and the former Soviet Union) to "return" to Germany and gain automatic admission to German citizenship, in contrast to long-term residents (such as guest workers and their offspring) who could acquire citizenship only under fairly exceptional circumstances, if at all. Over the past decade, between 200,000 and 250,000 such *Aussiedler* have entered Germany annually (with a higher, though exceptional volume in the period 1989–1990).

The new coalition government of SPD and Greens that took office in October 1998 promised a fundamental overhaul of the country's old citizenship laws. In the face of strong CDU opposition, featuring a controversial public petition campaign, as well as an electoral setback in state elections in Hesse in early 1999 that deprived it of a clear majority in the upper house of the country's parliament (*Bundesrat*), Chancellor Schröder's "red-green" coalition was forced to seek a legislative compromise with at least part of the political opposition. The outcome of these efforts was as yet unclear at the time of this writing, however.

Polling results paint an uncertain picture regarding German attitudes vis-à-vis foreigners, immigrants, and refugees, in part because opinion surveys on these matters are notoriously unreliable, with many respondents avoiding honest answers and focusing on what are assumed to be the "politically correct" attitudes. Whereas tolerance of foreigners decreases with age among western Germans, the opposite appears to be the case among eastern Germans, where younger generations might well consider immigrants and asylum seekers to be an unwelcome socioeconomic burden and an undesirable source of competition for already scarce employment.[38] More than half of the German population perceives "conflicts of interest" between themselves and various groups of foreigners and "outsiders," although almost half also expects economic and cultural advantages, though primarily from guest workers (*Gastarbeiter*) and not from asylum seekers.[39] A 1993 poll also showed some interesting east-west contrasts in attitudes toward foreigners. For example, 66 percent of western Germans but only 19 percent of eastern Germans stated that they "had a foreigner as a friend," while 3 percent of *Wessis* and 17 percent of *Ossis* indicated that they "could not imagine having a foreign friend." When asked whether "they would have understanding for violent riots in respect to asylum seekers," 91 percent in the west responded with "no" (8 percent with "yes"), while the corresponding percentages in the east were 82 and 18, respectively.[40] As some analysts have noted, German attitudes regarding foreigners will also continue to be significant in international perceptions of the "new" Federal Republic. Or, as Steven Muller has formulated it, "it will prove to be difficult for the Germans to develop a stable and self-confident national self-image in the face of the suspicious doubts of their neighbors."[41]

Although the element of *Deutschtum* and manifestations of what were once considered "typical" German characteristics still manifest themselves in contemporary Germany, observers like Jarausch have suggested that "[t]he identity debate is . . . muddled by a fundamental change in the connotation of Germanness during the last half-century," particularly as a result of the transformation of values in a "postmaterial" direction during and after the 1960s in the "old" FRG and a legacy of socialist socialization in the area of the former GDR.[42] In the case of the Federal Republic, West German values and orientations converged sufficiently with those prevailing in other parts of Western Europe to blur or erode specifically "German" characteristics.[43]

In addition to the importance of Germany's continued east-west contrast, to which we turn shortly, the question of (national) identity and what it means to be a German at the threshold of the twenty-first century is also shaped by contrasting perspectives between, broadly speaking, the Left and the Right. We have seen in previous chapters that these two parts of the German political and ideological spectrum have tended to articulate considerably different visions regarding the interpretation of history, the conduct of foreign policy, or the contours of domestic political and sociocultural life. In the 1980s, there was a partial but unintended and awkward "convergence" of revisionist conservatism and elements of the prodetente peace movement on a conceptualization of "German national interests" under conditions of renewed Cold War. Worried observers spoke of a potentially destabilizing German "neutralist nationalism."

In postunification Germany, many of the debates and alignments have been recast. The east-west divide does not equate with a Left-Right gap, despite the popularity of the Party of Democratic Socialism (successor party to the former East German SED) in some quarters in the new federal states, since eastern Germans overwhelmingly vote for parties that are largely built on western German foundations (including a by no means negligible presence of the conservative CDU). In altered postunification circumstances, the pattern of Left-Right contestation over aspects of Germany's identity and national agenda has acquired new contours, as Jarausch has outlined:

> Taken together, many seemingly disparate debates over particular topics are part of a broader process of redefining German national identity. The Right generally seeks to use unification in order to escape the burden of past guilt, reduce the influx of foreigners, serve Western business interests, safeguard the existence of male privileges and promote greater international assertiveness. Conversely the Left tries to cling to a sense of historical shame, create a multicultural society, support Eastern redistribution claims, advance affirmative action, and argue for circumspection abroad. Ironically, both sides represent different forms of traditionalism, since the former hopes to revive older national legacies, while the latter attempts to preserve the progressive heritage of the FRG.[44]

In their quest for a stable post-GDR identity, eastern Germans have fluctuated between all-German orientations and lingering *Ostalgie* throughout the 1990s. When asked in 1990, a few months before unification, whether they considered themselves to be either primarily "Germans" or "East Germans," 61 percent of GDR citizens expressed a primary identity as "Germans," and only 32 percent as "East Germans." In 1992, however, the results were virtually the reverse: Now only 35 percent defined themselves as "Germans," whereas fully 60 percent expressed a primary identity as "East Germans."[45] In 1993, an EMNID survey found that 45 percent of eastern Germans saw themselves as primarily "German," while 54 percent stressed the identity as *Ossi*. In comparison, in the same survey 81 percent of western Germans considered themselves to be "Germans," while only 19 percent stressed the idea of being "West German."[46] Intellectuals like Jens Reich began to refer to a specific *Ost-Identität* as a *Trotzidentität* (an identity of defiance and resistance). By contrast, LeGloannec spoke of a *Trostidentität*, that is, "an identity by default, an apolitical nostalgia, a utopia, what West Germany had been as a dream, for over forty years."[47]

In a poll taken in 1993 by the Allensbach Institute, "[o]nly 22 percent of West Germans and 11 percent of East Germans answered that they felt 'together like Germans.' Seventy-one percent of the old citizens and 85 percent of the new citizens of the Federal Republic saw themselves divided by 'opposing interests.'"[48] More recent polling results suggest a resurgence of a more general identification with "Germany" among the eastern Germans, however. Nevertheless, insofar as many eastern Germans see their region as a continued *Armenhaus Deutschlands* (poorhouse of Germany) and themselves as *Bürger zweiter Klasse* (second-class citizens), east-west contrasts in political culture that may have some of their roots in the Cold War era persist with added sharpness.

Some have suggested that a specifically eastern German sense of identity has many "functional" characteristics, triggered by the need for adaptation and integration. Welsh, Pickel, and Rosenberg have written, for example, that

[a] stronger eastern German identity is in fact not a somehow passive and negative reaction to a unification process gone sour. This would simply be inconsistent with what a majority of eastern Germans say. Rather, a growing collective consciousness is better understood as an adaptation strategy to the problems and conflicts that have been created by unification. Eastern German identity is not necessarily embraced as a way of opting out of the new Germany, of celebrating cultural distinctiveness, or of waxing nostalgic about a paradise lost. From a functional point of view it may instead be a constructive response: an Eastern German self-consciousness does not question the rules of the game in any fundamental sense but rather facilitates integration by empowering individuals and collective actors in the ongoing conflicts of interest, many of them along East-West lines.[49]

One indicator of national identity that a number of researchers have explored is the question of national pride. Survey results at the time of unification had detected a higher level of national pride and identification with "Germany" among eastern than among western Germans. This was explained as the abandonment of an identification with the discredited GDR among East Germans, coupled with a focus on "Germany" as a means of defining a sense of equality with West Germans and bypassing the need to identify with a still relatively alien "Federal Republic."

In a 1992 poll, 69 percent of western Germans and 71 percent of eastern Germans claimed to be "proud to be a German," while 22 percent of *Wessis* and only 13 percent of *Ossis* felt no such pride. A poll taken a year later showed some striking east-west differences in this area among younger citizens. While 47 percent of younger western Germans felt pride at being German (and 48 percent did not), the corresponding percentages among younger eastern Germans were 68 and 31, respectively.[50]

By 1995, however, western and eastern attitudes were roughly similar, at least as far as overall national identity was concerned. In its Eurobarometer survey of spring 1995, the European Commission sought to measure "pride in nationality and level of identification with national and European identity" and provided separate results for western and eastern Germany. The results, in percentages, were as follows, with eastern responses in parentheses: "very proud to be German"—13 (9); "fairly proud to be German"—32 (39); "not very proud to be German"—21 (24); "not at all proud to be German"—14 (12); focus on German "nationality only"—28 (34); focus on a mixture of German "nationality" first, followed by European identity—43 (44); focus on a mixture of European identity first, followed by German "nationality"—15 (12); European identity only—9 (5).[51] The results show considerable east-west similarity, with continued uneasiness in both parts of the country regarding the very notion of "national pride" on the one hand and a strong tendency to limit one's identity to German nationality only or, more frequently, to a mixture of German nationality and attachment to Europe, on the other hand.

Thomas Blank has reported on two interesting aspects of national pride: national history and national political institutions. Using a scale ranging from 1 ("not proud") to 5 ("very proud"), he found that in 1995 the following percentages of western Germans selected the various points on the scale when asked about their level of pride regarding German history: 32.8 (1), 22.2 (2), 29.2 (3), 11.9 (4), and 4.0 (5). The corresponding results among eastern Germans were 22.1 (1), 26.8 (2), 40.4 (3), 7.0 (4), and 3.8 (5). The data show a generally low level of pride in the nation's history among all Germans. As for pride in the country's "democratic institutions," the following percentages of western Germans selected the various points on the scale in a 1993 survey: 4.6 (1), 10.3 (2), 30.5 (3), 36.0 (4), and 18.5 (5). The eastern German results were 10.6 (1), 22.0 (2), 41.8 (3), 20.7 (4), and 4.9 (5). In this case, we notice a distinctly higher level of pride among western Germans.[52]

Throughout the postwar era, "Europe" provided most West Germans with a workable ersatz identity in the face of national division.[53] East Germans never had the opportunity to develop such a European identity, of course, and have been catching up with their western compatriots in this regard. Polling data from 1991 suggest an overall decline of pro-European sentiments in the German conception of identity, however. In a Eurobarometer poll conducted for the European Commission in that year, an average of 53 percent of EC citizens claimed to have a "frequent" or "occasional" sense of "being European." Western Germans, with 46 percent, and eastern Germans, with 34 percent, were clearly below this average. In fact, the poll found that the sense of being European was nowhere as weak as in the new German *Länder*.[54] Such polling data would suggest not a revival of older German nationalism perhaps, but rather a relative "normalization" of German attitudes, in line with more widespread "Euroskepticism" in the EC (today the EU), and a preoccupation with national needs and difficulties in the wake of unification. The result is a blending of national and European orientations, as the 1995 poll suggests.

Several additional aspects of national identity have been the subject of debate and, in some cases, opinion surveys. These include a variety of questions and issues. For example, what should the united country be called? At the time of unification, some suggested simply "Germany" or *Deutscher Bund*, but the designation "Federal Republic" has persisted. What would be the most appropriate national anthem? Here the third verse of the *"Deutschlandlied,"* adopted by the "old" FRG, continues to be used, despite suggested alternatives. Where should the country's capital and seat of government be located? This became the subject of considerable debate after unification, focused on the political symbolism, ideological connotations, and historical legacies of Bonn versus Berlin, until the *Bun-*

destag decided in favor of the latter in June 1991.[55] Also controversial have been the selection and political interpretation of key national holidays. October 3 is designated as "Day of German Unity" (*Tag der Einheit*), but there are other days with sensitive connotations as well, such as June 17 (anniversary of the 1953 East German uprising and original day of German unity in the "old" FRG); November 9 (marking the anniversaries of both the anti-Jewish pogrom of *Reichskristall-nacht* in 1938 and the opening of the Berlin Wall in 1989); and May 8 (a day of unconditional surrender or of liberation in 1945?).[56]

As Michael Mertes has suggested, there are still further questions about words and terminology, often with considerable implications for matters of identity and mental unity. This includes the debate over what one ought to call eastern Germany: the "former GDR," or the "new *Bundesländer*," or, as some nationalist revisionists would have it, *Mitteldeutschland* (in view of the "lost territories" behind the Oder-Neisse line)? What about the cumbersome need to continue distinguishing between an "old" and "new" Federal Republic? And then there is the ongoing debate about what happened in 1989 and 1990: Was it unification (*Einigung* or *Vereinigung*) or reunification (*Wiedervereinigung*)?[57]

Finally, and in conclusion, it should be stressed that the question of identity in contemporary Germany involves a complex and by no means static set of attachments and orientations, as Welsh, Pickel, and Rosenberg have noted:

> The postwar creation of two Germanys coupled with the leveling effects of industrialization has reduced the importance of traditional differences based on history, religion, class, and culture in German politics. This has encouraged the emergence of identities that are no longer seen as exclusive but as complementary and/or in competition with each other. The (re)emergence of regional ties at the *Land* level, attachments to some aspects of the old GDR *and* to the Federal Republic, as well as to Europe, more often than not complement rather than contradict each other. In other words, East and West German identities are only one of several competing identities.[58]

They add that "some particular social milieu patterns of the former GDR persist,"[59] but suggest that east-west patterns of difference do not ipso facto imply the absence of an effective, overarching sense of *national* identity.

One Nation, Two Societies?

There is a widespread consensus among many observers and analysts that contemporary Germany is characterized by considerable estrangement between *Ossis* and *Wessis*.[60] We have already encountered evidence of this condition in our examination of the state of German national identity. This estrangement is partly the result of some four decades of division and the accompanying socialization in two very different social and political systems, and partly the consequence of an unequal and uneven unification experience. Many eastern Germans have expressed the sense of being "second-class citizens" in the united Germany, a condition many expect will persist into the foreseeable future.[61] In a series of opinion surveys, for example, the EMNID institute explored this issue. When asked whether they expected to be second-class or equal citizens in the foreseeable future, 78, 84, and 80 percent of eastern German respondents chose the former in 1990, 1991, and 1993, respectively, while 21, 15, and 19 percent chose the latter option during those years.[62] In 1995, the results were largely similar, with 72 percent of the easterners seeing themselves as second-class citizens and 27 percent considering themselves equal. Interestingly, in this same survey 77 percent of *western* Germans considered the *Ossis* to be equal citizens, while 22 percent did sense eastern inequality in the united Germany.[63]

An EMNID survey published in the weekly magazine *Der Spiegel* in 1995 provided additional food for thought. Of all Germans, only 15 percent wished that unification had not taken place, whereas a solid 83 percent was of the opposite opinion. However, only about 31 percent of Germans believed that there was no "growing wall" in the citizens' heads, as opposed to a clear 67 percent who did sense an increasing *Mauer-im-Kopf* syndrome.[64] When asked for their overall evaluation of the unification process since 1990, the response "better than I expected" was selected by only 13 percent of the eastern and 25 percent of the western Germans. The answer "just like I expected" was chosen by 33 percent of *Ossis* and 28 percent of *Wessis*, while the view that things had turned out "worse than I expected" received support among 53 percent in the east and 43 percent in the west. Yet when asked whether they were better or worse off now, compared with their life in the former GDR, eastern Germans responded as follows: "much better" (9 percent), "better" (41 percent), "about the same" (27 percent), "worse" (18 percent), and "much worse" (5 percent).[65]

Evidence suggests that many eastern Germans rapidly lost their sense of support for privatization and the general characteristics of a free market economy after 1990, even though "objective" economic indicators pointed to a gradual improvement in conditions in the east. The level of mutual sympathy between western and eastern Germans dropped noticeably as the decade progressed. An IN-FAS poll taken in 1992 found that 65 percent of western Germans considered themselves to be "hard-working" (*fleißig*), but only 28 percent of them felt the same way about their eastern compatriots. At the same time, 95 percent of *Ossis* saw themselves as hard-working, while 94 percent of them saw the western Germans as "efficient" (*geschäftstüchtig*) and 79 percent considered the *Wessis* to be "selfish" (*egoistisch*). Furthermore, a poll conducted in 1991 suggested that 63 percent of eastern Germans felt that the western Germans were behaving in a "colonialist" manner, and a further 82 percent considered their western compatriots to be arrogant *Besserwessis* (western know-it-better types).[66]

Additional polling data provide further interesting insights into the sometimes paradoxical or contradictory state of public opinion in the reunited Germany.

Data gathered by the *Infratest dimap* institute in the course of the decade, for instance, show a steadily rising number of eastern Germans who see themselves as "winners" rather than "losers" in the unification process.[67] At the same time, however, this institute reported that as of 1997, some 70 percent of eastern Germans (and about 46 percent of *Wessis*) continued to complain that "western Germans have too little understanding for eastern Germans," while about 63 percent of western Germans (and some 36 percent of *Ossis*) claimed that "the efforts of western Germans for the reconstruction of the east are too little appreciated by eastern Germans." These latter two trends have been growing in the course of the decade. Asked whether the rapid unification process in 1990 was "right" or "not right," 51 percent of all Germans chose the former answer in 1997, while no less than 45 percent selected the latter response.[68]

Compared with their counterparts in the "old" FRG, the former GDR citizens have been far more impacted on a personal level by the advent of unity. Unemployment, bankruptcies, privatization, a new political and legal system, a competitive market economy, a new educational system, an information and media revolution, an unraveling social network, and a host of additional psychological and social ordeals and pressures—all in the former East Germany have been affected, even if to a variable degree. It is not surprising, therefore, that observers have noticed the crystallization of what some have called "a sense of community among citizens of the former GDR,"[69] partially built upon and yet also distinct from the official identity that prevailed in East Germany before the events of 1989–1990.

In this context the phenomenon of *Ostalgie* receives frequent attention and comment, but the same cannot be said for an equally noticeable *Westalgie* in the former West German territory: a "longing" for the certainties of the Cold War, the sense of stable affluence of the days before unification, the absence of whining and financially burdensome *Ossis*, and so forth.[70] For both eastern and western Germans, Wolfgang Thierse has a sobering and at the same time provocative message, however: "The end of the coziness behind the Wall has come." Using a German word-play, he calls for the division to be overcome by means of sharing (*die Überwindung der Teilung durch Teilen*).[71] Some of the anti-*Ossi* western German opinions are further enhanced by the proliferation of attitudes characteristic of what Countess Marion Dönhoff has called a *Raff-Gesellschaft* (a selfish "grabbing society"), which reduces the willingness to sacrifice for the "common good."[72] In other words, there is evidence of a Germany made up of two often equally nostalgic and mutually estranged and prejudiced communities, both suffering from a *Mauer-im-Kopf* (Wall-in-the-head) syndrome.[73]

During and shortly after unification, a number of observers suggested that a solid all-German identity could be built upon a surprising degree of east-west convergence in political culture, despite decades of national division. They argued that this unintended and indirect democratic socialization of former GDR citizens had been the result of the constant availability of information from Western (especially West German) media, despite official SED efforts to curtail or even eliminate the population's exposure to such subversive material. Subsequent research has presented a more nuanced picture, however, thus modifying the initial optimism. Noting the distinctly eastern German component in the Federal Republic's general political culture, for example, David Conradt has reminded us that "East Germans did not spend the last forty years just watching western television and waiting for the moment when they could become Wessis."[74]

In 1991 and 1995, the IPOS Institute in Mannheim conducted surveys among western and eastern Germans to measure their trust in public institutions. The West German political system had been introduced wholesale in the east, but how did the *Ossis* feel about these institutions, compared with their western compatriots? Aside from finding that trust in public institutions was by no means very high in either part of Germany (an issue to which we return later), the IPOS analysts noted a relative convergence of trust/distrust levels between *Wessis* and *Ossis* over the 1991–1995 period regarding such institutions as the Federal Constitutional Court (*Bundesverfassungsgericht*), the *Land* (state) government, the Federal Council (*Bundesrat*), the police, and the courts. In general, however, eastern levels of trust in these institutions still remained below western levels. Gaps in trust were particularly noticeable between *Wessis* and *Ossis* regarding the Constitutional Court, the police and the courts, the federal government, the *Bundestag*, television, political parties, the print media, and the churches. Whereas westerners hovered between neutrality and relative or considerable trust regarding most of these institutions, easterners showed either minimal trust, neutrality, or limited distrust. One could interpret such results as a glass half full or half empty: positively, in that they show a gradual increase in eastern trust regarding institutions that were by and large "imposed" by the west, or negatively, because this very sense of "imposition" from the outside continues to limit eastern trust in central political and societal institutions.[75] Regarding this latter possibility, some have suggested that lower eastern German trust in and acceptance of key political and economic institutions is not only or primarily the result of deficient prior socialization but perhaps also caused by an eastern sense of being treated with condescension and as socially unequal.[76]

The IPOS researchers also measured western and eastern "satisfaction with democracy and selected societal conditions" in 1991 and 1995, again allowing for a consideration of changes over time. The resulting east-west percentage gap in satisfaction levels (based on percentage responses of "very satisfied" and "satisfied"), with the western level higher in each instance, were as follows (with the 1995 gap noted in parentheses in each case): democracy—26 (15); educational opportunities—15 (27); equality of rights—8 (29); economic situation—73 (22); crime protection—5 (29). The data show a clear and even dramatic narrowing of differences in level of satisfaction with democracy and the economic situation, but an equally dramatic widening of differences regarding educational opportunities, equality of rights, and crime protection. It should be noted, though, that some of the narrowing of these gaps regarding satisfaction levels between east and west was the result of a noticeable increase in western dissatisfaction levels. A look at eastern satisfaction levels reveals attitudinal stability over the 1991–1995 period in only one area (democracy) and a downward turn in other areas that reflect a lingering or even growing sense of second-class citizenship and existential anxiety (again, 1995 results in parentheses): democracy—52 (53); educational opportunities—69 (57); equality of rights—79 (44); economic situation—14 (29); crime protection—58 (14).[77] Other opinion surveys have yielded evidence of an eastern German tendency to separate attitudes on economic issues into personal and more general categories: In 1992, for example, almost 50 percent of former GDR citizens agreed that their personal prosperity had increased (while 15 percent disagreed), yet the level of general support for a market economy stood at 44 percent, down from 77 percent in 1990.[78]

The foregoing discussion clearly suggests that, at least at the close of the 1990s, it is the socioeconomic effects of national unification that continue to play a major role in defining some of the basic contours of eastern *and* western German identities and attitudes. A number of observers have pointed to the paradox that the apparent divergence in subjective identity between eastern and western Germans has grown despite a general eastern acceptance of western political institutions as well as an increased eastern sense of personal economic well-being. To some observers, this would suggest that "there is no direct relationship between personal economic situation and eastern German identity."[79] Additional explanation may be sought in the fact that although eastern Germany has made noticeable economic progress, the area's general economic condition still continues to lag well behind that of the country's western half. Furthermore, the unmistakable presence of western German dominance in economics, politics, and culture serves as a constant, daily reminder to former GDR inhabitants that their region is dependent and vulnerable.[80]

The radical introduction of market economics after 1989–1990 led to severe dislocation, including a decline of employment in the east from about 9.3 million in 1989 to 6.2 million in 1992 (a drop of 34 percent); worsening economic opportunities for many women (almost 62 percent of the unemployed in eastern Germany in 1992 were women, for example); an income level in the east that was still stuck at roughly 60–70 percent of the western level in the mid-1990s; a turbulent process of privatization carried out under the auspices of the highly controversial *Treuhandanstalt* (trustee agency);[81] and continued property disputes that served to slow investment and generate anxiety for many families now living in possibly contested housing.[82] Although the objective degree of economic progress in the east achieved over a relatively short period of time is certainly quite dramatic, eastern perceptions remain far more mixed and reflective of continuing frustrations and anxieties.[83]

Polling data capture the evolving mood quite well. In a 1993 survey, the INFAS Institute found that 47 percent of western Germans were "optimistic" with regard to their "personal prospects," 40 percent were "partly optimistic," and 4 percent were "pessimistic." The corresponding percentages for eastern Germans were 44, 48, and 8, respectively. When asked about their sense of "political perspectives" for the reunited Germany, only 9 percent of western Germans were "optimistic," 60 percent were "partly optimistic," and 20 percent were "pessimistic." In this case, the eastern German percentages were 12, 61, and 26, respectively. Altogether, some 28 percent of *Wessis* and 32 percent of *Ossis* expressed unhappiness with reunification, even though a majority of 55 percent in the west and a plurality of 41 percent in the east continued to feel favorable toward the overall process.[84] And in its 1995 survey, the IPOS Institute found that while 38 percent of westerners and 15 percent of easterners expected a general "assimilation of living standards between East and West Germans" in up to five years, 41 percent of westerners and 48 percent of easterners assumed a period of five to ten years would be more likely. Reflecting a clear gap in optimism, 37 percent of easterners believed that more than ten years would be needed to achieve rough east-west equality, whereas only 17 percent of westerners felt this way.[85]

In addition to a more or less distinct eastern political consciousness and the continued impact of a turbulent economic transition, different analysts point to the more psychocultural manifestations of east-west German divergence and continued disunity.[86] This is where the "mental gap" and the *Mauer-im-Kopf* syndrome make themselves most clearly felt. A good deal of this estrangement is focused on attempts to interpret and come to grips with the past, as we shall see more fully later in this chapter. Considered in general terms, the matter has drawn the suggestion that since "the two Germanys were actively engaged in the struggle to shape a historically-derived sense of national identity into a serviceable vehicle for political identification" on either side of the Iron Curtain, "the forty years of division created two virtual mirror self-images, locked in mutual antagonism. Many of the current debates about the past can therefore be understood as efforts to negotiate a reconciliation of these long-held, contradictory norms of German identity."[87]

Controversy is created by what many eastern Germans perceive as a western German attempt at discrediting fully all aspects of the former GDR and imposing the "old" Federal Republic's Cold War self-image and "reading" of the German past on the reunited nation, especially on its eastern half and on Berlin in particular. These *Ossis* would argue that evidence of such attempts or tendencies can be found in controversies over monuments and memorials of the former GDR; the renaming of streets and other public sites; the presentation of the nation's history in such museums as the *Haus der Geschichte* in Bonn and the *Deutsches Historisches Museum* in Berlin; the expulsion of numerous presumably "tainted" academics and researchers from eastern universities and institutes;[88] an ongoing "westernization" with allegedly "colonialist" characteristics of eastern Germany's artistic, literary, and cultural life; and so forth.[89] In a critical evaluation of such developments, Welsh, Pickel, and Rosenberg argue that

[a]s the Federal Republic continues to rewrite its own history, many East Germans feel that they are being offered assimilation into a Western-defined "German identity" rather than allowed an active role in creating a common founding mythology for the unified state. At the same time, social, political, and especially economic conditions continue to reinforce clear distinctions of opportunity and status between East and West. Identity, however, cannot simply be dictated by a new elite. It must in some way connect with, confirm or be confirmed by the experience of the population.[90]

Against this general background of identity, unity, and continued east-west estrangement, a number of observers have pointed to the presence of what appear to be two somewhat distinct political cultures in the united Germany, in spite of evidence of gradual convergence between *Ossis* and *Wessis*.[91] Many of these differences are, of course, the result of a fundamental divergence in political socialization and experience, but some of them may also be the (temporary?) product of a unification process experienced by many eastern Germans as "imposed."

According to Martin and Sylvia Greiffenhagen, East Germany had produced a political culture that combined older, authoritarian German elements with contemporary socialist orientations, leading to a kind of "communist feudalism."[92] At the core of this political culture stood a mixture of *Schutz* (protection) and *Gehorsam* (obedience). While expecting absolute subservience of the citizenry, the state provided a fairly comprehensive existential protection to that same citizenry, thereby enhancing a mentality of citizen dependence on public institutions combined with a seriously underdeveloped sense of individualism and civic competence.[93] Most East Germans were forced into an attitude of passive resignation (*Anpassung*), which led to what analysts like Hans-Joachim Maaz have considered a psychological "deformation" (*Deformierung*) and a widely shared victimization and mental as well as emotional repression (*Verdrängung*).[94] This contrasts sharply with the development of a more explicitly liberal-democratic civic culture in the "old" Federal Republic, as we saw in Chapter 2.

Sketching the difference in mentality between eastern and western Germans, Jürgen Kocka has suggested that the former GDR citizens "hold old-fashioned virtues such as obedience, orderliness, modesty, cleanliness, and duty in higher esteem" than do citizens of the "old" FRG. Furthermore, "[w]ork represents a more central value to Germans in the East than in the West. East Germans tend less to hedonistic, postmaterialistic, and individualistic values than do West Germans—although the difference is less significant among the younger respondents."[95] He also notes that "East Germans are less likely to identify with political parties and party democracy, and are more sympathetic towards plebiscitary or grass-root democracy." Echoing the verdict reached by other observers as well, he concludes that "Easterners appear more 'German' than Westerners, in that they are more deeply rooted in older German traditions."[96]

Polling data have generated ample illustration of this contrast in political and social culture between western and eastern Germany. For example, in 1992 "law and order" (*Ruhe und Ordnung*) were seen as important by 35 percent of western and 51 percent of eastern Germans. On the issue of a perceived responsibility of the state to come to the assistance of citizens in case of sickness, need, unemployment, and retirement income, 51 percent of *Wessis* and 80 percent of *Ossis* agreed with this proposition. In a 1992 EMNID survey, 56 percent of western Germans supported a limitation on state involvement in the country's economic life, compared with 79 percent of eastern Germans who favored a high level of state economic activity.[97] Some of these eastern German attitudes have probably been enhanced, of course, by the sense of existential uncertainty generated by the turbulent aftermath of unification and a corresponding desire to have the state "come to the rescue."[98]

In addition to such divergent views on the welfare state and the role of the state in the country's economic life, eastern and western Germans also evince some clearly different attitudes regarding the desirable mode of political life. A number of observers have suggested that eastern Germany continues to be characterized by a tendency that was considered typical of traditional German political culture: a dislike of political conflict (referred to in German as a *politische Streitkultur* or *Konfliktkultur*), in favor of a search for consensus and harmony, perhaps imposed by the state in a relatively authoritarian context.[99] Just as some 40 percent of West Germans in the 1950s claimed to look back seminostalgically on the sense of community that the Third Reich had provided for them, so in the 1990s we find some 42 percent of eastern Germans who remember fondly a similar sense of community in the former GDR. Compared with western Germans, eastern Germans appear to lack the level of "social trust" (*soziales Vertrauen*) that constitutes a significant precondition for a sense of political efficacy and a more positive level of civic cooperation and participation.[100] Whereas in western Germany the level of social trust has risen from 13 percent in 1945 to 45 percent in the 1990s (accompanied by a corresponding decline of social distrust from 83 percent in 1945 to 34 percent in the 1990s), in eastern Germany the contemporary levels are at 29 percent "trust" and 48 percent "distrust."[101]

According to the Greiffenhagens, the eastern German sense of community is the product of older German tendencies that survived in a new setting throughout the history of the GDR. The traditional German sense of "dualism," juxtaposing an authoritarian public order with a privatized withdrawal into a world of culture, nature, association, and local community, was further enhanced and perpetuated by the GDR's petty-bourgeois character and forbidding totalitarian political structure.[102] The result was an orientation that mixed *Innerlichkeit* (introversion) and *Angst* (fear), and the development of a *Nischenkultur* (culture of niches) based on private networks of friendship and cooperation but lacking a more broadly based degree of social trust that is indispensable in a liberal-democratic civic culture. The sense of "community" that developed was further enhanced at the workplace, which generated a primary network of social contacts, leisure-time activities, and cultural opportunities. Some commentators (by no means all of them eastern German) have sought to draw a positive contrast between this sense of community in the former GDR and the "lonely crowd" produced by western individualism and normlessness (Durkheim's *anomie*), yet they forget that East Germany's *Nischengesellschaft* was what the Greiffenhagens call a *Notgemeinschaft*, that is, a less-than-voluntary response, based on need, to an omnipresent totalitarian state and thus part of a far less attractive political context.[103]

A further characteristic of East German political culture, with roots in traditional German conceptions of politics and with continued relevance for contemporary eastern German orientations, is a "decisionist" tendency (*Dezisionismus*), that is, an inclination to define politics in black-versus-white terms, to focus on clear choices and decisive action instead of deliberative uncertainty, acceptance of compromise, and tolerance of ambiguity (*Ambiguitätstoleranz*).[104] Unlike the "old" Federal Republic, where a Westernization of political culture promoted the development of greater pluralism and tolerance, the former GDR helped instill in many of its citizens an intolerance rooted in an ideology based on notions of irreconcilable class conflict and an authoritarian frame of mind grounded in a mixture of Prussian traditions and the contours of a Leninist *Kommandostaat* (command-state).[105]

As two prominent observers of Germany's political culture have pointed out, the considerable attitudinal chasm that separates many western and eastern Germans represents a major challenge in the process of creating a true sense of national unity in the "new" Federal Republic. It will take years to bridge the gap between "the eastern German labor society [*Arbeitsgesellschaft*] and the western German leisure society [*Freizeitgesellschaft*]" and between the "petty-bourgeois and materialist orientation" of the *Ossis* and the "bourgeois-postmaterialist perspective on life" that characterizes most *Wessis*.[106] The ongoing dynamics of modernization contribute to an inescapable western German dominance vis-à-vis the east for the foreseeable future. Furthermore, the impact of unification on eastern versus western Germans is inevitably disproportionate, with an almost exclusively west-to-east transfer of money, ideas, institutions, and elites. Both halves of Germany continue to evolve, and prospects for a gradual convergence remain good, despite contemporary evidence of politically significant animosity and resentment (as reflected in a sizable vote for the post-SED Party of Democratic Socialism in many parts of the east throughout the 1990s, for example).

A Stable Democracy?

The turbulent aftermath of unification, captured in the persistence of an east-west identity gap and the continuing problems of mutual estrangement between *Ossis* and *Wessis*, has (so far, at least) not generated the effect that has worried many observers of German domestic politics: a destabilization of democracy. In fact, in view of the challenges posed by the unexpected advent of unification, the Federal Republic continues to experience a striking political stability, the worried proclamations of pundits and pessimists notwithstanding. The relatively smooth transition, after sixteen years, from the Kohl regime to a novel *Rot-Grün* coalition between the SPD and the Bündnis90/Greens after the federal elections of September 1998 was a further positive sign for many analysts, although it should also be noted that this transition was quickly followed by considerable friction and turbulence in the new governing coalition.[107] At the same time, however, many observers inside and outside Germany are keenly aware of the profound need for political and socioeconomic reform in a country where an attachment to stability often turns into a posture of rigidity and where a worship of presumed tradition reflects a legacy of antimodernist *Angst* and undermines the pursuit of indispensable innovation.[108] Christoph Bertram, for example, has spoken of the "new German lethargy."[109] The new federal government promised reforms, but the proof of this particular pudding would also have to be in the tasting.

German society and culture are, indeed, on the whole quite conservative, due to a variety of reasons: long-standing psychocultural traditions, a legacy of political and social authoritarianism, a desire for stability and predictability in light of a highly turbulent national history, and a preoccupation with the maintenance of a secure foundation of postwar economic prosperity. These stability- and security-oriented attitudes find their reflection in diverse aspects of German political and socioeconomic life, such as the often conservative notion of the *Rechtsstaat*; the much-appreciated solidity of the deutsche mark; the desire to project reliability and predictability in foreign policy; the focus on order in the institutional arrangements governed by the constitution (*Grundgesetz*); a widely desired avoidance of conflict and promotion of social harmony; a continued linkage between state and church power; and persistent male dominance in much of the corporate and academic worlds.

In the face of the fundamental transformation of European affairs since the events of 1989–1991, with their far-reaching consequences for Germany's domestic order and international status and role, the long-standing and deep-seated German preoccupation with order and stability appears to have gained renewed momentum. Both *Wessis* and *Ossis* yearn for this order and stability, even if the criteria and standards by which they define and evaluate their objective diverge. Noting a "German preference for maximum stability" and a "jargon of harmony," Michael Mertes has examined German "political rhetoric" and composed a basic vocabulary that reflects a predilection for "continuity and harmony in domestic as well as foreign affairs."

> *Friede* (peace), along with its derivatives such as *sozialer Friede* (social peace), *innerer Friede* (domestic peace), and *Friedenspflicht* (literally, peace obligation, the banning of "wild" strikes); *Versöhnung* (reconciliation) and *Verständigung* (understanding, agreement); *Normalisierung* (normalization) and *Normalität* (normality); *Dialog* (dialogue) and *Ausgleich* (balance, compromise); *Partnerschaft* (partnership), along with its derivatives *Sozialpartnerschaft* (social partnership) and *Sicherheitspartner-*

schaft (security partnership); *Augenmass* (sense of proportion), *Vernunft* (common sense), and *Mitte* (literally center, meaning something like mainstream); *Kontinuität* (continuity), *Berechenbarkeit* (predictability), *Verlässlichkeit* (reliability), and *Behutsamkeit* (a mixture of caution and gentleness, the opposite of abruptness); [and] peculiar, difficult to translate neologisms like *konzertierte Aktion* (literally, concerted action), *Solidarpakt* (solidarity pact) or *Streitkultur* (culture of dispute; in this combination, the irenic *Kultur* neutralizes the abhorrent *Streit*).[110]

One might add that this terminology points to a political culture where *Macht* (power), *Feind* (enemy), and *Volk* (people in an ethnic sense), once central to an illiberal tradition, have given way to *Verantwortung* (responsibility), *Gegner* (opponent), and *Bürger* (citizens).

As we saw in Chapter 2, most analysts of political culture in the "old" Federal Republic pointed to a mixture of tradition and innovation in popular and elite attitudes and orientations. With the added complication of 16 million "new" citizens socialized by and in the former GDR, this observation still holds true today. In the following pages, we examine some of the recent findings and observations, all the while keeping in mind the sources and manifestations of east-west contrast discussed earlier.

Much of traditional German political culture was characterized by statist, authoritarian (*obrigkeitsstaatliche*) tendencies that found their perhaps strongest expression in Prussia, based on a clear separation of state and society (*Gesellschaft*), the power of a conservative civil service (*Beamtentum*), and the state's uncompromising expectation of obedience, loyalty, and subservience on the part of its apolitical *Untertanen* (subjects).[111] As the Greiffenhagens have noted, insulting the state and its symbols (*Verunglimpfung des Staates und seiner Symbole*) continues to be a punishable offense in Germany today. Statist intervention in many sectors of socioeconomic life remains a striking characteristic in the FRG, along with neocorporatist tendencies, a political style that favors legalistic solutions to problems, an elitist preoccupation with administrative competence, and a highly "bureaucratic-formalistic" political process.

The professional civil service, often still subject to a near-monopoly of jurists (*Juristenmonopol*), continues to enjoy considerable privilege and status in a society preoccupied with public order and managerial expertise, although there is some evidence that the "classical authoritarian bureaucrat is gradually dying out in Germany."[112] Civil servants serve the state, but is this state an entity unto itself or the democratic representative of the popular will and sovereignty? Today's civil servant (like all citizens) is to be loyal to the constitution, not to the state, but who is to be the judge of this loyalty (as the continuing controversy over the so-called *Extremistenbeschluß* of the 1970s, now also applied to former SED and/or current PDS members, shows all too clearly)? State and liberal-democracy have not yet been fully reconciled in Germany today (or, for that matter, in a number of other Western countries). Citizens expect a great deal from government, particularly in the east and most especially in the context of the modern welfare state, yet the old mentality of the *Untertan* has by and large disappeared.

The authoritarian aspects of prewar German political culture found much of their expression in the old, especially Prussian, notion of the *Rechtsstaat*.[113] In this tradition, the state defined and protected citizen rights, but this meant that a conception of citizenship along Western lines, based particularly on Anglo-Saxon, Lockean principles, by and large failed to take root. Observers have suggested that although the non- or even antidemocratic German *Rechtsstaat* is a thing of the past, a sometimes dangerous preoccupation with an inflexible and statist constitution has emerged in the contemporary Federal Republic. The deification of the state (*Staatsvergottung*) has been replaced by a deification of the constitution (*Verfassungsvergottung*), a focus characterized by normative rigidity and even absolutism instead of much-needed adaptability. Particularly questionable is the tendency to depend on the courts (most notably the Federal Constitutional Court) instead of the legislature to solve political questions that are turned into legalistic controversies. The "juridification" (*Verrechtlichung*) of political life reflects a desire for clarity and decisiveness as opposed to compromise and shifting attitudes, and corresponds with an oft-noted German fondness for regulations and order.

The continued prominence of the *Rechtsstaat* idea, though attached to a democratic constitution, also generates a considerable preoccupation with any and all potential subversion of the established order, particularly in light of Germany's disastrous experience with Nazi and Communist totalitarianism. The controversial law-and-order policies formulated in the early 1970s (*Extremistenbeschluß*, *Radikalenerlaß*, and *Berufsverbote*) have found their contemporary reflection in the considerable debate of recent years over the question of *Innere Sicherheit* (internal security), focused especially on the interception and tapping by public authorities of private communication in a battle against terrorism and organized crime (the so-called *großer Lauschangriff* issue). Much attention is directed at the legacy of the *Stasi*, East Germany's secret police, but the formerly West German and now all-German *Bundesnachrichtendienst* (BND), equivalent to the U.S. FBI, is not beyond controversy either.

The Greiffenhagens are aligned with those who worry that the democratic German *Rechtsstaat* could increasingly degenerate into a "security state" (*Sicherheitsstaat*) with renewed authoritarian inclinations, particularly in a context of growing citizen anxiety regarding crime (in eastern Germany even more so than in western Germany): Democracy and a preoccupation with law and order cannot be expected to be fully compatible under all circumstances. When all is said and done, however, contemporary German political life shows much evidence of considerable democratic solidity, especially in light of past tragedies and failures, based upon a remarkably successful constitution and a widespread support for the notion of "combative democracy" (*streitbare Demokratie*).[114]

The fairly high level of overall satisfaction with the existing democratic system expressed especially by western Germans in a series of recent polls, in spite of areas of dissatisfaction, is reflective of the development of a strong civic culture (*Bürgerkultur*) in the FRG after 1949.[115] Partly as a result of delayed democratic socialization, many aspects of this political culture are as yet more weakly developed among eastern Germans.[116] Furthermore, insofar as easterners' difficulties and dislocations associated with unification are blamed not only on a failed GDR but also on the "imposition" of western German political and economic structures and practices, the Federal Republic's eastern citizens greet both liberal democracy and market capitalism with a strong dose of skepticism, if not hostility.[117]

Most survey research results covering the past thirty to forty years point to a distinct (West) German increase in the level of general knowledge regarding politics, a growth in interest in political matters, a rise in the level of social trust among citizens, an increase in the sense of political self-confidence and efficacy, and an expansion in the degree and range of political participation. The attraction of reform- and protest-oriented political behavior has tended to fluctuate: A time of relative withdrawal ensued in the late 1970s and 1980s after a period of considerable fervor, with contemporary evidence suggesting the possible resurgence of protest and radical discontent in some quarters, particularly on the left (most notably associated with the PDS) and the far right (Republikaner, NPD, and DVU).[118] More generally, analysts have pointed to what Max Kaase has termed a "participatory revolution" in recent years, focused on new and in many ways "unconventional" (though not necessarily illegal) modes of political behavior.

We have noted that in spite of a consolidation of a flourishing civic culture, some observers note the lingering impact of older, authoritarian inclinations in some areas in Germany—for example, in an ambivalent attitude regarding the appropriateness of political opposition (influenced by a "decisionist" tendency coupled with an aversion to political dispute or *Konfliktscheu*) and an often negative opinion concerning the rights and influence of (political) minorities.[119] Nonetheless, the prevailing conclusion is, once again, that postwar Germany has experienced a dramatic and highly successful transformation in its political culture, and that contemporary German democracy is characterized by considerable stability. Many if not most indicators suggest a fundamental German convergence with developments in the political cultures of other Western, advanced industrialized or postindustrial societies.[120]

Certain additional specific aspects of contemporary Germany's political culture, some of them shared at least in part with other Western societies, warrant further comment and attention. In a context of postunification challenges, social anomie, and eastern German disorientation, and against the dark background of Nazi horrors, numerous observers have noted the proliferation of violent acts by neo-Nazi extremists and speculated about its implications for German democratic stability.[121] In the words of one analyst, "[t]he threat of the radical Right in contemporary Germany should not be downplayed," even if "Germany in the early 1990s [was] not the Germany of the early 1930s."[122] The violence occurs disproportionately in eastern Germany, particularly involving fairly organized groups, though plenty of incidents have shaken the country's western part as well.[123] Most of the perpetrators are by no means unemployed or without educational opportunity, so that simple economic explanations do not suffice. Nor is there any strong evidence that the violent gangs are in any way fundamentally committed to a coherent neo-Nazi ideology.

Many analysts have pointed to social anomie, to the rapid disintegration of social norms and networks, as a key explanatory variable.[124] The unraveling of previous (imposed) frameworks of identity in the east, along with a distinct post-unification erosion of earlier euphoria and optimism, appears to have had a particularly severe impact: A sense of inferiority vis-à-vis the "old" FRG and domineering *Wessis* leads to compensatory violence, especially against convenient, easily identifiable scapegoats. The failure of a ritualistic East German anti-Fascism, and the strong paramilitary aspects of youth socialization and inexperience with true multiculturalism in the former GDR, are also cited as contributing factors. Although it is reassuring that the vast majority of Germans in east and west strongly reject any kind of political violence quite firmly, the extremist excesses are by no means disconnected from deeper traumas and tendencies, such as the shadows of the Nazi past and authoritarian-nationalist remnants, that continue to characterize German society and culture at large. We saw this earlier in the context of questions regarding national identity and immigration policy.

Another area of considerable analytical interest, in Germany and beyond, is the transformation of basic values that appears to have occurred, particularly among younger generations, in Western "postindustrial" and "postmaterialist" society since the 1960s.[125] We noted some of these changed attitudes regarding work, career, consumption, lifestyles, and so forth, and the ways in which they almost "revolutionized" traditional German sociocultural patterns in West Germany, in earlier chapters. Helmut Klages and Thomas Gensicke have described this process of change as a shift from "values of duty and acceptance" (*Pflicht-und Akzeptanzwerte*) to "self-development values" (*Selbstentfaltungswerte*).[126] In the wake of unification, a number of analysts have investigated the extent to which the dynamics of modernization triggered a similar transformation in eastern Germany during the latter part of the Cold War, in spite of the absence of anything analogous to the upheaval generated in the West during the 1960s and 1970s. Although they have found that many of the more "traditional" values still linger among the *Ossis*, they also point to rapid changes among younger eastern German generations since 1990. Some have even suggested that preunification exposure to West German television caused a kind of modernization-through-osmosis in the former GDR, undermining official socialization efforts.[127]

An interesting area of attitudinal research has been the question of religious orientation.[128] Secularization has led to a striking decline of religious belief and practice in all of Germany, but in the eastern part even more strongly than in the west. According to Stephan Eisel, "[t]he often heard statement that Germany has become a more Protestant country through unification is not accurate. In truth, it has become more secular: in the West only about 54 percent describe themselves as 'religious'; in the East, where the Reformation began, it is barely 33 percent."[129] Since 1950, Catholic church membership in eastern Germany has dropped from 11 percent to 5.5 percent, while the more numerous Protestant segment of the population has declined from 80.6 percent to 27 percent. In today's eastern Germany, roughly 65 percent of the population no longer belongs to any parish. Furthermore, while almost 10 percent of western Germans claim never to have believed in God and a further 23 percent have lost an earlier sense of religiosity, more than 50 percent of eastern Germans declare themselves to be atheist, with an additional 25 percent professing to have abandoned their previous belief in God. Among German youth, only 22 percent of those in the east express a belief in life after death, as opposed to 56 percent of western youth.[130] While nonchurch, alternative forms of religiosity have seen some increase in western Germany, this is not (yet) the case in the east. Interestingly, evidence suggests that of all institutions and practices in the former GDR, the socialist *Jugendweihe* (a secular alternative to traditional Christian forms of confirmation) continues to be quite popular in the new federal states, albeit stripped of the earlier Communist baggage and connotations.[131]

There is also empirical evidence, however, that the value pattern prevalent among today's *Ossis* constitutes a blend of traditional and modern, of materialist and postmaterialist, and of socialist and capitalist elements. It is too early to tell whether this pattern is merely transitional or more permanent in nature. Finally, there are those who have suggested that Germans as a whole, in reaction to their previously authoritarian and highly traditional culture, are moving more strongly in the opposite direction than most other Western societies, even to the point of possibly risking a challenge to democratic stability and social order.

In Chapter 2, we surveyed the postwar partisan spectrum in the Federal Republic. Contemporary Germany is very much a *Parteiendemokratie*, that is, the power and role of the different political parties are quite central to the functioning of the system. The parties are, in fact, explicitly covered by the country's Basic Law. In East Germany, the SED ruled supreme, although a variety of smaller parties, without any significant power, joined it in a kind of "national front" coalition. These were the so-called bloc parties (or what the Germans tend to nickname *Blockflöten*), and we saw in the previous chapter that these GDR parties either merged with their western German counterparts or vanished altogether as the GDR crumbled. Despite the dominance of *Wessis* in each party's national organization, however, distinct eastern versus western perspectives, identities, and allegiances can be found in the CDU, SPD, FDP, and Bündnis90/Greens. The SED generated its own successor party, the PDS, and is an almost entirely eastern phenomenon, seeking to carve out a niche for itself in Germany's political landscape as the party of *Ossi* identity and protest.[132]

In the course of the 1990s, however, Germany's established parties have faced an increasingly disgruntled electorate, which blames them for the widespread sense of political stalemate, a lack of reform, and the country's lackluster economic performance (especially in the area of unemployment). In 1992, the most widely used political expression in Germany was *Politikverdrossenheit*, roughly translatable as a "sullen or morose attitude regarding politics."[133] It has since become a fixture in any discussion of the state of German political culture. Federal President Richard von Weizsäcker helped draw public attention to the issue, and his successor, Roman Herzog, continued to speak out on it as well.[134] Results of opinion surveys suggest that the reputation of politicians among the citizens continues to decline, that the political parties are seen as corrupt and/or incapable of solving the country's problems, and that the political establishment fails to provide the necessary *Bürgernähe* (closeness to citizens) and is perceived to be undermining the quality of German democracy.

Although voter turnout continues to be reasonably high, certainly compared with turnout in a range of other Western countries, some observers are wondering whether these developments in the Federal Republic's civic culture mark a gradual erosion of the popular legitimacy of some of the country's key institutions. Might the traditionally apolitical German, disdainful of partisan controversy and longing for consensus and harmony, be making a comeback? Some have argued that eastern Germans, operating with a mixture of traditional German values and GDR-era antipluralist socialization, might be especially at risk of drifting away from a solid civic culture.

Part of the problem also lies in the transformation and fragmentation of contemporary society, making it increasingly difficult for "traditional" parties to appeal successfully and credibly to disparate individuals and groups with often highly incompatible interests and expectations. Furthermore, the increasingly technocratic character of much current public policy, as well as a tendency to withdraw state involvement from a range of socioeconomic activities, undermines the erstwhile prominence and relevance of political parties and instead draws attention to the significance of other "players," such as administrative experts and private-sector actors. The emergence of alternative movements and groups is a further factor that has undermined the traditional prominence and power of political parties, and not only in Germany.

We saw in earlier chapters that the state occupied a central role in traditional German political culture and practice. The postwar democratization of (West) German society and political life changed many of the illiberal aspects of this tradition, yet the role of the state has continued to be quite significant, particularly in its regulatory aspects and with regard to the overall management of Germany's elaborate "social market economy." What is more, most Germans are still conditioned to expect an active role by the state in the country's socioeconomic life. A recent survey suggested that, depending on the particular issue, between 50 and 95 percent of western Germans expected the state to assume at least part of the responsibility. Among eastern Germans, against a background of four decades of state socialism, such expectations were even more pronounced, ranging between

90 and 99 percent.[135] Insofar as these expectations are at times unrealistically high, the tendency toward *Politikverdrossenheit* gains further impetus.

Faced with an increasingly costly and unmanageable welfare-state system, contemporary Germany is caught between those on the right who advocate a reduction in state involvement, and those on the left who prefer the retention (if not expansion) of a sizable public sector. Yet the situation is made more difficult by the fact that an active state is not necessarily capable of gaining and maintaining effective control over an increasingly complex modern society and economy. Along with other advanced democracies, the Federal Republic runs the risk of considerable social anomie and alienation (*Entfremdung*) coupled with "system demand overload," with potentially serious consequences for the overall health of the country's civic culture and the legitimacy of its key political institutions. Some might search for scapegoats on whom to blame their existential *Angst* or even turn to violence; most are more likely to look for simple solutions to complex problems or drift further into apolitical apathy.

A significant part of the sense of stalemate that characterizes contemporary German politics is the result of a persistent ideological standoff between the right and left segments of the ideological spectrum. Although the roots of this confrontation lie well before 1990, and in many ways before 1945, the sudden collapse of Communism in Central and Eastern Europe in the 1989–1991 period has added a further dimension. In Chapter 6, we examined the advent of the CDU-FDP coalition in 1982 and its subsequent attempt to bring about a neoconservative *geistig-moralische Wende* (intellectual-moral change) in West German life, focused on traditional values, questions of national identity, and a neoliberal shrinkage of the welfare state (*Entstaatlichung*).[136] Although the German intellectual climate has been, to some extent, more conservative since the mid-1980s, the ideological impact of the 1960s and 1970s has by no means been reversed, as the electoral success of the Greens and the proliferation of movements and citizens' initiatives (*Bürgerinitiativen*) amply demonstrate. At the same time, however, the demise of Communism and the unavoidable element of national(ist) regeneration inherent in the unexpected drama of unification have emboldened many conservatives, such as Odo Marquard, Hermann Lübbe, Robert Spaemann, Rainer Zitelmann, and Arnulf Baring, to articulate their views and agendas with greater self-confidence. Their efforts frequently include a provocative historical revisionism, linked to the *Historikerstreit* (historians' dispute) of the 1980s or Chancellor Kohl's desire for a more "normalized" attitude of German citizens vis-à-vis their country's past.[137]

By contrast, the predicament of those on the left is far more problematic, in light of the demise of Communism.[138] Although the more conservative popular attitudes that emerged by the late 1970s had already affected the SPD in the course of the 1980s, the disintegration of the GDR did much to discredit the very idea of "socialism" and undermine the utopian element in much left-wing thinking. In addition, the advent of national unity once again posed the issues of nationhood and nationalism that have so bedeviled the Social Democrats throughout twentieth-century German history.[139] Many conservatives sought to depict the SPD (often unfairly) as ideological sympathizers of Communism in general and the now-defunct GDR regime in particular, and thus as politically unreliable.

Furthermore, faced with a state that is unable to solve all the problems placed at its feet and a citizenry that has lost much of its erstwhile faith in socioeconomic progress and modernity, socialists in Germany and elsewhere continue to experience a profound sense of ideological disillusionment and disorientation. Calls for social solidarity are at times barely audible in the presence of widespread materialist and postmaterialist individualism, neoliberal capitalism, and an eroding welfare state. While on the one hand traditional class consciousness and union activism decline, the new, postindustrial environmentalism is on the other hand not an inherently social-democratic issue. Classical Social Democracy is closely associated with state power, yet as a result it has frequent difficulty in grasping the significance of non- or even antistate social movements and reform efforts.

Faced with this predicament, Social Democratic leaders and parties in Germany and beyond have striven to reposition themselves in a more "pragmatic center," focused on welfare-state reform, closer cooperation with business interests, reductions in state regulatory activity, and a relatively conservative reliability in foreign policy. The resulting, carefully calibrated appeal to traditionally left-wing constituencies and more moderate, independent, centrist voters has yielded electoral success for center-left parties throughout the Western world in the course of the 1990s, as shown by Bill Clinton and the Democratic Party in the United States, Tony Blair and New Labour in Great Britain, and Gerhard Schröder and the SPD in Germany, to name but the most noticed examples.[140]

We conclude by returning to the clear differences that remain between western Germany's consolidated civic culture and eastern Germany's still more tentative embrace of democratic values and attitudes. Aspects of older German political culture, along with socialist-authoritarian remnants and a lingering Ostalgie, will probably only slowly erode, somewhat along the lines of what occurred in the FRG after 1949, but even this is not absolutely certain. For most eastern Germans, who lacked a cohesive anti-Communist counterelite when the SED regime crumbled, democracy is a western German import article, if not a "semicolonial" imposition, along with economic models and structures: Its consolidation will require the passage of a still very turbulent and controversial time of transition. Flight, exile, and expulsion had robbed the former GDR of many potential democrats, leaving behind a largely semitraditional, petty-bourgeois popular political culture, partly attached to a Lutheran church establishment caught between principled opposition and pragmatic accommodation.[141] Insofar as the mass media (particularly television) play a key role in contemporary political socialization, western German dominance in this realm since 1989–1990 events (if not earlier in a more indirect way) has further strengthened the impact of "outside" elements (what Germans call *Überfremdung*) on the development of a new civic culture in the former GDR.[142]

In the final analysis, the future of German political culture inevitably remains open, particularly the outlook for increased convergence or continued divergence between the orientations of *Ossis* and *Wessis*. Posing the questions that will be decisive in this regard, Martin and Sylvia Greiffenhagen have asked:

> Will the political culture of the new federal states merely limp behind that of the western Germans, until it converges with it seamlessly? Or will a specific [political] culture develop in the east, which will differentiate itself durably from that of the western Germans? What would such a culture look like? And [consider] the reverse: will western German [political] culture change as a result of unification? Will it, in the long run, absorb elements of an eastern German culture? Will tendencies that are reminiscent of earlier phases of [German] political history be strengthened? Will the democracy of the Federal Republic as a whole be thrown back to an earlier stage in its development?—Many questions to which there are until now hardly any empirically solid answers.[143]

Though unable to provide secure answers to these kinds of questions in the early 1990s, Manfred Kuechler endeavored to strike a note of optimism, suggesting that "[w]ary of ideologies, the Germans—east and west—will probably choose to be pragmatic."[144]

Brown and Red Shadows on the Threshold of a New Century

Among the many things that Germans in both east and west have expected from unification, one of the most fundamental and yet elusive has been the achievement of national "normalcy." After a disastrous *Sonderweg* ("special path")—a path culminating in two world wars, the Weimar failure, Nazi tyranny, the Holocaust, postwar occupation, national division, and Communist dictatorship in the east—Germany today longs for democratic stability, economic well-being, true national unity, and peace with its numerous neighbors. Yet, even now the country cannot fully escape the traumas of its history. Although most East Germans were aware of the abnormality of their rather artificial Communist state throughout the Cold War, and always remained at least psychologically oriented toward the other German state, many inside and outside the Federal Republic had gradually come to think of West Germany as a more or less "normal" state. The goal of reunification was ritualistically professed, but fewer and fewer really expected to see it happen. The FRG found a home in the Western camp, but could never escape the reality of the GDR across the East-West divide. In retrospect, the division of Europe and of Germany was inevitably abnormal.[145]

More important perhaps, national division permitted both German states to be selective and even self-serving in the ways in which they confronted the dark pages of the nation's past. Paradoxically perhaps, the unification of East and West Germany, while giving rise to an ostensibly "new" German nation-state, also challenges a *united* German people to grapple with aspects of a shared past for the first time since the end of World War II.[146] For eastern Germans, but also to some extent for western Germans, this process of what is often referred to as *Vergangenheitsbewältigung* ("mastering the past") and *Geschichtsaufarbeitung* ("working through history") is given a complicated twist by the simultaneous need to come to grips with the legacy of Cold War division in general and the GDR's Communist dictatorship in particular.[147] Will the united Germany (again) display an "inability to mourn" the traumas left by a double dictatorial legacy?[148] Some, like Brigitte Rauschenbach, believe this to be the case, suggesting that "German history is marked by a collective syndrome of failed farewells" to vanished epochs and regimes, notably after World Wars I and II.[149]

In the final pages of this chapter, we look more closely at the ways in which the united Germany confronts the Nazi past, partly against the background of distinct attitudes and policies in the FRG and the GDR before 1990. We also examine the controversies surrounding East Germany's Communist legacy in the current Federal Republic. First, however, we review some major aspects of the role played by history and historiography in the ongoing construction of German identity.[150]

According to Konrad H. Jarausch, Hinrich C. Seeba, and David P. Conradt, "history plays a central role in the creation of national identity." Using a series of "political founding myths," each nation constructs a "master narrative that presents a highly selective but all the more compelling account of common destiny."[151] In the case of Germany, the master narrative came to an apparently violent and sudden end in 1945, collapsing along with the ignominious Third Reich. Occupation, division, and reorientation in two different ideological directions by the two German "successor states" seemingly terminated German national history. However,

[t]he unification of 1989–90 has offered an unexpected continuation of the erstwhile master narrative by providing a new redemption. While the Left now worries about the doubling of the burden of the past, the Right sees the return of unity as a chance to undo the effects of the cultural revolution of the 1960s and to restore a positive sense of identity. Many of the current debates on the Stasi legacy, the collaboration of writers, the morality of *Ostpolitik*, etc. can be understood as clumsy attempts to rewrite history in order to renationalize Germany.[152]

As the product of delayed nation-state formation, Germany was, especially before 1871, a "cultural project," in which language, "the liberal rhetoric of individual freedom," the mythical and "nostalgic dream" of empire, and an increasingly narrow definition of *Deutschtum* played a key role. In the end, "the creation of the Second Empire reinforced the intolerant aspects of German identity," including a spillover into Germanic irredentism and an aggressive nationalist-imperialist foreign policy. The liberal conception of nationhood and history was defeated, and would later be unable to break through successfully during the ill-fated Weimar Republic. Instead, Hitler's Third Reich recast earlier, illiberal conceptions in a yet more extreme, racialist mold.[153]

When World War II ended, German national identity and history seemed to come to an end.[154] While the new East German regime launched the construction of a new, anti-Fascist German state in close alliance with the Soviet Union, West Germans focused on the creation of their *Wirtschaftswunder* and a supposedly provisional Federal Republic, and found a new identity in the pursuit of European integration. Burdened with the traumas of the past and the challenges of the present, most Germans appeared to withdraw into a sense of apolitical privacy. Official attempts at "mastering the past" were incomplete and at times less than forthright, and encountered a climate of widespread popular silence, discomfort, and resentment.

Facing one another across the Iron Curtain, neither German state was able to provide fully what had been "the missing component in the German sense of national identity," namely, "a shared attachment to a particular state and political system."[155] As we saw in previous chapters, the sense of all-German identity gradually faded, particularly among younger generations, and the country's prewar history increasingly took on the character of "alien territory," an unfamiliar storehouse of failures, crimes, and no longer useful or acceptable values and traditions. In each German state, as Felix Philipp Lutz has outlined, a distinctive "historical consciousness" developed, with dynamic variation across generations, which has complicated the post-1989 unification process.[156] West Germans lacked a sense of national pride and grew indifferent vis-à-vis any notion of traditional nationalism and nation-state. By contrast, citizen pride in the FRG's constitution and political institutions grew from 7 percent in 1959 to 51 percent in 1988, while pride in the country's economy and welfare state also rose significantly during the same period (from 33 to 50 percent and from 6 to 39 percent, respectively). An additional indication of the emergence of an "FRG nationalism" came in a poll on the eve of the opening of the Berlin Wall in 1989: Sixty percent of the Federal Republic's citizens (compared with only 23 percent in 1951) indicated that they felt "joyful" or "happy" upon seeing the black-red-gold postwar flag, and "over 80 percent of West Germans felt that they could be just as proud of their country as the Americans, British, or French."[157] It is important to emphasize, however, that this resurgent "national identity" was almost entirely focused on the postwar Federal Republic, at the expense of more all-German orientations and in avoidance of almost all pre-1945 German history.

In spite of the legacy of the earlier so-called Hallstein Doctrine, which was based on the official West German claim of a still-existing single German nation-state legitimately represented only by the FRG (the *Staatskerntheorie*), the practical pursuit of reunification was reduced to a matter of political ritual, since it ceased to be, in most minds, a realistic prospect. Insofar as most West Germans developed a primary attachment to the practices and institutions of liberal democracy (along with pride in their prosperous welfare state), the perspective on German history appeared to become more selective, focused on those elements that were considered most relevant to the new political order. This orientation led, for example, to the prominence and popularity of the exhibition "Questions Regarding German History" (*Fragen an die deutsche Geschichte*), which opened in the Reichstag building in Berlin in 1971 and centered on aspects of German parliamentary history, and to dedication of official resources for activities in the area of "political education" (*politische Bildung*), especially in the German school system. On the other side of the national divide, the East German leadership endeavored to construct a specific GDR identity based on membership in the Communist camp, appropriation of a heroic anti-Fascist self-definition, and a generally selective reinterpretation of German national history, focused on those elements felt to be most usefully "progressive." In the end, however, this attempt at *Abgrenzung* vis-à-vis the Federal Republic and the all-German past would fail.

The presumably "postnational" Federal Republic was caught completely unprepared when the Communist edifice in Central and Eastern Europe came crashing down in 1989 and 1990 and the question of German reunification suddenly reemerged on the "national" and international agenda. In the words of three observers, "history returned with a vengeance, overthrowing communism, liberating suppressed populations, and redrawing the map of Eastern Europe. The democratic awakening proved not only exhilarating but also threatening, since it upset Cold War certainties and thereby reopened previously settled questions of German identity."[158]

What followed has been called by many observers contemporary Germany's need to deal with a "double mastering of the past" (*doppelte Vergangenheitsbewältigung*).[159] As Jarausch, Seeba, and Conradt have put it,

[i]n spite of the resumption of the national story, unification in effect doubled the burden of the German past in the twentieth century. As if the scars of the Nazi trauma were not enough, the collapse of the GDR added another failed dictatorship, set of collaborators or victims, and demands for restitution. Just as personal memories of the Third Reich had begun to fade, fresh recollections of suffering under communist repression took their place and the whole practical set of post-1945 problems such as purging the civil service, prosecuting criminal perpetrators, and compensating their victims appeared to have returned in 1990.[160]

Political and intellectual controversy erupted on a variety of fronts. West and East Germany had gone their separate ways in confronting (and avoiding) the legacy of Nazism and World War II after 1949.[161] Each state had even sought to project decisive features of the Nazi past onto the other: Thus West Germans might compare Nazi and Communist "totalitarianism," while the East German regime depicted Western capitalism as intimately tied to the Fascist disaster.[162] Yet now western and eastern Germans were compelled to revisit the past together. The commemorations of the fiftieth anniversaries of D-Day and of the war's end, in 1994 and 1995 respectively, with a united Germany torn by domestic debate over the meaning of May 1945 (surrender or liberation?) and partially excluded from international ceremonies, were vivid reminders of the lingering "abnormality" of the country's status in world affairs.

There were other controversies as well, such as the reevaluation of the resistance against Hitler, pitting conservative against left-wing interpretations, each with its own heroes and agenda, which in turn reflected the official attempts at appropriating the resistance (*Widerstand*) for narrow ideological purposes in the "old" FRG and the former GDR during the Cold War. Then there was the lively debate over Daniel Goldhagen's book *Hitler's Willing Executioners*, which sought to depict the deep roots of German anti-Semitism and the massive complicity of the German population at the time of the Holocaust.[163] The redesignation in 1993 of the *Neue Wache* in Berlin as Germany's "central memorial site for the victims of war and tyranny" (*Zentrale Gedenkstätte für die Opfer von Krieg und Gewaltherrschaft*) triggered a vigorous debate about what was to be commemorated, who should be designated a victim, and how such commemoration could best be carried out.[164]

At least in part associated with the *Neue Wache* issue has been the controversy over the creation of a national Holocaust memorial (*Denkmal für die ermordeten Juden Europas*) in Berlin.[165] More generally, sites of commemoration associated with the Nazi legacy continue to be a source of frequent contention in contemporary Germany.[166] In eastern Germany, several such sites, for example at Buchenwald and Sachsenhausen, have been redesigned in order to eliminate what are now seen as unacceptable interpretations imposed by the former GDR. Different aspects of the war, once more or less taboo subjects in one or both of the German states, are today being addressed more openly, for example, the role of the *Wehrmacht* in war crimes (focused on a highly controversial exhibition)[167] or the personal wartime experiences of ordinary German soldiers and civilians. This latter tendency, insofar as it suggests a focus on the fate of Germans as "victims," stands in obvious contrast to the emphasis on German complicity that is at the heart of the controversy over the Goldhagen book. In 1998, controversy erupted over a speech by the widely respected German author Martin Walser, who openly questioned what he perceived to be the frequent "manipulation," in Germany and beyond, of the Holocaust for political purposes. The fact that the controversy coincided with the rise to power of a new generation of German political leaders allegedly less willing to remain burdened by the past and eager to defend the "national interests" of a more "normal" Germany (for example, in budgetary negotiations in the EU) only added to the intensity of the debate.

Opinion surveys suggest that contemporary German popular attitudes regarding the Nazi era in general and the Holocaust in particular fall into three strands. One group, found primarily on the left side of the political spectrum, believes that even younger German generations carry moral responsibility for what was done in their country's name. Operating on the basis of a "Holocaust identity," they are alienated from many aspects of German nationhood and tradition, since these are considered to be directly linked to the Nazi catastrophe. A broader group, stretched across the middle of the spectrum, accepts a diffuse historical responsibility but is otherwise more "ambivalent" and would prefer to "draw a line under the terrible past." Jarausch, Seeba, and Conradt argue that "[t]he danger comes from the Right, where less than ten percent in the East and about double that number in the West resent the burden of guilt and show remnants of anti-Semitic biases."[168]

However, a distinction among different patterns of opinion in the German population regarding the Nazi era must also pay careful attention to variations among generations. As the Greiffenhagens have noted, there is a threefold generational division that is important here for the decades after 1945: first, those who grew up during the Weimar era, possibly served in various capacities in the Third Reich, and had a leading role in postwar reconstruction and the creation of the two German states; second, those whose youth occurred during the Nazi era and World War II; and third, those who were born after the war "but for whom the theme of National Socialism has remained alive until today."[169]

As time has evolved and generations have succeeded one another, opinions on Nazism and its legacy have changed. At the end of the 1940s, some 57 percent of the West German population still believed that National Socialism had been basically a good idea, but that it had been badly carried out. By the end of the 1970s, the number of the FRG's citizens holding this view had shrunk to 26 percent (still a sizable group, of course). By the 1980s, some 65 percent of West Germans considered the Third Reich a negative occurrence in German history, and 66 percent felt that Nazism had been harmful to the German people from its beginning. At the same time, however, surveys showed that 22 to 45 percent of the population (depending on the level of education) believed that had there been no war and no Holocaust, Hitler would have been among Germany's greatest statesmen. In addition, by the end of the 1980s more than 40 percent of the FRG's citizens expressed willingness to argue that National Socialism had had its good and bad aspects.[170] Unfortunately, comparable survey data for the former GDR is not available.

Aside from its persistent significance in the area of public opinion, the Nazi legacy continues to affect Germany's political culture, institutions, and practices more generally, despite the passage of many years.[171] We have seen in previous chapters how many aspects of West Germany's domestic political life and foreign policy were shaped by an often conscious reaction against the past, in an effort to preclude any possible repetition of the totalitarian nightmare. The Nazi legacy helped define many elements in the country's constitutional and legal order, and the "lessons" of the past were quickly invoked (often by both sides) during many political controversies. The creation and supervision of a democratic citizen military were another key consequence of the earlier catastrophe. Calls for an end to conscription and the creation of a volunteer/professional military are thus frequently rejected by reference to Germany's traumatic experience with an illiberal militarism. At the same time, as Ralf Dahrendorf and others have argued, the National Socialist era may have continuing significance inasmuch as it triggered a type of "modernization" that brought about a (perhaps largely unintended) "bourgeoisification" of German society. Yet other analysts, such as Count Peter Kielmansegg, locate the "revolutionary" breakthrough in modern German history not in Nazism but in the utter national disintegration caused by World War II. In spite of a "renationalization" of much political discourse, unification has so far not really altered, let alone diminished, the persisting impact of Nazism and its legacy.

The "second *Vergangenheitsbewältigung*," focused on the legacy of the Cold War in general and on the former GDR regime in particular, has caused many waves of controversy and debate in Germany, and will continue to do so for some years to come.[172] There are some key differences, of course, between the mastering of the East German past and the need to confront the Nazi legacy.[173] The latter concerned all Germans equally, but was carried out separately in the two postwar German states. The former has differential impact and implications for eastern as opposed to western Germans, yet is being carried out in a unified Germany dominated by western Germans who are thus easily seen as standing in judgment of their eastern compatriots.

The level of controversy is further sharpened by the fact that, as Heinrich August Winkler has pointed out, "[f]ew West Germans want to admit that the legacy of the second German dictatorship belongs to all Germans."[174] In a similar vein, Werner Weidenfeld has stressed that "[t]he double German past cannot be mastered separately [by eastern and western Germans], if one wishes to achieve internal unity jointly."[175] It is not surprising, therefore, that several prosecuted former SED leaders have dismissed their trials as examples of *Siegerjustiz* (victors' justice). Furthermore, despite the crimes committed against many innocent civilians by the East German regime before 1989–1990, particularly the incarceration of political dissidents and the casualties at the Berlin Wall and the inner-German border, most observers reject any attempt to treat the Nazi and SED systems as equivalent, references to shared totalitarian features notwithstanding. The circumstances surrounding each system's emergence, persistence, and ultimate demise are too divergent, and so are many aspects of the way in which each operated, as well as their ideological orientation.[176]

A shared aspect of *Vergangenheitsbewältigung* in both cases is the perceived need to effect what Jürgen Habermas has called a *Mentalitätswandel* (change of mentality), based on a direct as well as indirect learning process that draws lessons from a traumatic past and aims at preventing repetition. Yet such change is made more complicated by eastern resistance to perceived dominance by *Besserwessis*. This in turn has led some to recommend that remaining *Stasi* files be destroyed, that access to files be terminated, and/or that purges and prosecutions be brought to an end.[177]

An additional similarity between the two attempts at mastering the past lies certainly in the fact that political, ideological, and partisan calculations and motivations were and again are very much a part of the process. In a general sense, as Mary Fulbrook has noted, "[t]he social psychology of a postdictatorial society, with post hoc maneuverings among the roles of would-be victim and perpetrator, fellow-traveler and innocent, has many problematic facets."[178] For example, although (western German) Christian Democrats and Social Democrats generally favor the idea of prosecuting certain top GDR leaders, there is no full unanimity on how far one should take this process. And whereas CDU officials are eager to expose the SPD and its erstwhile *Ostpolitik* as accomplices of East German Communism during the Cold War, Social Democrats decry such efforts as an attempt at historical revisionism carried out for partisan and ideological reasons and point to many instances of SED-CDU contact. Considerable support for prosecution of GDR functionaries also comes from Bündnis90/Greens, which contains many former East German dissidents.

Not surprisingly, the "post-Communist" PDS is most vocal in its opposition to the current process of *Vergangenheitsbewältigung*, seeing it as but one more part of a western German domination over hapless *Ossis*. Unfortunately for the PDS, however, a fair number of these same *Ossis* seem often more adamant regarding the need for trials and purges than many a disinterested *Wessi*.[179] The federal official in charge of the mountains of *Stasi* files, Joachim Gauck, has argued, for example, that "[w]hile West German 'neocolonialism' does take place from time to time, the investigation of public servants for *Stasi* collaboration is a result of pressure from the East German democracy movement, legalized by two German parliaments, and cannot be explained as a Machiavellian scheme by the old Federal Republic."[180]

As controversy regarding the interpretation of the East German past continues, some analysts have criticized what they see as a disturbing tendency toward a "cheap revision of history."[181] Calling for *Aufklärung* (enlightenment) instead of *Abrechnung* (a settling of accounts amounting to revenge), Rüdiger Thomas has stressed that true understanding of the past cannot be achieved on the basis of imposed, ideological standards, but only by means of an appropriate degree of mutual empathy and joint effort between east and west in a still far from unified Germany, resulting in more balanced, nuanced understanding.[182] Along similar lines, former FRG President Richard von Weizsäcker has reminded all his fellow Germans that "the mastering of the time which [now] lies behind us remains a task for east and west together. Our shared historical roots in this century involve January 30, 1933 [Hitler's accession to power] along with its pre-history as well as its consequences."[183] In doing so, he pointed explicitly to the complicated yet un-mistakable link between Germany's two totalitarian experiences in the course of the twentieth century.

Another interesting angle of this entire process concerns the question whether the focus on the GDR will, either inadvertently or deliberately, come to over-shadow and replace a continuing need to come to grips with the Nazi past. Just as the Cold War permitted both German states to avoid some aspects of liability for the past by "recasting" themselves as important allies of their respective super-power patrons, so now the end of the Cold War and the demise of the GDR may provide some in the united Germany (and particularly in its western part) with an "opportunity" to shift attention to the legacy of East German Communism in-stead. Furthermore, in the pursuit of this new *Vergangenheitsbewältigung*, some Germans may feel compelled to act with extra thoroughness to atone for the pur-ported shortcomings of the early postwar confrontation with the Nazi legacy. Thus Tina Rosenberg has noted that "[m]any East Germans believed that West Germany, having failed to purge itself after the war, was now determined to make up for it by purging someone else."[184] Yet in taking such a step, the authorities risk committing injustice vis-à-vis many average eastern Germans whose degree of complicity (if any) might not at all warrant the level of legal punishment or professional retribution inflicted.

The areas of greatest controversy in the effort at mastering the East German past have been the (re)writing of history, control over and access to the files of the GDR's secret police *(Stasi)*, the prosecution of higher East German officials as well as border guards, the purging of public service employees, the debate over the ideological complicity of (especially, but not exclusively, East German) writ-ers and intellectuals,[185] the treatment of the Party of Democratic Socialism (suc-cessor party to the SED), and miscellaneous disputes over those things that sym-bolize or evoke the vanished GDR regime (monuments, memorials, street names, and so forth).

The end of the Cold War and the advent of national unity generated consider-able scholarly activity by historians, political scientists, and other social scientists anxious to shed light on the past and utilize newly available source material.[186] Much retrospective work on the former GDR has been done, often aimed at ex-plaining its ultimate collapse.[187] A good deal of what has been written has been very useful and of solid quality, but it is perhaps not surprising that the tempta-tion of a conservative rewriting of history has produced considerable controversy among scholars and necessarily affected the quality of some publications.[188] Much criticism has been leveled, especially by more liberal or left-wing commen-tators, at not only the effort by some to reclaim much of national history as a positive legacy for the reunited nation-state, but also the tendency to emphasize only or primarily those aspects of the former GDR that shed the most unfavor-able light upon it and enhance its post-facto delegitimation. Such controversies are but part of a larger political and intellectual climate in which one group seeks to discredit the GDR and treats its legacy (if not its former inhabitants) with barely disguised condescension, while another group seeks to defend at least selected aspects of the East German past, such as certain social achievements, and poses as the defender of the *Ossi* underdog.[189]

The postunification scholarly battle, particularly among historians, is often heavily focused on what some have called the "renationalization of German identity." This debate forms but part of the larger contention about the future contours and character of the *Berliner Republik*, perceived successor to what a number of conservatives consider to have been artificial, imposed eastern and western German regimes during the Cold War era (the *Bonner* or *Rheinische Republik* and the "so-called GDR").[190] Thus Jarausch, Seeba, and Conradt point out that

> [u]nder the banner of "normalization," the Right is vigorously promoting a return to a national identity. Viewing the nation as a "natural" category, many conservatives hail unification as the end of the aberration of division and therefore call for a self-conscious resumption of a chastened version of German traditions. . . . In contrast, a defensive Left tries to cling to its rejection of nationalism. Understanding the nation as a constructed category, intellectuals blame nationalism for the disasters of German history and warn insistently against falling back into national categories. . . . Between these fronts, some moderates are trying to establish a democratic patriotism. Aware of the terrible excesses of nationalism in the past, they nonetheless argue for a "new foundation of the German nation" in order to stabilize the enlarged FRG.[191]

Against this background, a lively and at times fierce debate erupted in the early 1990s about the proper way to combine a historiographical evaluation of the GDR past with a desire to pass judgment on the former Communist regime. Wolfgang Thierse, a leading participant in this debate, asked who should or could pass judgment and render a moral verdict. Arguing that "we cannot dispose of history by delegating it to the judiciary," he joined the prominent pastor Friedrich Schorlemmer in recommending especially to his fellow eastern Germans the creation of a "tribunal regarding the legacy of the SED- and Stasi-state." He envisioned such a tribunal as "a form of concentrated public discourse," as "a form of collective coming to terms with our past by us [*Ossis*] ourselves," as "a form of joint learning of that which could be learned at all from forty years of GDR," and as "a forum of political-moral self-education and self-renewal."[192]

An official attempt at historiography was launched by the *Bundestag* in 1992, when it created a special inquiry commission (*Enquete-Kommission zur "Aufarbeitung von Geschichte und Folgen der SED-Diktatur in Deutschland"*) to examine the East German past. The sizable report and its numerous appendices were completed in 1994, but the entire process became quite partisan at several crucial junctures, so that its ultimate value could yet turn out to be somewhat limited.[193] A second parliamentary commission was set up by the parliament in 1995 and submitted its report in 1998.[194] One of its outcomes was the creation of a federal foundation (*Bundesstiftung für die Aufarbeitung der SED-Diktatur*) aimed at providing former regime victims with an opportunity at rehabilitation and establishing additional means for German society at large of coming to terms with the past. Aside from setting up the parliamentary inquiry commissions, the *Bundestag* also passed legislation in 1992 and 1994 (the so-called *Unrechtsbereinigungsgesetze*) to effect a mixture of compensation and rehabilitation for victims of Communist injustice in the GDR.

The legacy of the *Stasi* and the disposition of its vast collection of files have been among the most prominent and at times controversial aspects of unification's aftermath.[195] The East German security police left a massive quantity of material: some 180 kilometers of files, one million pictures, 200,000 tapes, and six million names in a card system.[196] In 1990, shortly before unification, the democratizing GDR created an office to handle the matter. Led by Joachim Gauck, the so-called Gauck Agency (*Gauck-Behörde*) was continued after October 1990 and placed in charge of carrying out the provisions of the *Stasi-Unterlagen-Gesetz* (*StUG*), adopted by the *Bundestag* in 1991 in order to regulate the handling of the sensitive files.[197] By the mid-1990s, it had a total of about 3,000 employees, distributed across the main office in Berlin and fourteen branch offices in the five new *Länder*. Procedures were established to give citizens (and even foreign scholars)[198] access to their files. In addition, regulations gave employers the right to obtain a screening of any prospective employee, carried out by the agency. The screening of public employees and elected politicians has been particularly significant. By 1995, nearly 2 million applications for access had been submitted (including more than 700,000 by private citizens wishing to see their own files), and even these covered but a fraction of the more than 100 miles of *Stasi* files that are extant. The legacy of the thousands of "unofficial collaborators" (*inoffizielle Mitarbeiter*, or *IM*) has been especially sensitive, with many eastern Germans discovering that those who informed on them were close friends, relatives, or even spouses.

The various trials of former East German leaders and a number of border guards have been equally controversial and even more publicly noted.[199] Focused on the GDR as *Unrechtsstaat*, the full weight of the German *Rechtsstaat* tradition was brought to bear on these proceedings. The trials satisfied those who sought retributive justice, if not outright revenge, and who longed for the clarity of condemnation that only judicial verdicts might provide. Yet they also raised questions about ex post facto judgments—that is, the apparent violation of the old legal maxim *nulla poena sine lege,* which holds that nobody can be condemned for actions that were within the law at the time they were committed (and in the state in which they occurred). While accepting the fact that the GDR was a sovereign state, prosecutors generally sought to demonstrate that the actions of the accused had violated East German law and could thus be the focus of indictments under the provisions of the 1990 unification treaty. Among the defendants, the border guards who were prosecuted for shooting would-be refugees typically claimed to have acted on the basis of "superior orders," although that defense had to be used with care, in light of its rejection at the postwar Nuremberg trials.[200]

Leading East German officials, such as SED General-Secretary Erich Honecker, his successor Egon Krenz, *Stasi* chief Erich Mielke, spymaster Markus Wolf, and several other former ministers and generals accused the authorities of victors' justice (*Siegerjustiz*), suggested that the trials violated the *Rückwirkungsverbot* (the German equivalent of the *nulla poena sine lege* principle), and argued that the border had been a militarized Cold War frontier, ultimately subject to Soviet veto and thus not within East German sovereign control.[201] The proceedings against Honecker were cut short by his illness, exile to Chile, and subsequent death, while Mielke was convicted for two Weimar-era murders and received early release from detention for health reasons. Several generals received jail sentences, while the border guards were generally given either light or suspended sentences. The trial of Egon Krenz, Günter Schabowski, and Günther Kleiber in Berlin, known popularly as the *Politbüro-Prozeß*, which I attended as an observer in the summer of 1997, showed both the advantages and drawbacks of the judicial method of *Vergangenheitsbewältigung*: The desire for a verdict is satisfied, but the focus on those top leaders who are still available for prosecution might make them convenient scapegoats and permit many a small-time collaborator or *Mitläufer* to evade a sense of personal responsibility. With ideological sparks flying once more, the trial very much turned into an "epilogue of the Cold War." Reviewing the various trials held in the united Germany since 1990, Rosenberg concludes: "Trials that seek to do justice on a grand scale risk doing injustice on a small scale; their goal must be not Justice but justice bit by bit by bit. Trials, in the end, are ill suited to deal with the subtleties of facing the past. For that, Germans must turn elsewhere."[202]

In their analysis of the impact of historical memory on the question of German identity, Jarausch, Seeba, and Conradt conclude that "the debates about history have intensified in the wake of unification" and that "alternative memories confront one another in a battle for cultural hegemony over a united Germany." They point out that "[a]lthough remembrances of the Second World War, recollections of the Holocaust, and judgments about the GDR are separate arenas, these debates are linked by cross-cutting attitudes towards national identity."[203] It indeed can be argued that every country has its "ghosts of history" and that a debate over the meaning and lessons of the past is by no means a uniquely German phenomenon, but the fact remains that the twentieth century has left the Germans with a national history that is sufficiently complex and traumatic to guarantee the persistence of controversy for many years to come. As we have seen, these debates over the past are not merely the more or less harmless stuff of academic conferences and publications. Rather, insofar as they reflect differing conceptions of Germany as a modern nation-state and the definitive abandonment of an older, illiberal political tradition, they are intimately connected with the

Germans' unfinished search for a stable, national identity and the consolidation of a vibrant civic culture.

Notes

1. The series of cards was produced by VOLLER ERNST, Innsbrucker Str. 37, 10825 Berlin. Using similar imagery of marriage and family, Lothar Kettenacker has written that "[p]ost-natal depression is perhaps the best way to describe the mood in Germany six years after the event: an almost traumatic realization that, with new family responsibilities encroaching from all directions, the free and easy life-style of the old Federal Republic cannot be maintained any longer." Kettenacker, *Germany since 1945* (Oxford/New York: Oxford University Press, 1997), p. 213. A measure of the degree of unexpectedness of unification can be gained when considering the results of a poll conducted in 1986 asking respondents whether they expected reunification to occur within their lifetimes. Nearly 80 percent did not expect to see Germany reunified, and only about 10 percent believed that they would experience it. Reported in Martin and Sylvia Greiffenhagen, *Ein schwieriges Vaterland. Zur politischen Kultur im vereinigten Deutschland* (München: Paul List Verlag, 1993), p. 51.

2. The expression is taken from the title of the book by Konrad Jarausch, *The Rush to German Unity* (New York: Oxford University Press, 1994).

3. Not surprisingly, of course, reactions to unification among the Germans varied based on a person's generation, biography, region, and political/ideological orientation. See Greiffenhagen, *Ein schwieriges Vaterland*, pp. 49–55. As far as generations were concerned, older Germans were clearly more favorable to unification, having experienced a united Germany in their lifetimes, than were younger Germans, for whom the existence of two separate states had become fairly normal.

4. See Wolfgang Dümcke and Fritz Vilmar, eds., *Kolonialisierung der DDR. Kritische Analysen und Alternativen des Einigungsprozesses* (Münster: agenda Verlag, 1996); Fritz Vilmar and Wolfgang Dümcke, "Kritische Zwischenbilanz der Vereinigungspolitik. Eine unerledigte Aufgabe der Politikwissenschaft," *Aus Politik und Zeitgeschichte*, nr. 40, 27 September 1996. In a 1991 opinion survey, 63 percent of eastern Germans agreed that western Germans had "conquered the former GDR in colonialist style," while 36 percent disagreed with this assessment. Among western Germans, the percentages were 31 and 66, respectively—in other words, a mirror image. In the same survey, 82 percent of former GDR citizens agreed that western Germans behaved like *Besserwessis*, while only 18 percent disagreed. The percentages among western Germans on this question were 56 and 42, respectively. See "Nur noch so beliebt wie die Russen," *Der Spiegel*, nr. 30, 1991, p. 28.

5. Cited in Greiffenhagen, *Ein schwieriges Vaterland*, pp. 54–55.

6. Stephan Eisel, "The Politics of a United Germany," *Daedalus*, vol. 123, nr. 1, Winter 1994, p. 150 (emphasis in original).

7. Mary Fulbrook, "Aspects of Society and Identity in the New Germany," *Daedalus*, vol. 123, nr. 1, Winter 1994, p. 214.

8. See, for example, Helmut Klages and Thomas Gensicke, "Geteilte Werte? Ein deutscher Ost-West-Vergleich," in Werner Weidenfeld, ed., *Deutschland. Eine Nation— doppelte Geschichte* (Köln: Verlag Wissenschaft und Politik, 1993); John Ardagh, *Germany and the Germans* (London/New York: Penguin Books, 1991), especially Chapter 8. An in-

teresting comparative report on psychological feelings across a considerable range of issues, among adults and youth, can be found in Aike Hessel, Michael Geyer, Julia Würz, and Elmar Brähler, "Psychische Befindlichkeiten in Ost- und Westdeutschland im siebten Jahr nach der Wende," *Aus Politik und Zeitgeschichte*, nr. 13, 21 March 1997. See also Laurence H. McFalls, "Une Allemagne, deux sociétés distinctes: les causes et conséquences culturelles de la réunification," *Canadian Journal of Political Science/Revue canadienne de science politique*, vol. XXVI, nr. 4, December 1993.

9. Anne-Marie LeGloannec, "On German Identity," *Daedalus*, vol. 123, nr. 1, Winter 1994, p. 139.

10. In view of the narrower focus of this chapter, little attention is given to matters of socioeconomic policy, institutional developments, legal-constitutional questions, and so forth, that have characterized the German public policy agenda since the events of 1989–1990. The interested reader may wish to turn to the following sources for more extensive discussion on these issues: Christopher Anderson, Karl Kaltenthaler, and Wolfgang Luthardt, eds., *The Domestic Politics of German Unification* (Boulder, CO/London: Lynne Rienner Publishers, 1993), Part 2; Robert Hettlage and Karl Lenz, eds., *Deutschland nach der Wende. Eine Zwischenbilanz* (München: Verlag C. H. Beck, 1995); Ardagh, *Germany and the Germans*; Michael G. Huelshoff, Andrei S. Markovits, and Simon Reich, eds., *From Bundesrepublik to Deutschland: German Politics after Unification* (Ann Arbor: University of Michigan Press, 1993); Patricia Smith, ed., *After the Wall: Eastern Germany Since 1989* (Boulder, CO: Westview Press, 1998).

11. Greiffenhagen, *Ein schwieriges Vaterland*, p. 11.

12. As previous chapters have shown, this is by no means a "new" issue in Germany. For a recent overview of the question, see Stefan Berger, *The Search for Normality: National Identity and Historical Consciousness in Germany Since 1800* (Providence, RI/Oxford: Berghahn Books, 1997); Part II in this book addresses the most recent developments. On the more recent debate, see the review essay by A. James McAdams, "Germany After Unification: Normal at Last?" *World Politics*, vol. 49, January 1997. See also Peter Pulzer, "Unified Germany: A Normal State?" *German Politics*, vol. 3, nr. 1, April 1994.

13. Stephen R. Graubard, "Preface," *Daedalus*, vol. 123, nr. 1, Winter 1994, p. IX.

14. For a fundamental exploration of this theme, see Andreas Staab, *National Identity in Eastern Germany: Inner Unification or Continued Separation?* (Westport, CT/London: Praeger Publishers, 1998).

15. The notion of modernization as a conceptual tool in analyzing the transformation of eastern Germany is stressed, for example, by Werner Weidenfeld, "Deutschland nach der Vereinigung: Vom Modernisierungsschock zur inneren Einheit," in Weidenfeld, ed., *Deutschland*. He adds that modernization in the east is but part of a broader domestic as well as international modernization challenge. The theme is also addressed by Stefan Hradil, "Die Modernisierung des Denkens. Zukunftspotentiale und 'Altlasten' in Ostdeutschland," and Michael Vester, "Deutschlands feine Unterschiede. Mentalitäten und Modernisierung in Ost- und Westdeutschland," both in *Aus Politik und Zeitgeschichte*, nr. 20, 12 May 1995.

16. Greiffenhagen, *Ein schwieriges Vaterland*, p. 42.

17. On the phenomenon of the *Nischengesellschaft*, see Günter Gaus, *Wo Deutschland liegt. Eine Ortsbestimmung* (Hamburg: Hoffmann und Campe, 1983), pp. 156–233.

18. Reported in "Stolz aufs eigene Leben," *Der Spiegel*, nr. 27, 1995, p. 43. In a 1991 survey, large majorities or pluralities of eastern Germans pointed with regret to aspects of the

former GDR that were vanishing in the united Germany. See "Im Osten liegt die SPD noch vorn," *Der Spiegel*, nr. 48, 1991, p. 63.

19. Survey conducted in 1992 by the Allensbach Institut für Demoskopie, cited in Klaus Harpprecht, "Im Niemandsland," *Die Zeit*, nr. 38, 10 September 1998.

20. Helga A. Welsh, Andreas Pickel, and Dorothy Rosenberg, "East and West German Identities," in Konrad H. Jarausch, ed., *After Unity: Reconfiguring German Identities* (Providence, RI/Oxford: Berghahn Books, 1997), p. 105.

21. LeGloannec, "On German Identity," p. 138.

22. Data cited in Heinrich August Winkler, "Rebuilding of a Nation: The Germans Before and After Unification," *Daedalus*, vol. 123, nr. 1, Winter 1994, pp. 112–113.

23. Winkler, "Rebuilding of a Nation," p. 121. See also Winkler, "Die vollendete Verwestlichung der Republik," *Berliner Zeitung*, 22/23 November 1997, p. II, and the response by Andreas Krause, "Die Westbindung ist keine Einbahnstraße," *Berliner Zeitung*, 6/7 December 1997, p. IV, in which new and old aspects of the discussion regarding Germany's orientation toward as well as historical alienation from Western (democratic) traditions are debated.

24. Konrad Jarausch, "Reshaping German Identities," in Jarausch, ed., *After Unity*, p. 2. See also Steven Muller, "Democracy in Germany," *Daedalus*, vol. 123, nr. 1, Winter 1994, pp. 44–51; Axel Knoblich, Antonio Peter, and Erik Natter, eds., *Auf dem Weg zu einer gesamtdeutschen Identität?* (Köln: Verlag Wissenschaft und Politik, 1993), especially the contributions by Antonio Peter and Erik Natter; Eduard J. M. Kroker and Bruno Dechamps, eds., *Die Deutschen auf der Suche nach ihrer neuen Identität?* (Frankfurt/Main: Frankfurter Allgemeine Zeitung, Verlagsbereich Wirtschaftsbücher, 1993). According to the historian Christian Meier, contemporary Germany has no choice but to be a nation, yet it is confronted by enduring difficulties in this regard, including a notable unwillingness, in view of past traumas, to think of itself in national terms. See his *Die Nation die keine sein will* (München/Wien: Carl Hanser Verlag, 1991).

25. Fulbrook, "Aspects of Society and Identity in the New Germany," p. 211. According to Angela Stent, however, the identity challenge is clearly greater for eastern Germans, who have acceded to an already existing liberal-democratic Federal Republic. Writing in the early 1990s, she argued that "East Germans have yet to develop a viable German identity." Stent, "The One Germany," *Foreign Policy*, nr. 81, Winter 1990–91, p. 62.

26. Jarausch, "Reshaping German Identities," p. 9.

27. Greiffenhagen, *Ein schwieriges Vaterland*, p. 34.

28. Jarausch, "Reshaping German Identities," pp. 10, 11.

29. See also LeGloannec, "On German Identity." She explores the double nature of the "East German revolution" ("national and democratic") and shows how, as a result, the "national question" and the "constitutional question" have become "intimately intertwined" (pp. 132, 133). Hermann Glaser, while accepting the notion of "national" identity, calls for a *Pluralisierung von Identität* in the reunited Germany. Glaser, "Deutsche Identitäten. Gesellschaft und Kultur im vereinten Deutschland," *Aus Politik und Zeitgeschichte*, nr. 13–14, 22 March 1996.

30. See the discussion in Greiffenhagen, *Ein schwieriges Vaterland*, p. 37ff.

31. According to Christhard Hoffmann, one of the fundamental issues in the debate on German national identity is the question of "whether the self-understanding of the new German nation-state should express itself in political and social institutions . . . or in ethno-cultural categories." Hoffman, "Introduction: One Nation—Which Past? Historio-

graphy and German Identities in the 1990s," *German Politics and Society*, vol. 15, nr. 2, Summer 1997, p. 1.

32. See, for example, Jeffrey Peck, Mitchell Ash, and Christine Lemke, "Natives, Strangers, and Foreigners," in Jarausch, ed., *After Unity*; Klaus J. Bade, "Immigration and Social Peace in United Germany," *Daedalus*, vol. 123, nr. 1, Winter 1994; Marc Fisher, *After the Wall: Germany, the Germans and the Burdens of History* (New York: Simon & Schuster, 1995), Part III; Gert Krell, Hans Nicklas, and Änne Ostermann, "Immigration, Asylum, and Anti-Foreigner Violence in Germany," *Journal of Peace Research*, vol. 33, nr. 2, 1996; Ardagh, *Germany and the Germans*, Chapter 5; Joyce Marie Mushaben, *From Post-War to Post-Wall Generations: Changing Attitudes Toward the National Question and NATO in the Federal Republic of Germany* (Boulder, CO: Westview Press, 1998), Chapter 7. According to Thomas Blank, the distinction between patriotism, with its more tolerant face, and a more xenophobic nationalism is essential to a proper analysis of the issue. He argues that most empirical data show the greater prevalence of the former rather than the latter in contemporary Germany. Identification with Germany as a nation-state thus need not inherently imply the pursuit of a xenophobic *Deutschtum*. Blank, "Wer sind die Deutschen? Nationalismus, Patriotismus, Identität—Ergebnisse einer empirischen Längsschnittstudie," *Aus Politik und Zeitgeschichte*, nr. 13, 21 March 1997.

33. Greiffenhagen, *Ein schwieriges Vaterland*, p. 42.

34. For further discussion of attitudes of eastern German youth, see Ursula Meckel, "Jugend vor, während und nach dem Umbruch in der DDR: Erfahrungsbericht und Perspektiven," and Manuela Glaab, "Die junge Generation in den neuen Bundesländern: Ansichten zur doppelten Integration," both in Weidenfeld, ed., *Deutschland*; Alfred Klaus, "Zukunftskonzepte Jugendlicher im Spiegel der Zeit," in Knoblich, Peter, and Natter, eds., *Auf dem Weg zu einer gesamtdeutschen Identität?*

35. For a general discussion of right-wing extremism in the united Germany, see Christoph Butterwegge and Horst Isola, eds., *Rechtsextremismus im vereinten Deutschland. Randerscheinung oder Gefahr für die Demokratie?* (Bremen: Steintor Verlag, 1991).

36. *Deutschland Nachrichten* (published by the German Information Center in New York), 6 March 1998, p. 2.

37. See Peck, Ash, and Lemke, "Natives, Strangers, and Foreigners."

38. On the importance of economic conditions for the development of attitudes among eastern German youth, see Kerstin Seiring, "Ostdeutsche Jugendliche fünf Jahre nach der Wiedervereinigung," *Aus Politik und Zeitgeschichte*, nr. 20, 12 May 1995.

39. Data cited and discussed in Greiffenhagen, *Ein schwieriges Vaterland*, pp. 389–392.

40. Data cited in Winkler, "Rebuilding of a Nation," p. 121.

41. Muller, "Democracy in Germany," p. 55.

42. Jarausch, "Reshaping German Identities," p. 16.

43. In this context, see also Erwin K. Scheuch, *Wie deutsch sind die Deutschen? Eine Nation wandelt ihr Gesicht* (Bergisch-Gladbach: Bastei-Lubbe-Taschenbuch, 1992).

44. Jarausch, "Reshaping German Identities," p. 18.

45. Cited in Greiffenhagen, *Ein schwieriges Vaterland*, p. 369; and Markus L. Müller, "Identitätsprobleme der Menschen in der DDR seit 1989/90," in Dümcke and Vilmar, eds., *Kolonialisierung der DDR*, p. 228. An example of lingering *Ostalgie* can be seen in the great popularity in eastern Germany of books written by *Ossis*, such as former GDR prime minister Hans Modrow's *Ich wollte ein neues Deutschland* (Berlin: Karl Dietz Verlag, 1998). This trend was also noticeable at the major book fair in Leipzig in early 1998.

46. Cited in Müller, "Identitätsprobleme der Menschen in der DDR seit 1989/90," p. 229.

47. LeGloannec, "On German Identity," pp. 142–143. See also the discussion of eastern Germany's evolving identity in Thomas Gensicke, "Vom Staatsbewußtsein zur Oppositions-Ideologie: DDR-Identität im vereinten Deutschland," and Harald Pätzolt, "Junge Länder—junge Menschen? Ostdeutsche Identität im Wandel," both in Knoblich, Peter, and Natter, eds., *Auf dem Weg zu einer gesamtdeutschen Identität?*

48. Cited in Winkler, "Rebuilding of a Nation," p. 117.

49. Welsh, Pickel, and Rosenberg, "East and West German Identities," p. 135. Pointing in a somewhat similar direction, Hans-J. Misselwitz has written that "what emerges is a reflexive 'eastern German' identity, constructed against a background of a shared GDR experience and acquired within the structure of interests of the unified Germany." See his essay "DDR: Geschlossene Gesellschaft und offenes Erbe," in Weidenfeld, ed., *Deutschland*, p. 111.

50. Data cited in Winkler, "Rebuilding of a Nation," pp. 119–120.

51. Data reproduced in Welsh, Pickel, and Rosenberg, "East and West German Identities," p. 112 (Table 3). On attitudes regarding national and European identity among eastern German youth, see the discussion by Glaab, "Die junge Generation in den neuen Bundesländern." For further discussion of research regarding national pride in a more comparative, international perspective, see Robert von Rimscha, "Amerikaner sind besonders patriotisch, Deutsche sehr kritisch," *Der Tagesspiegel*, 4 July 1998, p. 2; "Patrioten gesucht," *Focus*, nr. 28, 6 July 1998, pp. 30–31. Both of these articles discuss a comparative study on national pride carried out by the National Opinion Research Center (NORC) at the University of Chicago.

52. See Blank, "Wer sind die Deutschen?" p. 43.

53. Steven Muller sees a darker side to this German "Europeanism" when he writes that "German intellectual and political leaders have sublimated their confusion [about national identity] by invoking the vision of supranational Europe" in a way that "offers an eerie parallel to their predecessors who, after Napoleon, tried to invoke a supranational pan-Germanism." Muller, "Democracy in Germany," p. 47. The comparison of European integration with pan-Germanism under a heading of "supranationalism" is analytically rather careless, however.

54. Cited in Greiffenhagen, *Ein schwieriges Vaterland*, p. 387.

55. On the debate, see *Berlin-Bonn. Die Debatte. Alle Bundestagsreden vom 20. Juni 1991* (Köln: Verlag Kiepenheuer & Witsch, 1991). See also Greiffenhagen, *Ein schwieriges Vaterland*, pp. 284–294.

56. See Greiffenhagen, *Ein schwieriges Vaterland*, pp. 47–48.

57. Michael Mertes, "Germany's Social and Political Culture," *Daedalus*, vol. 123, nr. 1, Winter 1994, pp. 1–2.

58. Welsh, Pickel, and Rosenberg, "East and West German Identities," p. 113 (italics in original).

59. Welsh, Pickel, and Rosenberg, "East and West German Identities," p. 113.

60. This "estrangement" (or what the Germans would call *Entfremdung*) is the focal point of much of the literature on postunification Germany. See, for example, Wolfgang Hardtwig and Heinrich August Winkler, eds., *Deutsche Entfremdung. Zum Befinden in Ost und West* (München: Verlag C. H. Beck, 1994). See also Joachim Gauck, "Noch lange fremd," *Der Spiegel*, nr. 40, 29 September 1997, pp. 46, 48, 51.

61. According to Daniel Hamilton, however, reality is a bit more complicated. In his view, "[m]any east Germans wage a constant personal battle between gratitude and bitterness, between the desire to 'Test the West'—as a popular cigarette ad goes—and the need to retain the familiar, all amidst strong feelings of having become second- or even third-class citizens." Hamilton, "Germany After Unification," *Problems of Communism,* vol. XLI, nr. 3, May-June 1992, p. 7.

62. See Müller, "Identitätsprobleme der Menschen in der DDR seit 1989/90," p. 227. See also, for example, "Zwietracht im einig Vaterland," *Der Spiegel,* nr. 6, 1991, p. 46; "Nur noch so beliebt wie die Russen," p. 28; "Erst vereint, nun entzweit," *Der Spiegel,* nr. 3, 1993, p. 59.

63. "Stolz aufs eigene Leben," p. 49.

64. In a 1993 survey, 64 percent of western Germans and 74 percent of eastern Germans agreed that a new, mental Wall was growing between the two halves of the united Germany. See "Erst vereint, nun entzweit," p. 52. Stephen Kinzer has spoken of a "wall of resentment"—see "A Wall of Resentment Now Divides Germany," *The New York Times,* 14 October 1994, pp. A1, A6).

65. See "Stolz aufs eigene Leben," p. 40ff.

66. Cited in Greiffenhagen, *Ein schwieriges Vaterland,* p. 372. See also "Stolz aufs eigene Leben," p. 46; Manfred Kuechler, "Political Attitudes and Behavior in Germany: The Making of a Democratic Society," in Huelshoff, Markovits, and Reich, eds., *From Bundesrepublik to Deutschland,* p. 47; "Nur noch so beliebt wie die Russen," p. 27; "Stärkste Partei: die Nichtwähler," *Der Spiegel,* nr. 9, 1993, p. 29. Hans-Joachim Maaz has criticized this *Kolonisierung* as a process that prevents a much-needed confrontation with the past in both parts of the united Germany: The arrogant West overpowers a once again submissive East, whereby both sides are able to avoid a more honest look at those legacies that continue to "deform" their respective mentalities. See Maaz, "Eine Therapie für Deutschland? Psychosoziale Aspekte im deutschen Einigungsprozeß," in Weidenfeld, ed., *Deutschland,* pp. 94–95.

67. The EMNID Institute found in 1995, however, that only 25 percent of eastern Germans saw themselves as "winners," 17 percent considered themselves "losers," and a solid 58 percent chose the answer "neither winner nor loser." "Stolz aufs eigene Leben," p. 46.

68. *Infratest dimap* data reported in "Vermehrte Zweifel der Deutschen am Zusammenwachsen des Landes" and "Ostdeutsche sehen sich eher als Gewinner," *Berliner Zeitung,* 4/5 October 1997, pp. 1, 5.

69. Welsh, Pickel, and Rosenberg, "East and West German Identities," p. 108. On this question of an "eastern" identity, see also Müller, "Identitätsprobleme der Menschen in der DDR seit 1989/90." Some even suggested that this eastern German identity reflected a sense of "ethnie." See Josefine Janert, "Jammernder Ossi und geiziger Wessi," *Der Tagesspiegel,* 4 August 1998, p. 21. One of the more provocative explorations of this theme is Hans-J. Misselwitz, *Nicht länger mit dem Gesicht nach Westen. Das neue Selbstbewußtsein der Ostdeutschen* (Bonn: Verlag J.H.W. Dietz Nachfolger, 1996), in which he seeks to trace for his fellow *Ossis* a path between a naive *Ostalgie* and an equally naive worship of everything West German in order to fulfill more completely the promise of the events of 1989–1990. According to Dorothee Wierling, for whom memory and identity are intimately connected phenomena, the eastern German sense of identity was enhanced by, or perhaps even a direct product of, the opening of east-west borders and the dynamics of unification. Wierling, "The East as the Past: Problems with Memory and Identity," *German Politics and Society,* vol. 15, nr. 2, Summer 1997. For a dissenting perspective, rejecting the

notion of an eastern identity as "nonsense" spread by *Wessis*, see Stefan Berg, "Die neue deutsche Sippenhaft," *Der Spiegel*, nr. 39, 1996.

70. For provocative comment on the issue of *Westalgie*, see Hans Michael Kloth, "Die ehemalige BRD," *Der Spiegel*, nr. 25, 16 June 1997, pp. 40, 43.

71. Wolfgang Thierse, "Wahrnehmungen zum deutschen Befinden in Ost und West," in Hardtwig and Winkler, eds., *Deutsche Entfremdung*, pp. 20, 25.

72. See, for example, the critical perspectives and accompanying appeals for increased civic virtue contained in Marion Dönhoff et al., *Weil das Land sich ändern muss. Ein Manifest* (Reinbek bei Hamburg: Rowohlt Verlag, 1992). Michael Mertes has argued that "remaining wedded to the West German status quo will not do with regard to the greatest experiment that the country has faced in its postwar history. This is a message that mainly the West Germans must understand; for their Eastern compatriots, momentous change has become an everyday experience." Mertes, "Germany's Social and Political Culture," p. 27. Yet he then adds that "[t]he challenge consists in exporting the 'Bonn Republic' to Berlin" (p. 28).

73. A fascinating record of an attempt by a western German to gain a sense of the mental as well as socioeconomic state of his eastern compatriots, and thereby overcome the hurdle of east-west estrangement, is the "diary" of Hans Dieter Baroth, *Aber jetzt ist überall Westen* (Berlin: Dietz Verlag, 1994), covering the early 1990s. An American interpretation of Germany in which the continued east-west psychological divide plays a central role is Fisher, *After the Wall*, especially Part II. See also the essay by Lothar Fritze, "Irritationen im deutsch-deutschen Vereinigungsprozeß," *Aus Politik und Zeitgeschichte*, nr. 27, 30 June 1995, which focuses on east-west misunderstandings and alienation and advocates an intensified process of mutual learning and empathy. Michael Minkenberg speaks of "The Wall After the Wall: On the Continuing Division of Germany and the Remaking of Political Culture," *Comparative Politics*, vol. 26, nr. 1, October 1993.

74. David Conradt, "Political Culture in Unified Germany: Will the Bonn Republic Survive and Thrive in Berlin?" *German Studies Review*, vol. XXI, nr. 1, February 1998, p. 98.

75. Data reproduced in Welsh, Pickel, and Rosenberg, "East and West German Identities," p. 111 (Table 1). See also the discussion of eastern and western German social and political attitudes in Petra Bauer-Kaase, "Germany in Transition: The Challenge of Coping with Unification," in M. Donald Hancock and Helga A. Welsh, eds., *German Unification: Process and Outcomes* (Boulder, CO: Westview Press, 1994). Dieter Fuchs traces divergences between eastern and western German attitudes toward liberal democracy in "The Political Culture of Unified Germany," paper published by the Wissenschaftszentrum Berlin für Sozialforschung (WZB), June 1998. The 1992 Allensbach survey cited by Klaus Harpprecht ("In Niemandsland") found that, at least at that time, 36 percent of eastern Germans (as opposed to 69 percent of western Germans) were willing to "defend" the sociopolitical order of the Federal Republic. Furthermore, compared with their western compatriots, easterners placed substantially greater emphasis on "equality" than "liberty."

76. See, for example, Detlef Pollack, "Das Bedürfnis nach sozialer Anerkennung. Der Wandel der Akzeptanz von Demokratie und Marktwirtschaft in Ostdeutschland," *Aus Politik und Zeitgeschichte*, nr. 13, 21 March 1997.

77. Data reproduced in Welsh, Pickel, and Rosenberg, "East and West German Identities," p. 111 (Table 2).

78. Data cited in Eisel, "The Politics of a United Germany," p. 160.

79. Welsh, Pickel, and Rosenberg, "East and West German Identities," p. 121.

80. Rather than condemning western dominance, Karl Otto Hondrich has argued that this is an inescapable predicament, rooted in the preunification period, and not necessarily the result of a deliberate western German drive for hegemony. See his "Dominanz in Deutschland: Ein Kernproblem der Vereinigung," in Weidenfeld, ed., *Deutschland.* He concludes that "[t]here is no alternative to western dominance. Dominance is the solution, not the problem" (p. 100).

81. By July 1993, the *Treuhand* agency had sold about 78 percent and liquidated about 17 percent of the former East German enterprises and businesses under its control. For a general, critical overview of the agency's work and legacy, see Michael Jürgs, *Die Treuhändler. Wie Helden und Halunken die DDR verkauften* (München/Leipzig: List Verlag, 1997). See also Peter H. Merkl, "An Impossible Dream? Privatizing Collective Property in Eastern Germany," in Hancock and Welsh, eds., *German Unification*; Ferdinand Protzman, "East Nearly Privatized, Germans Argue the Cost," *The New York Times,* 12 August 1994, pp. C1-C2.

82. The trends have been contradictory, depending on what is emphasized. See, for example, the largely positive flavor of "Auferstanden aus Ruinen," *Der Spiegel,* nr. 36, 1995, p. 118ff., in contrast with the far more pessimistic "'Vulkane sind überall,'" *Der Spiegel,* nr. 25, 1996, p. 94ff.

83. For a discussion of economic achievements and setbacks in eastern Germany after unification, see Manfred Wegner, "Die deutsche Einigung oder das Ausbleiben des Wunders," *Aus Politik und Zeitgeschichte,* nr. 40, 27 September 1996.

84. Polling data cited in Mertes, "Germany's Social and Political Culture," p. 9.

85. Data reproduced in Welsh, Pickel, and Rosenberg, "East and West German Identities," p. 119. See also "Zehn Jahre bis zum Wohlstand?" *Der Spiegel,* nr. 31, 1991, p. 41ff. During the first postunification year, Klaus von Dohnanyi was among those who pointed to the likelihood of continued east-west divergence and estrangement into the foreseeable future. In his words, "[u]nity is the wish, but division remains the reality, economically, socially, and psychologically." He added: "Why don't we admit together that which we all know anyway, namely that the unification of both German states is a high political gamble with an as yet unknown outcome?" See Dohnanyi, *Das Deutsche Wagnis. Über die wirtschaftlichen und sozialen Folgen der Einheit* (München: Droemersche Verlagsanstalt Th. Knaur Nachf., 1991), pp. 13, 14. In his conclusion, he argued that only a Germany reunited on a basis of social equality and justice could turn into a reliable and successful partner in an integrating Europe.

86. See, for example, Ulrich Becker, Horst Becker, and Walter Ruhland, *Zwischen Angst und Aufbruch. Das Lebensgefühl der Deutschen in Ost und West nach der Wiedervereinigung* (Düsseldorf/Wien/New York: Econ Verlag, 1992).

87. Welsh, Pickel, and Rosenberg, "East and West German Identities," p. 123.

88. See Jürgen Kocka, "Crisis of Unification: How Germany Changes," *Daedalus,* vol. 123, nr. 1, Winter 1994, pp. 181–183.

89. On some of these issues, see Welsh, Pickel, and Rosenberg, "East and West German Identities," pp. 122–134; Dirk Verheyen, "What's In a Name? Streetname Politics and Urban Identity in Berlin," *German Politics and Society,* vol. 15, nr. 3, Fall 1997; *Streit um die Neue Wache. Zur Gestaltung einer zentralen Gedenkstätte* (Berlin: Akademie der Künste, 1993); Christoph Stölzl, ed., *Die Neue Wache Unter den Linden. Ein deutsches Denkmal im Wandel der Geschichte* (Berlin: Verlag Koehler & Amelang, 1993); *Demontage . . . revolutionärer oder restaurativer Bildersturm?* (Berlin: Karin Kramer Verlag, 1992); Brian Ladd,

Ghosts of Berlin: Confronting German History in the Urban Landscape (Chicago/London: University of Chicago Press, 1997), especially Chapters 5 and 6.

90. Welsh, Pickel, and Rosenberg, "East and West German Identities," p. 133.

91. See, for example, the analysis and conclusions by Mushaben, *From Post-War to Post-Wall Generations*, Chapter 8.

92. In connection with the following, see also the Greiffenhagens' comparison of political culture in eastern and western Germany in "Eine Nation: Zwei politische Kulturen," in Weidenfeld, ed., *Deutschland*.

93. Greiffenhagen, *Ein schwieriges Vaterland*, p. 372.

94. Hans-Joachim Maaz's views, drawn from his work as a psychoanalyst, have not been uncontroversial, however. For examples of his writings, see "Eine Therapie für Deutschland?"; *Der Gefühlsstau. Ein Psychogramm der DDR* (Berlin: Argon Verlag, 1990); *Das gestürzte Volk. Die unglückliche Einheit* (Berlin: Argon Verlag, 1991); *Die Entrüstung. Deutschland, Deutschland. Stasi, Schuld und Sündenbock* (Berlin: Argon Verlag, 1992). Maaz has argued that the *Wende* of 1989–1990 did not amount to a true (mental) revolution, since one form of dependence (on the GDR regime) was rapidly replaced by another (on the West German model). Many authoritarian-repressive structures in the east have thus been able to persist. Formal democratization has taken place, but not (yet) a "democratization of the soul." Altogether, Maaz believes that the united Germany is faced with a serious "psychosocial crisis," featuring multiple fears and an eastern German hyperfixation on "salvation from the west" (he speaks of *Westgeilheit*) as key components.

95. Klages and Gensicke have argued, however, that this focus on "traditional" values of work and discipline among eastern Germans has been temporarily heightened by the need to cope with the challenges of capitalist transformation since 1990. See "Geteilte Werte?" p. 56. See also the report on eastern versus western German "life-styles" by Annette Spellerberg, "Lebensstil, soziale Schicht und Lebensqualität in West- und Ostdeutschland," *Aus Politik und Zeitgeschichte*, nr. 13, 21 March 1997.

96. Kocka, "Crisis of Unification," pp. 186, 187. See also Martin and Sylvia Greiffenhagen, "Die ehemalige DDR als das 'deutschere' Deutschland?" in Martin Greiffenhagen, Heinrich Tiemann, and Hans-Georg Wehling, eds., *Die neuen Bundesländer* (Stuttgart/Berlin/Köln: Verlag W. Kohlhammer, 1994).

97. Various poll data cited in Greiffenhagen, *Ein schwieriges Vaterland*, pp. 372, 373.

98. According to Wilhelm Bürklin, insofar as aspects of traditional eastern German political culture, some of them with roots in the pre-GDR era, continue to survive, they create a considerable potential for a persisting, dominant social-democratic subculture in the new federal states. See his essay "Perspektiven für das deutsche Parteiensystem: Politische Konfliktlinien und die sozialdemokratische Kultur," in Weidenfeld, ed., *Deutschland*.

99. On the following, see Greiffenhagen, *Ein schwieriges Vaterland*, p. 373ff. Hans-J. Misselwitz has suggested that this tendency in eastern German political culture was instrumental both in the initial attachment to the notion of Round Table negotiations as a preferred approach to reform and in the subsequent disenchantment with the notion of political parties. See his "DDR: Geschlossene Gesellschaft und offenes Erbe," pp. 108–109.

100. Greiffenhagen, "Eine Nation: Zwei politische Kulturen," pp. 40–41.

101. Data cited in Greiffenhagen, *Ein schwieriges Vaterland*, p. 373.

102. See Greiffenhagen, "Eine Nation: Zwei politische Kulturen," pp. 35–36. See also the discussion in Misselwitz, "DDR: Geschlossene Gesellschaft und offenes Erbe."

103. Greiffenhagen, *Ein schwieriges Vaterland,* pp. 374–375, 378. See also Mertes, "Germany's Social and Political Culture," p. 22.

104. See Greiffenhagen, "Eine Nation: Zwei politische Kulturen," p. 37.

105. Greiffenhagen, *Ein schwieriges Vaterland,* pp. 375–376.

106. See Greiffenhagen, *Ein schwieriges Vaterland,* pp. 377–381; quotes from p. 377. The stronger survival of traditional, "secondary" German virtues (duty, work, discipline, loyalty, thrift, and the like) among eastern Germans is often emphasized. See, for example, Greiffenhagen, "Eine Nation: Zwei politische Kulturen," pp. 34–35.

107. See Gunter Hofmann, "Ein Kulturbruch, mit links," *Die Zeit,* nr. 41, 1 October 1998.

108. For an analysis of Germany's contemporary economic challenges, see Kurt J. Lauk, "Germany at the Crossroads: On the Efficiency of the German Economy," *Daedalus,* vol. 123, nr. 1, Winter 1994.

109. Christoph Bertram, "Die neue deutsche Lethargie," *Die Zeit,* nr. 33, 8 August 1997, p. 1. See also the call for reformist enthusiasm in Uwe Jean Heuser and Gero von Randow, "So kommt Neues in die Welt," *Die Zeit,* nr. 42, 8 October 1998.

110. Mertes, "Germany's Social and Political Culture," pp. 6, 7. Mertes extends this observation into a claim that "the absence of an articulated Left/Right dichotomy makes Germany's political culture different from that of many other countries" (p. 13). This might be a possibly self-serving, conservative overstatement of contemporary German political reality, however. Mertes also sees the predilection for consensus and harmony as a useful compensation for the "lack of a relatively homogeneous elite." He notes a "culture of reticence" in German political life and suggests that "Germany, having reacquired her full sovereignty only in 1990, is not yet endowed with what might be called mental sovereignty" (pp. 15, 16, 17).

111. On the following discussion, see Greiffenhagen, *Ein schwieriges Vaterland,* p. 73ff.

112. Greiffenhagen, *Ein schwieriges Vaterland,* p. 83.

113. On the following discussion, see Greiffenhagen, *Ein schwieriges Vaterland,* pp. 86–104.

114. For a more concerned evaluation of western and/versus eastern German attitudes regarding "preferences of order," see Christian Welzel, "Vom Konsens zum Dissens? Politische Ordnungspräferenzen von Eliten und Bürgern im ost-westdeutschen Vergleich," paper published by the Wissenschaftszentrum Berlin für Sozialforschung (WZB), February 1998.

115. In connection with the state of Germany's civic culture, see Greiffenhagen, *Ein schwieriges Vaterland,* pp. 105–128; Gunther Mai, "Vom Obrigkeitsstaat zur Demokratiefähigkeit? Westdeutsche Einstellungen seit Kriegsende," in Knoblich, Peter, and Natter, eds., *Auf dem Weg zu einer gesamtdeutschen Identität?*

116. Dieter Fuchs, Hans-Dieter Klingemann, and Carolin Schöbel have suggested, however, that East German political activism at the time of the 1989–1990 *Wende* is likely to have laid the foundation for successful democratization of eastern German political culture in due course. See "Perspektiven der politischen Kultur im vereinigten Deutschland," *Aus Politik und Zeitgeschichte,* nr. 32, 2 August 1991.

117. These circumstances present a particular challenge in the area of civic education in the new federal states. See Bernhard Muszynski, "Politische Bildung im vereinigten Deutschland," *Aus Politik und Zeitgeschichte,* nr. 47, 17 November 1995; Petra Moritz,

"Politische Bildung aus ostdeutscher Sicht," *Aus Politik und Zeitgeschichte*, nr. 47, 17 November 1995. See also Günther Rüther, "Politische Bildung, politische Kultur und innere Einheit," *Deutschland Archiv*, vol. 28, nr. 7, July 1995.

118. For some speculation prior to the September 1998 federal elections, see Ingo Preissler, "Vor allem Arbeiter wählen rechtsextreme Parteien," *Berliner Zeitung*, 10 July 1998, p. 5; Renate Oschlies, "Berliner Studie: Jeder dritte Deutsche lehnt die Demokratie ab," *Berliner Zeitung*, 11 August 1998, p. 1. Nevertheless, none of the far-right parties managed to win enough votes to gain seats in the *Bundestag*.

119. Greiffenhagen, *Ein schwieriges Vaterland*, p. 114ff.

120. Much of this conclusion is based on an analysis of the impact of modernization on Germany. See, for example, Mertes, "Germany's Social and Political Culture," p. 18ff.; Greiffenhagen, *Ein schwieriges Vaterland*, p. 196ff. Werner Weidenfeld and Karl-Rudolf Korte describe the German commitment to democracy as solid but pragmatic rather than affective. See "Die pragmatischen Deutschen. Zum Staats- und Nationalbewußtsein in Deutschland," *Aus Politik und Zeitgeschichte*, nr. 32, 2 August 1991.

121. In this connection, see Greiffenhagen, *Ein schwieriges Vaterland*, pp. 140–155; Fulbrook, "Aspects of Society and Identity in the New Germany," p. 225ff.

122. Fulbrook, "Aspects of Society and Identity in the New Germany," pp. 226, 230.

123. Mertes reports that "[o]f the acts of xenophobic violence, 39.2 percent have been perpetrated in small towns (ten thousand to fifty thousand inhabitants), 20.5 percent in the rural areas, 22.3 percent in the metropoles, and 18 percent in medium-sized cities." Mertes, "Germany's Social and Political Culture," p. 21.

124. See, for example, Mertes, "Germany's Social and Political Culture," p. 21. Fulbrook, among others, emphasizes the element of anomie among eastern German youth as one of the root causes of the xenophobic violence. Fulbrook, "Aspects of Society and Identity in the New Germany," pp. 221–225. Some 70 percent of those perpetrating violence against foreigners in Germany in the early 1990s were younger than twenty years of age, while only 2.7 percent were older than thirty.

125. See the discussion in Greiffenhagen, *Ein schwieriges Vaterland*, pp. 156–173. See also Klages and Gensicke, "Geteilte Werte?" pp. 48–53. These changes have also affected the role traditionally played by the churches and religion in society and politics. See, on this issue, Greiffenhagen, *Ein schwieriges Vaterland*, pp. 208–220. Another, related area of interest is the lingering significance of the legacy of the 1960s for the value structure among contemporary middle- and younger-age generations. See Greiffenhagen, *Ein schwieriges Vaterland*, pp. 221–236. The Greiffenhagens question whether generational analysis of the kind used in western Germany is of much use when applied to the country's east, particularly due to the consistent socializing impact of SED rule over time and across generations in the former GDR (p. 46). On the issue of generations, see also Tilman Fichter, "Political Generations in Federal Germany," *New Left Review*, March/April 1991.

126. Klages and Gensicke, "Geteilte Werte?" p. 50.

127. See Klages and Gensicke, "Geteilte Werte?" pp. 53–56.

128. For a general overview of the role of religion and the churches in German political culture today, see Greiffenhagen, *Ein schwieriges Vaterland*, pp. 208–220.

129. Eisel, "The Politics of a United Germany," pp. 155–156.

130. Polling data cited in Greiffenhagen, *Ein schwieriges Vaterland*, p. 215. Without providing a source, Mertes presents the following statistics: "[a]mong young people, 43 percent in the West (4 percent in the East) claim to be Catholic, 43 percent in the West (17

percent in the East) acknowledge that they are Protestant, and 11 percent in the West (79 percent in the East) say they do not adhere to any religious community." Mertes, "Germany's Social and Political Culture," p. 21.

131. In 1993, for example, some 70,000 eastern German youth celebrated a new, post-unification version of the *Jugendweihe*.

132. A thorough analysis of the current German party system would exceed the confines of this chapter. An excellent source is David Conradt, Gerald R. Kleinfeld, George K. Romoser, and Christian Søe, eds., *Germany's New Politics: Parties and Issues in the 1990s* (Providence, RI/Oxford: Berghahn Books, 1995). See also Muller, "Democracy in Germany," pp. 41–44; Kettenacker, *Germany since 1945*, Chapter 6; Eckhard Jesse, "Das deutsche Parteiensystem nach der Vereinigung," *German Studies Review*, vol. XXI, nr. 1, February 1998; the essays on the different parties in *Aus Politik und Zeitgeschichte*, nr. 5, 24 January 1992, and nr. 6, 2 February 1996. On the PDS phenomenon, see also Ann L. Phillips, "Socialism with a New Face? The PDS in Search of Reform," *East European Politics and Societies*, vol. 8, nr. 3, Fall 1994. For a rather pessimistic view of the SPD and the German Left in general, shortly after unification, see Stephen Padgett and William Paterson, "The Rise and Fall of the West German Left," *New Left Review*, March/April 1991.

133. In this context, see Greiffenhagen, *Ein schwieriges Vaterland*, pp. 174–188.

134. On Herzog's pronouncements, see "'Einen Klotz hinhauen,'" *Der Spiegel*, nr. 18, 28 April 1997, p. 22ff.

135. See Greiffenhagen, *Ein schwieriges Vaterland*, p. 189ff. The demise of East Germany's all-encompassing authoritarian "welfare state" left many eastern Germans in a state of uncertainty regarding the contours of their personal as well as their society's future. See Michael Häder and Peter Ph. Mohler, "Zukunftsvorstellungen der Menschen als Erklärungsvariable für die Krise in der DDR und die gegenwärtige Situation in Ostdeutschland," *Aus Politik und Zeitgeschichte*, nr. 27, 30 June 1995.

136. See Greiffenhagen, *Ein schwieriges Vaterland*, pp. 237–251.

137. On the *Historikerstreit*, see Chapter 6. In connection with Kohl's interest in history, consider the controversy in the 1980s and 1990s over the *Haus der Geschichte* in Bonn and the *Deutsches Historisches Museum* in Berlin. See, for example, the material in Christoph Stölzl, ed., *Deutsches Historisches Museum. Ideen—Kontroversen—Perspektiven* (Frankfurt/Berlin: Propyläen Verlag, 1988); Charles S. Maier, *The Unmasterable Past: History, Holocaust, and German National Identity* (Cambridge/London: Harvard University Press, 1988), Chapter 5. See also Fisher, *After the Wall*, Chapter 4.

138. See the discussion in Greiffenhagen, *Ein schwieriges Vaterland*, pp. 252–267.

139. On this issue, see, for example, Stefan Berger, "Nationalism and the Left in Germany," *New Left Review*, nr. 206, July/August 1994.

140. For analysis, see Wolfgang Hartenstein and Rita Müller-Hilmer, "Der Linksruck," *Die Zeit*, nr. 41, 1 October 1998 (on the German elections); Werner A. Perger, "Linkes Europa," *Die Zeit*, nr. 43, 15 October 1998 (on the broader Western European picture).

141. See also Greiffenhagen, "Eine Nation: Zwei politische Kulturen," pp. 37–38.

142. See Greiffenhagen, *Ein schwieriges Vaterland*, p. 122ff.; Greiffenhagen, "Eine Nation: Zwei politische Kulturen," pp. 39–40.

143. Greiffenhagen, *Ein schwieriges Vaterland*, p. 128.

144. Kuechler, "Political Attitudes and Behavior in Germany," p. 50.

145. See Muller, "Democracy in Germany," pp. 33–37.

146. See Fisher, *After the Wall*, especially Part IV.

147. See Bernd Faulenbach, "Probleme des Umgangs mit der Vergangenheit im vereinten Deutschland: Zur Gegenwartsbedeutung der jüngsten Geschichte," in Weidenfeld, ed., *Deutschland.*

148. The allusion is to the well-known book by Alexander and Margarete Mitscherlich, *Die Unfähigkeit zu trauern. Grundlagen des kollektiven Verhaltens* (München: Piper Verlag, 1967).

149. Brigitte Rauschenbach, "Der Unfähigkeit zu trauern vierter Aufzug. Ein deutsches Trauerspiel mit offenem Ende," *Deutschland Archiv*, vol. 27, nr. 7, July 1994, p. 708.

150. See the essays in the special issue of *German Politics and Society* entitled "One Nation—Which Past? Historiography and German Identities in the 1990s," vol. 15, nr. 2, Summer 1997.

151. Konrad H. Jarausch, Hinrich C. Seeba, and David P. Conradt, "The Presence of the Past," in Konrad H. Jarausch, ed., *After Unity*, p. 25.

152. Jarausch, Seeba, and Conradt, "The Presence of the Past," p. 27.

153. Jarausch, Seeba, and Conradt, "The Presence of the Past," pp. 27–37, quotations on pp. 27, 30, 32, 35.

154. On the following, see Jarausch, Seeba, and Conradt, "The Presence of the Past," p. 37ff.

155. Jarausch, Seeba, and Conradt, "The Presence of the Past," p. 40.

156. Felix Philipp Lutz, "Verantwortungsbewußtsein und Wohlstandschauvinismus: Die Bedeutung historisch-politischer Einstellungen der Deutschen nach der Einheit," in Weidenfeld, ed., *Deutschland.* See also Faulenbach, "Probleme des Umgangs mit der Vergangenheit im vereinten Deutschland." Bodo v. Borries has explored the contrasts between the orientation of historical consciousness among youth in eastern and western Germany in "'Geschichtsbewußtsein' der Jugend in Deutschland: Ein Ost-West Vergleich," in Weidenfeld, ed., *Deutschland.*

157. Survey data reproduced in Jarausch, Seeba, and Conradt, "The Presence of the Past," pp. 46 (Table 1), 47.

158. Jarausch, Seeba, and Conradt, "The Presence of the Past," p. 47.

159. For a basic overview of some of the issues involved, and a comparison of post-1945 and post-1989 attempts at *Vergangenheitsbewältigung*, see Christa Hoffmann and Eckhard Jesse, "Die 'doppelte Vergangenheitsbewältigung' in Deutschland: Unterschiede und Gemeinsamkeiten," in Weidenfeld, ed., *Deutschland.* See also Ludwig Elm, *Nach Hitler. Nach Honecker. Zum Streit der Deutschen um die eigene Vergangenheit* (Berlin: Dietz Verlag, 1991).

160. Jarausch, Seeba, and Conradt, "The Presence of the Past," pp. 47–48.

161. In his fascinating study entitled *Divided Memory: The Nazi Past in the Two Germanys* (Cambridge, MA/London: Harvard University Press, 1997), Jeffrey Herf examines the "significance of political memories for the construction of democracy and dictatorship in post-1945 German history" and "how past beliefs and contemporaneous political interests in domestic and international politics shaped the narratives of the Nazi past told by postwar German political leaders," both in the FRG and the GDR (p. 2). "Long-established interpretive frameworks" (p. 4) shaped the postwar construction of memory and guided essential policy developments, yet within a context of Cold War confrontation, in which the Nazi legacy in turn played a considerable role. Herf concludes that "[i]n East no less than in West Germany, the end of the Nuremberg interregnum and the beginning of the Cold War reinforced provincial and divided memories of the war and the Holocaust. Once

the two German states were established, pursuit of their respective national interests in foreign policy also influenced national memory, though in very different ways" (pp. 383–384).

162. This is the focus of Antonia Grunenberg's "Antitotalitarianism Versus Antifascism—Two Legacies of the Past in Germany," *German Politics and Society*, vol. 15, nr. 2, Summer 1997.

163. Daniel Jonah Goldhagen, *Hitler's Willing Executioners: Ordinary Germans and the Holocaust* (New York: Vintage Books, 1997). See also Wolfgang Wippermann, *Wessen Schuld? Vom Historikerstreit zur Goldhagen-Kontroverse* (Berlin: Elefanten Press, 1997); Heiner Lichtenstein and Otto R. Romberg, eds., *Täter—Opfer—Folgen. Der Holocaust in Geschichte und Gegenwart* (Bonn: Bundeszentrale für politische Bildung, 1995). The reactions to Goldhagen's book by the German historiographical establishment were interesting, and partially tied to broader professional soul-searching regarding historians' involvement in the Nazi regime. See Volker Ullrich, "Späte Reue der Zunft," *Die Zeit*, nr. 39, 17 September 1998.

164. On the *Neue Wache* controversy, see Stölzl, ed., *Die Neue Wache Unter den Linden*; Streit um die Neue Wache; Daniela Büchten and Anja Frey, eds., *Im Irrgarten deutscher Geschichte. Die Neue Wache 1818–1993* (Berlin: Schriftenreihe des Aktiven Museums Faschismus und Widerstand in Berlin e.V., nr. 5, 1993).

165. On this controversy, see *Der Wettbewerb für das "Denkmal für die ermordeten Juden Europas." Eine Streitschrift* (Berlin: Verlag der Kunst; Neue Gesellschaft für Bildende Kunst, 1995).

166. For an excellent general discussion of the issue, see Peter Reichel, *Politik mit der Erinnerung. Gedächtnisorte im Streit um die nationalsozialistische Vergangenheit* (München/Wien: Carl Hanser Verlag, 1995).

167. On the exhibition, see Hans-Günther Thiele, ed., *Die Wehrmachtsausstellung. Dokumentation einer Kontroverse* (Bonn: Bundeszentrale für politische Bildung, 1997).

168. Jarausch, Seeba, and Conradt, "The Presence of the Past," p. 52. Lutz delineates five types of attitudes toward the Nazi past and its contemporary implications among West Germans. See "Verantwortungsbewußtsein und Wohlstandschauvinismus," p. 162ff.

169. Greiffenhagen, *Ein schwieriges Vaterland*, pp. 56–57.

170. Data cited in Greiffenhagen, *Ein schwieriges Vaterland*, p. 57.

171. In this connection, see Greiffenhagen, *Ein schwieriges Vaterland*, p. 58ff.

172. For an evaluation of some of the issues raised by this "second" *Vergangenheitsbewältigung*, see Bernward Baule and Rita Süssmuth, eds., *Eine deutsche Zwischenbilanz. Standpunkte zum Umgang mit unserer Vergangenheit* (München: Günter Olzog Verlag, 1997).

173. See Hoffmann and Jesse, "Die 'doppelte Vergangenheitsbewältigung' in Deutschland," p. 211ff. See also Tina Rosenberg, *The Haunted Land: Facing Europe's Ghosts After Communism* (New York: Vintage Books, 1996), Chapter 8. On the implications of similarities and differences for historiography, see Christoph Kleßmann, "Zwei Diktaturen in Deutschland—Was kann die künftige DDR-Forschung aus der Geschichtsschreibung zum Nationalsozialismus lernen?" *Deutschland Archiv*, vol. 25, nr. 6, June 1992. See also Friso Wielenga, "Schatten der deutschen Geschichte. Der Umgang mit der Nazi- und DDR-Vergangenheit in der Bundesrepublik Deutschland," *Deutschland Archiv*, vol. 27, nr. 10, October 1994; Friso Wielenga, *Schatten deutscher Geschichte. Der Umgang mit dem Nationalsozialismus und der DDR-Vergangenheit in der Bundesrepublik* (Vierow bei Greifswald:

SH-Verlag, 1995); Klaus Sühl, ed., *Vergangenheitsbewältigung 1945 und 1989. Ein unmöglicher Vergleich? Eine Diskussion* (Berlin: Verlag Volk & Welt, 1994).

174. Winkler, "Rebuilding of a Nation," p. 117.

175. Weidenfeld, "Deutschland nach der Vereinigung," p. 15.

176. See, for example, Greiffenhagen, *Ein schwieriges Vaterland*, pp. 64–65.

177. Greiffenhagen, *Ein schwieriges Vaterland*, pp. 66–68. For a rejection of an end to judicial proceedings, see Richard Schröder, "Schwamm drüber? Das reicht nicht," *Die Zeit*, nr. 35, 22 August 1997, p. 3.

178. Fulbrook, "Aspects of Society and Identity in the New Germany," p. 231.

179. A survey conducted in 1991 found that 75 percent of western Germans and 79 percent of eastern Germans favored a trial for former GDR leader Erich Honecker, for example. See "Zwietracht im einig Vaterland," p. 47.

180. Joachim Gauck, "Dealing with a Stasi Past," *Daedalus*, vol. 123, nr. 1, Winter 1994, p. 282.

181. LeGloannec, "On German Identity," p. 141.

182. Rüdiger Thomas, "Aufklärung statt Abrechnung: Anmerkungen zum Umgang mit der DDR-Geschichte," in Weidenfeld, ed., *Deutschland*.

183. Richard von Weizsäcker, "Arbeit an der Vergangenheit als wesentlicher Teil der deutschen Einigung," in Albrecht Schönherr, ed., *Ein Volk am Pranger? Die Deutschen auf der Suche nach einer neuen politischen Kultur* (Berlin: Aufbau Taschenbuch Verlag, n.d.), p. 186.

184. Rosenberg, *The Haunted Land*, p. 328.

185. On some of the controversies in this area, see Peter Monteath and Reinhard Alter, eds., *Kulturstreit—Streitkultur: German Literature Since the Wall* (Amsterdam/Atlanta, GA: Editions Rodopi, 1996), which examines the debates surrounding Christa Wolf and the late Heiner Müller particularly closely.

186. An interesting attempt at bridging the historiographical gap between east and west is Peter Bender's *Episode oder Epoche? Zur Geschichte des geteilten Deutschland* (München: Deutscher Taschenbuch Verlag, 1996). Bender stresses that postwar German history must focus properly on *both* German states, and tries to trace the many parallels in their development over time. He aims at interpreting the history of each state for the former inhabitants of the other.

187. Among this by now copious literature, see, for example, the excellent study by Charles S. Maier, *Dissolution: The Crisis of Communism and the End of East Germany* (Princeton, NJ: Princeton University Press, 1997); Jens Reich, "Warum ist die DDR untergegangen? Legenden und sich selbst erfüllende Prophezeiungen," *Aus Politik und Zeitgeschichte*, nr. 46, 8 November 1996; Jürgen Kocka and Martin Sabrow, eds., *Die DDR als Geschichte. Fragen—Hypothesen—Perspektiven* (Berlin: Akademie Verlag, 1994).

188. According to Konrad Jarausch, three approaches to the GDR past can be distinguished: the "apologetic-nostalgic approach," the "accusatory-polemical approach," and the "objective approach," with the latter involving extensive comparisons between the FRG and the GDR and between the GDR and other East bloc states. Jarausch, "The German Democratic Republic as History in United Germany: Reflections on Public Debate and Academic Controversy," *German Politics and Society*, vol. 15, nr. 2, Summer 1997.

189. Karl-Ernst Jeismann has suggested that three possible approaches in dealing with matters of historical consciousness in Germany are currently competing with one another. According to the "missionary model" (*Missionierungsmodell*), the GDR's legacy should be

dismissed and the western German view of the nation's history should be imposed. The "separation model" (*Separationsmodell*) would maintain a sense of east-west German divergence, allowing each part of the country its own legacy and memory. Jeismann favors the "integration model" (*Integrationsmodell*), however, based on a shared, comparative examination of the past that would require both parts of the country to transcend more narrowly focused perspectives. See his essay "Die Geschichte der DDR in der politischen Bildung: Ein Entwurf," in Weidenfeld, ed., *Deutschland.*

190. The weekly *Die Zeit* published a series of essays focused on this theme and its implications for German political life. See, for example, Harpprecht, "Im Niemandsland;" Thomas Assheuer, "Das Deutschlandspiel," *Die Zeit*, nr. 37, 3 September 1998; Andreas Schätzke, "Falsche Erwartung," *Die Zeit*, nr. 31, 23 July 1998; Richard Herzinger, "Das ungewisse Etwas," *Die Zeit*, nr. 42, 8 October 1998; Fritz Stern, "Ein neuer Anfang," and Martin Walser, "Bloß ein Etikett," both in *Die Zeit*, nr. 40, 24 September 1998. See also Christoph Bertram, "Germany Moves On," *Foreign Affairs*, vol. 77, nr. 4, July/August 1998. He concludes with confidence that "[t]he foundations of the Bonn Republic will not be dismantled when government and parliament settle in Berlin. Germany's democracy and tolerance, its federal confidence and its reserve as a nation, nourished over 50 years and now strongly rooted, are not in danger. The move back to Berlin is, thanks to Bonn, a move forward" (p. 194).

191. Jarausch, Seeba, and Conradt, "The Presence of the Past," pp. 55, 56. In this context, see also the discussion of patriotism by Mertes, "Germany's Social and Political Culture," p. 23ff. For a neoconservative discussion of German unification as a "trauma" for the German Left and a criticism of the alleged tradition of left-wing national self-hatred in Germany, see Rainer Zitelmann, "Wiedervereinigung und deutscher Selbsthaß: Probleme mit dem eigenen Volk," in Weidenfeld, ed., *Deutschland.* See also Brigitte Seebacher-Brandt, *Die Linke und die Einheit* (Berlin: Siedler Verlag, 1991). For an illustration of worries from the Left, see Günter Grass, *Lastenausgleich. Wider das dumpfe Einheitsgebot* (Darmstadt: Luchterhand Literaturverlag, 1990). See also the critical questioning of all notions of "nationhood" by Peter Sloterdijk, "Der starke Grund, zusammen zu sein," *Die Zeit*, nr. 2, 2 January 1998. On general developments in post-1990 German historiography, see Berger, *The Search for Normality*, Part II.

192. Wolfgang Thierse, "Schuld sind immer die anderen. Ein Plädoyer für die selbstkritische Bewältigung der eigenen Geschichte," in Schönherr, ed., *Ein Volk am Pranger?* p. 17. See also Friedrich Schorlemmer, "Das Dilemma des Rechtsstaates—Die juristischen Prozesse und das politische Tribunal" in the same volume. This small book contains reactions to Thierse and Schorlemmer and a general discussion about the ways in which the united Germany could and should confront the GDR past.

193. Highlights of the commission's report were published under the title *Getrennte Vergangenheit, gemeinsame Zukunft*, 4 volumes, edited by Ingrun Drechsler, Bernd Faulenbach, Martin Gutzeit, Markus Meckel, and Hermann Weber (München: Deutscher Taschenbuch Verlag, 1997).

194. See *Schlußbericht der Enquete-Kommission "Überwindung der Folgen der SED-Diktatur im Prozeß der deutschen Einheit"* (Bonn: Deutscher Bundestag, 13. Wahlperiode, Drucksache 13/11000, 10 June 1998).

195. See Stefan Wolle, "Im Labyrinth der Akten: Die archivalische Hinterlassenschaft des SED-Staates," in Weidenfeld, ed., *Deutschland.*

196. See Greiffenhagen, *Ein schwieriges Vaterland*, p. 71.

197. For further discussion, see Gauck, "Dealing with a Stasi Past;" Gauck, *Die Stasi-Akten. Das unheimliche Erbe der DDR* (Reinbek bei Hamburg: Rowohlt Taschenbuch Verlag, 1991).

198. See, for example, Timothy Garton Ash, *The File: A Personal History* (New York: Random House, 1997).

199. For an excellent analysis of the virtues and drawbacks of the judicial effort at coming to terms with the GDR past, see Rosenberg, *The Haunted Land*, pp. 329–351. See also "Schuld und Soße," *Der Spiegel*, nr. 6, 1997, p. 54ff., which evaluates her arguments. In addition, see Josef Isensee, ed., *Vergangenheitsbewältigung durch Recht. Drei Abhandlungen zu einem deutschen Problem* (Berlin: Duncker & Humblot, 1992), especially the essay by Günther Jakobs.

200. See Peter Schneider, "Facing Germany's Newer Past," *The New York Times*, 30 September 1991.

201. On the prosecution of Wolf, see "Suche nach Blut an den Händen," *Der Spiegel*, nr. 2, 1997, p. 32ff.

202. Rosenberg, *The Haunted Land*, p. 351.

203. Jarausch, Seeba, and Conradt, "The Presence of the Past," pp. 58, 59. See also Antonia Grunenberg, *Welche Geschichte wählen wir?* (Hamburg: Junius Verlag, 1992).

9

Tradition and Innovation in Contemporary German Foreign Policy

The unexpected and dramatic events that rocked Europe from Berlin to Moscow between 1989 and 1991 abruptly transformed the structures and patterns of international affairs that had marked the divided continent for more than four decades. The reemergence of a united Germany in the heart of Europe, along with the spectacular demise of the Soviet Union, constituted the most climactic episodes in this process of breathtaking change. Presumably "solved," or at least dormant, in a context of seemingly definitive national division, the old "German Question" suddenly reappeared on the European diplomatic landscape. The end of the Kohl era after the federal elections of September 1998, coupled with the creation of an unprecedented "red-green" coalition between the Social Democrats and the Greens, merely added renewed fuel to the considerable domestic and foreign interest in (and, at times, wariness regarding) the future direction of German diplomacy that has marked much of the 1990s.

Writing about this German Question, W. R. Smyser has suggested that

[e]ver since the dawn of the European state system, the countries of Europe and the world have faced two German questions. Now that the Cold War is over they must begin dealing with a third—and different—German question. The first question was how to treat a weak and divided Germany. . . . The second German question was

An earlier, slightly different version of this chapter appeared in Patricia Smith, ed., *After the Wall: Eastern Germany Since 1989* (Boulder, CO: Westview Press, 1998).

how to deal with a united and strong Germany. . . . Now there is a third and new German question: How should the world react to a Germany that is united, democratic, and responsible, that is not bent on aggression, but that remains powerfully influential and that has its own interests and pursues them?[1]

How has this "new" Germany defined and developed its foreign and security policies, and what have been the domestic as well as foreign reactions? How has unification changed the policies that had come to enjoy considerable public consensus in the "old" Federal Republic?

In 1993, three years after the reemergence of a single, united Germany on the European diplomatic stage, Andrei S. Markovits and Simon Reich published an essay with the direct and fairly provocative title "Should Europe Fear the Germans?" Pointing to the persistent scholarly and journalistic preoccupation with an often elusive German Question, they noted that the contemporary debate focuses on "the issue of the new Germany's role in a changing European and global environment," adding that the various "commentaries are divisible into two major categories: the majority optimistic, basically viewing Germany's unification as a boon to Germany, Europe, and global peace; and the minority pessimistic, worrying that a strong Germany will repeat the mistakes of its past."[2]

As far as the optimists are concerned, Markovits and Reich suggested that some of them, inspired and reassured by functionalist integration theory, perceive "a Germany tamed by its international ties."[3] In contrast to such external constraints on German international behavior, rooted in both NATO and the European Union, institutionally focused optimists emphasize "internal constraints [on] German dominance," pointing to "the acceptance of a system of federalism and democratic values as the new Germany assimilates the political structure of the old Federal Republic."[4] The underlying assumption is that the united Germany is in the end nothing more than a successful enlargement of the formerly West German Federal Republic. A third group of optimists, using a more sociological line of analysis, essentially argues that "the new German political and economic elites represent the postwar triumph of the bourgeoisie with its liberal and democratic values over the traditionally imperialist and aggressive ways of the feudal and aristocratic Junkers before 1945."[5] Much of this echoes the now-classic analysis of postwar West Germany by Ralf Dahrendorf.[6] In this view, contemporary "German economic, intellectual, and political elites have been acutely aware of their responsibility for Germany's terrible past and thus stand vigil, guarding against the reemergence of militarist, antiliberal, xenophobic, and cryptofascist tendencies in the new united Germany."[7]

As for the pessimists, Markovits and Reich suggest that their "anguish concerning prospective [German] hegemony, in view of Germany's unification and the vacuum in power and leadership created by American and Soviet withdrawals from Europe, takes two primary forms: one historical, the other cultural. In different ways, both stress evidence that predates 1945."[8] Worried by a German tradition of democratic failure in domestic politics and militarist and economic aggressiveness in foreign policy, the historical pessimists fear a resurgence of destabilizing German assertiveness, in part as the by-product of socioeconomic and political turmoil at home. For their part, cultural pessimists "reflect an angst—both within and outside Germany—about Germany's enhanced power and its new problems with the conjunction of reunification and global transformation" and are animated by "a concern that, freed of superpower constraints, the reunited Germany will relive old habits."[9]

Debating the Foundations of Policy

The opposing perspectives of optimists and pessimists sketched by Markovits and Reich and summarized above are not merely a matter of analysis and commentary by foreign observers. They find their reflection, at least in part, in an ongoing debate within a Germany searching for a clear sense of role and identity as central power in a post–Cold War Europe.[10] As Josef Janning has argued, "the most controversial notions in the intellectual debate on the country's future policy all have to do with different interpretations of the meanings of the past. In this discourse, traditionalists who perceive themselves as realists stand against modernists educated in a structural analysis of international affairs."[11]

In a deeper sense, this debate among Germans over their country's foreign policy is connected to a more fundamental philosophical and even ideological dispute between those who advocate a greater sense of German "normalcy," expressed in occasionally revisionist historiography and a positive attitude regarding "healthy" patriotism,[12] and those who would ultimately argue that post-Auschwitz Germany can never pretend or afford to be "normal." To the latter, the German *Sonderweg* ("special path") that culminated in Nazism and the Holocaust represents a shadow and burden that cannot and may not be pushed aside in favor of a partly revisionist and partly ahistorical sense of postunification "normalcy." The prominent philosopher Jürgen Habermas, for example, has raised strong questions about the tendency to seek a restoration of "normalcy" in Germany's domestic as well as foreign affairs.[13]

In the contemporary German foreign policy debate, "realists" or "traditionalists" emphasize the importance of underlying continuity in European diplomatic history and suggest the enduring relevance of classical balance-of-power and *Realpolitik* perspectives. Their views are not without influence in leading German policymaking circles, particularly in the Christian Democratic Party and its Bavarian sister party, the CSU. As Janning puts it, in the realist-traditionalist perspective, "states as actors—their interests and power, their constellations and coalitions—dominate and foreign policy is statecraft conducted to maximize nationally accountable benefits in a primarily anarchic environment."[14]

In contrast to the "realist" or "traditionalist" perspective, a considerable number of German scholars and commentators stress the importance of multilateralist and integrationist aspects of European as well as global affairs. Summarizing their line of analysis, Janning notes that for them "the integration of Germany in these supra-, multi- and transnational contexts is so fundamental that it transcends the analytical separation of national vs. integration policies. This has been proven in the four decades of West German integration and should remain the focus of the united country as well. Therefore any foreign policy, be it conducted from Bonn or Berlin, should be rooted in the development and nurturing of those institutions which have to steer these interdependencies."[15] The arguments advanced in this context span a considerable spectrum, including those who envisage a postnational Germany as "civilian" power in a transformed international political arena.[16]

And where does the general public in Germany stand? In the course of the 1990s, a series of in-depth opinion surveys have been carried out in order to obtain insight into the evolving state of the German public mind with regard to a variety of foreign and security policy issues.[17] The results show a deeply rooted pro-Western foreign policy culture. Respondents expressed a considerable and to some extent even growing level of support for NATO, but less solid backing for a continued U.S. military presence on German soil. Divergences in opinion between eastern and western Germans on these and other questions have narrowed at least somewhat in recent years, despite continuing contrasts on matters of security policy. Over time, this might suggest the possibility of a relative erosion of mental contrasts that were rooted in the Cold War era.

Most Germans support a more active NATO role in "out-of-area" operations, including crisis management in Eastern and Southeastern Europe and security guarantees for future new EU members in Central and Eastern Europe, yet a still deeply engrained "culture of reticence" blocks broader support for active German military participation in both NATO- and UN-sponsored missions. At least half of the German public favors the eastward expansion of NATO membership, with Central and Eastern Europe, along with Russia, increasingly defined as an area of "vital interest."

Overall support for further European integration as well as expanded EU membership remains strong, but worries about the implications for the FRG of a full Economic and Monetary Union (EMU), as envisaged in the Maastricht Treaty of 1991, have clearly grown over the past few years. The German public appears to be increasingly conscious of Germany's enhanced post–Cold War influence and responsibility, and of the corresponding importance of the country's national interests, yet support for a nonmilitary, multilateralized exercise of German power continues to be striking.

The argument advanced in this chapter is situated between the optimist and pessimist camps, and between the neorealist and integrationist perspectives, by stressing the extent to which postunification German foreign policy continues to evolve, thus precluding definitive evaluation, and by suggesting that Germany's post–Cold War foreign policy environment is characterized by a partial renationalizing "return of history," particularly to the East and Southeast, along with a continuing presence of Western integrationist constraints and commitments. These commitments, in turn, are the product of a genuine post-1945 reorientation in German foreign policy culture, although in a united Germany with its peculiar national sensitivities and vulnerabilities vis-à-vis an adjacent zone of post-Communist turmoil, they must coexist and even compete with more nationally focused inclinations and temptations.

The essence of Germany's foreign policy environment is the country's central, continental location.[18] West German and East German foreign policies were the product of defeated, traumatized, and slowly rehabilitated states of a partitioned nation on the front line of a Cold War dominated by superpower patrons and overshadowed by nuclear peril. With prospects for national reunification uncertain at best and wary neighbors eager to tame a restless and aggressive Germany once and for all, foreign policy options were limited. Each state became a loyal member of its respective "camp." The tradition of German *Schaukelpolitik*, whereby a united Germany had floated along its *Sonderweg* between East and West, gave way to *Westbindung* for the FRG and *Ostbindung* for the GDR.

The end of the Cold War has produced a united Germany once more, yet in a considerably transformed European setting (despite some suggestive similarities to an older Europe, especially in the post-Communist East).[19] Jochen Thies tries to capture the significance and implications of this mixture of continuity and change when he notes that "[h]istory starts to matter again. Germany cannot escape from it, nor can the country run away from the new realities of geography. There is no relief from being positioned in the middle of Europe. Germany has to accept the fact and must act in order to overcome the traumatic memories of the past when the middle position after Bismarck led to great European wars, bringing to an end the history of the German Reich, founded in 1871, after just two generations in 1945."[20]

Integrated more decisively into the Western world than ever before, constrained by a maze of military, economic, and political commitments and limitations, and guided by a considerably transformed foreign policy culture, today's Germany strives to combine its Western links and the imperatives of its Central European geopolitical location in a new type of policy, which may be called *Scharnierpolitik* ("hinge policy"). Eager to preserve and strengthen the achievements of postwar integration and reconciliation in the West and to extend these successes and benefits to a struggling and unstable East, Germany has assumed a leading role in the Western "outreach" effort to post-Communist Central and Eastern Europe (including the Commonwealth of Independent States, or CIS, in general and Russia in particular), within the frameworks of the European Union (EU), the North Atlantic Treaty Organization (NATO), and the Conference on Security and Cooperation in Europe (CSCE, with its organizational component, the Organization for Security and Cooperation in Europe, known as OSCE). The Federal Republic is in fact reaching out to the post–Cold War East in ways that are at times reminiscent of the U.S. approach to Western Europe (and western Germany) after 1945. In the view of W. R. Smyser, "Germany's principal foreign policy objective since unification has been to link East and West."[21] In other words, it is turning from a pair of Cold War front-line states into the strategic "hinge" between the continent's two halves.

Placed once more at the center of European affairs, Germany has, as Daniel Hamilton puts it, "embarked on an active policy of pan-European entente, seeking to build a stable political, economic, and security framework that can make Europe safe from its history. During the cold war, European stability had been organized from the periphery; the premise of European entente is that it must now be facilitated from the center. Germany, united and free, is the nation most able, anxious, and willing to spur its partners to commission the actual construction of a Common European Home and underwrite the accompanying *Hausordnung*."[22] In pursuit of these objectives, Germany's pivotal role gives it a unique weight vis-à-vis its neighbors on all sides, since its "significance within the European Community and the West increases its influence within the East while its growing sway in the East enhances its ability to shape Western institutions and policies."[23] In fact, Smyser argues, "Germany sits at the center of a vast network of contacts and communications across the Northern Hemisphere."[24]

Even prior to the end of the Cold War, some of these developments were in a way foreshadowed by the accelerating pace of *Deutschlandpolitik* between the FRG and the GDR during the 1970s and 1980s. In the words of Arnulf Baring, "[t]he slow return of West Germany to the old central European position started with détente."[25] At that time, such a policy matched the fundamental strategic and political interests of a divided nation benefiting from East-West detente. Today, the pursuit of *Scharnierpolitik* corresponds to a united Germany's fundamental national interest in promoting East-West reconciliation and integration. The alternative of inaction would amount to a more or less benign neglect of a politically turbulent and economically struggling power vacuum that could destabilize and threaten the entire continent. In fact, one might argue that the success of an activist German policy, pursued within multilateralist frameworks, is in the more general European interest as well. In this case, one might say that what is good for Germany is good for Europe. Germany's new *Scharnierpolitik* is still evolving, both in terms of definition and execution, thus rendering most proclamations of optimism or pessimism rather premature. Moreover, the impulses and dynamics underlying this policy reflect both "realist" and "integrationist" tendencies, characteristic of Germany's complex foreign policy environment.

As we saw in Chapter 4, factors of power, geography, identity, and developmental timing have historically combined to turn the question of Germany's place in the international arena into a fundamental problem for German foreign policy and a basic feature in the development of German foreign policy culture. In terms of its power, Germany has tended to be either too weak to alleviate the perennial security fears that permeate the country's foreign policy culture, or too strong to leave wary neighbors reassured about their own safety. The country's geopolitical location has often been profoundly associated with a sense of fluidity, vulnerability, and encirclement.

As a result, German diplomatic history can be seen as a series of attempts to deal with this geopolitical predicament and the consequences of delayed unification, against a background of changing regimes and domestic ideologies. Bismarck and some of the country's subsequent leaders emphasized the central continental "bridge" function of the German state, a focus that led to a preoccupation with the balance of power, flexible alliances, and the resulting pursuit of a "switching policy" (*Schaukelpolitik*) between East and West. Elements of this tradition resurfaced during the Cold War in the context of various German neutrality proposals. Other German leaders, especially Kaiser Wilhelm II and Adolf Hitler, adopted a far more explicit *Großmachtpolitik*, that is, the pursuit of an aggressive, militant great-power policy that undermined any sense of balance of power and made war with the country's neighbors all but inevitable. After World War II, West German chancellor Konrad Adenauer was particularly responsible for the creation of a third, largely unprecedented tradition in German foreign policy, focused on a mixture of "supranationalization," involving the surrender of major portions of German sovereignty to NATO and the European Community, and "Westernization," signaling the abandonment of the earlier, often anti-Western German *Sonderweg* in favor of close political and ideological association with the Western "camp" during the Cold War. Which tradition would prevail in post–Cold War Germany?

Upon the country's reunification in October 1990, Volker Rühe (CDU) remarked that the new Germany would undoubtedly be *östlicher und protestantischer* (more eastern and more Protestant). Rather than interpreting this observation solely as a commentary about German domestic politics, one can also consider it an interesting speculation about the geopolitical and cultural implications of reunification for the country's foreign policy. The demise of Communism and the Iron Curtain has placed the united Germany back in the center of the continent, yet the traditions and benefits of Adenauer's *Westpolitik* as well as the aversion against an exposed, nationalist diplomacy appear to have taken firm root in German foreign policy culture. Moreover, Germany's continued integration in Western economic, political, and security structures, and the country's inability to address, let alone solve, the challenges to the East independently from broader, multilateralist frameworks of "outreach," entail a series of real constraints that limit its foreign policy choice environment.

A Central European Germany is back, but it is no longer the Germany or the Europe of 1871, 1914, or even 1945. As the old Federal Republic's Bonn gives way to the newly united Germany's Berlin, the fully sovereign country's Western ties and interests are now indeed increasingly complemented by Eastern worries and interests.[26] Hence there is the clearly discernible emergence of a new, fourth vision or tradition in German foreign policy: a *Scharnierpolitik* that seeks to blend the geopolitical imperatives (and temptations) that once undergirded the *Schaukelpolitik* of the post-1871 era with the deeper philosophical orientations and principles developed through "supranationalization" and "Westernization" in the *Westpolitik* of the years between 1949 and 1989. We can grasp the broad outlines of this new direction in German foreign policy by examining post-1990 developments in the country's European integration and security policies.

Toward a Grand European Union?

Throughout the postwar period, as we have noted, the Federal Republic has been a prominent and convinced advocate of ever-closer European integration. A strong reaction against the excesses of previous nationalism, combined with a need to achieve international rehabilitation and alleviate the concerns of neighbors regarding the exercise of German power, served to generate a widely shared political consensus in West Germany in favor of the construction of an increasingly postnational European unity. Looking back from the 1990s, one can argue that the FRG's European policy has in fact been the product of mixed motivations: Philosophical and ideological conviction has been essential, but so have calculations of (West) German "national interest" and the imperatives imposed by international (especially Cold War) conditions.[27]

The advent of unification quickly raised questions among Germany's neighbors, however, about the future reliability of the country's commitment to continued, let alone expanded, European integration.[28] Preoccupation with the massive task of rebuilding the former GDR in a context of economic recession, in addition to the removal of earlier constraints on German national sovereignty— might these factors not give rise to a Germany less reticent in advancing its national interest and wielding the instruments of its considerable diplomatic and economic clout? Simon Bulmer and William E. Paterson admit that "German unification has certainly placed the question of the country's role in Europe back under the spotlight," but they argue that "the dramatic changes of 1989 have not yet led to a correspondingly dramatic change in Germany's role. . . . The principal response has seen the FRG reiterate its European identity; the Europeanization of Germany became once again a goal of policy."[29]

For years, the members of the European Community/Union have grappled with two fundamental objectives that have often been presented as in some ways mutually exclusive: further integration among the EC's existing members (known as "deepening") and membership expansion (referred to as "widening" or "broadening"). Great Britain, an outspoken opponent of further surrender of sovereignty to the Brussels "Eurocracy," has tended to emphasize the objective of broadened membership, as part of its vision of a more loosely constructed "intergovernmental" Europe of national states. France, meanwhile, has been more interested in the goal of further integration from time to time, seeking to promote a "supranational" Europe in which France might enhance the exercise of its power by means of the Franco-German axis. Other EC members have been scattered across and between these two camps. The Federal Republic has always been an advocate of both objectives, reflecting both a sense of policy conviction and a need to maintain amicable relations with two key European allies.[30] Prior to the end of the Cold War, West Germany championed the membership causes of Austria and the Scandinavian countries, and also lent crucial support to the creation of the Single European Act of 1986 and the initiation of the Europe 1992 project, which aimed at the comprehensive removal of fiscal, physical, and technical barriers that hindered the completion of a fully integrated internal EC market.

Reflecting both ideological orientation and a calculation of German interests, the Federal Republic continues to encourage the simultaneous pursuit of "deepening" and "widening" today. Hence the country has strongly supported the Maastricht Treaty of 1991, which launched the European Union (EU) and envisioned a common European currency (the euro) by the end of the decade and a Common Foreign and Security Policy (CFSP) among EU members.[31] Although, as Hans Schauer has suggested, Germany's postwar political elite has been quite favorable to supranational Europeanist visions and schemes (often in contrast to the more nationally sensitive British and French, for example), late 1990s developments and polling data nevertheless suggest at least a relative weakening of traditional "Europhoria" in the Federal Republic, among the political elite as well as the general public.[32] Worry about the exchange of a strong deutsche mark for a possibly weaker euro is particularly pronounced in this regard. It should also be noted here, if only in passing, that the urgency felt by many EC states regarding the creation of a more integrated European Union after 1989 was considerably enhanced by the unexpected advent of German unification and a resultant desire to maintain and deepen supranational restraints on a potentially "renationalized" united Germany.

As far as the process of "widening" is concerned, it is clear that the Federal Republic has emerged as the leading advocate of EU membership for several post-Communist Central and Eastern European countries, most notably Poland, the Czech Republic, Slovakia, and Hungary. More than is the case for other EU member states, Germany's support for eastward enlargement is an unmistakable reflection of its central geopolitical location and its desire to promote socioeconomic prosperity and stability on its eastern frontier. New market opportunities and a concern about the flow of "economic refugees" constitute significant motivating factors here.

The Federal Republic's current interest in the economic transformation of Eastern Europe has its roots in a long-standing tradition of German economic involvement in the region, going back centuries. After 1949, as the Cold War evolved, the FRG pursued a more active *Osthandel* (trade in the East) than any other Western country. Aside from its obvious geopolitical, economic, and financial significance to the countries to its east, Markovits and Reich have argued that "the newly united Germany's position will in due course become even more formidable by virtue of inheriting the former German Democratic Republic's close 'socialist' ties with Eastern Europe and the [former] Soviet Union." They add that Germany's economic "hegemony" in Central and Eastern Europe will (once again) be matched by an equally important degree of cultural dominance, whereby "German cultural hegemony in the region will assume a commercialized and capitalist character."[33]

The simultaneous pursuit of "deepening" and "widening" does entail a fundamental tension, however, which German policy will be unable to avoid. The result is the likelihood of a "two-speed" Europe, with a more fully integrated core surrounded by those countries that are primarily interested in or eligible for an intergovernmental European design. Official German policy continues to tread carefully in this area, eager to avoid a harmful split among EU members. However, the circulation of an unofficial but widely noted CDU discussion paper, produced by Wolfgang Schäuble and Karl Lamers (leader and foreign policy spokesman of the party's *Bundestagsfraktion*, respectively) and calling for acceptance of a "two-speed" EU, would suggest that the seeds of policy adjustment may indeed have been planted.[34]

In the pursuit of its European integration policies, the Federal Republic is able to draw upon a considerable reservoir of economic and diplomatic clout. This was already the case before 1990. The advent of unification and the demise of the Iron Curtain and many of the restrictions imposed by the Cold War have, however, further enlarged German influence and maneuverability. Although German economic growth rates have slowed markedly in the course of the 1990s, particularly as a result of the high costs associated with eastern German reconstruction, the German economy continues to perform a crucial "locomotive" function within the EU. The deutsche mark is clearly Europe's leading currency, playing a central role in the Exchange-Rate Mechanism (ERM) and slated to become the core element in the common European currency. Among European central banks, the *Bundesbank* occupies an often dominant position, which is in turn reflected in the decision to locate the European Central Bank (ECB, also dubbed the "Eurofed") in Frankfurt, Germany's financial capital. Qualification criteria for participation in the euro in 1999 and beyond have been heavily shaped by German policy preferences, in particular a desire to preserve the currency's health by placing restrictions on permissible national budget deficits and other inflation-inducing tendencies.

Germany's economic clout is not without its weak spots, however, such as the continued financial drain of eastern reconstruction, the less-than-optimal competitiveness of the German economy in a larger comparative perspective (sometimes referred to as the *Standort Deutschland* question), and the rather inflexible regulatory structure of the German economy. Nonetheless, as Bulmer and Paterson point out, "Germany is emerging as the core economy of the 'new Europe.'"[35] This considerable economic clout translates itself indirectly (and at times more directly) into EU policy, for example, by means of the FRG's role as economic policy "model," in EU budgetary negotiations, and in the articulation of membership criteria in the areas of a common currency and eastward expansion. In the final analysis, "German economic strength makes an important indirect contribution to the FRG's role in the EU."[36]

Germany's economic prominence, along with a newly gained reputation for political stability and reliability, forms the basis for a considerable degree of *diplomatic* clout in EU matters as well. The FRG's foreign policy choice environment has expanded, and so has the country's opportunity to play a more explicitly leading role, if it chooses to do so. According to Bulmer and Paterson, "[i]n the particular context of the EU, integration is no longer a means whereby Germany seeks to compensate for its semi-sovereignty. Now, with Germany's position in integration approaching 'normality,' integration has a much greater potential to be used to enhance German international power."[37]

Yet this potential is, in fact, exactly the basis for concern in some quarters in Europe: Will the EU increasingly turn into a vehicle for the exercise and projection of German power and the pursuit of national German interests? Will the newly united Germany merely be a "gentle giant," or is it the "emergent leader" of an EU shaped and run according to German interests and preferences? However, the fact that the explicitly national exercise of German power is even more certain in the absence of an EU and further integration suggests that skeptics and critics may consider themselves caught between a German-dominated EU and a far less predictable nonintegrated Europe in which German power would be exercised in an at best intergovernmental setting featuring renationalized foreign policies. Such wary observers are likely to take note of the emergence in some quarters in Germany of what one might call a "Teutonic Thatcherism," which suggests limits to further integration in favor of the pursuit of more intergovernmental scenarios, accompanied by a more explicit exercise of German power based on calculations of national interest.[38] Some of the rather forceful statements on the EU's future, particularly in the interconnected areas of budgetary restructuring and membership expansion, made by Germany's new "red-green" coalition government after the September 1998 national elections did appear to point in this direction.

Aware of the anxieties felt by many of Germany's neighbors, and convinced about the success and benefits of integration and multilateralism, the country's foreign policy making elite continues to stress its collaborative European commitment. In the past, West Germany sought to coordinate key aspects of its policy by means of the European Political Cooperation (EPC) mechanism launched in the 1970s. In the post-Maastricht era, the FRG is eager to see the promise of a Common Foreign and Security Policy fulfilled. When coordinating mechanisms fail, however, Germany is showing less and less hesitation in proceeding in a more unilateralist fashion, as was illustrated in 1991 by the country's assertiveness regarding the recognition of Slovenian and Croatian independence (although domestic public opinion pressures also played a role here).[39] As a result, one might argue that "German power will become more evident where European institutions prove to be too weak."[40]

Summarizing their conclusions regarding the united Germany's status and role in a deepening and widening European Union, Bulmer and Paterson write:

> German unification has certainly had a liberating effect on the *potential* for German diplomacy. German singularities, such as the situation of Berlin or domestic sensitivity to Cold War defence strategies, have disappeared; the FRG no longer has to employ European integration as a way of compensating for its diplomatic weaknesses. As a non-nuclear, largely civilian power the FRG is less disadvantaged by the new security circumstances. The "redefined" Europe post-1989 has Germany at its geographical core, a configuration likely to be reflected in the federal government's policy as entry of the Visegrad countries [Poland, the Czech Republic, Slovakia, and Hungary] into the EU approaches. These circumstances add to the existing character of Bonn's European diplomacy: the priority given to multilateral frameworks; the bilateralization of policy through the "inner core" of the Franco-German relationship; and the attempt to project a European identity as intrinsic to that of Germany.[41]

The result is a Germany that so far is more a "gentle giant" than assertive leader, with considerable economic and diplomatic clout, but more likely to exercise this power indirectly than directly. Echoing this conclusion, William Wallace agrees that "Germany is Europe's leading state" and the continent's "natural hegemon," but adds that although this "Germany may be Europe's central power, . . . it is also its reluctant leader."[42]

The Federal Republic's great interest in the EU's eastward expansion is not merely the result of calculations of economic interest. Equally important are concerns about instability and conflict in Central, Eastern, and Southeastern Europe, and the resultant flows of refugees, leading to a keen interest in an effective Western response. Consequently, German policy on questions of deepening and widening the European Union cannot be considered in isolation from the related and in some ways larger question of European security. It is in this context that the implications of the Cold War's end and German unification, leading to Germany's reemergence as a Central European power, become most noticeable.

Securing a Post–Cold War Europe

The dramatic events of the years 1989–1991, with the collapse of Eastern European Communism, the unification of Germany, and the demise of the USSR as watersheds, have not only transformed the political and economic stage on which the ongoing endeavor of European integration is played out. Perhaps more important, they have radically altered the general European security environment. In this new setting, the united Germany has an essential role to play. And once again, the impact of geopolitical imperatives on the country's policy is strikingly evident. James Sperling has tried to capture the significance of the transformation:

> The long European peace after the Second World War was the product of political-military bipolarity, the nuclear stalemate between the Soviet Union and the United States, and the division of Germany. German foreign and security policies were constrained by the triple imperative of acquiescing to American superiority in Europe without shattering its fragile political-security partnership with France, of suffering French pretentions to European leadership without jeopardizing the American protectorate or foreclosing the prospect of Franco-German codetermination, and of acknowledging Soviet interests in Europe without foregoing the objective of German unification. Today, the postwar bonds on German policy are dissolving; the threat of war between the major European states has receded into the background; political-military bipolarity has evaporated as has the ideological hostility that helped sustain it; Germany is unified and fully sovereign; and France, the United States, and Russia acknowledge Germany's leadership role in Europe and seek its partnership.[43]

Yet Sperling's description of contemporary conditions is open to at least some question. To what extent are those "postwar bonds on German policy" indeed "dissolving"? What is the likelihood of a continued degree of implicit bipolarity between an expanding NATO and a wary, turbulent Russia? Insofar as the East-West conflict of the Cold War era was partly rooted in deeper, historical divergence between the West and Slavic Russia, might not at least some degree of East-West estrangement continue to complicate the European diplomatic and security landscape? In view of the many ties, from NATO to the EU, that link Germany to immediate and more distant neighbors and partners, what does it mean to declare the country "fully sovereign"? And finally, is Germany willing and able to play the "leadership role" that, according to Sperling, its allies and partners expect it to perform?

It is essential to note that post–Cold War Europe faces security threats and dilemmas that are not easily summed up in traditional, military categories. With the immediate nuclear peril and the possibility of all-out military conflict between major European states receding, other challenges have come to the fore to preoccupy policymakers in Germany and elsewhere. These include ethnopolitical upheaval in the Balkans and inside the area of the former Soviet Union; large-scale flows of refugees fleeing conflict and/or seeking a share of the West's economic prosperity and opportunity; the threats posed by various forms of terrorism (including militant Islamic fundamentalism); the infiltration of economically oriented organized crime unleashed by a breakdown of law and order in the post-Communist societies of Central and Eastern Europe (including Russia); and other matters related to economic security (industrial espionage, resource and market access, financial stability, and so forth).

Any analysis of the united Germany's evolving security policy must, therefore, take account of several factors: the ties that continue to bind the country into NATO; the persistence of a Western-oriented "security policy culture" developed during the Cold War era; the new security challenges shared with other European/Western states; the security-related potential available through multilateral institutions other than NATO (especially the EU, the Western European Union, and the CSCE/OSCE); and, once again, the impact of the country's Central European geopolitical location. These and other factors characterize the environment in which today's German policymakers define Germany's interests, conceptualize the country's preferred role in security matters, and conceive of Germany's international identity in a post–Cold War world.

Considerations of power, role, and identity have caused German officials and political leaders to place special emphasis on the notion of Germany as a "civilian" power.[44] This entails caution in the use and display of military capability, rooted in an enduring reaction to the legacy of aggressive German militarism and a sensitivity to the perceptions of wary neighbors to the East and West. Upon unification, the country reaffirmed its commitment to the status of being a nonnuclear power and agreed to clear limitations on the overall size of its armed forces.[45] The notion of being a "civilian" power, focused on economic and political aspects of leadership, may be seen by many as a partial continuation of Germany's Cold War–era "self-containment." However, it is not without an element of convenient German self-interest either, as Sperling has noted: "Germany remains satisfied to contribute to the economic requirements of security and to accelerate the demilitarization of interstate relations, particularly in Europe—a development that plays to Germany's economic capacity and not coincidentally enhances German influence in the reconstruction and recasting of the European order."[46]

At the time of the Gulf War, a Germany that is still "susceptible to bouts of self-pity and urgent moralizing"[47] was the scene of vigorous debate and controversy regarding the possible use of German military force outside the NATO area.[48] Many argued that the country's Basic Law did not permit such use, and would have to be amended. However, the Federal Republic's Constitutional Court decided in 1994 that deployment of *Bundeswehr* troops in "out-of-area" operations was not at odds with the constitution. The argument was also made, particularly on the German Left, that German military activity ought to be limited to UN-sanctioned "blue helmet" operations at most. By contrast, Chancellor Helmut Kohl, Defense Minister Volker Rühe, and others in the CDU maintained that broader military ventures were both constitutional and in accordance with Germany's international obligations as well as its renewed status as a "normal" power in world affairs. As a result, there has been German military participation in the 1990s in a variety of settings and situations, although in the case of the Gulf War the country's primary contribution remained financial ($10.7 billion).[49] Nonetheless, even the more conservative CDU cannot escape the shadows of Germany's past. As a result, and despite all claims of "normalcy," German policymakers continue to look favorably upon their country's role and status as a "civilian" power.[50]

A further important component in the Federal Republic's official self-definition and self-conception today continues to be its Western orientation and commitment, reiterated and reemphasized by its leaders and representatives like a religious mantra. These foreign policy cultural orientations are reinforced by tangible links produced by the organizations of which the FRG is a member, particularly NATO and the EU. Although the presence of U.S. and other Allied forces on German soil has been radically reduced, ventures such as the Eurocorps (in which *Bundeswehr* troops serve alongside forces from several other Western European states) serve to reflect Germany's Western orientation and commitment and evince the modified sovereignty enjoyed by both the FRG and its partners.

A third important component in the Federal Republic's preferred role and identity is its multilateralist orientation.[51] A history of nationalist excesses and disasters, coupled with an awareness of the sensitivity of any unilateralist exercise of its strategic, Central European power, has induced among German policymakers a considerable appreciation of the substantive as well as cosmetic advantages of multilateralist initiatives and diplomacy. As Sperling puts it, "German policymakers have systematically translated German interests into the interests of the many over the course of the postwar period."[52] Similarly, Christoph Bertram has noted that "[o]f all Western countries, post-war Germany has been most conscious of the need to be part of a team in international affairs," although he argues also that "[t]he collective cosiness of German foreign policy exists no longer."[53] In the end, this is also the meaning of the often professed desire to become and remain a "European Germany" and avoid the impression of wanting to create a "German Europe." As a result, despite a growing sense of specific German interests in the geopolitical heart of a dynamically changing continent, Germany's leaders continue to show clear evidence of their preference for the pursuit of policy through multilateral channels, ranging from NATO to the European Union and the OSCE.

"Civilian," Western, and multilateralist—it is with these conceptions of its identity and role that the enlarged Federal Republic exercises its power in Europe today. In the realm of security policy, two areas of focus stand out in particular. First, there is the question of a stronger and clearer European pillar or identity in the Western alliance, coupled with the question of the future U.S. role in Europe. Second, there is the integration of Central and Eastern Europe into Western security institutions, tied to the issue of an integrating Europe's relationship with a post-Communist but still far from stabilized Russia. If the first area of policy tends to find the FRG caught between the Atlantic connection with the United States and the Euro-Gaullist ambitions of France, the second issue-area shows Germany in its quintessentially central continental role, eager to connect a vacuum-prone Eastern Europe with the Western security community without alienating or aggravating Russia.[54]

As with the "widening" versus "deepening" debate regarding the European Union, these issues on the German security policy agenda might suggest the necessity of making choices. Yet, once again, choices are exactly what the Federal Republic would very much like to avoid. Thus we notice a clear interest in the development of a stronger European defense identity coupled with a reemphasized commitment to the transatlantic linkage with the United States. Similarly, a desire for the effective security integration of Central and Eastern Europe into existing Western institutions is accompanied by a willingness to see the OSCE strengthened as a forum that might transcend Cold War products like NATO and serve to placate a wary Russia.

One might conclude that in the areas of European integration as well as European security, German diplomacy reveals a tendency to "genscher," in the words of Timothy Garton Ash, referring to the inclination of former (West) German Foreign Minister Hans-Dietrich Genscher to avoid unpleasant choices and pursue the reconciliation of seemingly incompatible goals. Ash has described "Genscherism" as an attempt "to maintain and improve Germany's ties with a wide range of states, which were themselves pursuing quite different and contradictory objectives. This complex balancing act involved saying somewhat different things in different places. Fudge was the hard core of Genscherism."[55]

In the context of the analysis presented in this chapter, one might, in fact, argue that this tendency of "genschering" is the behavioral expression of the logic inherent in *Scharnierpolitik*. In the realm of security policy, the Federal Republic thus serves as Europe's "hinge," preserving the gains and successes of Atlantic and Western European endeavors rooted in the Cold War era while seeking to extend and to some extent transform these by integrating its neighbors to the East and cultivating the goodwill of post-Soviet Russia. This *sowohl-als-auch* (A as well as B) quality of German policy is captured succinctly by Sperling when he writes that "[t]he political objectives of German foreign policy have not been fundamentally changed by the transformation of the European security order: Germany's foreign policy objectives remain the political and economic unification of Europe and the creation of a pan-European security system that preserves the indivisibility of German and American security."[56]

It remains to be seen, however, whether this "genscherist" inclination will continue to fit the requirements of policy in a postunification, post–Cold War era. At some point, choices may have to be made, because, as Elizabeth Pond has noted, "[b]alancing EU and transatlantic commitments, NATO and the European 'pillar,' France and the United States, western and eastern Europe, Central Europe and Russia, widening and deepening of the EU, joining NATO allies in out-of-area operations and doing the tough political spadework to make this step domestically acceptable—will be tricky."[57]

The North Atlantic Treaty Organization faced a serious "identity crisis" when the Cold War passed from the European scene. The newly unified Germany quickly showed its desire for a reformed alliance by urging the adjustment of

NATO strategy from a Cold War reliance on flexible response in the area of nuclear deterrence and forward defense in the conventional military field to a
post–Cold War focus on pan-European collective security and stability. Many of
the policy and posture adjustments adopted by the alliance at its London summit
meeting in July 1990 in fact corresponded with German preferences. In the
course of the 1990s, German officials became increasingly attracted to a subtle
but important redefinition of NATO as a political community with shared values
and common security interests, instead of the more explicitly military character
of the alliance's former, Cold War identity. This recasting of the organization's
identity dovetailed with the FRG's interest in the demilitarization of European affairs, the deepening of the links between NATO and the OSCE, and the reassurance of a Russia still suspicious of Western intentions. All of these objectives
could be pursued in and by an adjusted NATO without jeopardizing the security
link with the United States, which all German policymakers continue to see as indispensable to both the Federal Republic and all of Europe.[58]

The Organization for Security and Cooperation in Europe (OSCE) is an outgrowth of the Conference on Security and Cooperation in Europe (CSCE), which
in turn was launched in Helsinki in 1975 as the product of efforts at detente between East and West. The importance of the CSCE/OSCE has grown in the
post–Cold War era, with the demise of the Warsaw Pact and the Soviet Union, as the
Western alliance found itself confronted with the need to reach out to erstwhile opponents and construct a viable pan-European security order. Ever since the 1970s,
German governments have been prominent supporters of pan-European security
schemes, reflective of Germany's precarious Cold War status as a divided front-line
nation before 1990 and the united Germany's sensitive Central European position
today. The Federal Republic's interest in CSCE/OSCE results from a mixture of economic and military security calculations, since the organization "promises the insti-
tutionalization of a pan-European peace order based upon the principle of collective security" and "offers an additional mechanism for overcoming the 'prosperity
barrier' (*Wohlstandsgrenze*) between the nations of western and eastern Europe with
the establishment of a free-market regime throughout Europe."[59]

For a centrally located state like Germany, the CSCE/OSCE constitutes an ideal
umbrella organization. It includes all NATO partners, including the United
States, a variety of neutrals, and all former Warsaw Pact states. Furthermore, it
provides a valuable forum for consultation and cooperation alongside the more
fully established and integrated Western alliance. Along with the North Atlantic
Cooperation Council (NACC), launched by NATO in 1991 as a vehicle for
post–Cold War East-West consultation, the CSCE/OSCE is seen as a vital ingredient in the Western "security outreach" to Central and Eastern European states,
irrespective of which ones might in the end join NATO. There has so far been no
indication that the German government seriously considers the CSCE/OSCE to
be a full alternative to the Western alliance. Rather, the two organizations are seen
as eminently complementary. As far as the Federal Republic is concerned, "NATO

provides insurance against any military threat to the territorial integrity of Germany, while the CSCE makes a positive contribution to European security by integrating the former Warsaw Pact member states, including the former Soviet Union, into the western economic and political orbit."[60]

In the longer run, German-U.S. tension may result from the fact that for the U.S. government the CSCE/OSCE is likely to remain a useful but subordinate addition to the alliance and a forum to engage potential NATO members as well, whereas for the Federal Republic NATO may decline in importance, increasingly replaced by a strengthened CSCE/OSCE that corresponds more fully to Germany's Central European security calculations and preferences.[61]

Beyond its military security utility, the CSCE/OSCE is also seen as valuable in the area of economic security, where a centrally located Germany, prosperous but burdened by the costs of eastern reconstruction, finds itself a prime migration and asylum target of those in search of more promising economic opportunities. In this sense, the CSCE/OSCE is a complement to the European Union, providing a framework for economic integration and assistance. With the overt threat of military attack receding, it is these issues of economic insecurity and instability that have moved to the top of Germany's list of international concerns. In the post–Cold War era, the Federal Republic has been the largest recipient of asylum seekers and economic refugees on the one hand, and the primary donor of Western assistance to the former Communist bloc on the other hand. The CSCE/OSCE is important for the FRG because it can help ensure that Germany does not face a turbulent east alone.

It is clear, then, that the Federal Republic currently pursues a security policy that reflects the country's specific geopolitical location, focuses on concerns that range from the military and political to the economic, and utilizes (or, as some might say, juggles) a variety of existing institutions. In the words of Sperling, "[t]he German security strategy has three primary elements: self-containment of German power in order that Germany may use its power to influence its European neighbors to effect German policy objectives; the creation of an independent Europe capable of negotiating on an equal basis with the United States on economic issues; and the continued demilitarization of Europe that depends upon the sustained growth of democracy and the free market in the former member states of the Warsaw Pact."[62] Insofar as the CSCE/OSCE, EU, and WEU (West European Union) might gain weight in German security policy calculations, the future of NATO will become a significant issue. Yet for the time being, neither the CSCE/OSCE nor the EU/WEU is in a position to impart the security benefits the FRG continues to derive from membership in the Atlantic alliance and a special relationship with the United States.

As we enter a new century and a new millennium, however, one country may once more stand out as absolutely critical to the future shape of German foreign policy and the overall European political and security order: Russia. Even before the demise of the Soviet Union in 1991, the pivotal role played by Gorbachev in the drama of German unification served to open a new chapter in this crucial bilateral relationship. The basis was laid by the 1990 Treaty on Good-Neighborliness, Partnership, and Cooperation between the FRG and the USSR. As W. R. Smyser has put it, this "German-Soviet tie [created] new confluences within Europe's center even as it [renewed] old ones."[63] A political, military, and economic bargain was struck between the two powers, reflecting the interests and historical as well as geopolitical sensitivities of both sides. Arrangements were made for the withdrawal of Soviet troops from eastern Germany (with the Federal Republic covering the DM 8.4 billion price tag), the future military status of this GDR territory in a united Germany within NATO, and acceptable force levels and structures in the context of the Treaty on Conventional Forces in Europe (CFE), in addition to formal, mutual nonaggression pledges.

In addition to the military aspects of the new relationship, the Federal Republic became the Soviet Union's (and later Russia's) most significant Western economic partner, in areas ranging from trade to investment and financial aid. By 1991, Germany had pledged at least $40 billion in various kinds of financial and economic assistance, to be delivered over a number of years. Furthermore, the FRG has lobbied hard for Soviet/Russian interests at G-7 summits and in meetings of the International Monetary Fund (IMF).

At the same time, Germany is required to balance its special relationship with Russia with the concerns of wary neighbors in Central and Eastern Europe, who would be easily suspicious of undue German-Russian coziness at their expense and who are eager to receive their share of the Federal Republic's financial largesse, economic investment, and advocacy in favor of their membership in Western economic and security institutions. Furthermore, in its relations with these neighbors, Germany has had to settle or at least manage a series of thorny issues, ranging from the recognition of the Oder-Neisse border with Poland and the legacy of the 1938 Munich Agreement and its aftermath vis-à-vis the Czech Republic, to compensation for victims of Germany's wartime policies and actions in eastern neighboring countries and the ongoing problem of post–Cold War migration and organized crime.[64]

As far as NATO is concerned, the need to balance the simultaneous but not necessarily compatible importance of Russia and East-Central Europe on the scales of the Federal Republic's diplomacy represents a particular conundrum for German policymakers: how to reconcile support for alliance membership of Central and Eastern European states with due consideration for the hostile attitude of its strategic partner Russia regarding such eastward enlargement of an organization rooted in the Cold War. There is a further dilemma, of course: At what point do closer relations with Russia not only complicate Germany's role in Central and Eastern Europe, but also burden or even jeopardize the crucial partnerships with major Western powers such as France, the United Kingdom, and the United States? Under what circumstances might concerns or even fears of a German-Russian "neo-Rapallo" reemerge?

Yet the dictates of geopolitics and history will render a close German-Russian connection all but inescapable, with as yet unforeseeable consequences for those situated in between. In the words of Smyser:

> The new [German-Russian] tie will unfold in a historical context of hundreds of years of dramatically varying relations between the Russian and German peoples. Russian troops were in Berlin as enemies in 1759, as friends in 1814, and as conquerors in 1945. A Prussian expeditionary force joined in Napoleon's invasion of Russia in 1813, and the two German invasions of Russia during World Wars I and II alternated with periods of friendship. From the eighteenth through the twentieth centuries, the Germans and Russians have maintained a fascination for each other, a mixture of fear and attraction that may be unique in international affairs.[65]

Close relations with both the Soviet Union and various neighbors in Central and Eastern Europe formed an integral part of the former East Germany's Communist *Staatsräson*. Yet Germany's preoccupation with and interest in those to its east has deeper roots than the years of Cold War division and antagonism. The virtual absence of *Ossis* among the Federal Republic's foreign policy making elite is therefore not as consequential for the country's diplomatic orientations as one might think. In the end, the geopolitical imperatives are almost certainly far more compelling than the political biographies and ideological proclivities of leaders and diplomats in a Germany that today is "a creature of the West" but has "a foot in the East."[66]

Conclusion

In the course of the 1990s, the foreign policy of the reunited Germany has been subjected to close scrutiny and analysis by numerous German and non-German observers alike. The end of the Kohl Era in the fall of 1998 and the advent of a "red-green" coalition of SPD and Bündnis90/Greens, with Green leader Joschka Fischer as new foreign minister, merely enhanced this scrutiny and gave it a new twist, the insistence on policy continuity by the new government notwithstanding. As we saw at the outset, many analysts have approached their task with explicit or implicit assumptions or preconceptions about the outlook for German diplomacy, often rooted in worries about a return of history (the pessimists) or confidence in the country's definitive postwar transformation (the optimists). Different analyses stress different factors, policy objectives, and contextual variables, producing varying descriptions of the nature of contemporary German foreign policy and divergent characterizations of the contours of the country's power, role, and identity in European and world affairs.

Many of these characterizations suggest that despite unification and the reacquisition of full sovereignty, Germany still cannot be seen as a "normal" country. The legacy and trauma of a turbulent past continue to cast their shadows across the present. Any signs of any independent exercise or flexing of German power and muscle are quickly registered among the country's ever-sensitive neighbors. Domestic policy disputes regularly feature direct or indirect references to the implications of aspects of Germany's disastrous prewar past. In addition, the unique burdens of unification, along with the country's often precarious Central European location, are also factors that help shape a foreign policy that reflects particular predicaments and must meet some difficult challenges. Or, by contrast, Germany is singled out because it is expected to perform a special set of international tasks and provide a distinct degree of diplomatic leadership.

The assortment of perspectives on and evaluations of German foreign policy, scattered across the 1990s and some of them noted in this chapter, reminds us of the subjectivity and contingency of most analysis. Germany and Europe are experiencing rapid and dynamic changes that complicate the identification and projection of stable and durable patterns of policy into an uncertain future. The utility of historical criteria and examples may be limited and even misleading in an environment in which national and postnational frameworks of policy calculation and pre- and post-1989 institutional mechanisms complicate a messy diplomatic, economic, and military setting.

As far as the interpretation of German foreign policy is concerned, realists are pitted against postrealists and optimists against pessimists, with each case built on a necessarily selective evaluation of policies, pronouncements, and possibilities. It is frequently a matter of the glass being seen as half full or half empty, and (to stay with liquid metaphors) a question of old and new bottles filled with new or old wine. Underlying a clear majority of analyses is an incontrovertible fact, however: The united Germany is once again the principal power in the heart of the European continent. Whether this fact will be accompanied by a "return of history," or whether a new Germany will play its central role differently from in the past, cannot be answered definitively at this point, at least not at the end of the first postunification decade. Yet the resultant geopolitical imperatives for its foreign policy are inescapable, and form the core of the growing *Scharnierpolitik* with which the Federal Republic seeks to blend interest and allegiance as well as tradition and innovation, looking east and west and to the future.

Notes

1. W. R. Smyser, "Dateline Berlin: Germany's New Vision," *Foreign Policy*, nr. 97, Winter 1994/95, p. 140.

2. Andrei S. Markovits and Simon Reich, "Should Europe Fear the Germans?" in Michael G. Huelshoff, Andrei S. Markovits, and Simon Reich, eds., *From Bundesrepublik to Deutschland: German Politics after Unification* (Ann Arbor: University of Michigan Press, 1993), p. 271. The optimist versus pessimist outlook is also considered by Eckart Arnold, "German foreign policy and unification," *International Affairs*, vol. 67, nr. 3, 1991, p. 467ff.

3. Markovits and Reich, "Should Europe Fear the Germans?" p. 273.

4. Markovits and Reich, "Should Europe Fear the Germans?" pp. 273, 274.

5. Markovits and Reich, "Should Europe Fear the Germans?" p. 274.

6. Ralf Dahrendorf, *Society and Democracy in Germany* (New York: W. W. Norton & Co., [1965] 1979).

7. Markovits and Reich, "Should Europe Fear the Germans?" p. 274.

8. Markovits and Reich, "Should Europe Fear the Germans?" p. 275.

9. Markovits and Reich, "Should Europe Fear the Germans?" p. 276. For some examples of wary or pessimistic analysis, see Lanxin Xiang, "Is Germany in the West or in Central Europe?" *Orbis*, vol. 36, nr. 3, Summer 1992; Moishe Postone, "Germany's Future and Its Unmastered Past," in Huelshoff, Markovits, and Reich, eds., *From Bundesrepublik to Deutschland*, pp. 291–299; Alan Sked, "Cheap Excuses: Germany and the Gulf Crisis," *The National Interest*, nr. 24, Summer 1991, pp. 51–60. In their book *The German Predicament: Memory and Power in the New Europe* (Ithaca, NY/London: Cornell University Press, 1997), Markovits and Reich argue that the optimist and pessimist views of Germany and its future foreign policy are both "partially correct." They point to what they see as an "enormous disparity between Germany's structural power, particularly its economic power, and its domestic ideology," and "ideology of reluctance," which prevents the assumption of a more explicit and constructive international leadership role. By focusing on the significance of collective memory, they seek to uncover mass and elite attitudinal and ideological tendencies with relevance to the conduct of foreign policy (material in quotations taken from pp. xii and xiii).

10. See Philip H. Gordon, "The Normalization of German Foreign Policy," *Orbis*, vol. 38, nr. 2, Spring 1994, pp. 233–238; Gunther Hellmann, "Jenseits von 'Normalisierung' und 'Militarisierung': Zur Standortdebatte über die neue deutsche Außenpolitik," *Aus Politik und Zeitgeschichte*, nr. 1-2, 3 January 1997, pp. 24–33.

11. Josef Janning, "A German Europe—a European Germany? On the debate over Germany's foreign policy," *International Affairs*, vol. 72, nr. 1, 1996, p. 34.

12. In this context, see Roger Boyes and William Horsley, "The Germans as victims: a British view," *The World Today*, June 1995, pp. 110–114.

13. See Jürgen Habermas, *Die Normalität einer Berliner Republik. Kleine Politische Schriften VIII* (Frankfurt: Suhrkamp Verlag, 1995). Habermas focuses especially on the question of "lessons of history," and whether and how one might learn from history at all. He also makes an impassioned plea for a postnational perspective on world affairs.

14. Janning, "A German Europe—a European Germany?" p. 34. For some representative samples from the literature, see Christoph Bluth, "Germany: defining the national interest," *The World Today*, March 1995, pp. 51–55; the essays by Hans-Peter Schwarz, Arnulf Baring, Günther Gillessen, and Gregor Schöllgen in Arnulf Baring, ed., *Germany's New Position in Europe: Problems and Prospects* (Oxford/Providence: Berg Publishers, 1994); Hans-Peter Schwarz, *Die Zentralmacht Europas. Deutschlands Rückkehr auf die Weltbühne* (Berlin: Siedler Verlag, 1994); Gregor Schöllgen, *Angst vor der Macht. Die Deutschen und ihre Außenpolitik* (Berlin/Frankfurt: Verlag Ullstein, 1993); Michael Stürmer, "Deutsche Interessen," in Karl Kaiser and Hanns W. Maull, eds., *Deutschlands neue Außenpolitik. Band I: Grundlagen* (München: Oldenbourg Verlag, 1994), pp. 39–61. The essays on German foreign policy in Bertel Heurlin, ed., *Germany in Europe in the Nineties* (New York: St. Martin's Press, 1996), are also in part inspired by the realist tradition of analysis.

15. Janning, "A German Europe—A European Germany?" p. 36. See, for example, the writings of such scholars as Ernst-Otto Czempiel, Dieter Senghaas, Hanns W. Maull, and Werner Weidenfeld.

16. See the discussion in Karl Kaiser, "Das vereinigte Deutschland in der internationalen Politik," in Kaiser and Maull, eds., *Deutschlands neue Außenpolitik. Band I: Grundlagen*, pp. 1–14; Hanns W. Maull, "Zivilmacht Bundesrepublik Deutschland. 14 Thesen für eine neue deutsche Außenpolitik," *Europa-Archiv*, nr. 10, 1992, pp. 269–278.

17. In connection with the following discussion of German public opinion, see Ronald D. Asmus, *German Strategy and Opinion After the Wall, 1990–1993* (Santa Monica, CA: Rand Corporation, 1994); Ronald D. Asmus, *Germany's Geopolitical Maturation: Public Opinion and Security Policy in 1994* (Santa Monica, CA: Rand Corporation, 1995); Dieter Wulf, "Deutschland im Wandel. Außenpolitische Vorstellungen der Deutschen in West und Ost seit der Wiedervereinigung: Ergebnisse einer repräsentativen Studie," *Deutschland Archiv*, vol. 26, nr. 12, December 1993, pp. 1354–1360. See also Ludger Kühnhardt, "Wertgrundlagen der deutschen Außenpolitik," in Kaiser and Maull, eds., *Deutschlands neue Außenpolitik. Band I: Grundlagen*, pp. 99–127.

18. See Daniel Hamilton, "Germany After Unification," *Problems of Communism*, vol. XLI, nr. 3, May-June 1992, p. 13ff.

19. An attempt at comparing the post–Cold War shape of European affairs with conditions prevailing after 1815 and 1918, and their implications for the conduct of German foreign policy, is made by Josef Joffe, "German Grand Strategy After the Cold War," in Baring, ed., *Germany's New Position in Europe*.

20. Jochen Thies, "Germany and Eastern Europe Between Past and Future," in Baring, ed., *Germany's New Position in Europe*, p. 72.

21. Smyser, "Dateline Berlin: Germany's New Vision," p. 145.

22. Hamilton, "Germany After Unification," p. 13.

23. Hamilton, "Germany After Unification," p. 13.

24. Smyser, "Dateline Berlin: Germany's New Vision," p. 156.

25. Arnulf Baring, "'Germany, What Now?'" in Baring, ed., *Germany's New Position in Europe*, p. 7.

26. See Thies, "Germany and Eastern Europe Between Past and Future."

27. For an analysis of the interplay of philosophical conviction and calculated self-interest behind (West) German EC policy, reaching beyond the traditional neofunctionalist and intergovernmentalist theories in the study of integration to include fuller consideration of German domestic political and economic dynamics, see Michael G. Huelshoff, "Germany and European Integration: Understanding the Relationship," in Huelshoff, Markovits, and Reich, eds., *From Bundesrepublik to Deutschland*.

28. See Anne-Marie LeGloannec, "The Implications of German Unification for Western Europe," in Paul B. Stares, ed., *The New Germany and the New Europe* (Washington, DC: Brookings Institution, 1992).

29. Simon Bulmer and William E. Paterson, "Germany in the European Union: gentle giant or emergent leader?" *International Affairs*, vol. 72, nr. 1, 1996, p. 13. See also David Marsh, *Germany and Europe: The Crisis of Unity* (London: Heinemann Publishers, 1994), Chapter 6.

30. See Janning, "A German Europe—a European Germany?" p. 39ff.

31. On the sometimes haphazard and reactive development of German policy on European integration in the course of the 1990s, see Hartmut Mayer, "Early at the beach and

claiming territory? The evolution of German ideas on a new European order," *International Affairs*, vol. 73, nr. 4, 1997.

32. See Hans Schauer, "Nationale und europäische Identität. Die unterschiedlichen Auffassungen in Deutschland, Frankreich und Großbritannien," *Aus Politik und Zeitgeschichte*, nr. 10, 28 February 1997, pp. 3–13.

33. Markovits and Reich, "Should Europe Fear the Germans?" pp. 283, 284. For a discussion of the issues as seen from the Central and Eastern European perspective, see András Inotai, "Economic Implications of German Unification for Central and Eastern Europe," in Stares, ed., *The New Germany and the New Europe*.

34. CDU/CSU-Fraktion des Deutschen Bundestages, "Überlegungen zur Europapolitik," Bonn, 1 September 1994. In his analysis, Josef Janning refers to this school of thought as that of the "core protagonists." Janning, "A German Europe—a European Germany?" pp. 40–41. See also Christian Deubner, *Deutsche Europapolitik: Von Maastricht nach Kerneuropa?* (Baden-Baden: Nomos Verlagsgesellschaft, 1995), who argues for greater clarity regarding German interests in the context of revision of EU institutions and policies.

35. Bulmer and Paterson, "Germany in the European Union," p. 16, and p. 14ff. generally.

36. Bulmer and Paterson, "Germany in the European Union," p. 16.

37. Bulmer and Paterson, "Germany in the European Union," p. 17.

38. See, for example, the writings of Hans Arnold: *Europa am Ende? Die Auflösung von EG und NATO* (München/Zürich: Piper Verlag, 1993) and *Deutschlands Größe. Deutsche Außenpolitik zwischen Macht und Mangel* (München/Zürich: Piper Verlag, 1995).

39. For further discussion, see Bulmer and Paterson, "Germany in the European Union," pp. 17–18; Beverly Crawford, "German foreign policy and European political cooperation: the diplomatic recognition of Croatia in 1991," *German Politics and Society*, vol. 13, nr. 2, Summer 1995, pp. 1–34; Wolfgang Krieger, "Toward a Gaullist Germany? Some Lessons from the Yugoslav Crisis," *World Policy Journal*, vol. XI, nr. 1, Spring 1994, pp. 26–38; Hans-Dietrich Genscher, *Erinnerungen* (Berlin: Siedler Verlag, 1995), Chapter 19, published in English under the title *Rebuilding a House Divided: A Memoir by the Architect of Germany's Reunification* (New York: Broadway Books, 1998).

40. Bulmer and Paterson, "Germany in the European Union," p. 18.

41. Bulmer and Paterson, "Germany in the European Union," p. 30 (emphasis in original).

42. William Wallace, "Germany as Europe's leading power," *The World Today*, August/September 1995, pp. 162, 164. See also Jochen Thies, "Germany: Europe's reluctant Great Power," *The World Today*, October 1995, pp. 186–190. Harald Müller sees Germany somewhere between "new assertiveness" and "self-contained leadership." Müller, "German Foreign Policy After Unification," in Stares, ed., *The New Germany and the New Europe*, p. 161ff. See also the argument in Markovits and Reich, *The German Predicament*, which stresses collective memory in both Germany and its neighbors as a key reason for this reluctance.

43. James Sperling, "German Security Policy and the Future European Security Order," in Huelshoff, Markovits, and Reich, eds., *From Bundesrepublik to Deutschland*, p. 321. See also James Sperling, "German Security Policy in Post-Yalta Europe," in M. Donald Hancock and Helga A. Walsh, eds., *German Unification: Process and Outcomes* (Boulder, CO: Westview Press, 1994).

44. See the discussion by Hanns W. Maull, "Germany and Japan: The New Civilian Powers," *Foreign Affairs*, vol. 69, nr. 5, Winter 1990/91, pp. 91–106. Maull argues that "international relations are undergoing a profound transformation that offers an opportunity to take history beyond the world of the nation-state, with its inherent security dilemmas and its tendency to adjust to change through war. As a result of their own hubris, the farsightedness of the American victors in World War II and a series of historical accidents, Germany and Japan now in some ways find themselves representing this new world of international relations" (p. 93). See also Maull, "Zivilmacht Bundesrepublik Deutschland. 14 Thesen für eine neue deutsche Außenpolitik."

45. On recent German policy regarding nuclear disarmament, see Harald Müller, Alexander Kelle, Katja Frank, Sylvia Meier, and Annette Schaper, "The German Debate on Nuclear Weapons and Disarmament," *Washington Quarterly*, vol. 20, nr. 3, Summer 1997.

46. Sperling, "German Security Policy and the Future European Security Order," p. 323. On Germany's role as international economic power, see Norbert Kloten, "Die Bundesrepublik als Weltwirtschaftsmacht," in Kaiser and Maull, eds., *Deutschlands neue Außenpolitik. Band I: Grundlagen*, pp. 63–80.

47. Daniel Hamilton and James Clad, "Germany, Japan, and the False Glare of War," *Washington Quarterly*, Autumn 1991, p. 41.

48. See the discussion in Franz H. U. Borkenhagen, "Militarisierung deutscher Außenpolitik?" *Aus Politik und Zeitgeschichte*, nr. 33-34, 9 August 1996, pp. 3–9.

49. For further discussion of German policy during the Gulf War, see Genscher, *Erinnerungen*, Chapter 18.

50. For further discussion regarding the broader question of Germany's role and power in world affairs generally, see Hamilton and Clad, "Germany, Japan, and the False Glare of War." A fairly critical evaluation of German policy at the time of the Gulf War is presented by Sked, "Cheap Excuses." See also Jochen Thies, "Germany: tests of credibility," *The World Today*, June 1991, pp. 89–90.

51. This factor is especially emphasized in Beverly Crawford and Jost Halfmann, "Domestic Politics and International Change: Germany's Role in Europe's Security Future," in Beverly Crawford, ed., *The Future of European Security* (Berkeley: University of California at Berkeley, Center for German and European Studies, Research Series, Number 84, 1992).

52. Sperling, "German Security Policy and the Future European Security Order," p. 324.

53. Christoph Bertram, "The Power and the Past: Germany's New International Loneliness," in Baring, ed., *Germany's New Position in Europe*, pp. 92, 94.

54. For Central/Eastern European and Russian perspectives on the future European security order and Germany's policy on this question, see Slawomir A. Dabrowa, "Security Problems Facing Central and Eastern Europe After German Unification," and Sergei A. Karaganov, "Implications of German Unification for the Former Soviet Union," both in Stares, ed., *The New Germany and the New Europe*.

55. Timothy Garton Ash, "Germany's Choice," *Foreign Affairs*, vol. 73, nr. 4, July/August 1994, p. 72. See also Lothar Gutjahr, *German Foreign and Defence Policy after Unification* (London/New York: Pinter Publishers, 1994), Chapter 5.

56. Sperling, "German Security Policy and the Future European Security Order," p. 325.

57. Elizabeth Pond, "Germany Finds Its Niche as a Regional Power," *Washington Quarterly*, vol. 19, nr. 1, Winter 1996, p. 38. For his part, Ash outlines four basic options facing German foreign policy: "Carolingian Completion" (further deepening of the existing European Union around a Franco-German core), "Wider Europe" (widening the EU and

NATO to include Germany's eastern neighbors), "Moscow First" (the development of a new-old special relationship with Russia, which Ash describes as "the classic eastern option of German foreign policy"), and "World Power" (seeking the rights and duties of being a world power, such as a permanent seat on the UN Security Council). Ash, "Germany's Choice," p. 73ff. Ash concludes that Germany will "choose not to choose," but adds that "to choose not to choose does not mean you make no choices" (p. 79).

58. The role of the United States in European affairs since World War II and the importance of the German-U.S. connection are a key area of focus in Gregory F. Treverton, *America, Germany, and the Future of Europe* (Princeton, NJ: Princeton University Press, 1992). See also Dana H. Allin, "German-American Relations After the Cold War," in Gale A. Mattox and A. Bradley Shingleton, eds., *Germany at the Crossroads: Foreign and Domestic Policy Issues* (Boulder, CO: Westview Press, 1992); Alice Ackermann and Catherine McArdle Kelleher, "The United States and the German Question: Building a New European Order," in Dirk Verheyen and Christian Søe, eds., *The Germans and Their Neighbors* (Boulder, CO: Westview Press, 1993); and W. R. Smyser, *Germany and America: New Identities, Fateful Rift?* (Boulder, CO: Westview Press, 1993).

59. Sperling, "German Security Policy and the Future European Security Order," p. 329 (italics added).

60. Sperling, "German Security Policy and the Future European Security Order," p. 330.

61. One potential signal in this direction was the staging in March 1998 of a trilateral German-Russian-French summit conference (with more intended to follow) that excluded the United States and focused on continental European issues. For a discussion of the summit, see Steven Erlanger, "Germany Sits In With A New Team," *The New York Times*, 12 April 1998, p. WK3.

62. Sperling, "German Security Policy and the Future European Security Order," p. 338.

63. Smyser, "U.S.S.R.-Germany: A Link Restored," *Foreign Policy*, nr. 84, Fall 1991, p. 126.

64. For further discussion of the united Germany's relations with its immediate East-Central European neighbors, see the essays on Polish-German, Czech-German, and Hungarian-German relations by Arthur R. Rachwald, Milan Hauner, and Ivan Volgyes, respectively, in Verheyen and Søe, eds., *The Germans and Their Neighbors*. See also Stuart Drummond, "Germany: moving towards a new *Ostpolitik?*" *The World Today*, vol. 49, nr. 7, July 1993, pp. 132–135; Kazimierz Wóycicki, "Zur Besonderheit der deutsch-polnischen Beziehungen," *Aus Politik und Zeitgeschichte*, nr. 28, 5 July 1996, pp. 14–20; Jan Kren, "Tschechisch-deutsche Beziehungen in der Geschichte: Von Böhmen aus betrachtet," *Aus Politik und Zeitgeschichte*, nr. 28, 5 July 1996, pp. 21–27; Otto Kimminich, "Völkerrecht und Geschichte im Disput über die Beziehungen Deutschlands zu seinen östlichen Nachbarn," *Aus Politik und Zeitgeschichte*, nr. 28, 5 July 1996, pp. 28–38; Roland Freudenstein, "Poland, Germany and the EU," *International Affairs*, vol. 74, nr. 1, 1998.

65. Smyser, "U.S.S.R.-Germany: A Link Restored," p. 136.

66. Smyser, "U.S.S.R.-Germany: A Link Restored," p. 127.

Selected Bibliography

The following references are limited to (edited) books and other monographs. Articles from journals, magazines, and newspapers, and specific chapters in the various edited volumes, have been excluded. The reader may wish to peruse the extensive endnotes for each chapter for further bibliographic reference.

Adenauer, Konrad: *Bundestagsreden* (Bonn: Verlag AZ-Studio, 1967)

Albertin, Lothar, and Werner Link, eds.: *Politische Parteien auf dem Weg zur parlamentarischen Demokratie in Deutschland* (Düsseldorf: Droste Verlag, 1981)

Anderson, Christopher, Karl Kaltenthaler, and Wolfgang Luthardt, eds.: *The Domestic Politics of German Unification* (Boulder, CO/London: Lynne Rienner Publishers, 1993)

Angermann, Erich, and Marie-Luise Frings, eds.: *Oceans Apart?* (Stuttgart: Klett-Cotta, 1981)

Ardagh, John: *Germany and the Germans* (New York/London: Penguin Books, 1991; revised edition)

_____: *Germany and the Germans: An Anatomy of Society Today* (New York: Harper & Row, 1988)

Arnold, Hans: *Deutschlands Größe. Deutsche Außenpolitik zwischen Macht und Mangel* (München/Zürich: Piper Verlag, 1995)

_____: *Europa am Ende? Die Auflösung von EG und NATO* (München/Zürich: Piper Verlag, 1993)

Ash, Timothy Garton: *The File: A Personal History* (New York: Random House, 1997)

_____: *In Europe's Name: Germany and the Divided Continent* (New York: Vintage Books, 1994)

_____: *The Uses of Adversity: Essays on the Fate of Central Europe* (New York: Random House, 1989)

Ashkenasi, Abraham: *Modern German Nationalism* (New York: John Wiley and Sons, 1976)

_____: *Reformpartei und Außenpolitik* (Köln: Westdeutscher Verlag, 1968)

Asmus, Ronald D.: *Germany's Geopolitical Maturation: Public Opinion and Security Policy in 1994* (Santa Monica, CA: Rand Corporation, 1995)

_____: *German Strategy and Opinion After the Wall, 1990–1993* (Santa Monica, CA: Rand Corporation, 1994)

Auswärtiges Amt (Bonn), ed.: *Aussenpolitik der Bundesrepublik Deutschland. Dokumente von 1949 bis 1994* (Köln: Verlag Wissenschaft und Politik, 1995)

_____: *40 Jahre Außenpolitik der Bundesrepublik Deutschland: Eine Dokumentation* (Stuttgart: Verlag Bonn Aktuell, 1989)

Bahr, Egon: *Was wird aus den Deutschen? Fragen und Antworten* (Reinbek bei Hamburg: Rowohlt Taschenbuch Verlag, 1982)

Bahrmann, Hannes, and Christoph Links: *Wir sind das Volk. Die DDR zwischen 7. Oktober und 17. Dezember 1989. Eine Chronik* (Berlin/Weimar: Aufbau-Verlag Berlin, 1990)

Bailey, George: *Germans* (New York: Avon Books, 1972)

Baker, Kendall L., Russell J. Dalton, and Kai Hildebrandt: *Germany Transformed* (Cambridge, MA: Harvard University Press, 1981)

Bakker, G.: *Duitse Geopolitiek, 1919–1945* (Assen, Netherlands: Van Gorcum & Co., 1967)

Balfour, Michael: *Germany: The Tides of Power* (London/New York: Routledge, 1992)

Baring, Arnulf: *Unser neuer Größenwahn: Deutschland zwischen Ost und West* (Stuttgart: Deutsche Verlags-Anstalt, 1988)

Baring, Arnulf, ed.: *Germany's New Position in Europe: Problems and Prospects* (Oxford/Providence, RI: Berg Publishers, 1994)

Baule, Bernward, and Rita Süssmuth, eds.: *Eine deutsche Zwischenbilanz. Standpunkte zum Umgang mit unserer Vergangenheit* (München: Günter Olzog Verlag, 1997)

Becker, Ulrich, Horst Becker, and Walter Ruhland: *Zwischen Angst und Aufbruch. Das Lebensgefühl der Deutschen in Ost und West nach der Wiedervereinigung* (Düsseldorf/Wien/New York: Econ Verlag, 1992)

Bender, Peter: *Episode oder Epoche? Zur Geschichte des geteilten Deutschlands* (München: Deutscher Taschenbuch Verlag, 1996)

_____: *Die Ostpolitik Willy Brandts, oder Die Kunst des Selbstverständlichen* (Reinbek bei Hamburg: Rowohlt Taschenbuch Verlag, 1972)

Berger, Stefan: *The Search for Normality: National Identity and Historical Consciousness in Germany Since 1800* (Providence, RI/Oxford: Berghahn Books, 1997)

Berghahn, Volker, ed.: *Militarismus* (Köln: Kiepenheuer & Witsch, 1975)

Bergsträsser, Ludwig: *Geschichte der politischen Parteien in Deutschland* (München: G. Olzog Verlag, 1965)

Berlin-Bonn. Die Debatte. Alle Bundestagsreden vom 20. Juni 1991 (Köln: Verlag Kiepenheuer & Witsch, 1991)

Besson, Waldemar: *Die Außenpolitik der Bundesrepublik* (München: Piper, 1970)

Blackbourn, David, and Geoff Eley: *The Peculiarities of German History: Bourgeois Society and Politics in Nineteenth-Century Germany* (Oxford/New York: Oxford University Press, 1984)

Bleek, Wilhelm, and Hanns Maul, eds.: *Ein ganz normaler Staat? Perspektiven nach 40 Jahren Bundesrepublik* (München/Zürich: Piper Verlag, 1989)

Blumenwitz, Dieter, and Gottfried Zieger, eds.: *Die deutsche Frage im Spiegel der Parteien* (Köln: Verlag Wissenschaft und Politik, 1989)

Bracher, Karl Dietrich: *Zeit der Ideologien* (Stuttgart: Deutsche Verlags-Anstalt, 1982)

_____: *The German Dilemma* (London: Weidenfeld and Nicolson, 1974)

_____: *The German Dictatorship* (New York: Praeger, 1970)

Brandt, Peter, and Herbert Ammon, eds.: *Die Linke und die nationale Frage* (Reinbek bei Hamburg: Rowohlt Taschenbuch Verlag, 1981)

Brandt, Willy: *"was zusammengehört": Reden zu Deutschland* (Bonn: Verlag J.H.W. Dietz Nachf., 1990)

_____: *Plädoyer für die Zukunft* (Frankfurt: Europäische Verlagsanstalt, 1972)

_____: *Außenpolitik, Deutschlandpolitik, Europapolitik* (Berlin: Berlin-Verlag, 1968)

_____: *Brandt-Reden 1961–65* (Köln: Verlag Wissenschaft und Politik, 1965)

Bruns, Wilhelm: *Von der Deutschland-Politik zur DDR-Politik?* (Opladen: Leske & Budrich, 1989)

———: *Die Außenpolitik der DDR* (Berlin: Colloquium Verlag, 1985)

Büchten, Daniela, and Anja Frey, eds.: *Im Irrgarten deutscher Geschichte. Die Neue Wache 1818–1993* (Berlin: Schriftenreihe des Aktiven Museums Faschismus und Widerstand in Berlin e.V., nr. 5, 1993)

Burdick, Charles, Hans-Adolf Jacobsen, and Winfried Kudszus, eds.: *Contemporary Germany: Politics and Culture* (Boulder, CO: Westview Press, 1984)

Buruma, Ian: *The Wages of Guilt: Memories of War in Germany and Japan* (New York: Farrar, Straus, Giroux, 1994)

Butler, Rohan D'Olier: *The Roots of National Socialism* (London: Faber and Faber, 1941; New York: E. P. Dutton & Co., 1942)

Butterwegge, Christoph, and Horst Isola, eds.: *Rechtsextremismus im vereinten Deutschland. Randerscheinung oder Gefahr für die Demokratie?* (Bremen: Steintor Verlag, 1991)

Calleo, David: *The German Problem Reconsidered* (Cambridge: Cambridge University Press, 1978)

———: *Europe's Future: The Grand Alternatives* (New York: W. W. Norton, 1965/1967)

Childs, David: *The GDR: Moscow's German Ally* (London: Unwin Hyman, 1988)

Clemens, Clay: *Reluctant Realists: The Christian Democrats and West German Ostpolitik* (Durham, NC: Duke University Press, 1989)

Clement, Alain: *Gibt es ein deutsches Geschichtsbild?* (Studien & Berichte der Katholischen Akademie in Bayern, Heft 14, 1961)

Coffey, Joseph I., Klaus von Schubert, et al.: *Defense and Detente: U.S. and West German Perspectives on Defense Policy* (Boulder, CO: Westview Press, 1989)

Conradt, David P.: *The German Polity* (New York: Longman, 1982/1996)

Conradt, David, Gerald R. Kleinfeld, George K. Romoser, and Christian Søe, eds.: *Germany's New Politics: Parties and Issues in the 1990s* (Providence, RI/Oxford: Berghahn Books, 1995)

Cooney, James A., Gordon A. Craig, Hans-Peter Schwarz, and Fritz Stern, eds.: *The Federal Republic of Germany and the United States* (Boulder, CO: Westview Press, 1984)

Craig, Gordon A.: *The Germans* (New York: G. P. Putnam's Sons, 1982)

———: *From Bismarck to Adenauer: Aspects of German Statecraft* (Baltimore: Johns Hopkins University Press, 1958)

Cromwell, William C., N. Forman, and Josef Joffe: *Political Problems of Atlantic Partnership* (Bruges, Belgium: College of Europe, 1969)

Dahrendorf, Ralf: *Society and Democracy in Germany* (New York: W. W. Norton & Co., [1965] 1979)

Dalton, Russell J.: *Politics in West Germany* (Glenview, IL/Boston, MA: Scott, Foresman and Co., 1989)

Dann, Otto: *Nation und Nationalismus in Deutschland, 1770–1990* (München: Verlag C. H. Beck, 1996)

Demontage . . . revolutionärer oder restaurativer Bildersturm? (Berlin: Karin Kramer Verlag, 1992)

Der Wettbewerb für das "Denkmal für die ermordeten Juden Europas." Eine Streitschrift (Berlin: Verlag der Kunst; Neue Gesellschaft für Bildende Kunst, 1995)

Deubner, Christian: *Deutsche Europapolitik: Von Maastricht nach Kerneuropa?* (Baden-Baden: Nomos Verlagsgesellschaft, 1995)

Deutsch, Karl W., and Lewis Edinger: *Germany Rejoins the Powers* (Stanford: Stanford University Press, 1959)

Dietze, Gottfried: *Deutschland—Wo bist Du?* (München/Wien: Günter Olzog Verlag, 1980)

Dohnanyi, Klaus von: *Das Deutsche Wagnis. Über die wirtschaftlichen und sozialen Folgen der Einheit* (München: Droemersche Verlagsanstalt Th. Knaur Nachf., 1991)

Dönhoff, Marion Gräfin, et al.: *Weil das Land sich ändern muss. Ein Manifest* (Reinbek bei Hamburg: Rowohlt Verlag, 1992)

Drechsler, Ingrun, et al., eds.: *Getrennte Vergangenheit, gemeinsame Zukunft* (München: Deutscher Taschenbuch Verlag, 1997)

Dulles, Eleanor Lansing: *One Germany or Two* (Stanford: Hoover Institution Press, 1970)

Dümcke, Wolfgang, and Fritz Vilmar, eds.: *Kolonialisierung der DDR. Analysen und Alternativen des Einigungsprozesses* (Münster: agenda Verlag, 1996)

Eich, Hermann: *The Germans* (New York: Stein and Day, 1980)

Eisenmann, Peter, and Gerhard Hirscher, eds.: *Die deutsche Identität und Europa* (Mainz: v. Hase & Koehler Verlag, 1991)

Eisner, Erich: *Das europäische Konzept von Franz Josef Strauß* (Meisenheim am Glan: Verlag Anton Hain, 1975)

Eley, Geoff: *From Unification to Nazism: Reinterpreting the German Past* (Boston: Allen and Unwin, 1986)

Elm, Ludwig: *Nach Hitler. Nach Honecker. Zum Streit der Deutschen um die eigene Vergangenheit* (Berlin: Dietz Verlag, 1991)

Epstein, Klaus: *The Genesis of German Conservatism* (Princeton, NJ: Princeton University Press, 1966)

Erler, Fritz: *Politik für Deutschland* (Stuttgart: Seewald Verlag, 1968)

Evans, Richard J.: *Rethinking German History* (London: Allen and Unwin, 1987)

Faulenbach, Bernd: *Ideologie des deutschen Weges. Die deutsche Geschichte in der Historiographie zwischen Kaiserreich und Nationalsozialismus* (München: Beck Verlag, 1980)

Feiler, Oswald: *Moskau und die Deutsche Frage* (Krefeld: Sinus Verlag, 1984)

Fischer, Fritz: *Germany's Aims in the First World War* (New York: W. W. Norton & Co., [1961] 1967)

Fisher, Marc: *After the Wall: Germany, the Germans and the Burdens of History* (New York: Simon & Schuster, 1995)

Flynn, Gregory, ed.: *The Internal Fabric of Western Security* (Totowa, NJ: Allanheld, 1981)

Fogt, Helmut: *Politische Generationen* (Opladen: Westdeutscher Verlag, 1982)

Free, Lloyd: *Six Allies and a Neutral* (Glencoe, IL: Free Press, 1959)

Friedrich-Ebert-Stiftung: *Das Preußenbild der DDR im Wandel* (Bonn: Verlag Neue Gesellschaft, 1981)

Fritsch-Bournazel, Renata: *L'Allemagne: un enjeu pour l'Europe* (Brussels: Éditions Complexe, 1987)

_____: *Das Land in der Mitte. Die Deutschen im europäischen Kräftefeld* (München: Iudicium Verlag, 1986)

Fritsch-Bournazel, Renata, André Brigot, and Jim Cloos: *Les Allemands au Coeur de l'Europe* (Paris: Fondation pour les Études de Défense Nationale, 1983)

Fulbrook, Mary: *The Divided Nation: A History of Germany 1918–1990* (New York/Oxford: Oxford University Press, 1992)

_____: *A Concise History of Germany* (Cambridge: Cambridge University Press, 1990)

Funke, Manfred, et al., eds.: *Demokratie und Diktatur* (Bonn: Schriftenreihe der Bundeszentrale für politische Bildung, 1987)

Gatzke, Hans W.: *Germany and the United States* (Cambridge, MA: Harvard University Press, 1980)

Gauck, Joachim: *Die Stasi-Akten. Das unheimliche Erbe der DDR* (Reinbek bei Hamburg: Rowohlt Taschenbuch Verlag, 1991)

Gauly, Thomas M., ed.: *Die Last der Geschichte. Kontroversen zur deutschen Identität* (Köln: Verlag Wissenschaft und Politik, 1988)

Gaus, Günter: *Wo Deutschland liegt: eine Ortsbestimmung* (Hamburg: Hoffmann und Campe, 1983)

_____: *Texte zur deutschen Frage* (Darmstadt: Hermann Luchterhand Verlag, 1981)

Geiss, Imanuel, ed.: *July 1914: The Outbreak of the First World War. Selected Documents* (New York: Charles Scribner's Sons, 1967)

Genscher, Hans-Dietrich: *Rebuilding a House Divided: A Memoir by the Architect of Germany's Reunification* (New York: Broadway Books, 1998)

_____: *Erinnerungen* (Berlin: Siedler Verlag, 1995)

_____: *Deutsche Außenpolitik* (Stuttgart: Verlag Bonn Aktuell, 1981)

German Politics and Society (special issue entitled "One Nation—Which Past? Historiography and German Identities in the 1990s," vol. 15, nr. 2, Summer 1997)

Germany in Transition (*Daedalus*, vol. 123, nr. 1, Winter 1994)

Gerschenkron, Alexander: *Bread and Democracy in Germany* (Berkeley: University of California Press, 1943)

Giordano, Ralph: *Die zweite Schuld oder Von der Last Deutscher zu sein* (Hamburg: Rasch und Röhring Verlag, 1987)

Glees, Anthony: *Reinventing Germany: German Political Development Since 1945* (Oxford/Washington, DC: Berg Publishers, 1996)

Goldhagen, Daniel J.: *Hitler's Willing Executioners: Ordinary Germans and the Holocaust* (New York: Vintage Books, 1997)

Görtemaker, Manfred: *Unifying Germany, 1989–1990* (New York: St. Martin's Press, 1994)

Grass, Günter: *Lastenausgleich. Wider das dumpfe Einheitsgebot* (Darmstadt: Luchterhand Literaturverlag, 1990)

Graubard, Stephen R., ed.: *A New Europe?* (Boston: Houghton Mifflin Co., 1964)

Grebing, Helga: *Der 'deutsche Sonderweg' in Europa, 1806–1945. Eine Kritik* (Stuttgart: Verlag W. Kohlhammer, 1986)

Grebing, Helga, et al.: *Konservatismus–eine deutsche Bilanz* (München: Piper, 1971)

Greiffenhagen, Martin: *Die Aktualität Preussens* (Frankfurt: Fischer Taschenbuch Verlag, 1981)

_____: *Das Dilemma des Konservatismus in Deutschland* (München: Piper, 1971)

Greiffenhagen, Martin, and Sylvia Greiffenhagen: *Ein schwieriges Vaterland. Zur politischen Kultur im vereinigten Deutschland* (München: Paul List Verlag, 1993)

_____: *Ein schwieriges Vaterland* (Frankfurt: Fischer Taschenbuch Verlag, 1981)

Grewe, Wilhelm G.: *Deutsche Außenpolitik der Nachkriegszeit* (Stuttgart: Deutsche Verlags-Anstalt, 1960)

Gross, Johannes: *De Duitsers* (Baarn, Netherlands: Uitgeverij In den Toren, 1968)

Grosser, Alfred: *Das Deutschland im Westen* (München/Wien: Carl Hanser Verlag, 1985)

_____: *Geschichte Deutschlands seit 1945* (München: Deutscher Taschenbuch Verlag, 1979)

Grosser, Alfred, and Henri Menudier: *La Vie Politique en Allemagne Fédérale* (Paris: A. Colin, 1970)

Grunenberg, Antonia: *Welche Geschichte wählen wir?* (Hamburg: Junius Verlag, 1992)

Gruner, Wolf D.: *Die deutsche Frage in Europa 1800 bis 1990* (München/Zürich: Piper Verlag, 1993)

_____: *Die deutsche Frage. Ein Problem der europäischen Geschichte seit 1800* (München: Verlag C. H. Beck, 1985)

Gutjahr, Lothar: *German Foreign and Defence Policy after Unification* (London/New York: Pinter Publishers, 1994)

Habermas, Jürgen: *Die Normalität einer Berliner Republik. Kleine Politische Schriften VIII* (Frankfurt: Suhrkamp Verlag, 1995)

Haffner, Sebastian: *The Ailing Empire: Germany from Bismarck to Hitler* (New York: Fromm International Publishing Co., 1989)

Haftendorn, Helga: *Security and Detente* (New York: Praeger, 1985)

Haftendorn, Helga, Lothar Wilker, and Claudia Wörmann, eds.: *Die Aussenpolitik der Bundesrepublik Deutschland* (Berlin: Wissenschaftlicher Autoren-Verlag, 1982)

Hahn, Walter F.: *Between Westpolitik and Ostpolitik: Changing West German Security Views* (Beverly Hills/London: Sage Publications, 1975)

Hämäläinen, Pekka Kalevi: *Uniting Germany: Actions and Reactions* (Boulder, CO: Westview Press, 1994)

Hancock, M. Donald, and Helga A. Welsh, eds.: *German Unification: Process and Outcomes* (Boulder, CO: Westview Press, 1994)

Hanrieder, Wolfram F.: *Germany, America, Europe: Forty Years of German Foreign Policy* (New Haven/London: Yale University Press, 1989)

_____: *Fragmente der Macht. Die Außenpolitik der Bundesrepublik* (München: Piper, 1981)

_____: *The Stable Crisis* (New York: Harper & Row, 1970)

Hanrieder, Wolfram F., ed.: *West German Foreign Policy: 1949–1979* (Boulder, CO: Westview Press, 1980)

Hardtwig, Wolfgang, and Heinrich August Winkler, eds.: *Deutsche Entfremdung. Zum Befinden in Ost und West* (München: Verlag C. H. Beck, 1994)

Heimannsberg, Barbara, and Christoph J. Schmidt, eds.: *The Collective Silence: German Identity and the Legacy of Shame* (San Francisco: Jossey-Bass Publishers, 1993)

Heisenberg, Wolfgang, and Dieter S. Lutz, eds.: *Sicherheitspolitik kontrovers: Auf dem Weg in die neunziger Jahre* (Bonn: Schriftenreihe der Bundeszentrale für politische Bildung, 1987)

Herf, Jeffrey: *Divided Memory: The Nazi Past in the Two Germanys* (Cambridge, MA/London: Harvard University Press, 1997)

Hettlage, Robert, and Karl Lenz, eds.: *Deutschland nach der Wende. Eine Zwischenbilanz* (München: Verlag C. H. Beck, 1995)

Hillenbrand, Martin J.: *Germany in an Era of Transition* (Paris: Atlantic Institute for International Affairs, 1983)

Hillgruber, Andreas: *Deutsche Geschichte 1945–1982* (Stuttgart: Verlag W. Kohlhammer, 4th edition, 1983)

_____: *Germany and the Two World Wars* (Cambridge, MA/London: Harvard University Press, 1981)

_____: *Großmachtpolitik und Militarismus im 20. Jahrhundert* (Düsseldorf: Droste Verlag, 1974)

Hirsch, Kurt, ed.: *Deutschlandpläne* (München: Rütten & Löning Verlag, 1967)

"Historikerstreit": Die Dokumentation der Kontroverse um die Einzigartigkeit der nationalsozialistischen Judenvernichtung (München: Piper, 1987)

Hoffmann, Dierk, Karl-Heinz Schmidt, and Peter Skyba, eds.: *Die DDR vor dem Mauerbau. Dokumente zur Geschichte des anderen deutschen Staates, 1949–1961* (München/Zürich: Piper Verlag, 1993)

Hoffmann-Lange, Ursula, Helga Neumann, and Bärbel Steinkemper, eds.: *Konsens und Konflikt zwischen Führungsgruppen in der Bundesrepublik Deutschland* (Frankfurt: Peter D. Lang Verlag, 1980)

Holborn, Hajo: *Germany and Europe* (Garden City, NY: Doubleday, 1970)

Holm, Hans-Henrik, and Nikolaj Petersen, eds.: *The European Missiles Crisis: Nuclear Weapons and Security Policy* (New York: St. Martin's Press, 1983)

Hrbek, Rudolf: *Die SPD–Deutschland und Europa* (Bonn: Europa Union Verlag, 1972)

Huelshoff, Michael G., Andrei Markovits, and Simon Reich, eds.: *From Bundesrepublik to Deutschland: German Politics After Unification* (Ann Arbor: University of Michigan Press, 1993)

Iggers, George G.: *The German Conception of History: The National Tradition of Historical Thought from Herder to the Present* (Middletown, CT: Wesleyan University Press, 1983)

Isensee, Josef, ed.: *Vergangenheitsbewältigung durch Recht. Drei Abhandlungen zu einem deutschen Problem* (Berlin: Duncker & Humblot, 1992)

Jäckh, Ernst: *Deutschland. Das Herz Europas* (Stuttgart/Berlin/Leipzig: Deutsche Verlags-Anstalt, 1928)

Jacobsen, Hans-Adolf: *Von der Strategie der Gewalt zur Politik der Friedenssicherung* (Düsseldorf: Droste Verlag, 1977)

Jacobsen, Hans-Adolf, and Otto Stenzl, eds.: *Deutschland und die Welt* (München: Deutscher Taschenbuch Verlag, 1964)

Jahn, Hans Edgar: *Die deutsche Frage von 1945 bis heute* (Mainz: v. Hase & Köhler Verlag, 1985)

James, Harold: *A German Identity, 1770–1990* (London: Weidenfeld and Nicolson, 1990)

James, Harold, and Marla Stone, eds.: *When the Wall came down: reactions to German unification* (New York/London: Routledge, 1992)

Jarausch, Konrad: *The Rush to German Unity* (New York: Oxford University Press, 1994)

Jarausch, Konrad, ed.: *After Unity: Reconfiguring German Identities* (Providence, RI/Oxford: Berghahn Books, 1997)

Jeismann, Karl-Ernst, ed.: *Einheit–Freiheit–Selbstbestimmung: Die Deutsche Frage im historisch-politischen Bewußtsein* (Frankfurt/New York: Campus Verlag, 1988)

Jesse, Eckhard, ed.: *Bundesrepublik Deutschland und Deutsche Demokratische Republik* (Berlin: Colloquium Verlag, 1980/1985)

Joachimsen, Paul: *Vom deutschen Volk zum deutschen Staat. Eine Geschichte des deutschen Nationalbewußtseins* (Göttingen: Vandenhoeck & Ruprecht, 1967)

Jürgs, Michael: *Die Treuhändler. Wie Helden und Halunken die DDR verkauften* (München/Leipzig: List Verlag, 1997)

Kaiser, Karl, and Hanns W. Maull, eds.: *Deutschlands neue Außenpolitik. Band I: Grundlagen* (München: Oldenbourg Verlag, 1994)

Kaiser, Karl, and Roger Morgan, eds.: *Britain and West Germany* (London: Oxford University Press, 1971)

Käser, Steffen, ed.: *"Denk' ich an Deutschland . . . ": Grundlagen eines Dialoges beider deutscher Staaten* (Gerlingen: Bleicher Verlag, 1987)

Kennedy, Paul: *The Rise and Fall of the Great Powers* (New York: Random House, 1987)

Kettenacker, Lothar: *Germany since 1945* (Oxford/New York: Oxford University Press, 1997)

Kiep, Walther Leisler: *Good-Bye Amerika—Was Dann?* (Stuttgart-Degerloch: Seewald Verlag, 1972)

Klessman, Christoph: *Die doppelte Staatsgründung* (Bonn: Schriftenreihe der Bundeszentrale für politische Bildung, 1982)

Klotzbach, Kurt: *Der Weg zur Staatspartei* (Berlin/Bonn: Verlag J.H.W. Dietz Nachf., 1982)

Knabe, Hubertus, ed.: *Aufbruch in eine andere DDR* (Reinbek bei Hamburg: Rowohlt Taschenbuch Verlag, 1989)

Knapen, Ben: *Het Duitse Onbehagen* (Amsterdam: Uitgeverij Bert Bakker, 1983)

Knoblich, Axel, Antonio Peter, and Erik Natter, eds.: *Auf dem Weg zu einer gesamtdeutschen Identität* (Köln: Verlag Wissenschaft und Politik, 1993)

Koch-Hillebrecht, Manfred, ed.: *Das Deutschenbild* (München: Beck Verlag, 1977)

Kocka, Jürgen, and Martin Sabrow, eds.: *Die DDR als Geschichte. Fragen-Hypothesen-Perspektiven* (Berlin: Akademie Verlag, 1994)

Kohl, Hans: *The Mind of Germany* (New York: Harper & Row, 1965)

Kohl, Helmut: *Ich wollte Deutschlands Einheit* (Berlin: Propyläen Verlag, 1996)

_____: *Reden und Erklärungen zur Deutschlandpolitik* (Bonn: Presse- und Informationsamt der Bundesregierung, 1990)

_____: *Reden, 1982–1984* (Bonn: Presse- und Informationsamt der Bundesregierung, 1984)

Krieger, Leonard: *The German Idea of Freedom* (Chicago/London: University of Chicago Press, 1957)

Krisch, Henry: *The German Democratic Republic: The Search for Identity* (Boulder, CO: Westview Press, 1985)

Krockow, Christian Graf von: *Nationalismus als deutsches Problem* (München: Piper, 1970)

Kroker, Eduard J. M., and Bruno Dechamps, eds.: *Die Deutschen auf der Suche nach ihrer neuen Identität?* (Frankfurt am Main: Frankfurter Allgemeine Zeitung, Verlagsbereich Wirtschaftsbücher, 1993)

Kuiper, Jan C.: *De Angst der Patriotten* (Assen, Netherlands: Van Gorcum & Co., 1973)

Kunst, Hermann, Helmut Kohl, and Peter Egen, eds.: *Dem Staate verpflichtet* (Stuttgart/Berlin: Kreuz Verlag, 1980)

Ladd, Brian: *Ghosts of Berlin: Confronting German History in the Urban Landscape* (Chicago/London: University of Chicago Press, 1997)

Laqueur, Walter, and Robert Hunter, eds.: *European Peace Movements and the Future of the Western Alliance* (New Brunswick, NJ: Transaction Books, 1985)

Larrabee, F. Stephen, ed.: *The Two German States and European Security* (New York: St. Martin's Press, 1989)

Le Gloannec, Anne-Marie: *Die deutsch-deutsche Nation: Anmerkungen zu einer revolutionären Entwicklung* (München: printul Verlagsgesellschaft, 1991)

Leonhardt, Rudolf W.: *X-mal Deutschland* (München: Piper, 1961)

Lerner, Daniel, and Morton Gorden: *Euratlantica* (Cambridge, MA: MIT Press, 1969)

Lichtenstein, Heiner, and Otto R. Romberg, eds.: *Täter—Opfer—Folgen. Der Holocaust in Geschichte und Gegenwart* (Bonn: Bundeszentrale für politische Bildung, 1995)

Longerich, Peter, ed.: *"Was ist des Deutschen Vaterland?": Dokumente zur Frage der deutschen Einheit 1800–1990* (München/Zürich: Piper, 1990)

Loth, Wilfried: *Ost-West-Konflikt und deutsche Frage* (München: Deutscher Taschenbuch Verlag, 1989)

Löwenthal, Richard: *Gesellschaftswandel und Kulturkrise* (Frankfurt: Fischer Taschenbuch Verlag, 1979)

Löwke, Udo: *Für den Fall, daß . . . : SPD und Wehrfrage, 1949–1955* (Hannover: Verlag für Literatur & Zeitgeschehen, 1969)

Lübbe, Hermann: *Politische Philosophie in Deutschland* (Basel: B. Schwabe, 1963)

Maaz, Hans-Joachim: *Die Entrüstung. Deutschland, Deutschland. Stasi, Schuld und Sündenbock* (Berlin: Argon Verlag, 1992)

_____: *Das gestürzte Volk. Die unglückliche Einheit* (Berlin: Argon Verlag, 1991)

_____: *Der Gefühlsstau. Ein Psychogramm der DDR* (Berlin: Argon Verlag, 1990)

Maier, Charles S.: *Dissolution: The Crisis of Communism and the End of East Germany* (Princeton, NJ: Princeton University Press, 1997)

_____: *The Unmasterable Past: History, Holocaust, and German National Identity* (Cambridge, MA: Harvard University Press, 1988)

Marsh, David: *Germany and Europe: The Crisis of Unity* (London: Heinemann Publishers, 1994)

Matthias, Erich: *Sozialdemokratie und Nation* (Stuttgart: Deutsche Verlags-Anstalt, 1952)

Mattox, Gale A., and A. Bradley Shingleton, eds.: *Germany at the Crossroads: Foreign and Domestic Policy Issues* (Boulder, CO: Westview Press, 1992)

Mayer-Vorfelder, Gerhard, and Hubertus Zuber, eds.: *Union alternativ* (Stuttgart: Seewald Verlag, 1976)

McAdams, A. James: *Germany Divided: From the Wall to Reunification* (Princeton, NJ: Princeton University Press, 1993)

_____: *East Germany and Detente: Building Authority After the Wall* (Cambridge: Cambridge University Press, 1985)

McCauley, Martin: *The German Democratic Republic Since 1945* (New York: St. Martin's Press, 1983)

McClelland, Charles E., and Steven P. Scher, eds.: *Postwar German Culture* (New York: E. P. Dutton, 1974)

Meier, Christian: *Die Nation die keine sein will* (München/Wien: Carl Hanser Verlag, 1991)

Meinecke, Friedrich: *The German Catastrophe: Reflections and Recollections* (Cambridge, MA: Harvard University Press, 1950)

Merkl, Peter H.: *German Unification in the European Context* (University Park: Pennsylvania State University Press, 1993)

_____: *German Foreign Policies, West and East* (Santa Barbara, CA: ABC-CLIO Inc., 1974)

Merkl, Peter H., ed.: *The Federal Republic of Germany at Forty* (New York/London: New York University Press, 1989)

Merritt, Anna J., and Richard L. Merritt, eds.: *Public Opinion in Semisovereign Germany* (Urbana: University of Illinois Press, 1980)

Michalka, Wolfgang, ed.: *Die Deutsche Frage in der Weltpolitik* (Stuttgart: Steiner-Verlag-Wiesbaden, 1986)

Miller, Susanne: *Die SPD vor und nach Godesberg* (Bonn-Bad Godesberg: Verlag Neue Gesellschaft, 1974)

Mintzel, Alf, and Heinrich Oberreuter, eds.: *Parteien in der Bundesrepublik Deutschland* (Bonn: Schriftenreihe der Bundeszentrale für politische Bildung, 1990)

Misselwitz, Hans-J.: *Nicht länger mit dem Gesicht nach Westen. Das neue Selbstbewußtsein der Ostdeutschen* (Bonn: Verlag J.H.W. Dietz Nachfolger, 1996)

Mitscherlich, Alexander, and Margarete Mitscherlich: *Die Unfähigkeit zu trauern. Grundlagen des kollektiven Verhaltens* (München: Piper Verlag, 1967)

Mitter, Armin, and Stefan Wolle, eds.: *"Ich liebe euch doch alle!" Befehle und Lageberichte des MfS. Januar-November 1989* (Berlin: BasisDruck Verlagsgesellschaft, 1990)

Modrow, Hans: *Ich wollte ein neues Deutschland* (Berlin: Karl Dietz Verlag, 1998)

Mohler, Armin: *Vergangenheitsbewältigung, oder wie man den Krieg nochmals verliert* (Krefeld: Sinus-Verlag, 1980)

Möller, Walter, and Fritz Vilmar: *Sozialistische Friedenspolitik für Europa: Kein Frieden ohne Gesellschaftsreform in West und Ost* (Reinbek bei Hamburg: Rowohlt Taschenbuch Verlag, 1972)

Mommsen, Wolfgang J.: *Nation und Geschichte: Über die Deutschen und die deutsche Frage* (München/Zürich: Piper, 1990)

Monteath, Peter, and Reinhard Alter, eds.: *Kulturstreit-Streitkultur: German Literature Since the Wall* (Amsterdam/Atlanta, GA: Editions Rodopi, 1996)

Moore, Barrington: *Social Origins of Dictatorship and Democracy* (Boston: Beacon Press, 1966)

Mosse, George L.: *The Crisis of German Ideology* (New York: Grosset & Dunlap, 1964)

Müller-Roschach, Herbert: *Die deutsche Europapolitik* (Baden-Baden: Nomos Verlagsgesellschaft, 1974; Bonn: Europa Union Verlag, 1980)

Mushaben, Joyce Marie: *From Post-War to Post-Wall Generations: Changing Attitudes Toward the National Question and NATO in the Federal Republic of Germany* (Boulder, CO: Westview Press, 1998)

Naumann, Michael, ed.: *"Die Geschichte ist offen." DDR 1990: Hoffnung auf eine neue Republik* (Reinbek bei Hamburg: Rowohlt Taschenbuch Verlag, 1990)

Nawrocki, Joachim: *Relations Between the Two States in Germany* (Bonn: Press and Information Office of the Federal Government, n.d.)

Neumann, Erich P.: *Die Deutschen und die NATO* (Allensbach: Verlag für Demoskopie, 1969)

Niedhart, Gottfried, and Dieter Riesenberger, eds.: *Lernen aus dem Krieg? Deutsche Nachkriegszeiten, 1918–1945* (München: Verlag C. H. Beck, 1992)

Nipperdey, Thomas: *Nachdenken über die deutsche Geschichte* (München: Verlag C. H. Beck, 1986)

Noelle, Elisabeth, and Erich P. Neumann, eds.: *The Germans: Public Opinion Polls, 1947–1966* (Westport, CT: Greenwood Press, 1981)

Noelle-Neumann, Elisabeth, ed.: *The Germans: Public Opinion Polls, 1967–1980* (Westport, CT: Greenwood Press, 1981)

Opp, Karl-Dieter, Peter Voss, and Christiane Gern: *Origins of a Spontaneous Revolution: East Germany, 1989* (Ann Arbor: University of Michigan Press, 1995)

Parker, Geoffrey: *Western Geopolitical Thought in the 20th Century* (London: Croom Helm, 1985)

Paterson, William E.: *The SPD and European Integration* (Lexington, MA: Lexington Books, 1974)

Pfaltzgraff, Robert L., Kim Holmes, Clay Clemens, and Werner Kaltefleiter: *The Greens of West Germany* (Cambridge, MA/Washington, DC: Institute for Foreign Policy Analysis, 1983)

Pfetsch, Frank R.: *Die Außenpolitik der Bundesrepublik, 1949–1980* (München: Wilhelm Fink Verlag, 1981)

Plessner, Helmuth: *Die verspätete Nation* (Stuttgart: W. Kohlhammer Verlag, 1959; a new edition of the book was published in 1982 by Suhrkamp Verlag in Frankfurt am Main)

Plock, Ernest D.: *The Basic Treaty and the Evolution of East-West German Relations* (Boulder, CO: Westview Press, 1986)

Poppinga, Anneliese: *Konrad Adenauer: Geschichtsverständnis, Weltanschauung und politische Praxis* (Stuttgart: Deutsche Verlags-Anstalt, 1975)

Raina, Peter, ed.: *Internationale Politik in den siebziger Jahren* (Frankfurt: S. Fischer Verlag, 1973)

Ratifizieren oder nicht?: Die großen Reden der Debatte über die Ostverträge im Bundestag 23.–25. Februar 1972 (Hamburg: Hoffmann und Campe Verlag, 1972)

Rausch, Heinz: *Politische Kultur in der Bundesrepublik Deutschland* (Berlin: Colloquium Verlag Otto H. Hess, 1980)

Reichel, Peter: *Politik mit der Erinnerung. Gedächtnisorte im Streit um die nationalsozialistische Vergangenheit* (München/Wien: Carl Hanser Verlag, 1995)

_____: *Politische Kultur der Bundesrepublik* (Opladen: Leske & Budrich, 1981)

Reichel, Peter, ed.: *Politische Kultur in Westeuropa* (Bonn: Schriftenreihe der Bundeszentrale für politische Bildung, 1984)

Rein, Gerhard, ed.: *Die Opposition in der DDR* (Berlin: Wichern-Verlag, 1989)

Ritter, Gerhard: *The Sword and the Scepter: The Problem of Militarism in Germany* (Coral Gables, FL: University of Miami Press, 1969)

_____: *The German Problem: Basic Questions of German Political Life, Past and Present* (Columbus: Ohio State University Press, 1965)

Rosenberg, Tina: *The Haunted Land: Facing Europe's Ghosts After Communism* (New York: Vintage Books, 1996)

Rössler, Hellmuth: *Deutsche Geschichte. Schicksal des Volkes in Europas Mitte* (Güterloh: C. Bertelsmann, 1961)

Rüther, Günther, ed.: *Geschichte der christlich-demokratischen und christlich-sozialen Bewegungen in Deutschland* (Bonn: Schriftenreihe der Bundeszentrale für politische Bildung, 1987/1989)

Sauzay, Brigitte: *Le Vertige allemand* (Paris: O. Orban, 1985)

Schaffner, Bertram H.: *Father Land* (New York: Columbia University Press, 1948)

Schallück, Paul, ed.: *Germany: Cultural Developments since 1945* (München: Max Hüber Verlag, 1971)

Scharf, C. Bradley: *Politics and Change in East Germany* (Boulder, CO/London: Westview Press and Frances Pinter Publishers, 1984)

Scheel, Walter, ed.: *Nach Dreissig Jahren* (Stuttgart: Klett-Cotta Verlag, 1979)

_____: *Perspektiven deutscher Politik* (Düsseldorf/Köln: Diederichs, 1969)

Schelsky, Helmut: *Die skeptische Generation* (Düsseldorf: E. Diederich, 1963)

Scheuch, Erwin K.: *Wie deutsch sind die Deutschen? Eine Nation wandelt ihr Gesicht* (Bergisch-Gladbach: Bastei-Lubbe-Taschenbuch, 1992)

Schmidt, Helmut: *Freiheit Verantworten* (Düsseldorf: Econ-Verlag, 1983)

_____: *Der Kurs heißt Frieden* (Düsseldorf/Wien: Econ-Verlag, 1979)

_____: *Kontinuität und Konzentration* (Bonn-Bad Godesberg: Verlag Neue Gesellschaft, 1975)

Schmidt-Freytag, Carl G., ed.: *Die Autorität und die Deutschen* (München: Delp Verlag, 1966)

Schmitt, Carl: *The Concept of the Political* (New Brunswick, NJ: Rutgers University Press, 1976)

Schoenbaum, David, and Elizabeth Pond: *The German Question and Other German Questions* (New York: St. Martin's Press, 1996)

Schöllgen, Gregor: *Angst vor der Macht. Die Deutschen und ihre Außenpolitik* (Berlin/ Frankfurt: Verlag Ullstein, 1993)

Schomers, Michael: *Deutschland Ganz Rechts* (Köln: Kiepenheuer & Witsch, 1990)

Schönherr, Albrecht, ed.: *Ein Volk am Pranger? Die Deutschen auf der Suche nach einer neuen politischen Kultur* (Berlin: Aufbau Taschenbuch Verlag, n.d.)

Schössler, Dietmar, and Erich Weede: *West German Elite Views on National Security and Foreign Policy Issues* (Königstein: Athenäum-Verlag, 1978)

Schrenck-Notzing, Caspar von, and Armin Mohler, eds.: *Deutsche Identität* (Krefeld: Sinus Verlag, 1982)

Schubert, Klaus von, ed.: *Sicherheitspolitik der Bundesrepublik Deutschland: Dokumentation 1945–1977* (Köln: Verlag Wissenschaft und Politik, 1978 [vol. I] and 1979 [vol. II])

Schüddekopf, Charles, ed.: *"Wir sind das Volk!" Flugschriften, Aufrufe und Texte einer deutschen Revolution* (Reinbek bei Hamburg: Rowohlt Taschenbuch Verlag, 1990)

Schulz, Eberhard, and Peter Danylow: *Bewegung in der deutschen Frage?* (Bonn: Forschungsinstitut der Deutschen Gesellschaft für Auswärtige Politik, Arbeitspapiere zur Internationalen Politik, nr. 33, 1984)

Schulze, Hagen: *Wir sind was wir geworden sind. Vom Nutzen der Geschichte für die deutsche Gegenwart* (München/Zürich: Piper, 1987)

Schwarz, Hans-Peter: *Die Zentralmacht Europas. Deutschlands Rückkehr auf die Weltbühne* (Berlin: Siedler Verlag, 1994)

_____: *Die gezähmten Deutschen: Von der Machtbesessenheit zur Machtvergessenheit* (Stuttgart: Deutsche Verlags-Anstalt, 1985)

Schweigler, Gebhard: *West German Foreign Policy: the domestic setting* (New York: Praeger, 1984; Washington Papers nr. 106)

_____: *Nationalbewußtsein in der BRD und der DDR* (Düsseldorf: Bertelsmann Universitätsverlag, 1973)

Seebacher-Brandt, Brigitte: *Die Linke und die Einheit* (Berlin: Siedler Verlag, 1991)

Seidelmann, Reimund: *Die Entspannungspolitik der Bundesrepublik Deutschland* (Frankfurt/New York: Campus Verlag, 1982)

Sell, Friedrich: *Die Tragödie des deutschen Liberalismus* (Stuttgart: Deutsche Verlags-Anstalt, 1953)

Shirer, William L.: *The Rise and Fall of the Third Reich* (New York: Simon & Schuster, 1960)

Shlaes, Amity: *Germany: The Empire Within* (New York: Farrar, Straus & Giroux, 1991)

Smith, Gordon, William E. Paterson, and Stephen Padgett, eds.: *Developments in German Politics 2* (Durham, NC: Duke University Press, 1996)

Smith, Patricia, ed.: *After the Wall: Eastern Germany Since 1989* (Boulder, CO: Westview Press, 1998)

Smyser, W. R.: *Germany and America: New Identities, Fateful Rift?* (Boulder, CO: Westview Press, 1993)

_____: *German-American Relations* (Beverly Hills, CA: Sage Publications, Washington Papers nr. 74, 1980)

Snyder, Louis L.: *Roots of German Nationalism* (Bloomington: Indiana University Press, 1978)

Sodaro, Michael J.: *Moscow, Germany, and the West from Khrushchev to Gorbachev* (Ithaca, NY/London: Cornell University Press, 1990)

Sontheimer, Kurt: *Die verunsicherte Republik* (München: Piper, 1979)

_____: *Grundzüge des politischen Systems der Bundesrepublik Deutschland* (München: Piper, 1971)

Speier, Hans, and W. Phillips Davison, eds.: *West German Leadership and Foreign Policy* (Evanston, IL: Row, Peterson, 1957)

Spenle, Jean Edouard: *La Pensée allemande de Luther à Nietzsche* (Paris: A. Colin, 1967)

Spotts, Frederic: *The Churches and Politics in Germany* (Middletown, CT: Wesleyan University Press, 1973)

Stahl, Walter, ed.: *The Politics of Postwar Germany* (New York: Praeger, 1963)

Stares, Paul B., ed.: *The New Germany and the New Europe* (Washington, DC: Brookings Institution, 1992)

Stern, Fritz: *Dreams and Delusions: National Socialism in the Drama of the German Past* (New York: Vintage Books, 1989)

_____: *Gold and Iron: Bismarck, Bleichröder and the Building of the German Empire* (New York: Alfred A. Knopf, 1977)

_____: *The Failure of Illiberalism* (New York: Alfred A. Knopf, 1972)

_____: *The Politics of Cultural Despair* (Berkeley: University of California Press, 1963)

Sternberger, Dolf: *Verfassungspatriotismus* (Frankfurt am Main: Insel Verlag, 1990)

Stölzl, Christoph, ed.: *Die Neue Wache Unter den Linden. Ein deutsches Denkmal im Wandel der Geschichte* (Berlin: Verlag Koehler & Amelang, 1993)

_____: *Deutsches Historisches Museum. Ideen-Kontroversen-Perspektiven* (Frankfurt/Berlin: Propyläen Verlag, 1988)

Stöss, Richard: *Die extreme Rechte in der Bundesrepublik* (Opladen: Westdeutscher Verlag, 1989)

Streit um die Neue Wache. Zur Gestaltung einer zentralen Gedenkstätte (Berlin: Akademie der Künste, 1993)

Stürmer, Michael: *Dissonanzen des Fortschritts: Essays über Geschichte und Politik in Deutschland* (München/Zürich: Piper, 1986)

Sühl, Klaus, ed.: *Vergangenheitsbewältigung 1945 und 1989. Ein unmöglicher Vergleich? Eine Diskussion* (Berlin: Verlag Volk & Welt, 1994)

Szabo, Stephen F.: *The Diplomacy of German Unification* (New York: St. Martin's Press, 1992)

Szabo, Stephen F., ed.: *The Successor Generation: International Perspectives of Postwar Europeans* (Boston: Butterworths, 1983)

Taylor, A.J.P.: *Bismarck: The Man and the Statesman* (New York: Vintage Books, 1967)

_____: *The Course of German History* (London: H. Hamilton, 1945)

Teltschik, Horst: *329 Tage. Innenansichten der Einigung* (Berlin: Siedler Verlag, 1991)

Thadden, Rudolf von: *Fragen an Preußen* (München: Deutscher Taschenbuch Verlag, 1987)

Thiele, Hans-Günther, ed.: *Die Wehrmachtsausstellung. Dokumentation einer Kontroverse* (Bonn: Bundeszentrale für politische Bildung, 1997)

Thies, Wallace: *The Atlantic Alliance, Nuclear Weapons and European Attitudes* (Berkeley: University of California, Institute of International Studies, 1983)

Treitschke, Heinrich von: *Politics* (New York: Harcourt, Brace & World, 1963)

Treverton, Gregory F.: *America, Germany, and the Future of Europe* (Princeton, NJ: Princeton University Press, 1992)

Turner, Henry Ashby, Jr.: *The Two Germanies Since 1945* (New Haven, CT: Yale University Press, 1987)

Vali, Ferenc A.: *The Quest for a United Germany* (Baltimore: The Johns Hopkins Press, 1967)

Veblen, Thorstein: *Imperial Germany and the Industrial Revolution* (Ann Arbor: University of Michigan Press, [1915] 1966)

Venohr, Wolfgang, ed.: *Ohne Deutschland geht es nicht* (Krefeld: Sinus Verlag, 1985)

_____: *Die deutsche Einheit kommt bestimmt* (Bergisch Gladbach: Gustav Lübbe Verlag, 1982)

Verheyen, Dirk, and Christian Søe, eds.: *The Germans and Their Neighbors* (Boulder, CO: Westview Press, 1993)

Vogelsang, Thilo: *Das geteilte Deutschland* (München: Deutscher Taschenbuch Verlag, 1980)

Weber, Hermann: *DDR. Grundriß der Geschichte 1945–1990* (Hannover: Fackelträger-Verlag, 1991)

_____: *Geschichte der DDR* (München: Deutscher Taschenbuch Verlag, 1986)

Weber, Hermann, ed.: *DDR: Dokumente zur Geschichte der Deutschen Demokratischen Republik, 1945–1985* (München: Deutscher Taschenbuch Verlag, 1987)

Weber, Jürgen, and Peter Steinbach, eds.: *Vergangenheitsbewältigung durch Strafverfahren?* (München: G. Olzog Verlag, 1984)

Wehler, Hans-Ulrich: *Das deutsche Kaiserreich 1871–1918* (Göttingen: Vandenhoeck & Ruprecht, 1973)

Wehling, Hans Georg, ed.: *Politische Kultur in der DDR* (Stuttgart/Berlin/Köln: Verlag W. Kohlhammer, 1989)

Weidenfeld, Werner, ed.: *Deutschland. Eine Nation–doppelte Geschichte* (Köln: Verlag Wissenschaft und Politik, 1993)

_____: *Politische Kultur und deutsche Frage* (Köln: Verlag Wissenschaft und Politik, 1989)

_____: *Die Identität der Deutschen* (Bonn: Schriftenreihe der Bundeszentrale für politische Bildung, 1983)

_____: *Konrad Adenauer und Europa* (Bonn: Europa Union Verlag, 1976)

Weizsäcker, Richard von: *Von Deutschland aus* (München: Deutscher Taschenbuch Verlag, 1987)

Werner, Hans Detlef: *Klassenstruktur und Nationalcharakter* (Tübingen: Huth Verlag, 1967)

Wickert, Ulrich, ed.: *Angst vor Deutschland* (Hamburg: Hoffmann und Campe, 1990)

Wielenga, Friso: *Schatten deutscher Geschichte. Der Umgang mit dem Nationalsozialismus und der DDR-Vergangenheit in der Bundesrepublik* (Vierow bei Greifswald: SH-Verlag, 1995)

Willems, Emilio: *Der preußisch-deutsche Militarismus* (Köln: Verlag Wissenschaft und Politik, 1984)

Willms, Bernard: *Die deutsche Nation* (Köln-Lovenich: Edition Maschke Hohenheim, 1982)

Windsor, Philip: *Germany and the Management of Detente* (New York and Washington: Praeger, 1971)

Wippermann, Wolfgang: *Wessen Schuld? Vom Historikerstreit zur Goldhagen-Kontroverse* (Berlin: Elefanten Press, 1997)

Zelikow, Philip, and Condoleezza Rice: *Germany Unified and Europe Transformed: A Study in Statecraft* (Cambridge, MA/London: Harvard University Press, 1997)

Ziebura, Gilbert, ed.: *Grundfragen der deutschen Außenpolitik seit 1871* (Darmstadt: Wissenschaftliche Buchgesellschaft, 1975)

Zieger, Gottfried: *Die Haltung von SED und DDR zur Einheit Deutschlands 1949–1987* (Köln: Verlag Wissenschaft und Politik, 1988)

Zitelmann, Rainer, Karlheinz Weißmann, and Michael Großheim, eds.: *Westbindung. Chancen und Risiken für Deutschland* (Frankfurt: Verlag Ullstein/Propyläen Verlag, 1993)

Index

299